Religious Pluralism

For my students at the University College
of Cape Breton

Religious Pluralism in the West
An Anthology

Edited by
David George Mullan

BLACKWELL
Publishers

First published 1998

2 4 6 8 10 9 7 5 3 1

Blackwell Publishers Inc.
350 Main Street
Malden, Massachusetts 02148
USA

Blackwell Publishers Ltd
108 Cowley Road
Oxford OX4 1JF
UK

Library of Congress Cataloging-in-Publication Data

Religious pluralism in the West: an anthology / edited by David George Mullan.
    p.   cm.
    Includes bibliographical references and index.
    ISBN 0–631–20669–8. — ISBN 0–631–20670–1 (pbk.)
    1. Religious pluralism—History—Sources. 2. Religious pluralism—
Christianity—History—Sources.   I. Mullan, David George.
BL60.R448   1997   97–14136
291.1'72—dc21   CIP

British Library Cataloguing in Publication Data

A CIP catalogue record for this book is available from the British Library.

Typeset in 10½ on 12pt Ehrhardt
by Graphicraft Typesetters, Ltd, Hong Kong
Printed and bound in Great Britain by MPG Books Ltd, Bodmin, Cornwall

This book is printed on acid-free paper

CONTENTS

Preface   viii

Acknowledgments   x

Introduction: Philosophical and Historical Perspectives   1

1   The Ancient World   18
    The Bible   18
      Deuteronomy 13   18
      Matthew 13: 24–30, 36–43   20
      Luke 9: 51–6   20
      Luke 14: 15–24   20
      Acts 5: 33–9   21
    Ancient Greece   21
      Plato, *Laws* (*c.* 350)   21
    Roman Empire   24
      Tertullian, "Apology" and "Letter to Scapula" (197, 212)   24
      Lactantius, *The Divine Institutes* (*c.* 306)   28
      Julius Firmicus Maternus, *The Error of the Pagan Religions*
        (*c.* 346)   32
      Themistius, Oratio V to Jovian (364)   34
      John Chrysostom, Homily 46 on Matthew (*c.* 390)   36
      Augustine, Letter 93, Augustine to Vincentius,
        a schismatic bishop in Mauretania (408)   39

2   Medieval Europe   51
    Bishop Wazo, "Manichaeans at Châlons-sur-Marne"
      (*c.* 1043–48)   51

Thomas Aquinas, "Of Unbelief and Heresy" (*c.* 1271)   55
Marsilius of Padua, *Defensor Pacis* (1324)   73

3   The Renaissance and Reformations   82
Thomas More, "Of the Religions in Utopia" (1516)   82
Martin Luther, *Temporal Authority: To What Extent It
     Should Be Obeyed* (1523)   85
Balthasar Hübmaier, "Concerning Heretics and Those Who
     Burn Them" (1524)   94
Dirk Philips, "The Church of God" (*c.* 1560)   98
Sebastian Castellio, *Advice to a Desolate France* (1562)   100
Jacobus Acontius, *Stratagematum Satanae* (1565)   115
Juan de Mariana, "Not Fitting to Have Many Religions in
     One Province" (1599)   117

4   The Seventeenth Century   127
Arminius, "On Reconciling Religious Dissensions among
     Christians" (1606)   127
Thomas Helwys, *The Mistery of Iniquity* (1612)   132
Roger Williams, *The Bloudy Tenet* (1644)   136
Samuel Rutherford, "The State of the Question of
     Compulsion of Conscience, and Tolleration" (1649)   141
John Milton, *Civil Power in Ecclesiastical Causes* (1659)   152
Henry More, "Of Liberty of Conscience" (1660)   159
Pierre Bayle, *Philosophical Commentary* (1686)   165
John Locke, *A Letter Concerning Toleration* (1685)   174

5   The Eighteenth Century   185
Jean Jacques Rousseau, "On Civil Religion" (1762)   185
Voltaire, *Philosophical Dictionary* (1764)   187
Joseph Priestley, *An Essay on the First Principles of
     Government* (1771)   193
Claude Adrien Helvétius, *A Treatise on Man* (1772)   205
Moses Mendelssohn, *Jerusalem* (1783)   215
Thomas Jefferson, *Notes on the State of Virginia* (1781–2)   219

6   The Nineteenth Century   225
John Brownlow, *Liberty of Conscience* (*c.* 1826)   225
Felicité de Lamennais, *Words of a Believer* [*Paroles d'un
     Croyant*] (1834)   242
John Stuart Mill, *On Liberty* (1859)   244
Anonymous, *The Ultimate Principle of Religious Liberty* (1860)   252
Mandell Creighton, *Persecution and Tolerance* (1895)   257

7   The Twentieth Century   263
    Arthur Vermeersch, *Tolerance* (1912)   263
    Francesco Ruffini, *Religious Liberty* (1912)   271
    Reinhold Niebuhr, "The Test of Tolerance" (1943)   281
    Gustav Mensching, "The Unity of Religions" (1955)   296
    Carrillo de Albornoz, "Are There Theological Grounds for
        Religious Liberty?" (1963)   303
    Philip Wogaman, "An Unconscious Commitment in Search
        of Basis" (1967)   309
    John Rawls, "Equal Liberty" (1971)   313

8   Post-World War II Declarations   317
    Churches of Great Britain, *Human Rights and Religious
        Freedom* (1947)   318
    World Council of Churches, *Declaration on Religious Liberty*
        (Amsterdam, 1948)   326
    Universal Declaration of Human Rights (1948)   328
    Vatican II, *Dignitatis Humanae Personae* (1965)   329
    International Covenant on Civil and Political Rights (1976)   341
    *Declaration on the Elimination of all Forms of Intolerance and
        of Discrimination based on Religion or Belief* (1981)   341

Index   346

PREFACE

This anthology began its life in 1991 at the University College of Cape Breton when I undertook to teach a course charting the story of attitudes toward religious pluralism. I discovered that there is a vast and seemingly endless amount of literature on the subject, but no collection in any general sense. William Haller gathered together some important seventeenth-century documents,[1] Manfred Hoffmann has published some selected writings from the German Reformation,[2] but no one has done the same for the longer history. Thus I have concluded that there is a place for such a collection, and this is the fruit of three years of gathering and sifting.

My work was done in several locations, but primarily at home, in the library of the University College of Cape Breton. In addition, library staff, particularly Laura Peverill and Mary Campbell, have been never failing in their courtesy and helpfulness as they have dealt with a great many requests for inter-library loans.

I am grateful to several individuals in the United Kingdom who helped me to track down information about John Brownlow, namely Rosemary Rendel of the Catholic Record Society, London; the Reverend Petroc Howell, Diocesan Archivist, Birmingham; and Michael Hodgetts, Historical Director of Harvington Hall, Kidderminster, Worcs.

I benefited from comments supplied by Blackwell's readers; a longer book would have allowed me to incorporate their suggestions more completely. As it stands, I have had to narrow my focus all the more, meaning that I have generally left aside material of a legal nature (e.g., the Theodosian Code, papal pronouncements in the Middle Ages and the nineteenth century) and of a literary nature (e.g., Defoe's *Shortest Way with Dissenters*, Lessing's *Nathan the Wise*, Voltaire's *Calas Affair*, Marmontel's *Belisarius*).

I have appreciated the encouragement of scholars at the University College of Cape Breton and elsewhere, and the interest of students who have studied these documents with me. A number of research grants have bee supplied by the Committee on the Evaluation of Research Proposals UCCB, now the Research Evaluation Committee, under the Directo ı Research, Dr Robert Morgan.

Generally I have transcribed material without alteration, except for impos-ing American spelling throughout. However, I have set ease of reading and comprehension ahead of strict critical accuracy, and therefore, in a few instances, such as Rutherford's *Free Disputation*, I have found it desirable to make minor emendations to the text. That fact notwithstanding, older texts still bear the marks of non-standard orthography and capitalization, and I have not systematically attempted to suppress the idiosyncratic character of writings, particularly from the seventeenth century.

As part of the introduction to each selection, I have given details of the source used, together with suggestions for further reading.

Notes

1 William Haller (ed.), *Tracts on Liberty in the Puritan Revolution, 1638–1647*, 3 vols (New York: Columbia University Press, 1934).
2 Manfred Hoffmann, *Toleranz und Reformation* (Gütersloh: Gütersloher Verlagshaus Mohn, 1979).

ACKNOWLEDGMENTS

The editor and publishers gratefully acknowledge permission from the following to reproduce copyright material:

Abingdon Press for the extract from Philip Wogaman, *Protestant Faith and Religious Liberty*, copyright © 1967 Abingdon Press.

America Press, Inc., 106 West 156th Street, New York, NY 10019, for the extract from Walter M. Abbott (ed.), *The Documents of Vatican II* (Guild Press, 1966), copyright © 1966; all rights reserved.

Augsburg Fortress for the extract from W. I. Brandt (ed.), *Luther's Works*, vol. 45, copyright © 1962 Fortress Press.

Cambridge University Press for Appendix 1 from Herbert G. Wood, *Religious Liberty Today* (Cambridge, 1949).

David Campbell Publishers Ltd for the extracts from Book X of *The Laws of Plato*, translated by A. E. Taylor (J. M. Dent & Sons, 1934); and for the extract from Jean Jacques Rousseau, *The Social Contract and Discourses*, translated by G. D. H. Cole (J. M. Dent & Sons, 1913).

Columbia University Press for the extract from Walter Wakefield and Austin Evans (eds), *Heresies of the High Middle Ages*, copyright © 1969 Columbia University Press; and the extract from Marsilius of Padus *Defensor Pacis*, translated by Alan Gewirth, copyright © 1980 Columbia University Press.

Peter Lang Publishing, Inc. for the extract from Annie G. Tannenbaum (ed.), *Pierre Bayle's "Philosophical Commentary". A Modern Translation and Critical Interpretation* (Peter Lang, 1987).

National Council of Churches of Christ in the USA for the scripture extracts from the *Revised Standard Version of the Bible*, copyright 1946, 1952, 1971 the Division of Christian Education of the National Council of the Churches of Christ in the USA.

Oxford University Press for the extract from Ernest Barker (ed.), *From Alexander to Constantine: Passages and Documents Illustrating the History of Social and Political Ideas, 336 BC–AD 337* (Clarendon Press, 1956).

The Patmos Press for the extract from Sebastian Castellio, *Advice to a Desolate France*, translated by W. Valkhoff (Patmos Press, 1975).

SCM Press Ltd for the extract from George H. Williams and Angel M. Mergal (eds), *Spiritual and Anabaptist Writers*, Library of Christian Classics vol. xxv.

University of Alabama Press for the extract from Gustav Mensching, *Tolerance and Truth in Religion*, translated by H.-J. Klimkeit (University of Alabama Press, 1971).

The Voltaire Foundation for the extracts from Voltaire, *Philosophical Dictionary*, translated by Theodore Besterman (Penguin, 1972).

Westminster John Knox Press for the extract from George H. Williams and Angel M. Mergal (eds), *Spiritual and Anabaptist Writers* (Westminster Press, 1957); and the extract from Reinhold Niebuhr: *The Nature and Destiny of Man*, vol. 2.

World Council of Churches for the extracts from A. F. Carrillo de Albornoz, *The Basis of Religious Liberty* (SCM Press, 1963); and the extract from M. Searle Bates, *Religious Liberty: An Inquiry* (International Missionary Council, 1945).

Despite every effort to trace and contact copyright owners before publication this has not always been possible. If notified we will be pleased to rectify any errors or omissions at the earliest opportunity.

Introduction

PHILOSOPHICAL AND HISTORICAL PERSPECTIVES

The writer urged that we become persecutors as a matter of course as soon as we begin to feel very strongly upon any subject; we ought not therefore to do this; we ought not to feel very strongly even upon that institution which was dearer to the writer than any other – the Church of England. We should be Churchmen, but somewhat lukewarm Churchmen, inasmuch as those who care very much about either religion or irreligion are seldom observed to be very well bred or agreeable people. The Church herself should approach as nearly to that of Laodicea as was compatible with her continuing to be a Church at all, and each individual member should only be hot in striving to be as lukewarm as possible.
Samuel Butler, The Way of All Flesh *(1903), ch. 85[1]*

The title of this collection contains a word which may strike some as problematical, namely "pluralism." As Ian Markham has noted, it has come to be associated with a certain view of theology, represented by John Hick, where it "points to a transformed outlook to different religions: no longer are we able to speak of one tradition as being true and those that disagree as false, instead we must talk of different and equally valid ways to the Real."[2] More recently, James Wiggins has criticized this use of the term, and in its place has offered "religious diversity."[3] Markham's own preference, in a book which addresses in its own way the concerns identified here, is to speak of "plurality." However, these distinctions may be more imagined than real; Hick has edited a book which includes in its title the term "religious diversity," and he also makes use of the term "plurality" in the presentation of his ideas.[4] Thus I have retained the term as one which is valid for the simultaneous presence, however amicable or antagonistic, of more than one religion in a given society which, in the context of this work, is western.

Plurality of religions may not seem like much of a problem to us in the usual course of events, though this may for some, such as the American philosopher Richard Rorty, be predicated upon keeping religion off the public square;[5] while the appearance of religious intolerance, as in the instance of Salman Rushdie, may provoke passionate responses.[6] However, in western culture the general acceptance of pluralism does not have a lengthy history. Bernard Lewis reminds us that "tolerance is a new virtue, intolerance a new crime,"[7] while Franklin H. Littell has observed that "religious liberty . . . is a very recent experiment in social adjustment,"[8] and we might note that the experiment has not yet proven to be entirely successful. Indeed, "success" might be difficult to define. An essay by the historian T. K. Rabb seems to describe a historical process leading from intolerance through toleration to a situation where religions are equal – this might be akin to religious liberty – and where adherents do not draw conclusions about the superiority of the truth claims of their own beliefs.[9] However, a great many people who belong to the various traditions do assume that the teachings of their own religion, denomination, or sect are correct and that outsiders are in error, and any other approach must entail a denatured form of religion. The assumption that religious pluralism can stand only on a platform of an almost complete mistrust for one's own creed will prove to be a very poor one. Rather, Philip Wogaman's urging that each society and tradition must find the basis for religious liberty somewhere near its own heart is a necessary corrective.[10] At least in the short term, different answers are needed to deal with these situations in different cultures, whether in Britain, China, or the Sudan. Recently the University of Ulster was sued, successfully, by someone who claimed he had suffered discrimination due to his Roman Catholic religion.[11] A recent Amnesty International report (August 4, 1996) stated

> that religious groups in China were being restricted again and individuals persecuted. Strict official rules on religion had led to arbitrary detention of believers peacefully exercising their rights to worship. . . . Diplomats note that all religious groups must still register with the government and that the security authorities regularly carry out surveillance of religious activities.[12]

The Sudanese government is practicing forcible conversion of Christians and animists to Islam.[13]

Discussions about religious pluralism touch upon numerous aspects of political, social, and intellectual life, and to describe the history of how, in particular, western civilization has dealt with the issue supplies one means of telling the story of that civilization. If the essential qualities of the west are held to include the moral autonomy of the individual, limitations upon the powers of the state, and the existence within society of foci of meaning not determined by the state,[14] then our theme may be seen as fundamental to the emergence of that civilization.

It is not only Americans who have good reason to describe religious liberty as "the first liberty." A Baptist confession of 1646 declared that liberty of conscience, with specific reference to religion, is the dearest thing to "conscientious men," without which "all other liberties will not be worth the naming much less enjoying."[15] A twentieth-century Roman Catholic work on politics has expressed a similar notion: "If the civil power may justly determine the rights and activities of the Church, it may with greater reason exercise the same control" over every other kind of group, including unions and the whole array of voluntary associations.[16] These two statements have different emphases, the first looking to the freedom of the individual, the second to the freedom of an institution – or, perhaps, *institutions* – but of course the former cannot really exist without the capacity to establish the latter. Ernst Troeltsch argued that human rights and democracy have to be viewed as discrete elements, pointing to the wide range of rights acknowledged after the Glorious Revolution in England without democratic rule, and also to Calvinist New England and Rousseau's democracy which lacked that same extent of individual right in matters of religion.[17] However, in the case of England there were tendencies toward a further loosening of political control, to which non-conformity made its own contribution, while one may question also to what extent a society without religious freedom can be legitimately regarded as democratic. Surely that term must embody a range of possibilities of individual self-actualization.

However, even if one might succeed in suppressing the public expression of religious non-conformity, one cannot get at the inner person, and critics of persecution were quick to point out that persecution succeeded best in promoting hypocrisy. Some would perish in the flames for their beliefs; others would hide them behind a cloak of theological respectability.[18] Above the doorway to the Abbot House in Dunfermline, Scotland, an inscription reads:

> Sen Vord is Thrall and Thocht is fre
> Keip Veill Thy Tonge I Coinsell The.
>
> [Since word is thrall and thought is free
> Keep well thy tongue I counsel thee.]

Dimitry Pospielovsky wrote, before the fall of communism, that under the Soviet Union's constitution, the republic's people "may have the theoretical right to profess any religion, [but] they have not a constitutionally guaranteed right to *belong* to a religious organization or church," hence "the legal and constitutional right to profess any religion, if strictly interpreted, becomes the right to a *secret* personal religion without any external and visible manifestations."[19] But can religion be kept only as an interior matter, sequestered from a hostile world? Perhaps for a time, but few religious groups will be forever satisfied to operate in the penumbra of society. An integral part of religious liberty is that men and women must be free to engage in the public exercise of their faith, and to make converts to it, if at all possible. This public aspect, recognized by Locke, has found its place in the declarations of human rights familiar in the modern world, though it is by no means universally honored.[20] In 1980 the Baptist World Alliance presented a Declaration on Human Rights which upholds "the right to choose a religion freely and to maintain religious belief or unbelief without political advantage or disadvantage" as the first of twenty rights inherent in Christianity, and because of the religious basis for human rights, the practice of evangelization – itself the second right on the list – "is the key ingredient" in their promotion.[21]

The twentieth century, particularly since the Second World War, has witnessed widespread enunciation and affirmation of religious freedom, and not only by religious bodies whether sectarian or ecumenical in scope. The International Covenant on Civil and Political Rights, 1976 (Part III, Article 18) includes the following clauses:

1 Everyone shall have the right of freedom of thought, conscience and religion. This right shall include freedom to have or to adopt a religion or belief of his choice, and freedom, either individually or in community with others and in public or private, to manifest his religion or belief in worship, observance, practice and teaching.

2 No one shall be subject to coercion which would impair his freedom to have or to adopt a religion or belief of his choice.

3 Freedom to manifest one's religion or beliefs may be subject only to such limitations as are prescribed by law and are necessary to protect public safety, order, health, or morals or the fundamental rights and freedoms of others.[22]

In addressing religious pluralism, there are three prominent notions to be considered: intolerance, toleration, and liberty. Unfortunately, some writers take insufficient account of the content of these terms and the result is unnecessary obfuscation.

First, then, how do intolerance and toleration differ from each other? Actually, the distinction is rather limited, and it is important to point out that toleration is not the opposite of intolerance. To quote Thomas Paine (1791–2), "Toleration is not the *opposite* of Intolerance, but is the *counterfeit* of it. Both are despotisms."[23] The philosopher Preston King, who has provided the most nuanced discussion of the matter, states that intolerance is rooted in "an unequivocal objection."[24] The outcome of such hostility is to take necessary steps to suppress the offending practice or institution. The tolerant person is not one who has shed that unequivocal objection; indifference or relativism are not marks of toleration. As Jay Newman writes, "a certain kind of relativist is actually a *critic* of the spirit of tolerance, not a defender."[25] Rather, the tolerant state, church, person, is one who has decided, for whatever reason, that the required steps in ridding the world of *x* are either impracticable or undesirable. The objection, however, has not been effaced, and under different circumstances may once again seek a definitive resolution. Thomas Aquinas, writing about thirty years after the formal institution of the medieval inquisition, recognized the validity of permitting dissent when conditions pertaining to its suppression were not favorable.[26] Here is the *pragmatic* basis for toleration.[27] John Noonan, an American jurist, also writes of a *principled* ground, though this leads toward the notion of religious liberty, and to the distinction we shall return. Another problem arises also, an ethical problem. If toleration presupposes the sufferance of something toward which one harbours a serious objection, how can one justify *not* taking the necessary and plausible steps? Susan Mendus has defined this as the *paradox of toleration*,[28] and those who would practice toleration must take careful account of this issue, as did Heinrich Rommen in his book *The State in Catholic Thought*. He was against freedom of conscience which he thought a wrong ideology rooted in a denial of objective truth. On the other hand he deplored the hypocrisy of an imposed creed. He concluded that "we see at once that in this manner the political institution of freedom of conscience lives by its own practical merits and not by the philosophically and theologically wrong ideology that all subjective opinions are materially equal and that all creeds are equally true or false, as relativism contends."[29] Beyond the impossibility of relativism we should also note that sometimes what we commend to ourselves as toleration is nothing more than indifference, or worse, moral cowardice.[30]

Preston King states that "there is something intolerable about the concept of 'tolerance',"[31] while a Roman Catholic archbishop, speaking in 1966, declared:

> From the very outset I shall take my stand against religious tolerance: I pledge my full support for something more positive, more mature and of a higher order. I declare myself unequivocally in favour of religious freedom, in the most comprehensive and noble acceptation of this stirring term. . . .

Religious tolerance and religious freedom, therefore, are not interchangeable terms. The former is essentially a negative notion, while the latter is a positive one. Tolerance is the acceptance of a situation which one is unable or unwilling to alter here and now, but which may be altered in different circumstances. It does not guarantee religious freedom in the ultimate resort, but simply implies the absence of compulsion. Religious freedom, instead, signifies an irrevocably valid principle, implying a concrete affirmation of values, which the State, while not neglecting the just demands of public order, under no circumstances will allow to be molested. Tolerance implies the granting of a privilege which could be revoked. Religious freedom is the acknowledgment of an intrinsic – and therefore inviolable – right of the human person.[32]

Archbishop Cardinale's comment upon toleration is clarified in the story of the Huguenots in the seventeenth century. In 1598, for the sake of peace in his country, France's King Henry IV, a former Protestant turned Roman Catholic for the sake of gaining full possession of the crown, issued the Edict of Nantes, a decree of toleration for Huguenots. But what happened upon the arrival of another pharaoh, one who knew Joseph not? Toleration might then be rescinded, as it was in 1685 when Louis XIV, pursuing his motto of *un roi, une loi, une foi*, rescinded his ancestor's decree. The one who is tolerated lives on a bubble, waiting for a change in conditions and a repudiation of toleration. It is not a right, it is a permission. Thus the story of religious pluralism in the west must not be described as an ineluctable and triumphant upward march. It is a story with many twists and turns, and ups and downs.

One may think of toleration as a middle term between persecution and liberty, and a tolerant state may move in either direction; clearly there is no guarantee that liberty will be hatched from it. Where this does eventuate, the state simply surrenders any role in the determination of people's religion – well, almost, because in reality a complete and utter separation of church and state is not likely; western governments authorize Christian statutory holidays, not Muslim or Buddhist ones. Still, in Canada, the federal government does not *tolerate* Islam, Roman Catholicism, Greek Orthodoxy, the Pentecostal movement, or Judaism. It recognizes, in the wake of John Locke and a host of others, that the state is not a fit determiner of religious opinions, and that a stable society can be erected upon the foundation of religious pluralism in a context of liberty.

Intolerance can arise from several sources: concern for the security of society which, it is feared, may collapse if dissent is allowed to grow; the quest for power over people in as many spheres as possible; a desire to preserve and to defend a particular tradition; the agression which emerges from the missionary activities inherent in universalizing religions of the prophetic mold.[33] Michael Mullett, in his *Radical Religious Movements*, points out that in the older politics, the medieval state was intolerant of dissent because it was "adorned and inhibited by its religious legitimation,"[34] which was eroded by divergent opinions and structures; while the early modern state, having subordinated the church, relied upon the church's support which it received in exchange for suppressing dissent. Roland Bainton noted concisely that "to persecute, a man must believe that he is right, that the point in question is important, and that coercion is effective."[35] The persecutor, the intolerant man, has a firm belief in the rectitude and truth of something, hence he has an "unequivocal objection" to variant belief structures; the matter touches the integrity of social or political or other institutions, hence a threat to the world as he knows and loves it; and that by inflicting punishment he can either force compliance or eradicate the annoyance.

In 1757 David Hume published his essay on *The Natural History of Religion*. He wrote that early religions were marked by polytheism; indeed, there were 30,000 deities by the time of Hesiod (*c.* 700 BC). He also alleged, as others have since his time, that polytheism has a real tendency toward toleration and leads to "activity, spirit, courage, magnanimity, love of liberty, and all the virtues, which aggrandize a people." On the other hand, monotheism tends toward intolerance and "the monkish virtues of mortification, pennance, humility and passive suffering."[36]

Polytheism did have an inherent capacity for toleration. What is one more god to add to the existing pantheon? Also, the gods of the conquered might very well overlap with the gods of the conqueror, i.e., a sun god. However, let us look a little deeper into this issue, saving the most prominent example until last. In wider cultural perspective, one may consider the ancient Inca empire of the Andes. This was an expansionary state, and whenever new peoples were added, their chief sacred entity was enshrined in Cuzco and the cult administered by representatives of the respective people. However, while traditional worship was allowed, "conquered peoples were compelled to worship the Inca pantheon of nature gods."[37] The situation in ancient Rome was similar. Under the republic there was a wide range of deities dear to Romans, but the advent of the mystery cults from the east did bring about real anxiety. Late-night rituals inspired fears about subversion, and in 186 BC the Bacchanalia were suppressed in an orgy of blood.

It is quite plausible that the memory of that affair inspired fear of Christianity.[38] Christians were not subjected to continual persecution under the emperors. The empire could, of course, be savage toward its perceived enemies, but at least until the middle of the third century, there was little systematic or centrally directed persecution; it would flare up here and there and then subside again. However, Christians were always a potential target because they were outsiders. Their religion was distinct in so far as it was dogmatic; it focused on intellectual content and as it matured the level of doctrinal definition grew. This kind of religious teaching was different from the myriad competitors in the ancient Mediterranean world, though of itself, that would not likely have led to persecution. The real problem was that Christians, like Jews, were committed to an uncompromising monotheism which prohibited any kind of adoration of the imperial *genius*, hence they seemed disloyal and subversive.

Our final reflection upon pagan religious practice in this context is the vexed case involving Socrates who drank his famous cup of hemlock in 399 BC. He was tried in Athens on charges of atheism and corruption of the youth of the polis. Now, atheism is a protean term. Luther and others of his time assailed their enemies as atheists, not because they did not believe in God at all, but because they believed differently or else lived lives which were adjudged to be devoid of an appropriate moral sense of life lived out under the watchful eyes of God. Socrates was a believer in what we might call the irrational, though one can debate at what level that irrational (monotheistic?) force made contact with his own life. What it seems he did not believe in were the officially sanctioned gods of the Athenian polis, the denial of whom might, it was feared, lead to divine punishment of the entire community.[39] There were, of course, voices in Athens rather skeptical about the traditional pantheon; Socrates was not a lone ranger in this respect as he contradicted some of the theological views of a Sophocles, but Socrates was guilty of political sins as well as religious, and it is probable that his trial was a political one carried out in religious language. Nevertheless, it remains that while polytheism could present certain prospects for the invocation of religious toleration, it could also respond vigorously to perceived religious challenges, and it must be remembered that polytheism's tolerant spirit lacked a theoretical foundation. A pagan of the later Roman empire, Themistius, a Byzantine bureaucrat and educator, did offer a reasoned humanistic appeal for the toleration of various religious observances, but this was under threat of inundation by the imperial-backed Christianity of the late fourth century, and it has been noted that neither hellenistic nor ancient classical philosophy could have been invoked to establish this point of view.[40]

What then of monotheism, and in particular, Judaism and Christianity? Jay Newman has pointed to the ambivalence of the biblical material.[41] Clearly there is an intolerant spirit abroad; the assumption is of one truth (intolerance is a theological virtue, e.g., Elijah's assault on the priests of Ba'al in I Kings 18–19; tacit approval of Nebuchadnezzar's decree in favour of the religion of Shadrach, Meshach, and Abednego in Daniel 3). However, the monotheistic prophetic spirit in its full panoply of censoriousness still articulates a kind of perverse demand for religious freedom so that its re-formist word can be heard, though it never intended to lay down a defense of religious pluralism. The Christian scriptures display a similar conviction about the existence of Truth, but of course Christians were in no position to persecute in the apostolic era. The real interest about the scriptures in this debate is less in their own contemporary settings, but in the use later centuries would make of those sacred documents. We see Christians articu-lating the need for a cessation of persecution so long as they were its objects, but once in the driver's seat, Christians forgot Tertullian's appeal of *c.* 200 to natural right as a basis for worship rooted in individual conviction.[42] A century later, on the eve of his student Constantine's supremacy in the western empire, Lactantius again emphasized that worship must be volun-tary.[43] While this view would be maintained by some, the tide of Christian opinion was quickly toward a reversal of polarity, i.e., Christianity would begin to persecute pagans as pagans had formerly persecuted Christians. The first Christian to demand persecution of pagans was the convert Julius Firmicus Maternus who in *c.* 346 cited bloody biblical texts in favor of imperial suppression of pagan cults from which he had only recently been rescued![44] In the ensuing decades Christian theologians, most notably Augustine, would embrace the notion of a Christian magistrate supporting Christianity, and would read the Christian scriptures, even the parable of the tares, in terms of a correcting/persecuting spirit. It is interesting to note that this coincided with a shift in Christian theology toward an obsession with an ineradicable evil at the bottom of the human personality, hence the need for a supervisory state which would limit the damage done to true religion by schismatics and heretics. It is also worth recalling that in *c.* 200 Tertullian had uttered his famous dictum rebuking pagans for attributing every public calamity to the Christians: "If the Tiber rises as high as the city walls, if the Nile does not send its waters up over the fields, if the heavens give no rain, if there is an earthquake, if there is famine or pesti-lence, straightway the cry is, 'Away with the Christians to the lion!' What! shall you give such multitudes to a single beast?"[45] It would not be long until Roman law, in the service of a different deity, expressed the same fears, but with paganism at the point of the spear.

Shall we endure longer that the succession of the seasons be changed, and the temper of the heavens be stirred to anger, since the embittered perfidy of the pagans does not know how to preserve these balances of nature? For why has the spring renounced its accustomed charm? Why has the summer, barren of its harvest, deprived the laboring farmer of his hope of a grain harvest? . . . Why all these things, unless nature has transgressed the decree of its own law to avenge such impiety? In order that we may hereafter be compelled to sustain such circumstances, by a peaceful vengeance, as We have said, the venerable majesty of the Supernal Divinity must be appeased.[46]

One author has commented that the savagery of the Theodosian Code would come as no surprise to a successor to Diocletian, but "what is amazing is how with hardly a murmur the Church accepted as its own the very imperial scourge from which it had just escaped. The imperial thinking remained basic as long as the Byzantine Empire stood or had imitators. It permeated the orthodox churches. In the West, thanks to the immediate success of coercion, it was woven into catholic thought by St Augustine."[47] So triumphant was its success that at the end of the sixteenth century an inquisitor would find his own court first established in Eden. Paramo argued that the inquisition was founded by no less an authority than God himself in his search for Adam after the Fall; the *sanbenitos* worn by convicted heretics were just the same as the garb worn by Adam and Eve; their deprivation of pre-lapsarian benefits was an anticipation of the practice of confiscating the goods of heretics. In a later age, Christ became the first inquisitor of the evangelical law (*Legis Evangelicae*), to whose successors, the apostles, the jurisdiction of the inquisition was transferred. They were succeeded by bishops whose office carried with it the status of inquisitor against heretics.[48]

By the end of the fourth century, monotheism had proved itself to be not only intolerant, but also capable of persecution. Hume thought this inevitable, and over time, in the West Christianity has generally proven this in practice. Even so, however, the desire for domination has not always issued in bloody persecution. The only person executed for heresy in Christian antiquity was an Iberian, Priscillian. He was something of a Manicheean dualist, and was ultimately burned as a sorcerer in *c*. 385, suggesting that his crimes had a political odor to them. In any event, his execution evoked a strenuous protest from Bishop Martin of Tours. For the next 640 years there are no records of executions on religious grounds. In 1022 about 15 heretics were burned at Orléans in France, though the grounds are now held to have been clearly political. In the middle of the century the bishop of Liège made an unequivocal statement against persecution of heretics. Wazo wrote in answer to another bishop's query that "our Savior, who, mild and humble of heart, did not come to wrangle or contend but rather to suffer abuse, shameful treatment, blows, and finally death on the Cross."[49]

It was only in the final quarter of the twelfth century that persecution became an issue, and thus the historian confronts the task of explaining the emergence of a persecuting spirit, the intolerance of a partnership between church and state, out of a strictly ecclesiastical/ theological intolerance which lacked any kind of juridical/ political apparatus for coercion; in fact

R. I. Moore has argued that *c*. 1100 "Europe *became* a persecuting society" (i.e., it had not been for hundreds of years).[50]

The difficulty here is part of a larger problem which historians have defined as the closing of the medieval mind[51] after about 1175, a shift away from a degree of cultural openness and toward the familiar caricature of the closed middle ages, more ready to burn than to listen. From 1179 we have popes advocating rigorous measures against heretics, and from 1184 the papal voice spoke of heretics along with the Latin verb *exterminare*.[52] With the establishment of the Dominicans and the Franciscans early in the next century, along with the compliance of the Emperor, the formal institution of the inquisition followed in 1232. Indeed, under the terms of papal decrees of the late twelfth century, the bishop of Liège would have been deposed from office. It is not easy to explain this emergence of intolerance from a relatively lax context. Probably one would have to take note of the impact of the Crusades, the rise of the apparatus and personnel of governance, and even the arrival of the Cathar sect, whether a heresy or a distinct religion, whose appearance may have spurred the authorities to a re-examination of policy.

Whatever the explanations, there were willing supporters of a robust imposition of religious conformity, and Aquinas supplied a reasoned statement of the need to suppress heresy, to the point of death.[53] But one author has claimed to locate a deep tension within Thomist thought, and that because of the Angelic Doctor's high appraisal of the role of conscience.[54] Abelard had already made explicit the problem early in the twelfth century: "And so we say that those who persecuted Christ or his disciples, who they thought should be persecuted, sinned in deed, yet they would have sinned more gravely in fault if they had spared them against their own conscience."[55] Thus, as appeared also late in the seventeenth century in Pierre Bayle's *Philosophical Commentary*, while one may condemn the practice of persecution in the name of religion, the appeal to conscience can justify not only the practice of non-conformity but also its persecution. Bayle might well bewail the fate of his pastor-brother in a French prison, but one trajectory of his thought would indicate that logically he could only have affirmed the conscientious right of Louis XIV to enforce his policy of religious uniformity.[56] Thus conscience alone supplied a passionate but insufficient basis for the appeal for religious pluralism – but some contemporaries, notably leading Scottish covenanters of the mid-seventeenth century, argued that a good conscience is only that one informed by the Word of God properly interpreted.[57]

Protestants generally affirmed the superiority of the Bible to all other authorities. If this led to certainty of belief for some, others concluded that while scripture was perfect, it must be perceived by sin-blinded human beings, who could not hope to see truth with perfect clarity, and thus one must accept a diversity of opinion. This judgment of Jacobus Arminius of Leiden (1606) went far beyond the intentions of the mature Luther who once argued vigorously against coercion in religion, but a few years later had retreated to harsh punishments in order to defend the sometimes rather fragile fruit of his own labors. Lord Acton noted that "before a new authority can be set up in the place of one that exists, there is an interval when the right of dissent must be proclaimed."[58] Still, the Protestant principle was born, and it would be defended by John Milton in the seventeenth century and restated with characteristic energy by Reinhold Niebuhr in the twentieth. Luther's notion of *simul peccator et iustus* meant that humanity cannot be expected to seize the truth with unerring grasp; its perception of truth is ever partial and suspect, hence the dangers of coercion, since no one's judgment can be trusted to the nth degree. In any event, who should coerce? The state, made of men no less corruptible and corrupted than any others (Acontius)? Roger Williams obliterated these pretensions in his *Bloudy Tenent, of persecution* (1644) in which he made an interesting use of Calvinist predestinarian doctrine: if God has already predetermined each one's destiny, then what difference if the streets are full of heresy? None of the chosen can be lost, so let God mete out condign punishment at the eschaton. Williams tied this use of doctrine to an alternate mode of biblical interpretation which unhinged the New Testament from a dependence on the Old, and so his new Christian no longer sought the aid of a religiously committed magistrate; the only king of the church was Jesus Christ whose sole *modus operandi* in this age is spiritual, not carnal. Williams's restriction of the state to matters of personal security and the protection of property lies at the heart of John Locke's *Letter Concerning Toleration*. In fact, Locke's influential writing is arguably a condensed version of Williams's prolix and inelegant biblical exegesis.[59]

The Protestant principle would in due course undergo a thorough secularization through the Enlightenment, where French thinkers in particular could be unrelenting in their assault upon the bastions of priestcraft. Others, like the German playwright G. E. Lessing and the English philosopher Joseph Priestley were rather less acerbic, but they were unimpressed by religious dogmatism, focusing upon the ethical teachings of Christianity. In the nineteenth century John Stuart Mill articulated a philosophical justification of the unimpeded circulation of ideas (except for those ruled out by the harm principle) in his essay *On Liberty* (1859). This work expressed a fear of the power of societal disapproval and suppression of an unlimited variety of opinion expressed in the quest for individual autonomy.[60] Meanwhile, the Roman Catholic Church had not recovered from the setbacks of the Reformation only to surrender calmly before the onset of modern liberalism, nor did it intend to remain quiescent in the battle to hold at bay the forces unleashed in the French Revolution. There were indeed Catholic voices for religious liberty in England before emancipation in 1829, and in France the brilliant Lammenais condemned every vestige of persecution (1834) before drifting away from Roman Catholicism in despondency. These, however, were exceptions. Papal policy in the nineteenth century expressed both in decrees and diplomatic ventures was to repudiate religious plural- ism and to ensure the protection of the mind and faith of the flock.[61] Even between the world wars Ronald Arbuthnott Knox was aggravating Eng- lish Protestants with talk of restrictive religious laws if ever a Catholic regime were in a position to implement such: "a body of Catholic patriots, entrusted with the Government of a Catholic State, will not shrink even from repressive measures in order to perpetuate the secure domination of Catholic principles among their fellow-countrymen."[62]

Thus, one of the significant seismic events in Christianity in the twenti- eth century was the decree flowing from the Second Vatican Council, late in 1965, *Dignitatis humanae vitae*. If the magisterium of the Roman Catholic Church was late to embrace the notion, when acceptance of religious liberty came, its expression was clear and confident, though there were not a few opponents within that church. The decree represented something close to a repudiation of centuries of teaching and practice, and, while not drawing back from the church's claims to possession of the truth, *Dignitatis* locates religious liberty in the human person: "The Synod further declares that the right to religious freedom has its foundation in the very dignity of the human person, as this dignity is known through the revealed Word of God and by reason itself. This right of the human person to religious freedom is to be recognized in the constitutional law whereby society is governed."[63] However, suspicion dies hard, and one Protestant theologian has expressed concern over apparent loopholes which might allow a recrudescence of Catholic action prejudicial to religious pluralism.[64]

The selections which follow describe a number of different attitudes, aris- ing from diverse intellectual and social foundations. There are humanistic ideas about freedom in the quest for truth; skepticism about the attainab- ility of truth; the Bible as proof text for diametrically opposed positions; non-dogmatic views of Christianity which care little for doctrine, and more for morality which may not depend upon a particular religion; disputes over the nature and function of conscience; fear of pluralism leading to social breakdown and of persecution destroying human vitality. One finds a panor- ama of theological and philosophical perspectives, by no means all compat- ible with each other, but all the while illuminating the human condition, of which these entwined issues are essential components; thus the significance found within these covers is not just historical but profoundly existential and current. One cannot foresee the day when the question of religious pluralism will cease to merit careful consideration and vigorous debate. The editor dares to hope that this anthology will further awareness of and conversation about intolerance, toleration, and liberty.

Notes

1   Samuel Butler, *The Way of All Flesh* (Ware, Herts.: Wordsworth Editions, 1994), p. 327.
2   Ian S. Markham, *Plurality and Christian Ethics* (Cambridge: Cambridge University Press, 1994), pp. 9–10.
3   James B. Wiggins, *In Praise of Religious Diversity* (New York: Routledge, 1996), pp. 5–6.
4   John Hick and Hasan Askari (eds), *The Experience of Religious Diversity* (Aldershot: Gower, 1985); John Hick, "The Non-Absoluteness of Christianity," in John Hick and Paul F. Knitter (eds), *The Myth of Christian Uniqueness: Toward a Pluralistic Theology of Religions* (Maryknoll, NY: Orbis Books, 1987), p. 23.
5   Richard Rorty, "Religion as Conversation-Stopper," *Common Knowledge*, 3 (1994), p. 2.
6   Richard Webster, *A Brief History of Blasphemy: Liberalism, Censorship and "The Satanic Verses"* (Southwold: The Orwell Press, 1990).
7   Bernard Lewis, *The Jews of Islam* (Princeton, NJ: Princeton University Press, 1984), pp. 3–4.
8   Franklin H. Littell, "Religious Liberty: The Present Challenge," in Charles Wei-hsun Fu and Gerhard E. Spiegler (eds), *Movements and Issues in World Religions: A Sourcebook and Analysis of Developments since 1945. Religion, Ideology, and Politics* (Westport, CT: Greenwood Press, 1987), p. 201.
9   Theodore K. Rabb, "Religious Toleration during the Age of Reformation," in Malcolm R. Thorpe and Arthur J. Slavin (eds), *Politics, Religion and Diplomacy in Early Modern Europe: Essays in Honor of De Lamar Jensen*, vol. xxvii (Kirksville, MO: Sixteenth-Century Essays & Studies, 1994), pp. 305–19.
10   Philip Wogaman, *Protestant Faith and Religious Liberty* (Nashville, TN: Abingdon Press, 1967), p. 29.
11   *The Times Higher Education Supplement*, November 18, 1994.
12   Reported in *The Times*, August 5, 1996, p. 9.
13   *The Times*, October 11, 1995, editorial, "Canterbury and Khartoum: Dr Carey Stands up for Sudan's Christians."
14   Stephen L. Carter, *The Culture of Disbelief: How American Law and Politics Trivialize Religious Devotion* (New York: Basic Books, 1993), p. 40: "the religions as autonomous communities of resistance and as independent sources of meaning." See also David Tracy, *Plurality and Ambiguity: Hermeneutics, Religion, Hope* (San Francisco, CA: Harper & Row, 1987), p. 84: "Above all, the religions are exercises in resistance."

15 "A Confession of Faith of Seven Congregations or Churches of Christ in London," in Edward Bean Underhill (ed.), *Confessions of Faith, and other Public Documents, Illustrative of the History of the Baptist Churches of England in the 17th Century* (London, 1854), p. 45.

16 John A. Ryan and Moorhouse F. X. Millar, *The State and the Church* (New York: Macmillan, 1924), p. 59.

17 Ernst Troeltsch, "Die Bedeutung des Protestantismus für die Entstehung der modernen Welt," in *Historische Zeitschrift*, 3rd series, 1 (1906), p. 38. I am grateful to Professor Dr Diethelm Klippel, Universität Bayreuth, for bringing this essay to my attention, and also for sending me a copy. It may be found in English translation in Ernst Troeltsch, *Protestantism and Progress: A Historical Study of the Relation of Protestantism to the Modern World*, tr. W. Montgomery (Boston, MA: Beacon Press, 1958 [1912]), p. 118.

18 Perez Zagorin, *Ways of Lying: Dissimulation, Persecution, and Conformity in Early Modern Europe* (Cambridge, MA: Harvard University Press, 1990).

19 Dimitry V. Pospielovsky, *A History of Marxist-Leninist Atheism and Soviet Antireligious Policies*, vol. 1 of *A History of Soviet Atheism in Theory and Practice, and the Believer* (New York: St Martin's Press, 1987), p. 2.

20 Ninan Koshy, *Religious Freedom in a Changing World* (Geneva: WCC Publications, 1992), pp. 24ff.

21 Cyril E. Bryant and Ruby J. Burke (eds), *Celebrating Christ's Presence through the Spirit: Official Report of the Fourteenth Congress, Baptist World Alliance, Toronto, 1980* (Nashville, TN: Broadman Press, 1981), pp. 248–9.

22 This covenant was intended to be incorporated into United Nations treaty provisions and made obligatory on member states which ratified it. The full text may be consulted in Charles Humana (ed.), *World Human Rights Guide* (New York: Pico Press, 1984), pp. 18–23.

23 Thomas Paine, *The Rights of Man*, in *Writings*, 4 vols, ed. M. D. Conway (New York: G. P. Putnam's Sons, 1894–6), vol. II, p. 325.

24 Preston King, *Toleration* (London: George Allen & Unwin, 1976), pp. 25–6.

25 Jay Newman, *Foundations of Religious Tolerance* (Toronto: University of Toronto Press, 1982), p. 22.

26 Aquinas, *Summa Theologica*, II/II, Question 10, Answer 11.

27 See John T. Noonan, Jr, "Principled or Pragmatic Foundations for the Freedom of Conscience?" *Journal of Law and Religion*, 5 (1987), pp. 203–12.

28 Susan Mendus, *Toleration and the Limits of Liberalism* (Atlantic Highlands, NJ: Humanities Press, 1989), pp. 18–21. See also Bernard Williams, "Toleration: An Impossible Virtue?" in David Heyd (ed.), *Toleration: An Elusive Virtue* (Princeton, NJ: Princeton University Press,1996), pp. 18–27.

29 Heinrich A. Rommen, *The State in Catholic Thought* (St Louis, MO: Herder, 1950 [1945]), p. 438.

30 Mieczyslaw Maneli, *Freedom and Tolerance* (New York: Octagon, 1984), p. 351; Newman, *Foundations of Religious Tolerance*, pp. 21–3.

31 King, *Toleration*, p. 9.

32 H. E. Cardinale, *Religious Tolerance, Freedom and Inter-Group Relations in the Light of Vatican Council II* (London: Council of Christians and Jews, 1966),

pp. 5, 7. The author, a Roman Catholic archbishop, was apostolic delegate to Great Britain. The occasion was the Robert Waley Cohen Memorial Lecture for 1966.

33 Gustav Mensching, *Tolerance and Truth in Religion*, tr. H.-J. Klimkeit (University, Alabama: University of Alabama Press, 1971 [German orig. 1955]), pp. 29–42.

34 Michael A. Mullett, *Radical Religious Movements in Early Modern Europe* (London: George Allen & Unwin, 1980), p. xii.

35 Introduction by Roland H. Bainton, in Sebastian Castellio, *Concerning Heretics* [1554], tr. Bainton (New York: Octagon, 1965 [1935]), p. 12.

36 David Hume, *The Natural History of Religion*, cited in James Sambrook, *The Eighteenth Century: The Intellectual and Cultural Context of English Literature, 1700–1789*, 2nd edn (London: Longman, 1993), p. 49.

37 Stuart J. Fiedel, *Prehistory of the Americas*, 2nd edn (Cambridge: Cambridge University Press, 1992), p. 345. See also George A. Collier, Renato I. Rosaldo and John D. Wirth (eds), *The Inca and Aztec States 1400–1800: Anthropology and History* (New York: Academic Press, 1982), pp. 108–9.

38 Livy, *History of Rome*, bk 39; Stephen Benko, *Pagan Rome and the Early Christians* (London: B. T. Batsford, 1985), p. 11.

39 James Beckman, *The Religious Dimensions of Socrates' Thought* (Waterloo, Ont.: Wilfrid Laurier University Press, 1979), pp. 58–9. See also I. F. Stone, *The Trial of Socrates* (Boston: Little, Brown, 1988), esp. pp. 231–47.

40 V. Valdenberg, "Discours politiques de Thémistius dans leur rapport avec l'antiquité," tr. H. Grégoire, *Byzantion*, 1 (1924), pp. 579–80.

41 Jay Newman, *On Religious Freedom* (Ottawa: University of Ottawa Press, 1991), chs 2 and 3. See also Markham, *Plurality and Christian Ethics*, ch. 10.

42 Tertullian, *To Scapula*, ch. 2.

43 Lactantius, *The Divine Institutes*, V: 21.

44 Julius Firmicus Maternus, *The Error of the Pagan Religions*, ed. Clarence A. Forbes, vol. 37 of *Ancient Christian Writers* (New York: Newman Press, 1970).

45 Tertullian, *Apology*, ch. 40.

46 *The Theodosian Code and Novels and the Sirmondian Constitution*, ed. Clyde Pharr (Princeton, NJ: Princeton University Press, 1952), p. 490 (from the year 438).

47 N. Q. King, "*Compelle Intrare* and the Plea of the Pagans," *Modern Churchman*, n.s., 4 (1960–1), p. 112.

48 Ludovico of Paramo, *De origini et progressu officii sanctae inquisitionis, eiusque dignitate & utilitate* (Madrid, 1598), pp. 83–7.

49 Walter Wakefield and Austin Evans (eds), *Heresies of the High Middle Ages: Selected Sources Translated and Annotated* (New York: Columbia University Press, 1969), p. 91.

50 R. I. Moore, *The Formation of a Persecuting Society: Power and Deviance in Western Europe, 950–1250* (Oxford: Basil Blackwell, 1990), p. 5; emphasis in original.

51 Friedrich Heer, *The Medieval World: Europe 1100–1350*, tr. Janet Sondheimer (New York: Mentor, 1961), p. 146; John Boswell, *Christianity, Social Tolerance, and Homosexuality* (Chicago: University of Chicago Press, 1980), pp. 269ff.

52   Pope Alexander III, "Third Lateran Council" (1179), in Henry Joseph Schroeder (ed.), *Disciplinary Decrees of the General Councils* (St Louis, MO: Herder, 1937), pp. 234–5; Pope Lucius III, "Ad abolendam" (1184), in George G. Coulton, *The Death Penalty for Heresy from 1184 to 1921* (London, 1924), pp. 49–50; Wakefield and Evans (eds), *Heresies of the High Middle Ages*; Edward Peters (ed.), *Heresy and Authority in Medieval Europe* (Philadelphia: University of Pennsylvania Press, 1980).

53   Thomas Aquinas, *Summa Theologica*, II/II, Questions 10–11.

54   Eric D'Arcy, *Conscience and its Right to Freedom* (London: Sheed and Ward, 1961); *Summa Theologica*, I/II, Question 19, Article 5.

55   Peter Abelard, *Ethics*, ed. D. E. Luscombe (Oxford: Clarendon, 1971), p. 67.

56   Walter Rex, *Essays on Pierre Bayle and Religious Controversy* (The Hague: Martinus Nijhoff, 1965), pp. 180–1; John Kilcullen, *Sincerity and Truth: Essays on Arnauld, Bayle, and Toleration* (Oxford: Clarendon, 1988), pp. 89ff.

57   E. g. Samuel Rutherford, *A Free Disputation Against Pretended Liberty of Conscience* (London, 1649), p. 10.

58   Lord Acton, "The Protestant Theory of Persecution," in *Essays on Freedom and Power*, ed. Gertrude Himmelfarb (Gloucester, MA: Peter Smith, 1972 [1948]), p. 116.

59   Winthrop S. Hudson, "John Locke – Preparing the Way for the Revolution," *Journal of Presbyterian History*, 42 (1964), pp. 19–38; see also his "John Locke: Heir of Puritan Political Theorists," in George L. Hunt (ed.), *Calvinism and the Political Order* (Philadelphia, PA: Westminster, 1965).

60   Mendus, *Toleration and the Limits of Liberalism*.

61   Pope Gregory XVI, "Mirari vos" (1832), in Claudia Carlen (ed.), *The Papal Encyclicals*, 5 vols (Wilmington, NC: McGrath, 1981), vol. I, 235–41; Pius IX, "Quanta Cura and the Syllabus of Errors" (1864), in Anne Fremantle (ed.), *The Papal Encyclicals in their Historical Context* (New York: G. P. Putnam's Sons, 1956), pp. 135–52; Leo XIII, "Libertas" (1888), in Carlen (ed.), *Papal Encyclicals*, vol. II, pp. 169–81. See also John A. Ryan, "Condemnation of L'Avenir," *Catholic Historical Review*, 23 (1937), pp. 31–9; Peter Doyle, "Pope Pius IX and Religious Freedom," in W. J. Sheils (ed.), *Persecution and Toleration* (Oxford: Basil Blackwell, 1984), pp. 329–41.

62   *The Belief of Catholics* (New York: Harper & Brothers, 1927), p. 242. In the 5th edn (London: Sheed and Ward, 1957), pp. 203–4, the statement was softened: "Such considerations would reasonably be invoked if a body of Catholic patriots, entrusted with the government of a Catholic State, should deny to the innovator the right of spreading his doctrines publicly, and so endangering the domination of Catholic principles among their fellow-countrymen." See Cecil John Cadoux, *Roman Catholicism and Freedom* (London: Independent Press, 1936), pp. 50–92.

63   *Dignitatis Humanae Personae*, in Walter M. Abbott (ed.), *The Documents of Vatican II* (New York: Guild Press, 1966), pp. 675–96.

64   Wogaman, *Protestant Faith and Religious Liberty*, pp. 36–7.

1

THE ANCIENT WORLD

The Bible

These selections cover both the ancient Hebrew and early Christian texts. If some may seem obscure, they are included here because of the use made by later commentators – the example *par excellence* is Matthew 13, the parable of the tares, which would exercise numerous writers from antiquity to the seventeenth century, from North Africa to England to the remote forests of the Trans-Volga.[1] There is also a question whether a religion which makes claims to absolute truth can be other than a persecuting religion, if conditions permit. Many of the readings presented in subsequent sections of the anthology may be viewed as commentaries on this question.

SOURCE: Scripture passages are taken from the *Revised Standard Version of the Bible*, copyright 1946, 1952, 1971 by the Division of Christian Education of the National Council of the Churches of Christ in the USA. Reproduced with permission.
LITERATURE: Gustav Mensching, *Tolerance and Truth in Religion*, tr. H.-J. Klimkeit (University, AL: University of Alabama Press, 1971 [German orig. 1955]), esp. pp. 29–35; Jay Newman, *On Religious Freedom* (Ottawa: University of Ottawa Press, 1991), chs 2 and 3.

Deuteronomy 13

(1) If a prophet arises among you, or a dreamer of dreams, and gives you a sign or a wonder, and the sign or wonder which he tells you comes to pass, and if he says, "Let us go after other gods," which you have not known,

"and let us serve them," you shall not listen to the words of that prophet or to that dreamer of dreams; for the Lord your God is testing you, to know whether you love the Lord your God with all your heart and with all your soul. You shall walk after the Lord your God and fear him, and keep his commandments and obey his voice, and you shall serve him and cleave to him. But that prophet or that dreamer of dreams shall be put to death, because he has taught rebellion against the Lord your God, who brought you out of the land of Egypt and redeemed you out of the house of bondage, to make you leave the way in which the Lord your God commanded you to walk. So you shall purge the evil from the midst of you.

(6)   If your brother, the son of your mother, or your son, or your daughter, or the wife of your bosom, or your friend who is as your own soul, entices you secretly, saying 'Let us go and serve other gods,' which neither you nor your fathers have known, some of the gods of the peoples that are round about you, whether near you or far off from you, from the one end of the earth to the other, you shall not yield to him or listen to him, nor shall your eye pity him, nor shall you spare him, nor shall you conceal him; but you shall kill him; your hand shall be first against him to put him to death, and afterwards the hand of all the people. You shall stone him to death with stones, because he sought to draw you away from the Lord your God, who brought you out of the land of Egypt, out of the house of bondage. And all Israel shall hear, and fear, and never again do any such wickedness as this among you.

(12)   If you hear in one of your cities, which the Lord your God gives you to dwell there, that certain base fellows have gone out among you and have drawn away the inhabitants of the city, saying, "Let us go and serve other gods," which you have not known, then you shall inquire and make search and ask diligently; and behold, if it be true and certain that such an abominable thing has been done among you, you shall surely put the inhabitants of that city to the sword, destroying it utterly, all who are in it and its cattle, with the edge of the sword. You shall gather all its spoil into the midst of its open square, and burn the city and all its spoil with fire, as a whole burnt offering to the Lord your God; it shall be a heap for ever, it shall not be built again. None of the devoted things shall cleave to your hand; that the Lord may turn from the fierceness of his anger, and show you mercy, and have compassion on you, and multiply you, as he swore to your fathers, if you obey the voice of the Lord your God, keeping all his commandments which I command you this day, and doing what is right in the sight of the Lord your God.

Matthew 13: 24–30, 36–43

Another parable he put before them, saying, "The kingdom of heaven may be compared to a man who sowed good seed in his field; but while men were sleeping, his enemy came and sowed weeds among the wheat, and went away. So when the plants came up and bore grain, then the weeds appeared also. And the servants of the householder came and said to him, 'Sir, did you not sow good seed in your field? How then has it weeds?' He said to them, 'An enemy has done this.' The servants said to him, 'Then do you want us to go and gather them?' But he said, 'No; lest in gathering the weeds you root up the wheat along with them. Let both grow together until the harvest; and at harvest time I will tell the reapers, Gather the weeds first and bind them in bundles to be burned, but gather the wheat into my barn.'"

... Then he left the crowds and went into the house. And his disciples came to him, saying, "Explain to us the parable of the weeds of the field." He answered, "He who sows the good seed is the Son of man; the field is the world, and the good seed means the sons of the kingdom; the weeds are the sons of the evil one, and the enemy who sowed them is the devil; the harvest is the close of the age, and the reapers are angels. Just as the weeds are gathered and burned with fire, so will it be at the close of the age. The Son of man will send his angels, and they will gather out of his kingdom all causes of sin and all evildoers, and throw them into the furnace of fire; there men will weep and gnash their teeth. Then the righteous will shine like the sun in the kingdom of their Father. He who has ears, let him hear."

Luke 9: 51–6

When the days drew near for him to be received up, he set his face to go to Jerusalem. And he sent messengers ahead of him, who went and entered a village of the Samaritans, to make ready for him; but the people would not receive him, because his face was set toward Jerusalem. And when his disciples James and John saw it, they said, "Lord, do you want us to bid fire come down from heaven and consume them?" But he turned and rebuked them. And they went on to another village.

Luke 14: 15–24

When one of those who sat at table with him heard this, he said to him, "Blessed is he who shall eat bread in the kingdom of God!" But he said to him, "A man once gave a great banquet, and invited many; and at the time for the banquet he sent his servant to say to those who had been invited, 'Come; for all is now ready.' But they all alike began to make excuses. The first said to him, 'I have bought a field, and I must go out and see it; I pray you, have me excused.' And another said, 'I have bought five yoke of oxen, and I go to examine them; I pray you, have me excused.' And another said, 'I have married a wife, and therefore I cannot come.' So the servant came and reported this to his master. Then the householder in anger said to his servant, 'Go out quickly to the streets and lanes of the city, and bring in the poor and maimed and blind and lame.' And the servant said, 'Sir, what you commanded has been done, and still there is room.' And the master said to the servant, 'Go out to the highways and hedges, and compel people to come in [*compelle intrare*], that my house may be filled. For I tell you, none of those men who were invited shall taste my banquet.'"

Acts 5: 33–9

When they heard this they were enraged and wanted to kill them [Peter and the apostles]. But a Pharisee in the council named Gamaliel, a teacher of the law, held in honor by all the people, stood up and ordered the men to be put outside for a while. And he said to them, "Men of Israel, take care what you do with these men. For before these days Theudas arose, giving himself out to be somebody, and a number of men, about four hundred, joined him; but he was slain and all who followed him were dispersed and came to nothing. After him Judas the Galilean arose in the days of the census and drew away some of the people after him; he also perished, and all who followed him were scattered. So in the present case I tell you, keep away from these men and let them alone; for if this plan or this undertaking is of men, it will fail; but if it is of God, you will not be able to overthrow them. You might even be found opposing God!"

Ancient Greece

Plato, *Laws* (*c.* 350)

This late work by Plato (c. 428–c. 348) discusses the rule of law and reflects an attempt to improve upon the political reality of the Athenian polis. With respect to the laws about religion in book X, Plato takes for granted the numerous but uncodified Athenian laws against impiety and gives them greater definition. He accepts that the well-governed state must necessarily advance the cause of religion which will buttress the rule of law. Some have seen here the lineaments of the medieval inquisition.[2] While this is probably excessive, there is a clear statement of the state's readiness to act against expressed opinions contrary to established religious belief and practice. But his net was not such as to capture Socrates, whose trial for alleged impiety Plato thought a travesty.[3]

SOURCE: *The Laws of Plato*, tr. A. E. Taylor (London: J. M. Dent & Sons, 1934), Book X, sections 907–10, pp. 301–4.
LITERATURE: Glenn R. Morrow, *Plato's Cretan City: A Historical Interpretation of the "Laws"* (Princeton, NJ: Princeton University Press, 1960), pp. 470–96.

Athenian: Then I presume we may say our three propositions, that there are gods, that they are mindful of us, that they are never to be seduced from the path of right, are sufficiently demonstrated.

Clinias: Indeed you may, and my friend and I concur with your arguments.

Athenian: Still I confess they have been delivered with some heat due to eagerness to triumph over these bad men. But the source of this zeal, my dear Clinias, was apprehension that if they get the better of the argument, the wicked may fancy themselves free to *act* as they will, seeing how many strange ideas they entertain about the gods. This is what prompted me to speak with more than common vigor; if I have done never so little to influence such men toward self-reprobation and attraction towards the opposite type of character, the prelude to our laws against impiety will have been spoken to good purpose.

Clinias: Well, let us hope so; but if not, at least the cause will bring no discredit on a legislator.

Athenian: So our preamble may properly be followed by a sentence which will express the sense of our laws, a general injunction to the ungodly to turn from their ways to those of godliness. For the disobedient our law against *impiety* may run as follows: If any man commit impiety of word or act, any person present shall defend the law by giving information to the magistrates, and the first magistrates under whose notice the matter comes shall bring the case before the court appointed to deal with such offenses as the law directs. Any official failing to take action on information received shall himself be liable to be proceeded against for impiety at the suit of anyone willing to vindicate the law. In the case of conviction, the court shall impose a particular penalty on the offender for each act of impiety. Imprisonment shall form part of the penalty in all cases. And whereas there are three prisons in the State, a *common gaol* in the market-place for the majority of cases, for safe custody of the persons of the commonalty, a second attached to the Nocturnal Council and known as the *house of correction*, and a third in the heart of the country in the most solitary and wildest situation available, and called by some designation suggestive of *punishment*; and whereas also there are three causes of impiety, those we have already specified, and each such cause gives rise to two types of offense, there will be in all six classes of offenders against religion to be discriminated, who require different and dissimilar treatment. For though a man should be a complete unbeliever in the being of the gods, if he have also a native uprightness of temper, such persons will detest evil men; their repugnance to wrong disinclines them to commit wrongful acts; they shun the unrighteous and are drawn to the upright. But those in whom the conviction that the world has no place in it for gods is conjoined with incontinence of pleasure and pain and the possession of a vigorous memory and a keen intelligence share the malady of atheism with the other sort, but are sure to work more harm, where the former do less, in the way of mischief to their fellows. The first man may probably be free-spoken enough about gods, sacrifices, and oaths, and perhaps, if he does not meet with his deserts, his mockery may make converts of others. But the second, who holds the same creed as the other, but is what is popularly called a "man of parts", a fellow of plentiful subtlety and guile – that is the type which furnishes our swarms of diviners and fanatics for all kinds of imposture; on occasion also it produces dictators, demagogues, generals, contrivers of private Mysteries, and the arts and tricks of the so-called "sophist". Thus there are numerous types of these atheists, but two which legislation must take into account, the hypocritical, whose crimes deserve more than one death, or even two, and the others, who call for the combination of admonition with confinement. Similarly, the belief in divine indifference gives rise to two further types, and that in divine venality to another two. These distinctions once recognized, the law shall direct the judge to commit those whose fault is due to folly apart from viciousness of temper or disposition to the house of correction for a term of not less than five years. Throughout this period they shall have no communication with any citizen except the members of the Nocturnal Council, who shall visit them with a view to admonition and their soul's salvation. When the term of confinement has expired, if the prisoner is deemed to have returned to his right mind, he shall dwell with the right-minded, but if not, and he be condemned a second time on the same charge, he shall suffer the penalty of death. As for those who add the character of a beast of prey to their atheism or belief in divine indifference or venality, those who in their contempt of mankind bewitch so many of the living by the pretence of evoking the dead and the promise of winning over the gods by the supposed sorceries of prayer, sacrifice, and incantations, and thus do their best for lucre to ruin individuals, whole families, and communities, the law shall direct the court to sentence a culprit convicted of belonging to this class to incarceration in the central prison, where no free citizen whatsoever shall have access to him, and where he shall receive from the turnkeys the strict rations prescribed by the Curators of the Laws. At death he shall be cast out beyond the borders without burial, and if any free citizen has a hand in his burial, he shall be liable to a prosecution for impiety at the suit of any who cares to take proceedings. But should he leave children fit to be citizens, the guardians of orphans shall provide for them also, no worse than for other orphans, from the date of the father's conviction.

Moreover we must frame a law applicable to all these offenders alike, and designed to alleviate the sin of most of them against religion in word or act – to say nothing of the folly of the sinners – by the prohibition of illegal ceremonial.

In fact the following law should be enacted for all cases without exception. No man shall possess a shrine in his private house; when a man feels himself moved to offer sacrifice, he shall go to the public temples for that purpose and deliver his offerings to the priests of either sex whose business it is to consecrate them. He may join with himself in the prayers any persons whose company he may desire. This regulation shall be adopted for the reasons following. The founding of a sanctuary or cult is no light task; to discharge it properly demands some serious thought. But it is the common way, especially with all women, with the sick universally, with persons in danger or any sort of distress, as on the other hand with those who have enjoyed a stroke of good fortune, to dedicate whatever comes to hand at the moment and vow sacrifices and endowments to gods, spirits, and sons of gods, as prompted by fears of portents beheld in waking life, or by dreams. Similarly, the recollection of endless visions and the quest of a specific for them commonly leads to a filling of every house and village with shrines and altars erected in clear spaces or wherever such persons are minded to place them. All these are grounds for conformity with the law now proposed, and there is the further ground that it serves as a check on the ungodly. It prevents them from fraud in this matter itself, from setting up shrines and altars in their own houses, under the delusion that they are winning the privy favor of Heaven by offerings and prayers, thus indefinitely aggravating their criminality and bringing guilt before God on themselves and the better men who tolerate their conduct, until the whole community reaps the harvest of their impiety – as in a sense it deserves. Our legislator, in any case, shall be clear before God, for his enactment shall run thus: No citizen to possess a shrine in his private dwelling-house; in the case of proved possession, or worship at any shrine other than the public, if the possessor, whether man or woman, have committed no serious act of impiety, he that discovers the fact shall proceed to lay an information before the Curators of the Law, who shall direct the private shrine to be removed to a public temple, and, in the case of disobedience, impose penalties until the removal is effected. Any person proved guilty of a sin against piety which is the crime of a grown man, not the trivial offense of a child, whether by dedicating a shrine on private ground or by doing sacrifice to any gods whatsoever in public, shall suffer death for doing sacrifice in a state of defilement. What offenses are or are not puerile shall be decided by the Curators, who shall bring the offenders accordingly before the courts and inflict the penalty.

Roman Empire

Tertullian, "Apology" and "Letter to Scapula" (197, 212)

Little is known of this Carthaginian, but it would appear that he had received a classical education and that he was a convert to Christianity from paganism. Tertullian argued that the free choice of religion was a natural right. He ridiculed forced religion, and complained that in the myriad religions of the empire, only the Christians were to be denied their own. He insisted that Christians were free of malice, they were not subversive, and they loved their persecutors, who would in due course be punished by the one true God.

SOURCE: Tertullian, *The Writings*, 3 vols, ed. A. Roberts and J. Donaldson [*Ante-Nicene Christian Library*] (Edinburgh, 1869–70), I, pp. 102–3, 121–2, 46–7, 48–9.

LITERATURE: Rudolph Arbesmann, "General Introduction" to Tertullian, *Apologetical Works*, and Minucius Felix, *Octavius* (Washington, DC: Catholic University of America Press, 1950) [*Fathers of the Church*, vol. 10]; Gerald Lewis Bray, *Holiness and the Will of God: Perspectives on the Theology of Tertullian* (London: Marshall, Morgan and Scott, 1979).

Apology

(24)   This whole confession of these beings [your gods when exorcised], in which they declare that they are not gods, and in which they tell you that there is no God but one, the God whom we adore, is quite sufficient to clear us from the crime of treason, chiefly against the Roman religion. For if it is certain the gods have no existence, there is no religion in the case. If there is no religion, because there are no gods, we are assuredly not guilty of any offense against religion. Instead of that, the charge recoils on your own head: worshipping a lie, you are really guilty of the crime you charge on us, not merely by refusing the true religion of the true God, but by going the further length of persecuting it. But now, granting that these objects of your worship are really gods, is it not generally held that there is one higher and more potent, as it were the world's chief ruler, endowed with absolute power and majesty? For the common way is to apportion deity, giving an imperial and supreme domination to one, while its offices are put into the hands of many, as Plato describes great Jupiter in the heavens, surrounded by an array at once of deities and demons. It behoves us, therefore, to show equal respect to the procurators, prefects, and governors of the divine empire. And yet how great a crime does he commit, who, with the object of gaining higher favor with the Caesar, transfers his endeavors and his hopes to another, and does not confess that the appellation of God as of Emperor belongs only to the Supreme Head, when it is held a capital offense among us to call, or hear called, by the highest title any other than Caesar himself! Let one man worship God, another Jupiter; let one lift suppliant hands to the heavens, another to the altar of Fides; let one – if you choose to take this view of it – count in prayer the clouds, and another the ceiling panels; let one consecrate his own life to his God, and another that of a goat. For see

that you do not give a further ground for the charge of irreligion, by taking away religious liberty, and forbidding free choice of deity, so that I may no longer worship according to my inclination, but am compelled to worship against it. Not even a human being would care to have unwilling homage rendered to him; and so the very Egyptians have been permitted the legal use of their ridiculous superstition, liberty to make gods of birds and beasts, nay, to condemn to death any one who kills a god of their sort. Every province even, and every city, has its god. Syria has Astarte, Arabia has Dusares, the Norici have Belenus, Africa has its Caelestis, Mauritania has its own princes. I have spoken, I think, of Roman provinces, and yet I have not said their gods are Roman; for they are not worshipped at Rome any more than others who are ranked as deities over Italy itself by municipal consecration, such as Delventinus of Casinum, Visidianus of Narnia, Ancharia of Asculum, Nortia of Volsinii, Valentia of Ocriculum, and Hostia of Satrium, Father Curis of Falisci, in honor of whom, too, Juno got her surname. In fact, we alone are prevented having a religion of our own. We give offense to the Romans, we are excluded from the rights and privileges of Romans, because we do not worship the gods of Rome. It is well that there is a God of all, whose we all are, whether we will or no. But with you liberty is given to worship any god but the true God, as though He were not rather the God all would worship, to whom all belong.

(40) On the contrary, *they* deserve the name of faction who conspire to bring odium on good men and virtuous, who cry out against innocent blood, offering as the justification of their enmity the baseless plea, that they think the Christians the cause of every public disaster, of every affliction with which the people are visited. If the Tiber rises as high as the city walls, if the Nile does not send its waters up over the fields, if the heavens give no rain, if there is an earthquake, if there is famine or pestilence, straightway the cry is, "Away with the Christians to the lion!" What! shall you give such multitudes to a single beast? . . .

To Scapula

(1) We are not in any great perturbation or alarm about the persecutions we suffer from the ignorance of men; for we have attached ourselves to this sect, fully accepting the terms of its covenant, so that, as men whose very lives are not their own, we engage in these conflicts, our desire being to obtain God's promised rewards, and our dread lest the woes with which He threatens an unchristian life should overtake us. So we shrink not from the

grapple with your utmost rage, coming even forth of our own accord to the contest; and condemnation gives us more pleasure than acquittal. We have sent therefore this tract to you in no alarm about ourselves, but in much concern for you and for all our enemies, to say nothing of our friends. For our religion commands us to love even our enemies, and to pray for those who persecute us, aiming at a perfection all its own, and seeking in its disciples something of a higher type than the commonplace goodness of the world. For all love those who love them; it is peculiar to Christians alone to love those that hate them. Therefore, mourning over your ignorance, and compassionating human error, and looking on to that future of which every day shows threatening signs, necessity is laid on us to come forth in this way also, that we may set before you the truths you will not listen to openly and publicly.

(2) We are worshippers of one God, of whose existence and character nature teaches all men; at whose lightnings and thunders you tremble, whose benefits minister to your happiness. You think that others, too, are gods, the same we know to be devils. However, it is a fundamental human right, a privilege of nature, that every man should worship according to his own convictions: one man's religion neither harms nor helps another man. It is assuredly no part of religion to compel religion – to which free-will and not force should lead us – the sacrificial victims even being required of a willing mind. You will render no real service to your gods by compelling us to sacrifice. For they can have no desire of offerings from the unwilling, unless they are animated by a spirit of contention, which is a thing altogether undivine. Accordingly the true God bestows His blessings alike on wicked men and on His own elect; upon which account He has appointed an eternal judgment, when both thankful and unthankful will have to stand before His bar. Yet you have never detected us – sacrilegious wretches though you reckon us to be – in any theft, far less in any sacrilege. But the robbers of your temples, all of them swear by your gods, and worship them; they are not Christians, and yet it is they who are found guilty of sacrilegious deeds. We have not time to unfold in how many other ways your gods are mocked and despised by their own votaries. So, too, treason is falsely laid to our charge, though no one has ever been able to find followers of Albinus, or Niger, or Cassius, among Christians; while the very men who had sworn by the genii of the emperors, who had offered and vowed sacrifices for their safety, who had often pronounced condemnation on Christ's disciples, are till this day found traitors to the imperial throne . . .

(3) However, as we have already remarked, it cannot but distress us that no state shall bear unpunished the guilt of shedding Christian blood; as you

see, indeed, in what took place during the presidency of Hilarian, for when there had been some agitation about places of sepulture for our dead, and the cry arose, "No *areae* – no burial grounds for the Christians," it came about that their own *areae*, their threshing-floors, were awanting, for they gathered in no harvests. As to the rains of the bygone year, it is abundantly plain of what they were intended to remind men – of the deluge, no doubt, which in ancient times overtook human unbelief and wickedness; and as to the fires which lately hung all night over the walls of Carthage, they who saw them know what they threatened; and what the preceding thunders pealed, *they* who were hardened by them can tell. All these things are signs of God's impending wrath, which we must needs publish and proclaim in every possible way; and in the meanwhile we must pray it may be only local. Sure are *they* to experience it one day in its universal and final form, who interpret otherwise these samples of it. That sun, too, in the metropolis of Utica, with light all but extinguished, was a portent which could not have occurred from an ordinary eclipse, situated as the lord of day was in his height and house. You have the astrologers, consult them about it. We can point you also to the deaths of some provincial rulers, who in their last hours had painful memories of their sin in persecuting the followers of Christ. Vigellius Saturninus, who first here used the sword against us, lost his eyesight. Claudius Lucius Herminianus in Cappadocia, enraged that his wife had become a Christian, had treated the Christians with great cruelty: well, left alone in his palace, suffering under a contagious malady, he boiled out in living worms, and was heard exclaiming, "Let nobody know of it, lest the Christians rejoice, and Christian wives take encouragement." Afterwards he came to see his error in having tempted so many from their stedfastness by the tortures he inflicted, and died almost a Christian himself. In that doom which overtook Byzantium, Caecilius Capella could not help crying out, "Christians, rejoice!" Yes, and the persecutors who seem to themselves to have acted with impunity shall not escape the day of judgment. For you we sincerely wish it may prove to have been a warning only, that, immediately after you had condemned Mavilus of Adrumetum to the wild beasts, you were overtaken by those troubles, and that even now for the same reason you are being called to a blood-reckoning. But do not forget the future.

Lactantius, *The Divine Institutes* (*c.* 306)

Sometimes called the "Christian Cicero," Lactantius (c. 240–c. 325) was able to speak of his religion in terms familiar to Romans. A native of

North Africa, he was appointed by Diocletian as teacher of Latin rhetoric in Nicomedia. Upon his conversion *c.* 300 he lost his position, though he was never subjected to physical abuse during the time of persecution. Thereafter he tutored Constantine's son Crispus. He shares with Eusebius the distinction of being a great historian of the early Christian empire. Later writers for religious liberty would cite him as a representative of the anti-compulsion opinion of ancient Christianity, while advocates of intolerance would have to reinterpret his inconvenient words.

SOURCE: Lactantius, *Works*, 2 vols, ed. A. Roberts and J. Donaldson [*Ante-Nicene Christian Library*] (Edinburgh, 1871), vol. I, pp. 338–41, 343.

LITERATURE: Introductory material by M. F. McDonald in Lactantius, *The Divine Institutes, Books I–VII* (Washington, DC, 1964) [vol. 49 of *Fathers of the Church*], pp. ix–xxv, 3–14.

Book V   Concerning justice

(20) . . . It is befitting that they [pagans] should undertake the defense of their gods, lest, if our affairs should increase (as they do increase daily), theirs should be deserted, together with their shrines and their vain mockeries; and since they can effect nothing by violence (for the religion of God is increased the more it is oppressed), let them rather act by the use of reason and exhortations.

Let their priests come forth into the midst, whether the inferior ones or the greatest; their flamens, augurs, and also sacrificing kings, and the priests and ministers of their superstitions. Let them call us together to an assembly; let them exhort us to undertake the worship of their gods; let them persuade us that there are many beings by whose deity and providence all things are governed; let them show how the origins and beginnings of their sacred rites and gods were handed down to mortals; let them explain what is their source and principle; let them set forth what reward there is in their worship, and what punishment awaits neglect; why they wish to be worshipped by men; what the piety of men contributes to them, if they are blessed: and let them confirm all these things not by their own assertion (for the authority of a mortal man is of no weight), but by some divine testimonies, as we do. There is no occasion for violence and injury, for religion cannot be imposed by force; the matter must be carried on by words rather than by blows, that the will may be affected. Let them unsheath the weapon of their intellect; if their system is true, let it be asserted. We are prepared to hear, if they teach; while they are silent, we certainly pay no credit to them, as we do not yield to them even in their rage. Let them imitate us in setting forth the system of the whole matter: for we do not entice, as they say; but we teach, we prove, we show. And thus no one is detained by us against his will, for he is unserviceable to God who is destitute of faith and devotedness; and yet no one departs from us, since the truth itself detains him. Let them teach in this manner, if they have any confidence in the truth; let them speak, let them give utterance; let them venture, I say, to discuss with us something of this nature; and then assuredly their error and folly will be ridiculed by the old women, whom they despise, and by our boys. For, since they are especially clever, they know from books the race of the gods, and their exploits, and commands, and deaths, and tombs; they may also know that the rites themselves, in which they have been initiated, had their origin either in human actions, or in casualties, or in deaths. It is the part of incredible madness to imagine that they are gods, whom they cannot deny to have been mortal; or if they should be so shameless as to deny it, their own writings, and those of their own people, will refute them; in short, the very beginnings of the sacred rites will convict them. They may know, therefore, even from this very thing, how great a difference there is between truth and falsehood; for they themselves with all their eloquence are unable to persuade, whereas the unskilled and the uneducated are able, because the matter itself and the truth speaks.

Why then do they rage, so that while they wish to lessen their folly, they increase it? Torture and piety are widely different; nor is it possible for truth to be united with violence, or justice with cruelty. But with good reason they do not venture to teach anything concerning divine things, lest they should both be derided by our people and be deserted by their own. For the common people for the most part, if they ascertain that these mysteries were instituted in memory of the dead, will condemn them, and seek for some truer object of worship.

Hence "rites of mystic awe"[4] were instituted by crafty men, that the people may not know what they worship. But since we are acquainted with their systems, why do they either not believe us who are acquainted with both, or envy us because we have preferred truth to falsehood? But, they say, the public rites of religion must be defended. Oh with what an honorable inclination the wretched men go astray! For they are aware that there is nothing among men more excellent than religion, and that this ought to be defended with the whole of our power; but as they are deceived in the matter of religion itself, so also are they in the manner of its defense. For religion is to be defended, not by putting to death, but by dying; not by cruelty, but by patient endurance; not by guilt, but by good faith: for the former belong to evils, but the latter to goods; and it is necessary for that which is good to have place in religion, and not that which is evil. For if you wish to defend religion by bloodshed, and by tortures, and by guilt, it will no longer be defended, but will be polluted and profaned. For nothing is so much a matter of free-will as religion; in which, if the mind of the worshipper is disinclined to it, religion is at once taken away, and ceases to exist. The right method therefore is, that you defend religion by patient endurance or by death; in which the preservation of the faith is both pleasing to God Himself, and adds authority to religion. For if he who in this earthly warfare preserves his faith to his king in some illustrious action, if he shall continue to live, becomes more beloved and acceptable, and if he shall fall, obtains the highest glory, because he has undergone death for his leader; how much more is faith to be kept towards God, the Ruler of all, who is able to pay the reward of virtue, not only to the living, but also to the dead! Therefore the worship of God, since it belongs to heavenly warfare, requires the greatest devotedness and fidelity. For how will God either love the worshipper, if He Himself is not loved by him, or grant to the petitioner whatever he shall ask, when he draws nigh to offer his prayer without sincerity or reverence? But these men, when they come to offer sacrifice, present to their gods nothing from within, nothing of their own – no uprightness of mind, no reverence or fear. Therefore, when the worthless sacrifices are completed, they leave their religion altogether in the temple, and with the temple, as they had found it; and neither bring with them anything of it, nor take anything back. . . .

(21) . . . But that is not a sacrifice which is extorted from a person against his will. For unless it is offered spontaneously, and from the soul, it is a curse; when men sacrifice, compelled by proscription, by injuries, by prison, by tortures. If they are gods who are worshipped in this manner, if for this reason only, they ought not to be worshipped, because they wish to be worshipped in this manner: they are doubtless worthy of the detestation of men, since libations are made to them with tears, with groaning, and with blood flowing from all the limbs.

But we, on the contrary, do not require that any one should be compelled, whether he is willing or unwilling, to worship our God, who is the God of all men; nor are we angry if any one does not worship Him. For we trust in the majesty of Him who has power to avenge contempt shown towards Himself, as also He has power to avenge the calamities and injuries inflicted on His servants. And therefore, when we suffer such impious things, we do not resist even in word; but we remit vengeance to God, not as they act who would have it appear that they are defenders of their gods, and rage without restraint against those who do not worship them. From which it may be understood how it is not good to worship their gods, since men ought to have been led to that which is good by good, and not by evil; but because this is evil, even its office is destitute of good. . . .

Julius Firmicus Maternus, *The Error of the Pagan Religions* (*c.* 346)

Little is known about this fourth-century convert to Christianity. He was a Sicilian of the senatorial class who as a pagan in the mid-330s wrote an extensive work on astrology. About a decade later he wrote a vigorous diatribe against the still-dominant paganism in which he called upon the *sacratissimi imperatores* to destroy every vestige of pagan religion. This work might conceivably have served the purposes of later generations of persecutors, but its surviving ninth- or tenth-century manuscript lay unknown in a German monastery until discovered by Matthias Flacius who published it in 1562.

SOURCE AND LITERATURE: Julius Firmicus Maternus, *The Error of the Pagan Religions*, ed. Clarence A. Forbes (New York: Newman Press, 1970), pp. 107–8, 110–11, 114–17.

Chapter 28

And so let that filth which you are accumulating be washed away. Seek the native springs, seek the clean waters, so that there Christ's blood with the Holy Spirit may wash you white after your many stains.

But a higher authority is needed to enable full conviction to restore wretched human creatures to sound thinking, so that in minds cured and renewed in health there may remain no vestige of the quondam pestilential disease. So through the mouth of the prophets and by the divine utterance of God we are informed what idols are and what reality they possess. All the particulars must be given here so that it will not look as if an idea were being advanced on the basis of my own temerity, when the idea is really transmitted to me by divine magisterium and certified by the voice of heaven. . . . [Hereafter follow a number of quotations from the Old Testament and Revelation.]

Take away, yes, calmly take away, Most Holy Emperors, the adornments of the temples. Let the fire of the mint or the blaze of the smelters melt them down, and confiscate all the votive offerings to your own use and ownership. Since the time of the destruction of the temples you have been, by God's power, advanced in greatness. You have overthrown your enemies, enlarged the Empire, and, to add greater luster to your exploits, altering and scorning the fixed order of the seasons you have done in the winter what was never done before or will be again: you have trodden upon the swollen and raging waters of the Ocean. The wave of a sea already become almost unknown to us has trembled beneath your oars, and the Briton has quailed before the unexpected visage of the Emperor. What more would you have? Vanquished by your exploits, the elements have bowed to you. . . .

Why are you so prone to sacrilege, and why do you stop up your ears? Why in the heat of obstinate madness do you rush like this to your own doom and death? God made you free; it is in your power either to live or perish. Why do you hurl yourself over the precipice? Since you are on a slippery path and on the very point of falling, do at last plant carefully your faltering steps. Lo, the sentence is pronounced; lo, the penalty is decreed. Long has the divine leniency spared your crimes, long has it pretended to overlook your wickedness. You are coming to the critical point where hope and prayers fail; and that you may be more plainly instructed, learn the upshot of the punishment. On this topic there is a complete and systematic pronouncement in the Apocalypse, for it is written as follows: "If any man adores the beast and his image and has received a mark on his forehead and on his hand, he also drinks of the wine of the wrath of God mingled in the cup of his wrath, and shall be punished with fire and brimstone before the eyes of the Lamb. And the smoke of their torments shall ascend up for ever and ever; neither shall they have rest day nor night, whoever adore the beast and his image" [Revelation 14: 9–11].

Chapter 29

But on you also, Most Holy Emperors, devolves the imperative necessity to castigate and punish this evil, and the law of the Supreme Deity enjoins on you that your severity should be visited in every way on the crime of idolatry. Hear and store up in your sacred intelligence what is God's commandment regarding this crime.

In Deuteronomy this law is written, for it says: . . . [13: 6–10] He bids spare neither son nor brother, and thrusts the avenging sword through the body of a beloved wife. A friend too He persecutes with lofty severity, and the whole populace takes up arms to rend the bodies of sacrilegious men.

Even for whole cities, if they are caught in this crime, destruction is decreed; and that your providence may more plainly learn this, I shall quote the sentence of the established law. In the same book the Lord establishes the penalty for whole cities with the following words, for He says: . . . [13: 12–18].

To you, Most Holy Emperors, the Supreme Deity promises the rewards of His mercy and decrees a multiplication on the greatest scale. Therefore do what He bids; fulfill what He commands. Your first efforts have been crowned abundantly with major rewards. While in the status of neophytes in the faith you have felt the increase of the divine favor. Never has the worshipful hand of God abandoned you; never has He refused you aid in your distress. The ranks of your foemen have been laid low, and always the arms that warred against you have been dropped at sight of you. Proud peoples have been subjugated and the Persian hopes have collapsed. Cruelty in its evil array has been unable long to stand against you. You have seen God's power, both of you, each by a different event; on you has been conferred a celestial crown of victory, and by your happy success our troubles are relieved.

These rewards, Most Holy Emperors, the Supreme Deity has given you in recognition of your faith; as you are repaid for the time being with these distinctions, He invites you in to the secrets of the worshipful law. With a pure heart, a devout conscience, and incorrupt mind let your clemency ever fix its gaze upon heaven, ever look for help from God, implore the worshipful godhead of Christ, and offer spiritual sacrifices to the God of salvation for the welfare of the world and your own. So will all things come to you in happy success: victories, riches, peace, plenty, health, and triumphs, so that borne forward by the power of God you may govern the world in fortunate sovereignty.

Themistius, Oratio V to Jovian (364)

The advent of Christian emperors brought about a bifurcation in the traditional unity of religious and political life. Now an incongruous situation of a Christian bearing the title *pontifex maximus* had arisen, and Themistius (317–c. 388), a pagan educator and bureaucrat at Constantinople, set out to articulate the imperial role in religious life based upon the resources of the classical humanist tradition. The emperor would uphold culture, not a sect, and thus might embody in himself values common to both pagan and Christian. Themistius encouraged Jovian to practice toleration and permit the divinely ordained flowering of individual diversity, anticipating, as Barker has noted, John Stuart Mill. In a later discourse for Valens (374), Themistius clearly denied any imperial power in the realm of religion. In terms of paganism at least, one may agree with Valdenberg that, here, Themistius had no predecessors.

SOURCE: Ernest Barker (ed.), *From Alexander to Constantine: Passages and Documents Illustrating the History of Social and Political Ideas, 336 BC–AD 337* (Oxford: Clarendon Press, 1956), pp. 378–80. Reproduced with permission of Oxford University Press.

LITERATURE: V. Valdenberg, "Discours politiques de Thémistius dans leur rapport avec l'antiquité," tr. H. Grégoire, *Byzantion*, 1 (1924), pp. 557–80; Lawrence J. Daly, "Themistius' Plea for Religious Tolerance," *Greek, Roman and Byzantine Studies*, 12 (1971), pp. 65–79.

You, and you only, as it appears, are aware that a king is not able to apply compulsion to his subjects in all things. There are some things which have escaped the yoke of necessity – things which are stronger than threats or commands; and among them are all the virtues, and especially the virtue of reverence for the Divine. *You* have recognized in your wisdom that a man in whom the movement of the mind is to be really and truly unforced, self-governing, and voluntary must be a leader in these good things. If it is not possible even for you, Sire, to bring it about that a man should be kind by rule and prescription without choosing internally to be so, how much more is it impossible to make a man reverent and dear to heaven by inspiring him with fear of transitory necessities and poor weak bugbears, which time has often brought in its course and as often carried away? We stand most foolishly convicted if we do honor to the purple instead of to God, and change our worship as easily and as often as the tide veers in the Euboean channel. . . .

Not such are you, most godlike of kings. You, "autocrat" and self-governor in all things, as you are and will be to the end, assign by law to all men their share in the rights of worship; and in this, too, you emulate God, who has made it a common attribute of the nature of men that they should be duly disposed to piety, but has made the *mode* of their worship depend on the will of each. To apply the compulsion of necessity is to deprive man of a power which has been granted to him by God. This is the reason why the laws of Cheops and Cambyses hardly lasted as long as their makers, but the law of God and *your* law remains unchanged for ever – that the mind of each and every man should be free to follow the way of worship which it thinks [to be best]. This is a law against which no confiscation, no crucifixion, no death at the stake has ever yet availed; you may hale and kill the body, if so be that this come to pass; but the mind will escape you, taking with it freedom of thought and the right of the law as it goes, even if it is subjected to force in the language used by the tongue.

Nor is your army, Sire, all ordered on one and the same scheme. Some are infantry and some cavalry; some bear arms, and some carry slings; some have their station by your person, some near it, others far away from it; some are content if they are known to the bodyguard, and some cannot get so far. But all depend, none the less, on you and on your judgment; and this is true not only of the men in the army but also of all other men – all who serve you otherwise than in war – farmers, orators, administrators, philosophers, and

all the rest. Bethink you, Sire, that the Author of the universe rejoices
in this diversity. It is His will that Syria should have one sort of polity,
Greece another, and Egypt another; nay, Syria itself is not all alike, but
divided into small parts. No man conceives things in exactly the same way
as his neighbor; one has his opinion, and another that. Why, then, attempt
to force men to the impossible?

John Chrysostom, Homily 46 on Matthew (c. 390)

Chrysostom (349–407) was born in Antioch (Syria) where he received a
good classical education, including the art of rhetoric. He accepted baptism in 368, and thereafter pursued the ascetic life for some years. He
returned to Antioch where he was ordained deacon (381) and presbyter
(386). His vigorous preaching earned him a considerable following; Arians
and Jews were particular targets of his sermons. In 398 he was elected
bishop of Constantinople, but his enemies engineered his fall in 403; he
died in exile.

SOURCE: *The Homilies of S. John Chrysostom, Archbishop of Constantinople, on the
Gospel of Matthew*, tr. G. Prevost, 3 vols (Oxford, 1841–3), vol. II, pp. 628–31.
LITERATURE: Robert L. Wilken, *John Chrysostom and the Jews: Rhetoric and Reality in
the Late 4th Century* (Berkeley, CA: University of California Press, 1983).

What is the difference between this, and the Parable before it [the parable
of the sower, Matthew 13: 18–23]? There He speaks of them that have not
at all holden with Him, but have started aside, and have thrown away the
seed; but here He means the societies of the heretics. For in order that not
even this might disturb His disciples, He foretells it also, after having
taught them why He speaks in Parables. The former Parable then means
their not receiving Him; this, their receiving corrupters too. For indeed this
also is a part of the devil's craft, by the side of the truth always to bring in
error, painting thereon many resemblances, so as easily to cheat the deceivable.
Therefore He calls it not any other seed, but tares; which in appearance are
somewhat like wheat.

Then He mentions also the manner of his device. For "while men slept,"
saith He. It is no small danger, which He hereby suspends over our rulers,
to whom especially is entrusted the keeping of the field; and not the rulers
only, but the subjects too.

And He signifies also that the error comes after the truth, which the
actual event testifies. For so after the Prophets, were the false prophets; and

after the Apostles, the false apostles; and after Christ, Antichrist. For unless the devil see what to imitate, or against whom to plot, he neither attempts, nor knows how. Now then also, having seen that "one brought forth a hundred, another sixty, another thirty," he proceeds after that another way. That is, not having been able to carry away what had taken root, not to choke, nor to scorch it up, he conspires against it by another craft, privily casting in his own inventions.

And what difference is there, one may say, between them that sleep, and them that resemble the wayside? That in the latter case he immediately caught it away; yea, he suffered it not even to take root; but here more of his craft was needed.

And these things Christ saith, instructing us to be always wakeful. For, saith He, though thou quite escape those harms, there is yet another harm. For as in those instances *the wayside*, and *the rock*, and *the thorns*, so here again sleep occasions our ruin; so that there is need of continual watchfulness. Wherefore He also said, "He that endureth to the end, the same shall be saved" [Matthew 10: 22].

Something like this took place even at the beginning. Many of the Prelates, I mean, bringing into the Churches wicked men, disguised heresiarchs, gave great facility to the laying that kind of snare. For the devil needs not even to take any trouble, when he hath once planted them among us.

And how is it possible not to sleep? one may say. Indeed, as to natural sleep, it is not possible; but as to that of our moral faculty, it is possible. Wherefore Paul also said, "Watch ye, stand fast in the faith" [1 Corinthians 16: 13].

After this He points out the thing to be superfluous too, not hurtful only; in that, after the land hath been tilled, and there is no need of any thing, then this enemy sows again; as the heretics also do, who for no other cause than vain glory inject their proper venom.

And not by this only, but by what follows likewise, He depicts exactly all their acting. For, "When the blade was sprung up," saith He, "and brought forth fruit, then appeared the tares also;" which kind of thing these men also do. For at the beginning they disguise themselves; but when they have gained much confidence, and some one imparts to them the teaching of the word, then they pour out their poison.

But wherefore doth He bring in the servants, telling what hath been done? That He may pronounce it wrong to slay them.

And he calls him *an enemy*, because of his harm done to men. For although the despite is against us, in its origin it sprang from his enmity, not to us, but to God. Whence it is manifest, that God loves us more than we love ourselves.

And see from another thing also, the malicious craft of the devil. For he did not sow before this, because he had nothing to destroy, but when all had been fulfilled, that he might defeat the diligence of the Husbandman; in such enmity against Him did he constantly act.

And mark also the affection of the servants. I mean, what haste they are in at once to root up the tares, even though they do it indiscreetly; which shows their anxiety for the crop, and that they are looking to one thing only, not to the punishment of that enemy, but to the preservation of the seed sown. For of course this other is not the urgent consideration.

Wherefore how they may for the present extirpate the mischief, this is their object. And not even this do they seek absolutely, for they trust not themselves with it, but await the master's decision, saying, "Wilt Thou"?

What then doth the Master? He forbids them, saying, "Lest haply ye root up the wheat with them." And this He said, to hinder wars from arising, and blood and slaughter. For it is not right to put a heretic to death, since an implacable war would be brought into the world. By these two reasons then He restrains them; one, that the wheat be not hurt; another, that punishment will surely overtake them, if incurably diseased. Wherefore, if thou wouldest have them punished, yet without harm to the wheat, I bid thee wait for the proper season.

But what means, "Lest ye root up the wheat with them?" Either He means this, If ye are to take up arms, and to kill the heretics, many of the saints also must needs by overthrown with them; or that of the very tares it is likely that many may change and become wheat. If therefore ye root them up beforehand, ye injure that which is to become wheat, slaying some, in whom there is yet room for change and improvement. He doth not therefore forbid our checking heretics, and stopping their mouths, and taking away their freedom of speech, and breaking up their assemblies and confederacies, but our killing and slaying them.

But mark thou His gentleness, how He not only gives sentence and forbids, but sets down reasons.

What then, if the tares should remain until the end? "Then I will say to the reapers, Gather ye together first the tares, and bind them in bundles to burn them." He again reminds them of John's words [Matthew 3: 12], introducing Him as Judge; and He saith, So long as they stand by the wheat, we must spare them, for it is possible for them even to become wheat; but when they have departed, having profited nothing, then of necessity the inexorable punishment will overtake them. "For I will say to the reapers," saith He, "Gather ye together first the tares." Why, *first*? That these may not be alarmed, as though the wheat were carried off with them. And bind them in bundles to burn them, but gather the wheat into My barn."

Augustine, Letter 93, Augustine to Vincentius, a schismatic bishop in Mauretania (408)

As the bishop of Hippo in North Africa, Augustine (354–430) entered into conflict with the schismatic Donatists. In working out a response to the sometimes violent fanaticism of these who rejected catholic claims to be the authentic church, Augustine gradually developed a theory of state intervention in the struggle against the enemies of the catholic faith; in his Retractions he wrote that once he had been opposed to the use of coercion against schismatics, but this was because he "had not yet learned either how much evil their impunity would dare or to what extent the application of discipline could bring about their improvement."[5] He was not without a forerunner in this enterprise; Optatus had written in c. 367 against the same opponents and taken some steps toward justifying the punishment of the schismatics.[6] But it was Augustine who would undergird the theological construction of coercion for centuries to come. In fact, it was only in the sixteenth century that his ideas would find serious and sustained opposition and then in the late seventeenth century receive a full frontal assault from Pierre Bayle.

SOURCE: Augustine, *Letters*, vol. I in *Works*, 15 vols, ed. Marcus Dods (Edinburgh, 1872), vol. VI, pp. 395–404, 409–13.

LITERATURE: Emilien Lamirande, *Church, State and Toleration: An Intriguing Change of Mind in Augustine* (Villanova, PA: Villanova University Press, 1975); Peter Brown, *Augustine of Hippo* (Berkeley, CA: University of California Press, 1969 [1967]), esp. ch. 21; John A. Rohr, "Religious Toleration in St. Augustine," *Journal of Church and State*, 9 (1967), pp. 51–70; R. A. Markus, *Saeculum: History and Society in the Theology of St. Augustine* (Cambridge: Cambridge University Press, 1988 [1970]), esp. ch. 5.

Chapter 1

(1)   I have received a letter which I believe to be from you to me: at least I have not thought this incredible, for the person who brought it is one whom I know to be a Catholic Christian, and who, I think, would not dare to impose upon me. But even though the letter may perchance not be from you, I have considered it necessary to write a reply to the author, whoever he may be. You know me now to be more desirous of rest, and earnest in seeking it, than when you knew me in my earlier years at Carthage, in the lifetime of your immediate predecessor Rogatus. But we are precluded from this rest by the Donatists, the repression and correction of whom, by the

powers which are ordained of God, appears to me to be labor not in vain. For we already rejoice in the correction of many who hold and defend the Catholic unity with such sincerity, and are so glad to have been delivered from their former error, that we admire them with great thankfulness and pleasure. Yet these same persons, under some indescribable bondage of custom, would in no way have thought of being changed to a better condition, had they not, under the shock of this alarm, directed their minds earnestly to the study of the truth; fearing lest, if without profit, and in vain, they suffered hard things at the hands of men, for the sake not of righteousness, but of their own obstinacy and presumption, they should afterwards receive nothing else at the hand of God than the punishment due to wicked men who despised the admonition which He so gently gave and His paternal correction; and being by such reflection made teachable, they found not in mischievous or frivolous human fables, but in the promises of the divine books, that universal Church which they saw extending according to the promise throughout all nations: just as, on the testimony of prophecy in the same Scriptures, they believed without hesitation that Christ is exalted above the heavens, though He is not seen by them in His glory. Was it my duty to be displeased at the salvation of these men, and to call back my colleagues from a fatherly diligence of this kind, the result of which has been, that we see many blaming their former blindness? For they see that they were blind who believed Christ to have been exalted above the heavens although they saw Him not, and yet denied that His glory is spread over all the earth although they saw it; whereas the prophet has with so great plainness included both in one sentence, "Be Thou exalted, O God, above the heavens, and Thy glory above all the earth" [Psalm 108: 5].

(2)   Wherefore, if we were so to overlook and forbear with those cruel enemies who seriously disturb our peace and quietness by manifold and grievous forms of violence and treachery, as that nothing at all should be contrived and done by us with a view to alarm and correct them, truly we would be rendering evil for evil. For if any one saw his enemy running headlong to destroy himself when he had become delirious through a dangerous fever, would he not in that case be much more truly rendering evil for evil if he permitted him to run on thus, than if he took measures to have him seized and bound? And yet he would at that moment appear to the other to be most vexatious, and most like an enemy, when, in truth, he had proved himself most useful and most compassionate; although, doubtless, when health was recovered, he would express to him his gratitude with a warmth proportioned to the measure in which he had felt his refusal to indulge him in his time of frenzy. Oh, if I could but show you how many we have even from the Circumcelliones, who are now approved Catholics,

and condemn their former life, and the wretched delusion under which they believed that they were doing in behalf of the Church of God whatever they did under the promptings of a restless temerity, who nevertheless would not have been brought to this soundness of judgment had they not been, as persons beside themselves, bound with the cords of those laws which are distasteful to you! As to another form of most serious distemper, – that, namely, of those who had not, indeed, a boldness leading to acts of violence, but were pressed down by a kind of inveterate sluggishness of mind, and would say to us: "What you affirm is true, nothing can be said against it; but it is hard for us to leave off what we have received by tradition from our fathers," – why should not such persons be shaken up in a beneficial way by a law bringing upon them inconvenience in worldly things, in order that they might rise from their lethargic sleep, and awake to the salvation which is to be found in the unity of the Church? How many of them, now rejoicing with us, speak bitterly of the weight with which their ruinous course formerly oppressed them, and confess that it was our duty to inflict annoyance upon them, in order to prevent them from perishing under the disease of lethargic habit, as under a fatal sleep!

(3)   You will say that to some these remedies are of no service. Is the art of healing, therefore, to be abandoned, because the malady of some is incurable? You look only to the case of those who are so obdurate that they refuse even such correction. Of such it is written, "In vain have I smitten your children: they received no correction" [Jeremiah 2: 30]: and yet I suppose that those of whom the prophet speaks were smitten in love, not from hatred. But you ought to consider also the very large number over whose salvation we rejoice. For if they were only made afraid, and not instructed, this might appear to be a kind of inexcusable tyranny. Again, if they were instructed only, and not made afraid, they would be with more difficulty persuaded to embrace the way of salvation, having become hardened through the inveteracy of custom: whereas many whom we know well, when arguments had been brought before them, and the truth made apparent by testimonies from the words of God, answered us that they desired to pass into the communion of the Catholic Church, but were in fear of the violence of worthless men, whose enmity they would incur; which violence they ought indeed by all means to despise when it was to be borne for righteousness' sake, and for the sake of eternal life. Nevertheless the weakness of such men ought not to be regarded as hopeless, but to be supported until they gain more strength. Nor may we forget what the Lord Himself said to Peter when he was yet weak: "Thou canst not follow Me now, but thou shalt follow Me afterwards" [John 13: 36]. When, however, wholesome instruction is added to means of inspiring salutary fear, so that not only the light of truth may dispel

the darkness of error, but the force of fear may at the same time break the bonds of evil custom, we are made glad, as I have said, by the salvation of many, who with us bless God, and render thanks to Him, because by the fulfillment of His covenant, in which He promised that the kings of the earth should serve Christ, He has thus cured the diseased and restored health to the weak.

Chapter 2

(4)   Not every one who is indulgent is a friend; nor is every one an enemy who smites. Better are the wounds of a friend than the proffered kisses of an enemy [Proverbs 27: 6]. It is better with severity to love, than with gentleness to deceive. More good is done by taking away food from one who is hungry, if, through freedom from care as to his food, he is forgetful of righteousness, than by providing bread for one who is hungry, in order that, being thereby bribed, he may consent to unrighteousness. He who binds the man who is in a frenzy, and he who stirs up the man who is in a lethargy, are alike vexatious to both, and are in both cases alike prompted by love for the patient. Who can love us more than God does? And yet He not only gives us sweet instruction, but also quickens us by salutary fear, and this unceasingly. Often adding to the soothing remedies by which He comforts men the sharp medicine of tribulation, He afflicts with famine even the pious and devout patriarchs, disquiets a rebellious people by more severe chastisements, and refuses, though thrice besought, to take away the thorn in the flesh of the apostle, that He may make His strength perfect in weakness [2 Corinthians 12: 7–9]. Let us by all means love even our enemies, for this is right, and God commands us so to do, in order that we may be the children of our Father who is in heaven, "who maketh His sun to rise on the evil and on the good, and sendeth rain on the just and on the unjust" [Matthew 5: 45]. But as we praise these His gifts, let us in like manner ponder His correction of those whom He loves.

(5)   You are of opinion that no one should be compelled to follow righteousness; and yet you read that the householder said to his servants, "Whomsoever ye shall find, compel them to come in" [Luke 14: 23]. You also read how he who was at first Saul, and afterwards Paul, was compelled, by the great violence with which Christ coerced him, to know and to embrace the truth; for you cannot but think that the light which our eyes enjoy is more precious to men than money or any other possession. This light, lost suddenly by him when he was cast to the ground by the heavenly voice, he did not recover until he became a member of the Holy Church.

You are also of opinion that no coercion is to be used with any man in order to his deliverance from the fatal consequences of error; and yet you see that, in examples which cannot be disputed, this is done by God, who loves us with more real regard for our profit than any other can; and you hear Christ saying, "No man can come to me except the Father draw him" [John 6: 44], which is done in the hearts of all those who, through fear of the wrath of God, betake themselves to Him. You know also that sometimes the thief scatters food before the flock that he may lead them astray, and sometimes the shepherd brings wandering sheep back to the flock with his rod.

(6) Did not Sarah, when she had the power, choose rather to afflict the insolent bondwoman? And truly she did not cruelly hate her whom she had formerly by an act of her own kindness made a mother; but she put a wholesome restraint upon her pride [Genesis 16: 5]. Moreover, as you well know, these two women, Sarah and Hagar, and their two sons Isaac and Ishmael, are figures representing spiritual and carnal persons. And although we read that the bondwoman and her son suffered great hardships from Sarah, nevertheless the Apostle Paul says that Isaac suffered persecution from Ishmael: "But as then he that was born after the flesh persecuted him that was born after the Spirit, even so it is now" [Galatians 4: 29]; whence those who have understanding may perceive that it is rather the Catholic Church which suffers persecution through the pride and impiety of those carnal men whom it endeavors to correct by afflictions and terrors of a temporal kind. Whatever therefore the true and rightful Mother does, even when something severe and bitter is felt by her children at her hands, she is not rendering evil for evil, but is applying the benefit of discipline to counteract the evil of sin, not with the hatred which seeks to harm, but with the love which seeks to heal. When good and bad do the same actions and suffer the same afflictions, they are to be distinguished not by what they do or suffer, but by the causes of each: e.g., Pharaoh oppressed the people of God by hard bondage; Moses afflicted the same people by severe correction when they were guilty of impiety: their actions were alike; but they were not alike in the motive or regard to the people's welfare – the one being inflated by the lust of power, the other inflamed by love. Jezebel slew prophets, Elijah slew false prophets; I suppose that the dessert of the actors and of the sufferers respectively in the two cases was wholly diverse.

(7) Look also to the New Testament times, in which the essential gentleness of love was to be not only kept in the heart, but also manifested openly: in these the sword of Peter is called back into its sheath by Christ, and we are taught that it ought not to be taken from its sheath even in Christ's defense [Matthew 26: 52]. We read, however, not only that the Jews beat

the Apostle Paul, but also that the Greeks beat Sosthenes, a Jew, on account
of the Apostle Paul. Does not the similarity of the events apparently join
both; and, at the same time, does not the dissimilarity of the causes make a
real difference? Again, God spared not His own Son, but delivered Him up
for us all. Of the Son also it is said, "who loved me, and gave Himself for
me" [Galatians 2: 20]; and it is also said of Judas that Satan entered into him
that he might betray Christ. Seeing, therefore, that the Father delivered up
His Son, and Christ delivered up His own body, and Judas delivered up his
Master, wherefore is God holy and man guilty in this delivering up of
Christ, unless that in the one action which both did, the reason for which
they did it was not the same? Three crosses stood in one place: on one was
the thief who was to be saved; on the second, the thief who was to be
condemned; on the third, between them, was Christ, who was about to save
the one thief and condemn the other. What could be more similar than
these crosses? What more unlike than the persons who were suspended on
them? Paul was given up to be imprisoned and bound, but Satan is unquestionably worse than any gaoler: yet to him Paul himself gave up one man for
the destruction of the flesh, that the spirit might be saved in the day of the
Lord Jesus. And what say we to this? Behold, both deliver a man to bondage; but he that is cruel consigns his prisoner to one less severe, while he
that is compassionate consigns him to one who is more cruel. Let us learn,
my brother, in actions which are similar to distinguish the intentions of the
agents; and let us not, shutting our eyes, deal in groundless reproaches, and
accuse those who seek men's welfare as if they did them wrong. In like
manner, when the same apostle says that he had delivered certain persons
unto Satan, that they might learn not to blaspheme, did he render to these
men evil for evil, or did he not rather esteem it a good work to correct evil
men by means of the evil one?

(8) If to suffer persecution were in all cases a praiseworthy thing, it would
have sufficed for the Lord to say, "Blessed are they which are persecuted,"
without adding "for righteousness' sake" [Matthew 5: 10]. Moreover, if to
inflict persecution were in all cases blameworthy, it would not have been
written in the sacred books, "Whoso privily slandereth his neighbour, him
will I persecute" [Psalm 101: 5]. In some cases, therefore, both he that
suffers persecution is in the wrong, and he that inflicts it is in the right. But
the truth is, that always both the bad have persecuted the good, and the
good have persecuted the bad: the former doing harm by their unrighteousness, the latter seeking to do good by the administration of discipline;
the former with cruelty, the latter with moderation; the former impelled by
lust, the latter under the constraint of love. For he whose aim is to kill is not
careful how he wounds, but he whose aim is to cure is cautious with his

lancet; for the one seeks to destroy what is sound, the other that which is decaying. The wicked put prophets to death; prophets also put the wicked to death. The Jews scourged Christ; Christ also scourged the Jews. The apostles were given up by men to the civil powers; the apostles themselves gave men up to the power of Satan. In all these cases, what is important to attend to but this: who were on the side of truth, and who on the side of iniquity; who acted from a desire to injure, and who from a desire to correct what was amiss?

Chapter 3

(9)   You say that no example is found in the writings of evangelists and apostles, of any petition presented on behalf of the Church to the kings of the earth against her enemies. Who denies this? None such is found. But at that time the prophecy, "Be wise now, therefore, O ye kings; be instructed, ye judges of the earth: serve the Lord with fear," was not yet fulfilled. Up to that time the words which we find at the beginning of the same Psalm were receiving their fulfillment, "Why do the heathen rage, and the people imagine a vain thing? The kings of the earth set themselves, and the rulers take counsel together against the Lord, and against His Anointed" [Psalm 2]. Truly, if past events recorded in the prophetic books were figures of the future, there was given under King Nebuchadnezzar a figure both of the time which the Church had under the apostles, and of that which she has now. In the age of the apostles and martyrs, that was fulfilled which was prefigured when the aforesaid king compelled pious and just men to bow down to his image, and cast into the flames all who refused. Now, however, is fulfilled that which was prefigured soon after in the same king, when, being converted to the worship of the true God, he made a decree throughout his empire, that whosoever should speak against the God of Shadrach, Meshach, and Abednego, should suffer the penalty which their crime deserved. The earlier time of that king represented the former age of emperors who did not believe in Christ, at whose hands the Christians suffered because of the wicked; but the later time of that king represented the age of the successors to the imperial throne, now believing in Christ, at whose hands the wicked suffer because of the Christians.

(10)   It is manifest, however, that moderate severity, or rather clemency, is carefully observed towards those who, under the Christian name, have been led astray by perverse men, in the measures used to prevent them who are Christ's sheep from wandering, and to bring them back to the flock, when by punishments, such as exile and fines, they are admonished to consider

what they suffer, and wherefore, are taught to prefer the Scriptures which they read to human legends and calumnies. For which of us, yea, which of you, does not speak well of the laws issued by the emperors against heathen sacrifices? In these, assuredly, a penalty much more severe has been appointed, for the punishment of that impiety is death. But in repressing and restraining you, the thing aimed at has been rather that you should be admonished to depart from evil, than that you should be punished for a crime. For perhaps what the apostle said of the Jews may be said of you: "I bear them record that they have a zeal of God, but not according to knowledge: for, being ignorant of the righteousness of God, and going about to establish their own righteousness, they have not submitted themselves to the righteousness of God" [Romans 10: 2–3]. For what else than your own righteousness are you desiring to establish, when you say that none are justified but those who may have had the opportunity of being baptized by you? In regard to this statement made by the apostle concerning the Jews, you differ from those to whom it originally applied in this, that you have the Christian sacraments, of which they are still destitute. But in regard to the words, "being ignorant of God's righteousness, and going about to establish their own righteousness," and "they have a zeal of God, but not according to knowledge," you are exactly like them, excepting only those among you who know what is the truth, and who in the wilfulness of their perversity continue to fight against truth which is perfectly well known to them. The impiety of these men is perhaps even a greater sin than idolatry. Since, however, they cannot be easily convicted of this (for it is a sin which lies concealed in the mind), you are all alike restrained with a comparatively gentle severity, as being not so far alienated from us. And this I may say, both concerning all heretics without distinction, who, while retaining the Christian sacraments, are dissenters from the truth and unity of Christ, and concerning all Donatists without exception. . . .

Chapter 5

(16)   You now see therefore, I suppose, that the thing to be considered when any one is coerced, is not the mere fact of the coercion, but the nature of that to which he is coerced, whether it be good or bad: not that any one can be good in spite of his own will, but that, through fear of suffering what he does not desire, he either renounces his hostile prejudices, or is compelled to examine truth of which he had been contentedly ignorant; and under the influence of this fear repudiates the error which he was wont to defend, or seeks the truth of which he formerly knew nothing, and now willingly

holds what he formerly rejected. Perhaps it would be utterly useless to assert this in words, if it were not demonstrated by so many examples. We see not a few men here and there, but many cities, once Donatist, now Catholic, vehemently detesting the diabolical schism, and ardently loving the unity of the Church; and these became Catholic under the influence of that fear which is to you so offensive by the laws of emperors, from Constantine, before whom your party of their own accord impeached Caecilianus, down to the emperors of our own time, who most justly decree that the decision of the judge whom your own party chose, and whom they preferred to a tribunal of bishops, should be maintained in force against you.

(17) I have therefore yielded to the evidence afforded by these instances which my colleagues have laid before me. For originally my opinion was, that no one should be coerced into the unity of Christ, that we must act only by words, fight only by arguments, and prevail by force of reason, lest we should have those whom we knew as avowed heretics feigning themselves to be Catholics. But this opinion of mine was overcome not by the words of those who controverted it, but by the conclusive instances to which they could point. For, in the first place, there was set over against my opinion my own town, which, although it was once wholly on the side of Donatus, was brought over to the Catholic unity by fear of the imperial edicts, but which we now see filled with such detestation of your ruinous perversity, that it would scarcely be believed that it had ever been involved in your error. There were so many others which were mentioned to me by name, that, from facts themselves, I was made to own that to this matter the word of Scripture might be understood as applying: "Give opportunity to a wise man, and he will be yet wiser" [Proverbs 9: 9]. For how many were already, as we assuredly know, willing to be Catholics, being moved by the indisputable plainness of truth, but daily putting off their avowal of this through fear of offending their own party! How many were bound, not by truth – for you never pretended to that as yours – but by the heavy chains of inveterate custom, so that in them was fulfilled the divine saying: "A servant (who is hardened) will not be corrected by words; for though he understand, he will not answer"! [Proverbs 29: 19] How many supposed the sect of Donatus to be the true Church, merely because ease had made them too listless, or conceited, or sluggish, to take pains to examine Catholic truth! How many would have entered earlier had not the calumnies of slanderers, who declared that we offered something else than we do upon the altar of God, shut them out! How many, believing that it mattered not to which party a Christian might belong, remained in the schism of Donatus only because they had been born in it, and no one was compelling them to forsake it and pass over into the Catholic Church!

(18)   To all these classes of persons the dread of those laws in the promulgation of which kings serve the Lord in fear has been so useful, that now
some say we were willing for this some time ago; but thanks be to God, who
has given us occasion for doing it at once, and has cut off the hesitancy of
procrastination! Others say: We already knew this to be true, but we were
held prisoners by the force of old custom: thanks be to the Lord, who has
broken these bonds asunder, and has brought us into the bond of peace!
Others say: We knew not that the truth was here, and we had no wish to
learn it; but fear made us become earnest to examine it when we became
alarmed, lest, without any gain in things eternal, we should be smitten with
loss in temporal things: thanks be to the Lord, who has by the stimulus of
fear startled us from our negligence, that now being disquieted we might
inquire into those things which, when at ease, we did not care to know!
Others say: We were prevented from entering the Church by false reports,
which we could not know to be false unless we entered it; and we would not
enter unless we were compelled: thanks be to the Lord, who by His scourge
took away our timid hesitation, and taught us to find out for ourselves how
vain and absurd were the lies which rumor had spread abroad against His
Church: by this we are persuaded that there is no truth in the accusations
made by the authors of this heresy, since the more serious charges which
their followers have invented are without foundation. Others say: We thought,
indeed, that it mattered not in what communion we held the faith of Christ;
but thanks to the Lord, who has gathered us in from a state of schism, and
has taught us that it is fitting that the one God be worshipped in unity.

(19)   Could I therefore maintain opposition to my colleagues, and by resisting them stand in the way of such conquests of the Lord, and prevent the
sheep of Christ which were wandering on your mountains and hills – that
is, on the swellings of your pride – from being gathered into the fold of
peace, in which there is one flock and one Shepherd? Was it my duty to
obstruct these measures, in order, forsooth, that you might not lose what
you call your own, and might without fear rob Christ of what is His: that
you might frame your testaments according to Roman law, and might by
calumnious accusations break the Testament made with the sanction of
Divine law to the fathers, in which it was written, "In thy seed shall all the
nations of the earth be blessed" [Genesis 26: 4]: that you might have
freedom in your transactions in the way of buying and selling, and might be
emboldened to divide and claim as your own that which Christ bought by
giving Himself as its price: that any gift made over by one of you to another
might remain unchallenged, and that the gift which the God of gods has
bestowed upon His children, called from the rising of the sun to the going
down thereof, might become invalid: that you might not be sent into exile

from the land of your natural birth, and that you might labor to banish Christ from the kingdom bought with His blood, which extends from sea to sea, and from the river to the ends of the earth? Nay verily; let the kings of the earth serve Christ by making laws for Him and for His cause. Your predecessors exposed Caecilianus and his companions to be punished by the kings of the earth for crimes with which they were falsely charged: let the lions now be turned to break in pieces the bones of the calumniators, and let no intercession for them be made by Daniel when he has been proved innocent, and set free from the den in which they meet their doom; for he that prepareth a pit for his neighbor shall himself most justly fall into it.

Chapter 6

(20)   Save yourself therefore, my brother, while you have this present life, from the wrath which is to come on the obstinate and the proud. The formidable power of the authorities of this world, when it assails the truth, gives glorious opportunity of probation to the strong, but puts dangerous temptation before the weak who are righteous; but when it assists the proclamation of the truth, it is the means of profitable admonition to the wise, and of unprofitable vexation to the foolish among those who have gone astray. "For there is no power but of God: whosoever therefore resisteth the power, resisteth the ordinance of God; for rulers are not a terror to good works, but to the evil. Wilt thou then not be afraid of the power? Do that which is good, and thou shalt have praise of the same" [Romans 13: 1–3]. For if the power be on the side of the truth, and correct any one who was in error, he that is put right by the correction has praise from the power. If, on the other hand, the power be unfriendly to the truth, and cruelly persecute any one, he who is crowned victor in this contest receives praise from the power which he resists. But you do not that which is good, so as to avoid being afraid of the power; unless perchance this is good, to sit and speak against not one brother [Psalm 50: 20], but against all your brethren that are found among all nations, to whom the prophets, and Christ, and the apostles bear witness in the words of Scripture, "In thy seed shall all the nations of the earth be blessed" [Genesis 26: 4]; and again, "From the rising of the sun even unto the going down of the same, a pure offering shall be offered unto My name; for My name shall be great among the heathen, saith the Lord" [Malachi 1: 11]. Mark this: "saith the Lord;" not saith Donatus, or Rogatus, or Vincentius, or Ambrose, or Augustine, but "saith the Lord;" and again, "All tribes of the earth shall be blessed in Him, and all nations shall call Him blessed. Blessed be the Lord God, the God of Israel, who only doeth wondrous things; and blessed be His glorious name for ever, and

the whole earth shall be filled with His glory: so let it be, so let it be" [Psalm 72: 17–19]. And you sit at Cartennae, and with a remnant of half a score of Rogatists you say, "Let it not be! Let it not be!"

Notes

1　Roland H. Bainton, "The Parable of the Tares as the Proof Text for Religious Liberty to the End of the Sixteenth Century," *Church History*, 1 (1932), pp. 67–89; J. L. I. Fennell, "The Attitude of the Josephians and the Trans-Volga Elders to the Heresy of the Judaisers," *The Slavonic and East European Review*, 29 (1951), p. 498.

2　F. M. Cornford, *The Unwritten Philosophy and Other Essays*, ed. N. K. C. Guthrie (Cambridge: Cambridge University Press, 1950), p. 66. Plato is not mentioned in Edward Peters, *Inquisition* (Berkeley, CA: University of California Press, 1989).

3　Plato, *Epistles*, p. 7. Socrates (469–399 BC) was indicted in 399 BC on the following charge:

> This indictment and affidavit is sworn by Meletus, the son of Meletus of Pitthos, against Socrates, the son of Sophroniscus of Alopece: Socrates is guilty of refusing to recognize the gods the state recognizes, and of introducing other new divinities. He is also guilty of corrupting the youth. The penalty demanded is death.
>
> > Thomas C. Brickhouse and Nicholas D. Smith, *Socrates on Trial*
> > (Princeton, NJ: Princeton University Press, 1990), p. 30.

His defense is recorded in the *Apology*, where it is made clear that while he was no atheist his notions of the divinity may well have exposed him to charges under the various measures taken against impiety in Athens, a Greek city not to be outdone in its respect for religion. It would appear that Socrates withheld his support for the local gods and thus would have been perceived as undermining "the state's sacred credentials." James Beckman, *The Religious Dimensions of Socrates' Thought* (Waterloo, Ont.: Wilfrid Laurier University Press, 1979), p. 59. See also I. F. Stone, *The Trial of Socrates* (Boston, MA: Little, Brown, 1988).

4　Virgil, *Aeneid*, vol. III, p. 112.

5　Augustine, *The Retractions*, tr. Mary I. Bogan [vol. 60 of *Fathers of the Church*] (Washington, DC: Catholic University of America Press, 1968), p. 129.

6　*The Work of St Optatus, Bishop of Milevis, against the Donatists*, tr. O. R. Vassall-Phillips (London: Longmans, Green, 1917), vol. XV, pp. 164ff.

2

MEDIEVAL EUROPE

Bishop Wazo, "Manichaeans at Châlons-sur-Marne" (*c.* 1043–48)

Wazo was bishop of Liège between 1042 and 1048. He was a widely respected figure consulted by a number of persons, including Bishop Roger who sought his counsel on the matter of the appearance of the dualistic heresy in his diocese. Wazo's interesting refusal of the sword coincided with a vigorous assertion of the independence of ecclesiastical jurisdiction; thus he has been viewed as a precursor of the Hildebrandine reforms later in the century.

SOURCE: Walter Wakefield and Austin Evans (eds), *Heresies of the High Middle Ages* (New York: Columbia University Press, 1969), pp. 89–93.
LITERATURE: Roland H. Bainton, "The Parable of the Tares as the Proof Text for Religious Liberty to the End of the Sixteenth Century," *Church History*, 1 (1932), pp. 74–5; Gerd Tellenbach, *Church, State and Christian Society at the Time of the Investiture Contest*, tr. R. F. Bennett (Toronto: University of Toronto Press, 1991 [1936]), pp. 103–5.

Moreover, apostolic sublimity deemed our bishop worthy of frequent correspondence, which he was wont to receive most reverently and to answer humbly, if it happened that a question was put to him therein. Various bishops, too, appealed to their distinguished colleague by letter, in which they drew upon his wisdom in various matters. No one of them, provided his questions bore upon some useful subject, was refused a careful reply to his inquiries. The bishop of Châlons, among them, felt the need to consult His Holiness because of a danger to the souls entrusted to his care, a danger which he outlined in his letter as follows: In a certain region of his diocese there were some countryfolk who eagerly followed the evil teachings of

Manichaeans and frequented their secret conventicles, in which they engaged in I know not what filthy acts, shameful to mention, in a certain religious rite. And they lyingly asserted that the Holy Spirit is given by a sacrilegious imposition of hands; to buttress their faith in this error, they most falsely proclaimed Him to have been sent by God only in their heresiarch Mani, as though Mani were none other than the Holy Spirit. By this they fell into that blasphemy which, according to the Voice of Truth, can be forgiven neither here nor in the hereafter [Matthew 12: 31–2].

These people, it was said, constrained whomever they could to join their number. They abhorred marriage and not only avoided the eating of meat but also considered it wicked to kill any animal at all, assuming as justification for their error the command of God against killing in the Old Law. If it happened that any ignorant, tongue-tied persons were enrolled among the partisans of this error, it was stoutly asserted that at once they became more eloquent than even the most learned Catholics, so that it almost seemed as if the really true eloquence of the wise could be overcome by their garrulity. The bishop also added that he personally was more grieved over the daily seduction of others than by the damnation of these persons.

The troubled bishop asked the advice of the sure repository of wisdom as to the best procedure to adopt in dealing with such persons: whether or not the sword of earthly authority should be directed against them, lest, were they not exterminated, the whole lump be corrupted by a little leaven. In reply, our bishop writes, among other things:

"In regard to those of whom you wrote, their error is indeed evident, brought into the open by the holy fathers of old and confuted by their brilliant discussion. For, to pass over the most insensate blasphemies with which they deceive themselves in respect of the Holy Spirit, your Esteemed Self may perceive how they go out of their way to entangle themselves with numerous incongruities, by misinterpreting the commandment of the Lord which in the Old Law says, 'Thou shalt not kill' [Exodus 20: 13]. Unless they realize that therein only homicide was forbidden, they would find forbidden to them in like manner the use of those things which they think it lawful to eat, such as grain, vegetables, and wine. These things, as is their nature, have grown from seeds consigned to the earth in their own kind of life, and, unless destroyed in their prime, they could not serve the needs of mankind. Even if we make no mention of worldly authors, the Psalmist is witness to this fact when he says: 'And he destroyed their vineyards with hail' [Psalm 78: 47]. So too the Apostle: 'Senseless man, that which thou sowest is not quickened, except it die first' [1 Corinthians 15: 36]. And Truth himself says, 'Unless the grain of wheat falling into the ground die, itself remaineth alone' [John 12: 24–5]. It stands to reason, therefore, that of necessity they acknowledge that what manifestly can be killed by accident has had life. Therefore, let them choose what they will: either let them believe the Catholic interpretation, that only in respect of man was it written, 'Thou shalt not kill,' and with us lawfully avail themselves of the abundance of beasts for slaughter; or, if they insist on denying themselves this, we, by the very terms of their own error, will deny to them the use of bread, vegetables, and other things of this sort, because these things, did they not suffer death after their own fashion, could nowise be adapted to support human fallacies.

"Although Christian piety despises these tenets and although it condemns the sacrilege of the Arian heresy, nevertheless, in emulation of our Savior, who, mild and humble of heart, did not come to wrangle or contend but rather to suffer abuse, shameful treatment, blows, and finally death on the Cross, we are commanded for a time to bear with such things in some measure. For, as the Blessed Gregory says, no Abel will maintain his innocence whom the malice of a Cain has not harassed, nor will the grape dissolve into the savor of the wine unless it is crushed by the heel. Moreover, to be prepared for doing what the merciful and compassionate Lord, who does not judge sinners straightway but waits patiently for repentance, desires to be done about such persons, let us hearken to what He deemed fitting to teach His disciples – nay, rather us – when in His Gospel He expounded the parable of the field of wheat and the cockle. He said: 'The man that soweth the good seed in his field is the Son of Man. And the good seed are the children of the kingdom. And the field is the world. And the man, the enemy, that sowed the cockle is the devil. And the cockle are the children of the wicked one. But the harvest is the end of the world. And the reapers are the angels' [Matthew 13: 37–9]. What, moreover, but the role of preachers is signified by the servants who wish to gather up the cockle when it first appears? Do not preachers, as they seek to separate good from evil in Holy Church, attempt as it were to root out the cockle from the good seed of the field? But with notable discretion that Goodman of the house restrains their reckless zeal, saying: 'Do not so; lest perhaps gathering up the cockle you root up the wheat also together with it. Suffer both to grow until the harvest, and in the time of the harvest I will say to the reapers: Gather up first the cockle and bind it into bundles to burn, but the wheat gather ye into my barn' [Matthew 13: 29–30]. What does the Lord reveal by these words but His patience, which He wishes His preachers to display to their erring fellow men, particularly since it may be possible for those who today are cockle, tomorrow to be converted and be wheat?

"The fervor of spiritual zeal burning in your breast for souls deceived by devilish fraud shows that you surely are numbered among these servants. Out of this zeal you strive with the hoe of judicial decision to rid the grainfield of cockle, that the good be not corrupted by evil. But lest you do this hastily, lest it be done before its time, the holy text is rather to be obeyed, so that although we think we are practicing righteousness by punishing transgressors, whose impiety is veiled under semblance of strict life, we do no disservice to Him, who desires not the death of sinners nor rejoices in the damnation of the dying, but rather knows how to bring sinners back to repentance through His patience and long-suffering. Therefore, heeding the words of the Maker, let the decision of the arena wait; let us not seek to remove from this life by the sword of secular authority those whom God himself, Creator and Redeemer, wishes to spare, as He has revealed, to the end that they many turn again to His will from the snares of the devil in which they were entrapped. Thus, because it is indubitably proper for us to reserve such persons to the last harvest of that Goodman of the house, for whatever He may command His harvesters to do about them, so also, for our part, it behooves us to await the harvesters in fear and trembling. For perchance that harvest may disclose to be wheat some of those who grow as cockle in the field of this world, and it is possible for omnipotent God to make those whom we now consider to be enemies of the way of the Lord superior even to us in that heavenly home. Certainly we read that Saul, raging more than all the others, assisted at the stoning of the blessed first martyr, Stephen, and the martyr apostle now rejoices to recognize as a superior apostle the one who once was his persecutor.

"Moreover, we must meanwhile bear in mind that we who are called bishops do not receive at ordination the sword which belongs to the secular power and for that reason we are enjoined by God our Father not to do unto death but rather to quicken unto life. There is, however, another point about the aforesaid schismatics which should be carefully heeded, one of which you are not at all unmindful. They and those associating with them should be deprived of Catholic communion. Let it be officially and publicly announced to all others, so that, heeding the warning of the prophet, they may leave their midst and eschew their most unclean sect, for 'He that toucheth pitch shall be defiled with it' [Ecclesiasticus 13: 1]."

So very earnestly did the man of God, after the example of the Blessed Martin,[1] strive to impress these ideas that in a measure he curbed the habitual headstrong madness of the French, who yearned to shed blood. For he had heard that they identified heretics by pallor alone, as if it were certain fact that those who have a pale complexion are heretics. Thus, through error coupled with cruelty, many truly Catholic persons had been killed in the past.

This being the situation and because nothing of like reasonableness can be advanced in rebuttal of such clear reasoning supported by Gospel decree, let them to whom it is unknown see how reprehensible was the deed when certain partisans of a comparable sect had been seized at Goslar. After much discussion of their vagaries and a proper excommunication for obstinacy in error, they were also sentenced to be hanged. When we carefully invest- igated the course of this examination, we could learn no other reason for their condemnation than that they refused to obey some one of the bishops when he ordered them to kill a chicken. For I can truly say, and I will not keep silent, that if it had happened in his time, our Wazo would have agreed not at all with this verdict, after the example of the Blessed Martin, who, in order to intercede for Priscillianists condemned by edict of the depraved Emperor Maximin on advice of the priests who basely flattered him, pre- ferred to incur a slur on his most excellent virtue than to be unsolicitous even for heretics who were soon to die. We say these things not because we seek to defend the error of heretics, but to show that we do not approve of that which is nowhere sanctioned in the Sacred Laws.

Thomas Aquinas, "Of Unbelief and Heresy" (c. 1271)

The Italian Aquinas (1224/5–74) was the greatest theologian of his time, and his influence has continued through subsequent centuries. He made significant borrowings from the philosophy of Aristotle in an attempt to synthesize revelation with reason. Aquinas lived in the age of the Inquisi- tion, and his attitude toward religious pluralism is generally compatible with the aims of that institution. While maintaining the natural right of parents to determine the religion of the child, he did not see the individual determination of religious commitment as a right. Rather, the wrongful- ness of the compulsion of the non-Christian resided in the harm it might perpetrate upon the good health of the church; real faith was willing faith, and compulsion would propagate hypocrisy. Toleration of public worship by infidels other than Jews might be permitted only to avoid a greater evil; Jews, given their nearer proximity to Christianity, might be granted wider latitude. As for the departure of the baptized from orthodox belief, her- etics were worse than counterfeiters and should be put to death. D'Arcy has queried whether these attitudes are consistent with Aquinas' views on the priority of acting in conformity with the dictates of conscience, how- ever erroneous.[2]

SOURCE: *The Summa Theologica of St Thomas Aquinas*, 22 vols (London: Burns Oates & Washbourne, 1914–24), vol. IX, pp. 129–58.

LITERATURE: Eric D'Arcy, *Conscience and its Right to Freedom* (London: Sheed and Ward, 1961).

Part II, Second Part   Question X

Sixth Article   Whether the unbelief of pagans or heathens is graver than other kinds?

We proceed thus to the Sixth Article:

Objection 1 It would seem that the unbelief of heathens or pagans is graver than other kinds. For just as bodily disease is graver, according as it endangers the health of a more important member of the body, so does sin appear to be graver, according as it is opposed to that which holds a more important place in virtue. Now that which is most important in faith, is belief in the unity of God, from which the heathens deviate by believing in many gods. Therefore their unbelief is the gravest of all.

Objection 2 Further, Among heresies, the more detestable are those which contradict the truth of faith in more numerous and more important points: thus the heresy of Arius, who severed the Godhead, was more detestable than that of Nestorius who severed the humanity of Christ from the Person of God the Son. Now the heathens deny the faith in more numerous and more important points than Jews and heretics; since they do not accept the faith at all. Therefore their unbelief is the gravest.

Objection 3 Further, Every good diminishes evil. Now there is some good in the Jews, since they believe in the Old Testament as being from God, and there is some good in heretics, since they venerate the New Testament. Therefore they sin less grievously than heathens, who receive neither Testament.

On the contrary, It is written [2 Peter 2: 21]: "It had been better for them not to have known the way of justice, than after they have known it, to turn back." Now the heathens have not known the way of justice, whereas heretics and Jews have abandoned it after knowing it in some way. Therefore theirs is the graver sin.

I answer that, As stated above (A.5), two things may be considered in unbelief. One of these is its relation to faith: and from this point of view, he who resists the faith after accepting it, sins more grievously against faith, than he who resists it without having accepted it, even as he who fails to fulfill what he has promised, sins more grievously than if he had never promised it. In this way the unbelief of heretics, who confess their belief in the Gospel, and resist that faith by corrupting it, is a more grievous sin than that of the Jews, who have never accepted the Gospel faith. Since, however, they accepted the figure of that faith in the Old Law, which they corrupt by their false interpretations, their unbelief is a more grievous sin than that of the heathens, because the latter have not accepted the Gospel faith in any way at all.

The second thing to be considered in unbelief is the corruption of matters of faith. In this respect, since heathens err on more points than Jews, and these in more points than heretics, the unbelief of heathens is more grievous than the unbelief of the Jews, and that of the Jews than that of heretics, except in such cases as that of the Manichees, who, in matters of faith, err even more than heathens do.

Of these two gravities the first surpasses the second from the point of view of guilt; since, as stated above (A.1) unbelief has the character of guilt, from its resisting faith rather than from the mere absence of faith, for the latter, as was stated (ibid.) seems rather to bear the character of punishment. Hence, speaking absolutely, the unbelief of heretics is the worst.

This suffices for the Replies to the Objections.

Seventh Article   Whether one ought to dispute with unbelievers in public?

We proceed thus to the Seventh Article:

Objection 1   It would seem that one ought not to dispute with unbelievers in public. For the Apostle says [2 Timothy 2: 14]: "Contend not in words, for it is to no profit, but to the subverting of the hearers." But it is impossible to dispute with unbelievers publicly without contending in words. Therefore one ought not to dispute publicly with unbelievers.

Objection 2   Further, The law of Martianus Augustus confirmed by the canons expresses itself thus: "It is an insult to the judgment of the most religious synod, if anyone ventures to debate or dispute in public about matters which have once been judged and disposed of." Now all matters of faith have been decided by the holy councils. Therefore it is an insult to the councils, and consequently a grave sin to presume to dispute in public about matters of faith.

Objection 3   Further, Disputations are conducted by means of arguments. But an argument is a reason in settlement of a dubious matter: whereas things that are of faith, being most certain, ought not to be a matter of doubt. Therefore one ought not to dispute in public about matters of faith.

On the contrary, It is written [Acts 9: 22, 29] that "Saul increased much more in strength, and confounded the Jews," and that "he spoke . . . to the gentiles and disputed with the Greeks."

I answer that, In disputing about the faith, two things must be observed; one on the part of the disputant, the other on the part of his hearers. On the part of the disputant, we must consider his intention. For if he were to dispute as though he had doubts about the faith, and did not hold the truth of faith for certain, and as though he intended to prove it with arguments, without doubt he would sin, as being doubtful of the faith and an unbeliever. On the other hand, it is praiseworthy to dispute about the faith in order to confute errors, or for practice.

On the part of the hearers we must consider whether those who hear the·
disputation are instructed and firm in the faith, or simple and wavering. As
to those who are well instructed and firm in the faith, there can be no danger in disputing about the faith in their presence. But as to simple-minded
people, we must make a distinction; because either they are provoked and
molested by unbelievers, for instance Jews or heretics, or pagans who strive
to corrupt the faith in them, or else they are not subject to provocation
in this matter, as in those countries where there are no unbelievers. In the
first case it is necessary to dispute in public about the faith, provided there
be those who are equal and adapted to the task of confuting errors; since
in this way simple people are strengthened in the faith, and unbelievers are
deprived of the opportunity to deceive, while if those who ought to withstand the perverters of the truth of faith were silent, this would tend to
strengthen error. Hence Gregory says [*Pastor*, II, 4]: "Even as a thoughtless
speech gives rise to error, so does an indiscreet silence leave those in error
who might have been instructed." On the other hand, in the second case it
is dangerous to dispute in public about the faith, in the presence of simple
people, whose faith for this very reason is more firm, that they have never
heard anything differing from what they believe. Hence it is not expedient
for them to hear what unbelievers have to say against the faith.

Reply: Objection 1   The Apostle does not entirely forbid disputations,
but such as are inordinate, and consist of contentious words rather than of
sound speeches.

Reply: Objection 2   That law forbade those public disputations about the
faith, which arise from doubting the faith, but not those which are for the
safeguarding thereof.

Reply: Objection 3   One ought to dispute about matters of faith, not as
though one doubted about them, but in order to make the truth known, and
to confute errors. For, in order to confirm the faith, it is necessary sometimes to dispute with unbelievers, sometimes by defending the faith, according to 1 Peter 3: 15: "Being ready always to satisfy everyone that asketh you
a reason of that hope and faith which is in you." Sometimes again, it is
necessary, in order to convince those who are in error, according to Titus
1: 9: "That he may be able to exhort in sound doctrine and to convince the
gainsayers."

Eighth Article   Whether unbelievers ought to be compelled to the faith?

We proceed thus to the Eighth Article:

Objection 1   It would seem that unbelievers ought by no means to be
compelled to the faith. For it is written [Matthew 13: 28] that the servants
of the household, in whose field cockle had been sown, asked him: "Wilt

thou that we go and gather it up?" and that he answered: "No, lest perhaps gathering up the cockle, you root up the wheat also together with it:" on which passage Chrysostom says [Hom. 46. in Matth.]: "Our Lord says this so as to forbid the slaying of men. For it is not right to slay heretics, because if you do you will necessarily slay many innocent persons." Therefore it seems that for the same reason unbelievers ought not to be compelled to the faith.

Objection 2 Further, We read in the Decretals [Dist. 45., can., *De Judaeis*]: "The holy synod prescribes, with regard to the Jews, that for the future, none are to be compelled to believe." Therefore, in like manner, neither should unbelievers be compelled to the faith.

Objection 3 Further, Augustine says [*Tract. 26. in Joan.*] that "it is possible for a man to do other things against his will, but he cannot believe unless he is willing." But the will cannot be compelled. Therefore it seems that unbelievers ought not to be compelled to the faith.

Objection 4 It is said in God's person [Ezekiel 18: 32 (33: 11)]: "I desire not the death of the sinner" (Vulg. – "of him that dieth"). Now we ought to conform our will to the Divine will, as stated above (I.–II, Q.XIX, AA.9, 10). Therefore we should not even wish unbelievers to be put to death.

On the contrary, It is written [Luke 14: 23]: "Go out into the highways and hedges; and compel them to come in." Now men enter into the house of God, i.e. into Holy Church, by faith. Therefore some ought to be compelled to the faith.

I answer that, Among unbelievers there are some who have never received the faith, such as the heathens and the Jews: and these are by no means to be compelled to the faith, in order that they may believe, because to believe depends on the will: nevertheless they should be compelled by the faithful, if it be possible to do so, so that they do not hinder the faith, by their blasphemies, or by their evil persuasions, or even by their open persecutions. It is for this reason that Christ's faithful often wage war with unbelievers, not indeed for the purpose of forcing them to believe, because even if they were to conquer them, and take them prisoners, they should still leave them free to believe, if they will, but in order to prevent them from hindering the faith of Christ.

On the other hand, there are unbelievers who at some time have accepted the faith, and professed it, such as heretics and all apostates: such should be submitted even to bodily compulsion, that they may fulfill what they have promised, and hold what they, at one time, received.

Reply: Objection 1 Some have understood the authority quoted to forbid, not the excommunication but the slaying of heretics, as appears from the words of Chrysostom. Augustine too, says [*Ep. ad Vincent*, 93] of himself:

"It was once my opinion that none should be compelled to union with Christ, that we should deal in words, and fight with arguments. However this opinion of mine is undone, not by words of contradiction, but by convincing examples. Because fear of the law was so profitable, that many say: Thanks be to the Lord Who has broken our chains asunder." Accordingly the meaning of Our Lord's words, "Suffer both to grow until the harvest," must be gathered from those which precede, "lest perhaps gathering up the cockle, you root up the wheat also together with it." For, as Augustine says [*Contra Ep. Parmen*, III, 2] "these words show that when this is not to be feared, that is to say, when a man's crime is so publicly known, and so hateful to all, that he has no defenders, or none such as might cause a schism, the severity of discipline should not slacken."

Reply: Objection 2 Those Jews who have in no way received the faith, ought by no means to be compelled to the faith: if, however, they have received it, they ought to be compelled to keep it, as is stated in the same chapter.

Reply: Objection 3 Just as taking a vow is a matter of will, and keeping a vow, a matter of obligation, so acceptance of the faith is a matter of the will, whereas keeping the faith, when once one has received it, is a matter of obligation. Wherefore heretics should be compelled to keep the faith. Thus Augustine says to the Count Boniface [*Ep.* 185]: "What do these people mean by crying out continually: 'We may believe or not believe just as we choose. Whom did Christ compel?' They should remember that Christ at first compelled Paul and afterwards taught him."

Reply: Objection 4 As Augustine says in the same letter, "none of us wishes any heretic to perish. But the house of David did not deserve to have peace, unless his son Absalom had been killed in the war which he had raised against his father. Thus if the Catholic Church gathers together some to the perdition of others, she heals the sorrow of her maternal heart by the delivery of so many nations."

Ninth Article   Whether it is lawful to communicate with unbelievers?

We proceed thus to the Ninth Article:

Objection 1 It would seem that it is lawful to communicate with unbelievers. For the Apostle says [1 Corinthians 10: 27]: "If any of them that believe not, invite you, and you be willing to go, eat of anything that is set before you." And Chrysostom says [Hom. 25 *super Epist. ad Heb.*]: "If you wish to go to dine with pagans, we permit it without any reservation." Now to sit at table with anyone is to communicate with him. Therefore it is lawful to communicate with unbelievers.

Objection 2 Further, The Apostle says [1 Corinthians 5: 12]: "What have I to do to judge them that are without?" Now unbelievers are without. When, therefore, the Church forbids the faithful to communicate with certain people, it seems that they ought not to be forbidden to communicate with unbelievers.

Objection 3 Further, A master cannot employ his servant, unless he communicate with him, at least by word, since the master moves his servant by command. Now Christians can have unbelievers, either Jews, or pagans, or Saracens, for servants. Therefore they can lawfully communicate with them.

On the contrary, It is written [Deuteronomy 7: 2, 3]: "Thou shalt make no league with them, nor show mercy to them; neither shalt thou make marriages with them:" and a gloss on Leviticus 15: 19, "The woman who at the return of the month," etc., says: "It is necessary to shun idolatry, that we should not come in touch with idolaters or their disciples, nor have any dealings with them."

I answer that, Communication with a particular person is forbidden to the faithful, in two ways: first, as a punishment of the person with whom they are forbidden to communicate; secondly, for the safety of those who are forbidden to communicate with others. Both motives can be gathered from the Apostle's words [1 Corinthians 5: 6]. For after he had pronounced sentence of excommunication, he adds as his reason: "Know you not that a little leaven corrupts the whole lump?" and afterwards he adds the reason on the part of the punishment inflicted by the sentence of the Church when he says [verse 12]: "Do not judge them that are within?"

Accordingly, in the first way the Church does not forbid the faithful to communicate with unbelievers, who have not in any way received the Christian faith, viz. with pagans and Jews, because she has not the right to exercise spiritual judgment over them, but only temporal judgment, in the case when, while dwelling among Christians they are guilty of some misdemeanor, and are condemned by the faithful to some temporal punishment. On the other hand, in this way, i.e., as a punishment, the Church forbids the faithful to communicate with those unbelievers who have forsaken the faith they once received, either by corrupting the faith, as heretics, or by entirely renouncing the faith, as apostates, because the Church pronounces sentence of excommunication on both.

With regard to the second way, it seems that one ought to distinguish according to the various conditions of persons, circumstances and time. For some are firm in the faith; and so it is to be hoped that their communicating with unbelievers will lead to the conversion of the latter rather than to the aversion of the faithful from the faith. These are not to be forbidden to communicate with unbelievers who have not received the faith, such as pagans or Jews, especially if there be some urgent necessity for so doing.

But in the case of simple people and those who are weak in the faith, whose perversion is to be feared as a probable result, they should be forbidden to communicate with unbelievers, and especially to be on very familiar terms with them, or to communicate with them without necessity.

This suffices for the Reply to the First Objection.

Reply: Objection 2   The Church does not exercise judgment against unbelievers in the point of inflicting spiritual punishment on them: but she does exercise judgment over some of them in the matter of temporal punishment. It is under this head that sometimes the Church, for certain special sins, withdraws the faithful from communication with certain unbelievers.

Reply: Objection 3   There is more probability that a servant who is ruled by his master's commands, will be converted to the faith of his master who is a believer, than if the case were the reverse: and so the faithful are not forbidden to have unbelieving servants. If, however, the master were in danger, through communicating with such a servant, he should send him away, according to Our Lord's command [Matthew 18: 8]: "If . . . thy foot scandalize thee, cut it off, and cast it from thee."

With regard to the argument in the contrary sense the reply is that the Lord gave this command in reference to those nations into whose territory the Jews were about to enter. For the latter were inclined to idolatry, so that it was to be feared lest, through frequent dealings with those nations, they should be estranged from the faith: hence the text goes on [verse 4]: "For she will turn away thy son from following Me."

Tenth Article   Whether unbelievers may have authority or dominion over the faithful?

. . . .

Eleventh Article   Whether the rites of unbelievers ought to be tolerated?

We proceed thus to the Eleventh Article:

Objection 1   It would seem that rites of unbelievers ought not to be tolerated. For it is evident that unbelievers sin in observing their rites: and not to prevent a sin, when one can, seems to simply consent therein, as a gloss observes on Romans 1: 32: "not only they that do them, but they also that consent to them that do them." Therefore it is a sin to tolerate their rites.

Objection 2   Further, The rites of the Jews are compared to idolatry, because a gloss on Galatians 5: 1, "Be not held again under the yoke of bondage," says: "The bondage of that law was not lighter than that of idolatry." But it would not be allowable for anyone to observe the rites of idolatry, in fact Christian princes at first caused the temples of idols to be closed, and afterwards, to be destroyed, as Augustine relates [*De Civitate Dei*, vol. XVIII, p. 54]. Therefore it follows that even the rites of Jews ought not to be tolerated.

Objection 3 Further, Unbelief is the greatest of sins, as stated above (A.3). Now other sins such as adultery, theft and the like, are not tolerated, but are punishable by law. Therefore neither ought the rites of unbelievers to be tolerated.

On the contrary, Gregory says, speaking of the Jews: "They should be allowed to observe all their feasts, just as hitherto they and their fathers have for ages observed them."

I answer that, Human government is derived from the Divine government, and should imitate it. Now although God is all-powerful and supremely good, nevertheless He allows certain evils to take place in the universe, which He might prevent, lest, without them, greater goods might be forfeited, or greater evils ensue. Accordingly in human government also, those who are in authority, rightly tolerate certain evils, lest certain goods be lost, or certain greater evils be incurred: thus Augustine says [*De Ordine*, vol. II, 4]: "If you do away with harlots, the world will be convulsed with lust." Hence, though unbelievers sin in their rites, they may be tolerated, either on account of some good that ensues therefrom, or because of some evil avoided. Thus from the fact that the Jews observe their rites, which, of old, foreshadowed the truth of the faith which we hold, there follows this good – that our very enemies bear witness to our faith, and that our faith is represented in a figure, so to speak. For this reason they are tolerated in the observance of their rites.

On the other hand, the rites of other unbelievers, which are neither truthful nor profitable are by no means to be tolerated, except perchance in order to avoid an evil, e.g., the scandal or disturbance that might ensue, or some hindrance to the salvation of those who if they were unmolested might gradually be converted to the faith. For this reason the Church, at times, has tolerated the rites even of heretics and pagans, when unbelievers were very numerous.

This suffices for the Replies to the Objections.

Twelfth Article   Whether the children of Jews and of other unbelievers ought to be baptized against their parents' will?

We proceed thus to the Twelfth Article:

Objection 1 It would seem that the children of Jews and of other unbelievers ought to be baptized against their parents' will. For the bond of marriage is stronger than the right of parental authority over children, since the right of parental authority can be made to cease, when a son is set at liberty; whereas the marriage bond cannot be severed by man, according to Matthew 19: 6: "What . . . God had joined together let no man put asunder." And yet the marriage bond is broken on account of unbelief: for the Apostle says [1 Corinthians 7: 15]: "If the unbeliever depart, let him depart. For a brother or sister is not under servitude in such cases:" and a canon says that "if the unbelieving partner is unwilling to abide with the other, without insult to their Creator, then the other partner is not bound to cohabitation." Much more, therefore, does unbelief abrogate the right of unbelieving parents' authority over their children: and consequently their children may be baptized against their parents' will.

Objection 2 Further, One is more bound to succor a man who is in danger of everlasting death, than one who is in danger of temporal death. Now it would be a sin, if one saw a man in danger of temporal death and failed to go to his aid. Since, then, the children of Jews and other unbelievers are in danger of everlasting death, should they be left to their parents who would imbue them with their unbelief, it seems that they ought to be taken away from them and baptized, and instructed in the faith.

Objection 3 Further, The children of a bondsman are themselves bondsmen, and under the power of his master. Now the Jews are bondsmen of kings and princes: therefore their children are also. Consequently kings and princes have the power to do what they will with Jewish children. Therefore no injustice is omitted if they baptize them against their parents' wishes.

Objection 4 Further, Every man belongs more to God, from Whom he has his soul, than to his carnal father, from whom he has his body. Therefore it is not unjust if Jewish children be taken away from their parents, and consecrated to God in Baptism.

Objection 5 Further, Baptism avails for salvation more than preaching does, since Baptism removes forthwith the stain of sin and the debt of punishment, and opens the gate of heaven. Now if danger ensue through not preaching, it is imputed to him who omitted to preach, according to the words of Ezekiel 33: 6 about the man who "sees the sword coming and sounds not the trumpet." Much more therefore, if Jewish children are lost through not being baptized are they accounted guilty of sin, who could have baptized them and did not.

On the contrary, Injustice should be done to no man. Now it would be an injustice to Jews if their children were to be baptized against their will, since they would lose the rights of parental authority over their children as soon as these were Christians. Therefore these should not be baptized against their parents' will.

I answer that, The custom of the Church has very great authority and ought to be jealously observed in all things, since the very doctrine of catholic doctors derives its authority from the Church. Hence we ought to abide by the authority of the Church rather than by that of an Augustine or a Jerome or of any doctor whatever. Now it was never the custom of the Church to baptize the children of Jews against the will of their parents, although in times past there have been many very powerful catholic princes like Constantine and Theodosius, with whom most holy bishops have been on most friendly terms, as Sylvester with Constantine, and Ambrose with Theodosius, who would certainly not have failed to obtain this favor from them if it had been at all reasonable. It seems therefore hazardous to repeat this assertion, that the children of Jews should be baptized against their parents' wishes, in contradiction to the Church's custom observed hitherto.

There are two reasons for this custom. One is on account of the danger to faith. For children baptized before coming to the use of reason, afterwards when they come to perfect age, might easily be persuaded by their parents to renounce what they had unknowingly embraced; and this would be detrimental to the faith.

The other reason is that it is against natural justice. For a child is by nature part of its father: thus, at first, it is not distinct from its parents as to its body, so long as it is enfolded within its mother's womb; and later on after birth, and before it has the use of its free-will, it is enfolded in the care of its parents, which is like a spiritual womb, for so long as man has not the use of reason, he differs not from an irrational animal; so that even as an ox or a horse belongs to someone who, according to the civil law, can use them when he likes, as his own instrument, so, according to the natural law, a son, before coming to the use of reason, is under his father's care. Hence it would be contrary to natural justice, if a child, before coming to the use of reason, were to be taken away from its parents' custody, or anything done to it against its parents' wish. As soon, however, as it begins to have the use of its free-will, it begins to belong to itself, and is able to look after itself, in matters concerning the Divine or the natural law, and then it should be induced, not by compulsion but by persuasion, to embrace the faith: it can then consent to the faith, and be baptized, even against its parents' wish; but not before it comes to the use of reason. Hence it is said of the children of the fathers of old that they were saved in the faith of their parents; whereby we are given to understand that it is the parents' duty to look after the salvation of their children, especially before they come to the use of reason.

Reply: Objection 1 In the marriage bond, both husband and wife have the use of the free-will, and each can assent to the faith without the other's consent. But this does not apply to a child before it comes to the use of reason: yet the comparison holds good after the child has come to the use of reason, if it is willing to be converted.

Reply: Objection 2 No one should be snatched from natural death against the order of civil law: for instance, if a man were condemned by the judge to temporal death, nobody ought to rescue him by violence: hence no one ought to break the order of the natural law, whereby a child is in the custody of its father, in order to rescue it from the danger of everlasting death.

Reply: Objection 3 Jews are bondsmen of princes by civil bondage, which does not exclude the order of natural or Divine law.

Reply: Objection 4 Man is directed to God by his reason, whereby he can know Him. Hence a child before coming to the use of reason, in the natural order of things, is directed to God by its parents' reason, under whose care it lies by nature: and it is for them to dispose of the child in all matters relating to God.

Reply: Objection 5 The peril that ensues from the omission of preaching, threatens only those who are entrusted with the duty of preaching. Hence it had already been said (Ezekiel 3: 17): "I have made thee a watchman to the children (*vulg.* – house) of Israel." On the other hand, to provide the sacraments of salvation for the children of unbelievers is the duty of their parents. Hence it is they whom the danger threatens, if through being deprived of the sacraments their children fail to obtain salvation.

Question XI   Of Heresy

We must now consider heresy: under which head there are four points of inquiry: (1) Whether heresy is a kind of unbelief? (2) Of the matter about which it is. (3) Whether heretics should be tolerated? (4) Whether converts should be received?

First Article   Whether heresy is a species of unbelief?

We proceed thus to the First Article:

Objection 1 It would seem that heresy is not a species of unbelief. For unbelief is in the understanding, as stated above (Q.X, A.2). Now heresy would seem not to pertain to the understanding, but rather to the appetitive power; for Jerome says on Galatians 5: 19: "The works of the flesh are manifest: Heresy is derived from a Greek word meaning choice, whereby a man makes choice of that school which he deems best." But choice is an act of the appetitive power, as stated above [I–II, Q.XIII, A.1]. Therefore heresy is not a species of unbelief.

Objection 2 Further, Vice takes its species chiefly from its end; hence the Philosopher says [*Ethic*, v, 2] that "he who commits adultery that he may steal, is a thief rather than an adulterer." Now the end of heresy is temporal profit, especially lordship and glory, which belong to the vice of pride or covetousness: for Augustine says [*De Util. Credendi*, I] that "a heretic is one who either devises or follows false and new opinions, for the sake of some temporal profit, especially that he may lord and be honored above others." Therefore heresy is a species of pride rather than of unbelief.

Objection 3 Further, Since unbelief is in the understanding, it would seem not to pertain to the flesh. Now heresy belongs to the works of the flesh, for the Apostle says [Galatians 5: 19]: "The works of the flesh are manifest, which are fornication, uncleanness," and among the others, he adds, "dissensions, sects," which are the same as heresies. Therefore heresy is not a species of unbelief.

On the contrary, Falsehood is contrary to truth. Now a heretic is one who devises or follows false or new opinions. Therefore heresy is opposed to the truth, on which faith is founded; and consequently it is a species of unbelief.

I answer that, The word *heresy* as stated in the first objection denotes a choosing. Now choice as stated above [I–II, Q.XIII, A.3] is about things directed to the end, the end being presupposed. Now, in matters of faith, the will assents to some truth, as to its proper good, as was shown above [Q.IV, A.3]: wherefore that which is the chief truth, has the character of last end, while those which are secondary truths, have the character of being directed to the end.

Now, whoever believes, assents to someone's words; so that, in every form of belief, the person to whose words assent is given seems to hold the chief place and to be the end as it were; while the things by holding which one assents to that person hold a secondary place. Consequently he that holds the Christian faith aright, assents, by his will, to Christ, in those things which truly belong to His doctrine.

Accordingly there are two ways in which a man may deviate from the rectitude of the Christian faith. First, because he is unwilling to assent to Christ; and such a man has an evil will, so to say, in respect of the very end. This belongs to the species of unbelief in pagans and Jews. Secondly, because, though he intends to assent to Christ, yet he fails in his choice of those things wherein he assents to Christ, because he chooses, not what Christ really taught, but the suggestions of his own mind.

Therefore heresy is a species of unbelief, belonging to those who profess the Christian faith, but corrupt its dogmas.

Reply: Objection 1 Choice regards unbelief in the same way as the will regards faith, as stated above.

Reply: Objection 2 Vices take their species from their proximate end, while, from their remote end, they take their genus and cause. Thus in the case of adultery committed for the sake of theft, there is the species of adultery taken from its proper end and object; but their ultimate end shows that the act of adultery is both the result of the theft, and is included under it, as an effect under its cause, or a species under its genus, as appears from what we have said about acts in general [I–II, Q.XVIII, A.7]. Wherefore, as to the case in point also, the proximate end of heresy is adherence to one's own false opinion, and from this it derives its species, while its remote end reveals its cause, viz. that it arises from pride or covetousness.

Reply: Objection 3 Just as heresy is so called from its being a choosing [Greek *hairein*, to cut off], so does sect derive its name from its being a cutting off (*secando*), as Isidore states [*Etym*, VIII, 3]. Wherefore heresy and sect are the same thing, and each belongs to the works of the flesh, not indeed by reason of the act itself of unbelief in respect of its proximate object, but by reason of its cause, which is either the desire of an undue end in which way it arises from pride or covetousness, as stated in the second objection, or some illusion of the imagination (which gives rise to error, as the Philosopher [Aristotle] states in *Metaph.*, IV; *Ed. Did.*, III, 5), for this faculty has a certain connection with the flesh, in as much as its act is dependent on a bodily organ.

Second Article   Whether heresy is properly about matters of faith?

We proceed thus to the Second Article:

Objection 1 It would seem that heresy is not properly about matters of faith. For just as there are heresies and sects among Christians, so were there among the Jews and Pharisees, as Isidore observes [*Etym*, VIII, 3–5]. Now their dissensions were not about matters of faith. Therefore heresy is not about matters of faith, as though they were its proper matter.

Objection 2 Further, The matter of faith is the thing believed. Now heresy is not only about things, but also about words, and about interpretations of the Holy Writ. For Jerome says in Galatians 5: 20 that "whoever expounds the Scriptures in any sense but that of the Holy Ghost by Whom they were written, may be called heretic, though he may not have left the Church:" and elsewhere he says that "heresies spring up from words spoken amiss." Therefore heresy is not properly about the matter of faith.

Objection 3 Further, We find the holy doctors differing even about matters pertaining to the faith, for example Augustine and Jerome, on the question about the cessation of the legal observances: and yet this was without any heresy on their part. Therefore heresy is not properly about the matter of faith.

On the contrary, Augustine says against the Manichees: "In Christ's Church, those are heretics, who hold mischievous and erroneous opinions, and when rebuked that they may think soundly and rightly, offer a stubborn resistance, and, refusing to mend their pernicious and deadly doctrines, persist in defending them." Now pernicious and deadly doctrines are none but those which are contrary to dogmas of faith, whereby "the just man liveth" [Romans 1: 17]. Therefore heresy is about matters of faith, as about its proper matter.

I answer that, We are speaking of heresy now as denoting a corruption of the Christian faith. Now it does not imply a corruption of the Christian faith, if a man has a false opinion in matters that are not of faith, for instance, in questions of geometry and so forth, which cannot belong to the faith by any means; but only when a person has a false opinion about things belonging to the faith.

Now a thing may be of faith in two ways, as stated above [I, Q.XXXII, A.4; II–II, Q.I, A.6, *ad* I: Q.II, A.5], in one way, directly and principally, e.g., the articles of faith; in another way, indirectly and secondarily, e.g., those matters, the denial of which leads to the corruption of some article of faith; and there may be heresy in either way, even as there can be faith.

Reply: Objection 1 Just as the heresies of the Jews and Pharisees were about opinions relating to Judaism or Pharisaism, so also heresies among Christians are about matters touching the Christian faith.

Reply: Objection 2 A man is said to expound Holy Writ in another sense than that required by the Holy Ghost, when he so distorts the meaning of Holy Writ, that it is contrary to what the Holy Ghost has revealed. Hence it is written [Ezekiel 13: 6] about the false prophets: "They have persisted to confirm what they have said," viz. by false interpretations of Scripture. Moreover a man professes his faith by the words that he utters, since confession is an act of faith, as stated above [Q.III, A.1]. Wherefore inordinate words about matters of faith may lead to corruption of the faith; and hence it is that Pope Leo says in a letter to Proterius, Bishop of Alexandria: "The enemies of Christ's cross lie in wait for our every deed and word, so that, if we but give them the slightest pretext, they may accuse us mendaciously of agreeing with Nestorius."

Reply: Objection 3 As Augustine says [*Ep.*, 43] and we find it stated in the *Decretals* [XXIV., qu. 3, can. *Dixit Apostolus*]: "By no means should we accuse of heresy those who, however false and perverse their opinion may be, defend it without obstinate fervor, and seek the truth with careful anxiety, ready to mend their opinion, when they have found the truth," because, to wit, they do not make a choice in contradiction to the doctrine of the Church. Accordingly, certain doctors seem to have differed either in matters the holding of which in this or that way is of no consequence, so far as faith is concerned, or even in matters of faith, which were not as yet defined by the Church; although if anyone were obstinately to deny them after they had been defined by the authority of the universal Church, he would be deemed a heretic. This authority resides chiefly in the Sovereign

Pontiff. For we read: "Whenever a question of faith is in dispute, I think, that all our brethren and fellow bishops ought to refer the matter to none other than Peter, as being the source of their name and honor, against whose authority neither Jerome nor Augustine nor any of the holy doctors defended their opinion." Hence Jerome says [*Exposit. Symbol.*]: "This, most blessed Pope, is the faith that we have been taught in the Catholic Church. If anything therein has been incorrectly or carelessly expressed, we beg that it may be set aright by you who hold the faith and see of Peter. If however this, our profession, be approved by the judgment of your apostleship, whoever may blame me, will prove that he himself is ignorant, or malicious, or even not a catholic but a heretic."

Third Article   Whether heretics ought to be tolerated?

We proceed thus to the Third Article:

Objection 1   It seems that heretics ought to be tolerated. For the Apostle says [2 Timothy 2: 24–5]: "The servant of the Lord must not wrangle, . . . with modesty admonishing them that resist the truth, if peradventure God may give them repentance to know the truth, and they may recover themselves from the snares of the devil." Now if heretics are not tolerated but put to death, they lose the opportunity of repentance. Therefore it seems contrary to the Apostle's command.

Objection 2   Further, Whatever is necessary in the Church should be tolerated. Now heresies are necessary in the Church, since the Apostle says [1 Corinthians 11: 19]: "There must be . . . heresies, that they . . . , who are reproved, may be manifest among you." Therefore it seems that heretics should be tolerated.

Objection 3   Further, The Master commanded his servants [Matthew 13: 30] to suffer the cockle "to grow until the harvest," i.e., the end of the world, as a gloss explains it. Now holy men explain that the cockle denotes heretics. Therefore heretics should be tolerated.

On the contrary, The Apostle says [Titus 3: 10–11]: "A man that is a heretic, after the first and second admonition, avoid: knowing that he, that is such an one, is subverted."

I answer that, with regard to heretics two points must be observed: one, on their own side, the other, on the side of the Church. On their own side there is the sin, whereby they deserve not only to be separated from the Church by excommunication, but also to be severed from the world by death. For it is a much graver matter to corrupt the faith which quickens the soul, than to forge money, which supports temporal life. Wherefore if forgers of money and other evil-doers are forthwith condemned to death by the secular authority, much more reason is there for heretics, as soon as

they are convicted of heresy, to be not only excommunicated but even put
to death.

On the part of the Church, however, there is mercy which looks to the
conversion of the wanderer. Wherefore she condemns not at once, but
"after the first and second admonition," as the Apostle directs: after that, if
he is yet stubborn, the Church no longer hoping for his conversion, looks to
the salvation of others, by excommunicating and separating him from the
Church, and furthermore delivers him to the secular tribunal to be exterminated thereby from the world by death. For Jerome commenting on Galatians
5: 9, "A little leaven," says: "Cut off the decayed flesh, expel the mangy
sheep from the fold, lest the whole house, the whole paste, the whole body,
the whole flock, burn, perish, rot, die. Arius was but one spark in Alexandria,
but as that spark was not at once put out, the whole earth was laid waste
by its flame."

Reply: Objection 1   This very modesty demands that the heretic should
be admonished a first and second time: and if he be unwilling to retract, he
must be reckoned as already *subverted*, as we may gather from the words of
the Apostle quoted above.

Reply: Objection 2   The profit that ensues from heresy is beside the
intention of heretics, for it consists in the constancy of the faithful being put
to the test, and "makes us shake off our sluggishness, and search the Scriptures more carefully," as Augustine states [*De Gen. cont. Manich*, I, 1].
What they really intend is the corruption of the faith, which is to inflict very
great harm indeed. Consequently we should consider what they directly
intend, and expel them, rather than what is beside their intention, and so,
tolerate them.

Reply: Objection 3   According to *Decret*. XXIV [qu. III, can. *Notandum*],
"to be excommunicated is not to be uprooted." A man is excommunicated,
as the Apostle says (1 Corinthians 5: 5) that his "spirit may be saved in the
day of Our Lord." Yet if heretics be altogether uprooted by death, this is
not contrary to Our Lord's command, which is to be understood as refer-
ring to the case when the cockle cannot be plucked up without plucking
up the wheat, as we explained above [Q.X, A.8, *ad* 1], when treating of
unbelievers in general.

*Fourth Article   Whether the church should receive those who
return from heresy?*

We proceed thus to the Fourth Article:

Objection 1   It would seem that the Church ought in all cases to receive
those who return from heresy. For it is written [Jeremiah 3: 1] in the person
of the Lord: "Thou hast prostituted thyself to many lovers; nevertheless

return to Me saith the Lord." Now the sentence of the Church is God's sentence, according to Deuteronomy 1: 17: "You shall hear the little as well as the great: neither shall you respect any man's person, because it is the judgment of God." Therefore even those who are guilty of the prostitution of unbelief which is spiritual prostitution, should be received all the same.

Objection 2 Further, Our Lord commanded Peter [Matthew 18: 22] to forgive his offending brother *not* only "till seven times, but till seventy times seven times," which Jerome expounds as meaning that "a man should be forgiven, as often as he has sinned." Therefore he ought to be received by the Church as often as he has sinned by falling back into heresy.

Objection 3 Further, Heresy is a kind of unbelief. Now other unbelievers who wish to be converted are received by the Church. Therefore heretics also should be received.

On the contrary, The Decretal *Ad abolendam* [*De Haereticis*, cap. IX] says that "those who are found to have relapsed into the error which they had already abjured, must be left to the secular tribunal." Therefore they should not be received by the Church.

I answer that, In obedience to Our Lord's institution, the Church extends her charity to all, not only to friends, but also to foes who persecute her, according to Matthew 5: 44: "Love your enemies; do good to them that hate you." Now it is part of charity that we should both wish and work our neighbor's good. Again, good is twofold; one is spiritual, namely the health of the soul, which good is chiefly the object of charity, since it is this chiefly that we should wish for one another. Consequently, from this point of view, heretics who return after falling no matter how often, are admitted by the Church to Penance whereby the way of salvation is opened to them.

The other good is that which charity considers secondarily, viz. temporal good, such as the life of the body, worldly possessions, good repute, ecclesiastical or secular dignity, for we are not bound by charity to wish others this good, except in relation to the eternal salvation of them and of others. Hence if the presence of one of these goods in one individual might be an obstacle to eternal salvation in many, we are not bound out of charity to wish such a good to that person, rather should we desire him to be without it, both because eternal salvation takes precedence of temporal good, and because the good of the many is to be preferred to the good of one. Now if heretics were always received on their return, in order to save their lives and other temporal goods, this might be prejudicial to the salvation of others, both because they would infect others if they relapsed again, and because, if they escaped without punishment, others would feel more assured in lapsing into heresy. For it is written [Ecclesiastes 8: 11]: "For because sentence is not speedily pronounced against the evil, the children of men commit evils without any fear."

For this reason the Church not only admits to Penance those who return from heresy for the first time, but also safeguards their lives, and sometimes by dispensation, restores them to the ecclesiastical dignities which they may have had before, should their conversion appear to be sincere: we read of this as having frequently been done for the good of peace. But when they fall again, after having been received, this seems to prove them to be inconstant in faith, wherefore when they return again, they are admitted to Penance, but are not delivered from the pain of death.

Reply: Objection 1   In God's tribunal, those who return are always received, because God is a searcher of hearts, and knows those who return in sincerity. But the Church cannot imitate God in this, for she presumes that those who relapse after being once received, are not sincere in their return; hence she does not debar them from the way of salvation, but neither does she protect them from the sentence of death.

Reply: Objection 2   Our Lord was speaking to Peter of sins committed against oneself, for one should always forgive such offenses and spare our brother when he repents. These words are not to be applied to sins committed against one's neighbor or against God, for it is not left to our discretion to forgive such offenses, as Jerome says on Matthew 18: 15, "If thy brother shall offend against thee." Yet even in this matter the law prescribes limits according as God's honor or our neighbor's good demands.

Reply: Objection 3   When other unbelievers, who have never received the faith are converted, they do not as yet show signs of inconstancy in faith, as relapsed heretics do; hence the comparison fails.

Marsilius of Padua, *Defensor Pacis* (1324)

Marsilius, or Marsiglio, (c. 1280–1342) defended the powers of the secular ruler, which, like those of the subordinate church, flowed from the people. His services were welcomed by the Emperor Ludwig of Bavaria. Opinion about his sentiments concerning religion and coercion vary. Ruffini praised him as a forerunner of modern liberty of conscience and worship; more realistically, Lecler called him a pseudo-defender of such liberty. In any event, Marsilius succeeds in freeing religious opinion from threat of ecclesiastical persecution, although the role of the state remains ambiguous.

SOURCE: Marsilius of Padua, *Defensor Pacis*, tr. Alan Gewirth (Toronto: University of Toronto Press, 1980 [1956]), pp. 166–70, 173–5, 177–8.

LITERATURE: Alexander Passerin D'Entrèves, *The Medieval Contribution to Political Thought: Thomas Aquinas, Marsilius of Padua, Richard Hooker* (Oxford: Oxford University Press, 1939), ch. 4.

Discourse II

Chapter 9

(4)   In agreement with the mind of the Apostle in the second epistle to the Corinthians, Chapter 1, this was also clearly the view of St John Chrysostom in his book of *Dialogues*, also entitled *On the Priestly Dignity*, Book II, Chapter III. For the sake of brevity, we shall not here repeat those of his remarks which we quoted in Chapter V of this discourse, paragraph 6, but shall here cite what he adds to the aforesaid passage. This, then, is what Chrysostom wrote:

> There is great need of art, then, for this purpose, to help persuade men, when they are ill, to offer themselves willingly to the medicine of the priests, and not only this, but to be grateful for being cured. For a man will either break his bandages, which he certainly has free power to do, and will make his illness worse, or he will spurn the words which were to act as a surgical knife, and by his contempt will add to himself another wound, so that an opportunity for cure becomes the means of a worse disease. For there is no one who can cure a person against his will.

And then after several further remarks, which the pastor of souls ought to note in his corrective, although not coercive, function, Chrysostom continues:

> If a man is led away from the right faith, great exhortation, industry, and patience are required of the priest, because he cannot lead the erring person back to the path by force, but will try to persuade him to return to the true faith, from which he originally strayed.

See, then, how this saint separates the judgment of priests from that of rulers, in that the judgment of priests neither is nor ought to be coercive; and he gives the reasons which we have often stated: first, that coercive power is given by the laws or legislators, and was not granted to the priests of his time or province; and second, that even if coercive power were granted to them, in vain would they exercise it on their subjects, for coercion is of no spiritual help toward eternal salvation. And Chrysostom said the same thing in writing on the words of the ninth chapter of Luke [v. 23]: "If anyone wishes to come after me, let him deny himself." I have, however, omitted this passage here because the discussion has been sufficient, and for the sake of brevity.

(5)   This again was clearly the view of St Hilary in his epistle to the emperor Constantine, wherein he wrote, among other things: "God taught

rather than demanded knowledge of himself; in his precepts he counseled that the heavenly works be admired, but he spurned the use of coercive authority to impose avowal of himself." See, then, that God wants men to be taught knowledge and avowal of himself, that is, by faith; he does not want anyone to be coerced, but spurns this. And the same point is reiterated a little below: "God does not require a forced avowal." And farther below Hilary says the same thing in the person of all priests: "I cannot accept anyone unless he is willing, hear anyone unless he prays, bless anyone unless he proffers himself." God, then, does not want a forced avowal of himself, nor does he want anyone to be dragged thereto by the violent action of compulsion of someone else. Hence in Hilary's epistle against Auxentius, the bishop of Milan, whom he held to be an Arian and who, as he says, used armed force to make men profess his own opinion concerning, or rather contrary to, the catholic faith, Hilary, reproving him even if what he had taught had been true, writes as follows: "First we may grieve over the hardships of our age, and bemoan the stupid opinions of these times, whereby human institutions are believed to prop God's power, and one labors to protect the church of Christ by secular maneuvering." And again, in the same epistle: "But now – O sorrow! – earthly arguments are used to justify divine faith and Christ is indeed shown to be helpless when he is made dependent upon canvassing. The church frightens men with exile and imprisonment and uses coercion to induce belief in itself – that church which was once believed in amid exile and imprisonment." And when Hilary speaks of the "church," he means the college of priests or bishops and the other ministers of the temple, who are called clergymen.

(6)   This too was clearly the view of Ambrose in his second epistle to the emperor Valentinianus, entitled *To the People,* when he said: "I shall be able to weep, I shall be able to lament, I shall be able to grieve; against arms, soldiers, and Goths, my tears are my weapons, for such are the munitions of the priest; in any other way I neither can nor should resist." See, then, that the priest should not, even if he could, use weapons or coercive force against anyone, or command or urge that they be used, especially against the Christian faithful; but the whole world can observe that certain priests have followed the opposite course, against the teaching of the sacred canon and of the saints.

(7)   According to the truth, therefore, and the clear intention of the Apostle [he has cited, *inter alia,* 2 Corinthians 1: 23] and the saints [including John Chrysostom, *On the Priestly Dignity* and Hilary, *Epistle to Constantine*], who were the foremost teachers of the church or faith, it is not commanded that anyone, even an infidel, let alone a believer, be compelled in this world

through pain or punishment to observe the commands of the evangelic law, especially by a priest; and hence the ministers of this law, the bishops or priests, neither can nor should judge anyone in this world by a judgment in the third sense, or compel an unwilling person, by any pain or punishment, to observe the commands of divine law, especially without authorization by the human legislator; for such coercive judgment in accordance with divine law must not be exercised or executed in this world, but only in the future one. Hence in the nineteenth chapter [19: 28] of Matthew: "But Jesus said to them," that is, to the apostles: "Verily I say unto you, that ye which have followed me, in the regeneration when the son of man shall sit on the throne of his glory, ye also shall sit upon twelve thrones, judging the twelve tribes of Israel." See, then, when it was that the apostles were going to sit with Christ as judges in the third sense, namely, in the other world, not in this one. Whereon the gloss: "'in the regeneration,' that is, when the dead will rise up alive again." Hence, according to the gloss: "There are two regenerations, the first from water and the holy spirit, the second in resurrection." Hence "ye shall sit," and the gloss according to Augustine says: "When he who was in the guise of a servant and who was judged," that is, Christ, who was in this world judged by coercive judgment, and did not himself judge, "will exercise judiciary power," that is, in the resurrection, "you shall be judges with me." See, then, that according to Christ's words in the gospel and the exposition of the saints, Christ did not in this world exercise judiciary, that is, coercive, power, which we called judgment in the third sense, but rather, in the guise of a servant, he underwent such judgment by another man; and when he will exercise such coercive judiciary power in the other world, then, and not before, will the apostles sit with him to make such judgments.

(8)   Hence it is indeed to be wondered why any bishop or priest, whoever he be, assumes for himself greater or other authority than that which Christ or his apostles wanted to have in this world. For they, in the guise of servants, were judged by the secular rulers. But their successors, the priests, not only refuse to be subject to the rulers, contrary to the example and command of Christ and of the apostles, but they even claim to be superior to the supreme rulers and powers in coercive jurisdiction. Christ, however, said in the tenth [10: 18] chapter of Matthew: "And ye shall be brought before governors and kings for my sake"; but he did not say: Ye shall be governors or kings. And further on [10: 24] he adds: "The disciple is not over his master, nor the servant above his lord." Therefore, no coercive judgment, rulership, or dominion can or ought to be exercised in this world by any priest or bishop as such. This was also clearly the view of the famous Philosopher [Aristotle] in the *Politics*, Book IV, Chapter 12, for he said:

"Hence not all those who are elected or chosen by lot are to be regarded as rulers. Consider the priests in the first place. These must be regarded as different from the political rulers. And also there are the masters of choruses and heralds, and also ambassadors who are elected. And of the superintendent functions some are political, being exercised over all the citizens with regard to some action." And a little below he adds: "And other offices are economic."

(9)   What we have said is also borne out by this, that if Christ had wanted the priests of the New Law to be judges according to it, in the third sense of judge, that is, with coercive judgment, settling by such verdicts men's contentious acts in this world, then he would have given in this law special commands about such acts, just as he did in the Old Law in the case of Moses, whom God, by his own utterance and not through man, made ruler and coercive judge of the Jews, as it is told in the seventh chapter [7: 35] of the Acts. For this reason, also, God gave to Moses a law prescribing what must be observed in and for the status of the present life for the purpose of settling human disputes; a law which contained special commands about such matters, and was in this respect analogous to human law in some part of it. Accordingly, men were compelled and forced to observe these commands in this world through pain or punishment by Moses and by the coercive judges who took his place, but not by any priest, as is quite clear form the eighteenth chapter of Exodus. But such commands were not given by Christ in the evangelic law; rather, he took for granted the commands which were or would be given in human laws, and he commanded every human soul to observe these and to obey the men who ruled in accordance with them, at least in those commands which were not opposed to the law of eternal salvation. Hence in the twenty-second chapter [22: 21] of Matthew and the eleventh [actually 12: 17] of Mark: "Render unto Caesar the things that are Caesar's," by "Caesar" signifying any ruler. So too the Apostle said in the thirteenth chapter [13: 1] of Romans, and it bears repeating: "Let every soul be subject to the higher powers." So too in the first epistle to Timothy, last chapter [6: 1]: "Even to infidel lords," and the gloss thereon according to Augustine, which we quoted in Chapter V of this discourse, paragraph 8. From all these it is quite evident that Christ, the Apostle, and the saints held the view that all men must be subject to the human laws and to the judges according to these laws. . . .

Chapter 10

(1)   Concerning what we have said doubts may well arise. For if only the ruler by the legislator's authority has jurisdiction over all forms of

compulsion in the present life, through coercive judgment, and the infliction and exaction of penalties in property and in person, as was shown
above, then it will pertain to this ruler to make coercive judgments over
heretics or other infidels or schismatics, and to inflict, exact, and dispose of
the penalties in property and in person. But this seems inappropriate. For
it might seem that it pertains to the same authority to inquire into a crime
and to judge and correct the crime; but since it pertains to the priest, the
presbyter or bishop, and to no one else, to discern the crime of heresy, it
would seem to follow that the coercive judgment or correction of this and
similar crimes also pertains to the priest or bishop alone. Moreover, the
judging and punishing of a criminal might seem to pertain to the person
against whom or against whose law the criminal has sinned. But this person
is the priest or bishop. For he is the minister or judge of divine law, against
which essentially the heretic, schismatic, or other infidel sins, whether this
sinner be a group or an individual. It follows, therefore, that this judgment
pertains to the priest, and not to the ruler. And this clearly seems to be the
view of St Ambrose in his first epistle to the Emperor Valentinian; but since
he seems to adhere to this view through the whole epistle, I have omitted to
quote from it for the sake of brevity.

(2)   But now let us say, in accordance with our previous conclusions, that
any person who sins against divine law must be judged, corrected, and
punished according to that law. But there are two judges according to it.
One is a judge in the third sense, having coercive power to punish transgressors of this law; and this judge is Christ alone, as we showed by James,
Chapter 4, in the preceding chapter. But Christ willed and decreed that all
transgressors of this law should be coercively judged and punished in the
future world only, not in this one, as the preceding chapter made sufficiently clear. There is another judge according to this law, namely, the
priest or bishop, but he is not a judge in the third sense, and may not
correct any transgressor of divine law in this world and punish him by
coercive force; this was clearly shown in Chapters V and IX of this discourse by the authority and the invincible reasoning of the Apostle and the
saints. However, the priest is a judge in the first sense of the word, and he
has to teach, exhort, censure, and rebuke sinners or transgressors of divine
law, and frighten them by a judgment of the future infliction of damnation
and punishment upon them in the world to come by the coercive judge,
Christ, as we showed in Chapters VI and VII of this discourse, where the
power of the priestly keys was discussed, and in the preceding chapter,
where we compared the physician of bodies with the priests, "who are the
physicians of souls", as Augustine said by the authority of the prophet
and as the Master [Peter Lombard] repeats in Book IV, Distinction 18,

Chapter IX. Since, then, the heretic, the schismatic, or any other infidel is a transgressor of divine law, if he persists in this crime he will be punished by that judge to whom it pertains to correct transgressors of divine laws as such, when he will exercise his judicial authority. But this judge is Christ, who will judge the living, the dead, and the dying, but in the future world, not in this one. For he has mercifully allowed sinners to have the opportunity of becoming deserving and penitent up to the very time when they finally pass from this world at death. But the other judge, namely, the pastor, bishop or priest, must teach and exhort man in the present life, must censure and rebuke the sinner and frighten him by a judgment or prediction of future glory or eternal damnation; but he must not coerce, as is plain from the previous chapter.

(3)   Now if human law were to prohibit heretics or other infidels from dwelling in the region, and yet such a person were found there, he must be corrected in this world as a transgressor of human law, and the penalty fixed by that law for such transgression must be inflicted on him by the judge who is the guardian of human law by the authority of the legislator, as we demonstrated in Chapter XV of Discourse I. But if human law did not prohibit the heretic or other infidel from dwelling among the faithful in the same province, as heretics and Jews are now permitted to do by human laws even in these times of Christian peoples, rulers, and pontiffs, then I say that no one is allowed to judge or coerce a heretic or other infidel by any penalty in property or in person for the status of the present life. And the general reason for this is as follows: no one is punished in this world for sinning against theoretic or practical disciplines precisely as such, however much he may sin against them, but only for sinning against a command of human law. For if human law did not prohibit anyone from becoming drunk, or making and selling shoes according to his means or desires, or practicing medicine, or teaching, or working at other such functions as he pleased, then no one who became drunk, or who acted wrongly in any occupation, would be punished. . . .

(7)   For a person is not punished by the ruler solely for sinning against divine law. For there are many mortal sins even against divine law, such as fornication, which the human legislator knowingly permits, and which the bishop or priest does not, cannot, and should not prohibit by coercive force. But if the heretic's sin against divine law is such as human law also prohibits, then he is punished in this world as a sinner against human law. For this latter sin is the precise or primary essential cause why a person is punished in this life, for where this is given, the effect is given, and where it is removed, so is the effect. And conversely, he who sins against human

law will be punished in the other world as sinning against divine law, not as sinning against human law. For many things prohibited by human law are nevertheless permitted by divine law; for example, if a person does not repay a loan at the established date because of inability due to accident, illness, forgetfulness, or some other obstacle, he will not be punished for this in the other world by the coercive judge of divine law, and yet he is justly punished for it in this world by the coercive judge of human law. But if any person has sinned against divine law, he will be punished in the other world regardless of whether or not his act, such as fornication, is permitted by human law; and hence sinning against divine law is the primary essential cause, which in philosophy is usually called the cause "as such," of the punishment which is inflicted for and in the status of the future world; since where this cause is given, the effect is given, and where it is removed, so is the effect.

(8)   Therefore, the judgment over heretics, schismatics, and other infidels, and the power to coerce them, to exact temporal punishment from them, and to assign the pecuniary mulcts to oneself or to the community, and not to anyone else, belongs only to the ruler by authority of the human legis-lator, and not to any priest or bishop, even though it be divine law which is sinned against. For although the latter is indeed a law in its relation to men in and for the status of the present life, yet it is not a law in the last sense as having coercive power over anyone in this world; this is evident from the preceding chapter and Chapter V of this discourse. It is, however, a law in the third sense, as was made clear in Chapter X of Discourse I. And the priests are its judges, in the first sense of "judge," in this world, and they have no coercive power, as was shown in Chapter V of this discourse and in the preceding chapter by the words of the Apostle, Ambrose, Hilary, and Chrysostom. For if the priests were coercive judges or rulers over heretics because the latter sin against the discipline of which the priests are the teachers and the performers of certain operations upon others in accordance with it, then in similar fashion the goldsmith would be coercive judge and ruler over the counterfeiter of golden works, which is quite absurd; sim-ilarly too the physician would coerce those who act wrongly with respect to the art of medicine; and there would be as many rulers as there are func-tions or offices of the state against which it is possible to sin. But the impossibility or uselessness of this multiplicity of rulers was shown in Chapter XVII of Discourse I. For persons who committed such sins against the offices of the state would not on that account be coerced or punished, unless something else intervened, namely, a command of human law or of the legislator. For if such sins were not prohibited by human law, then those who committed them would not be punished.

Notes

1   Martin, bishop of Tours, protested against imperial proceedings which led to the execution in *c*. 385 of the heretic Priscillian.

2   "We must therefore conclude that, absolutely speaking, every will at variance with reason, whether right or erring, is always evil" (*Summa Theologica*, vol. I/II, Q.19, A.5). Must not one therefore follow reason/conscience in the formation of religious belief? Aquinas does not address this formulation of the problem.

3

THE RENAISSANCE AND
REFORMATIONS

Thomas More, "Of the Religions in Utopia" (1516)

More (1478–1535) was an English humanist and civil servant under Henry
VIII, rising to the position of Lord Chancellor in 1529. He was executed
in 1535 when he refused to assent to the king's elevation to the headship
of the church. His most famous writing is *Utopia*, a piece of humanist
criticism of sixteenth-century policies and mores. Not less than other
sections of this remarkable work, the piece on religion in Utopia has
spawned a good deal of debate among commentators. This is because
the apparently liberal attitude expressed here – before Luther's rise to
fame, it should be noted – does not seem to describe More's own career
in government where he was engaged in the prosecution of heretics. But
while Utopia was a fine expression of virtuous and enlightened non-
Christian society, its attitudes might certainly be expected to undergo
some amendment if and when it became a Christian society. As it was,
Utopia's wise founder did not grant total religious freedom, and in fact, the
non-Christian but committed searcher-after-truth Utopus represents as
much of the mind of the author as could be expected. In his later work,
A Dialogue Concerning Heresies (1529), More wrote ominously: "And yet
were heresye well worthy to be as sore punyshed as any other faute
syth there is no faute that more offendeth god"; and that princes "shall
not suffer theyr people to be seduced and corrupted by heretykes."[1] In
More's mind, a Christianized Utopus would have approved this statement
unreservedly.

SOURCE: Thomas More, *Utopia*, tr. G. C. Richards (Oxford: Basil Blackwell, 1923),
pp. 105–9.
LITERATURE: Edward L. Surtz, *The Praise of Wisdom: A Commentary on the Religious
and Moral Problems and Backgrounds of St Thomas More's "Utopia"* (Chicago,

IL: Loyola University Press, 1957), ch. 3; J. A. Guy, "Sir Thomas More and the Heretics," *History Today*, 30 (Feb. 1980), pp. 11–15.

There are different kinds of religion not only in various parts of the island, but also in each city. Some worship the Sun; others the Moon, others one of the planets as God. Some reverence a man who in former times was conspicuous for virtue or glory, not only as God, but as the supreme God. But the majority, and those the wiser among them, do nothing of the kind, but believe in one unknown Divine Power, eternal, incomprehensible, inexplicable, far beyond the reach of human intellect, diffused throughout the universe not in bulk but in power and potency. Him they call Father, to Him alone they attribute the beginnings, the growth, the progress, the changes and the ends of all things, and to no other do they give divine honors. Nay, all the others too, though varying in their belief, agree with them in this respect, that they think there is one supreme Being, to Whom we owe it that the whole world was made and is governed; and all alike call Him in their native language, Mythra; but in this respect they disagree, that He is looked on differently by different people, each thinking that whatever that be which he regards as supreme is that same nature, to Whose unique power and majesty the sum of all things by common consent is attributed. But gradually they are all beginning to depart from this medley of superstitions and are coming to agree together in that one religion which seems to surpass the rest in reasonableness. Nor is there any doubt that the other beliefs would have all disappeared long ago, had not anything untoward which chance brought upon men when they were thinking of changing their religion, been construed by fear as having not happened by chance but been sent from heaven, the Deity, Whose worship they were proposing to forsake, thus avenging an intention so impious towards Himself.

But when they heard from us the name of Christ, His teaching, His example, His miracles, and the no less wonderful constancy of the many martyrs, whose blood freely shed drew so many nations into their fellowship in many parts of the world, you cannot think how readily disposed they were to join it, whether through the secret inspiration of God, or because they thought it nearest to that belief which has the widest prevalence among them. But I think this, too, was of no small weight, that they heard from us that Christ approved the common way of living which they follow, and that it is still in use among the truest societies of Christians. But whatever it was that influenced them, not a few agreed to adopt our religion and received holy baptism.

But as among us four (for that was all that was left, two of our company having died), there was, I am sorry to say, no priest, they were instructed in all other matters, but so far lack those sacraments, which with us only a

priest can give; however, they understand what they are, and desire them
with the greatest earnestness. Nay, they are even debating earnestly among
themselves whether without the sending of a Christian bishop one chosen
out of their own number may receive valid orders, and it seemed that they
would choose one, but when I left, they had not yet done so. Even those
who do not agree with the religion of Christ, do not try to deter others from
it and do not oppose the instruction of any. One only of our company was
interfered with, while I was there. He, as soon as he was baptized, in spite
of our protests, began to speak publicly of Christ's religion with more zeal
than discretion, and began to be so warm in his preaching, that not only did
he prefer our worship to any other, but condemned all others as profane in
themselves, and the followers of them impious and sacrilegious, and loudly
declared they were worthy of eternal punishment. When he had long been
preaching in this style, they arrested him, not for despising their religion,
but for stirring up strife among the people, tried and convicted him, and
sentenced him to exile. They count this among their most ancient institutions, that no one shall suffer for his religion. At the very beginning King
Utopus – having heard that before his arrival the inhabitants had been
continually quarrelling about religion, and having observed that the dissensions between the individual sects in fighting for their country had given
him the opportunity of overcoming them all – after he had gained the
victory, first ordained that it should be lawful for every man to follow what
religion he chose; that each might strive to bring others over to his own,
provided that he quietly and peaceably supported his own by reasoning and
did not bitterly try to demolish that of others; if his persuasions were not
successful, he was to use no violence and refrain from abuse, but if he
contended too vehemently in expressing his views, he was to be punished
by exile or enslavement.

Utopus ordained this not merely from regard to peace, which he saw to
be utterly destroyed by constant wrangling and implacable hatred, but
because he thought that this peace was in the interest of religion itself. On
religion he did not venture to dogmatize himself, being doubtful whether
God did not inspire different people with different views, and desire a
varied and manifold worship. But assuredly he thought it both insolence
and folly to require by violence and threats that all should agree with what
you believe to be true; moreover, if it should be the case that one religion
is true and all the rest false, he foresaw that if the matter were dealt with
reasonably and moderately, truth by its own natural force would come out
and be clearly seen; but if there were contention and armed violence were
employed, seeing that the worst men are always the most obstinate, the best
and holiest religion would be overwhelmed because of the conflicting false
religions, like corn overgrown by thorns and bushes. So he left it all an open

matter and made it free to each to choose what he should believe, save that he strictly gave injunction that no one should fall so far below the dignity of human nature as to believe that the soul perishes with the body, or that the world is the mere sport of chance and not governed by any divine providence.

This is why they believe that after this life vices are punished and virtue is rewarded; and if anyone thinks otherwise they do not even regard him as a human being, seeing that he has lowered the lofty nature of his soul to the level of the brute beasts; so far are they from classing him among their citizens, whose laws and customs he would treat with contempt if it were not for fear. For who can doubt that he will strive either to evade by craft the common laws of his country, or to break them by violence, in order to serve his own private greed, when he has nothing to fear but the law, and no hope beyond the body? Wherefore one of this mind is excluded from office, is entrusted with no function, and is not put in charge of any public function; he is generally looked upon as of a mean and low disposition. But they do not punish him in any way, being convinced that it is in no man's power to believe whatever he chooses; nor do they compel him by threats to disguise his views, and they do not allow any deceptions or lies in the matter, for them they hate exceedingly as being next door to actual wrong-doing. They forbid him to argue in support of his opinion, at any rate before the common people, but in private before the priests and men of weight and importance they not only permit but encourage it, being sure that such madness will in the end give way to reason.

There are others too, and not so very few, who are not interfered with, because they are not bad men and there is something to be said for their view; these believe that animals have immortal souls, but not to be compared with ours in dignity and not destined to equal felicity.

Martin Luther, *Temporal Authority: To What Extent It Should Be Obeyed* (1523)

This passage from the "early" Luther (1483–1546) actually embodies much of medieval (including Thomistic) thought on the subject of religious freedom, but reworks those notions in such a way as to anticipate the commonplaces of later thought – the inviolability of conscience, the hypocrisy engendered by compulsion, and the nature of tolerance as the ranking of priorities. But Luther would not retain this mind for long. With his own vision threatened by more radical thoughts and actions, in two years he distinguished between the freedoms of conscience and worship, the magistrate having power of compulsion to hinder public expressions of heresy. In 1530 he would sanction the death penalty for blasphemy, even without the presence of sedition, and in the following year he affirmed the ancient Justinian Code's strictures against blasphemy, redefined to include a variety of doctrinal errors. Later, when Castellio reacted to the burning of Servetus in Geneva in 1553, he cited a number of passages from the reformers which were favorable to his own argument for freedom of religion; among those works was this one by Luther.[2]

SOURCE: Reprinted from *Luther's Works*, vol. 45, ed. W. I. Brandt (Philadelphia, PA: Fortress Press, 1962) pp. 104–18. Copyright © 1962 Fortress Press; reproduced by permission of Augsburg Press.
LITERATURE: Roland Bainton, "The Struggle for Religious Liberty," *Church History*, 10 (1941), pp. 95–124; Joseph Lecler, *Toleration and the Reformation*, tr. T. L. Westow, 2 vols (New York: Association Press, 1960), vol. I, pp. 147–64; William A. Mueller, *Church and State in Luther and Calvin: A Comparative Study* (Garden City, NY: Anchor Books, 1965 [1954]), ch. 4; Henry Loewen, *Luther and the Radicals* (Waterloo, Ont.: Wilfrid Laurier University Press, 1974), ch. 7.

We come now to the main part of this treatise. Having learned that there must be temporal authority on earth, and how it is to be exercised in a Christian and salutary manner, we must now learn how far its arm extends and how widely its hand stretches, lest it extend too far and encroach upon God's kingdom and government. It is essential for us to know this, for where it is given too wide a scope, intolerable and terrible injury follows; on the other hand, injury is also inevitable where it is restricted too narrowly. In the former case, the temporal authority punishes too much; in the latter case, it punishes too little. To err in this direction, however, and punish too little is more tolerable, for it is always better to let a scoundrel live than to put a godly man to death. The world has plenty of scoundrels anyway and must continue to have them, but godly men are scarce.

It is to be noted first that the two classes of Adam's children – the one in God's kingdom under Christ and the other in the kingdom of the world under the governing authority, as was said above – have two kinds of law. For every kingdom must have its own laws and statutes; without law no kingdom or government can survive, as everyday experience amply shows. The temporal government has laws which extend no further than to life and property and external affairs on earth, for God cannot and will not permit anyone but himself to rule over the soul. Therefore, where the temporal authority presumes to prescribe laws for the soul, it encroaches upon God's government and only misleads souls and destroys them. We want to make this so clear that everyone will grasp it, and that our fine gentlemen, the princes and bishops will see what fools they are when they seek to coerce the people with their laws and commandments into believing this or that.

When a man-made law is imposed upon the soul to make it believe this or that as its human author may prescribe, there is certainly no word of God for it. If there is no word of God for it, then we cannot be sure whether God wishes to have it so, for we cannot be certain that something which he does not command is pleasing to him. Indeed, we are sure that it does not please him, for he desires that our faith be based simply and entirely on his divine word alone. He says in Matthew 18 [16: 18], "On this rock I will build my church"; and in John 10 [vv. 27, 14, 5], "My sheep hear my voice and know me; however, they will not hear the voice of a stranger, but flee from him." From this it follows that with such a wicked command the temporal power is driving souls to eternal death. For it compels them to believe as right and certainly pleasing to God that which is in fact uncertain, indeed, certain to be displeasing to him since there is no clear word of God for it. Whoever believes something to be right which is wrong or uncertain is denying the truth, which is God himself. He is believing in lies and errors, and counting as right that which is wrong.

Hence, it is the height of folly when they command that one shall believe the Church, the fathers, and the councils, though there be no word of God for it. It is not the church but the devil's apostles who command such things, for the church commands nothing unless it knows for certain that it is God's word. As St Peter puts it, "Whoever speaks, let him speak as the word of God" [1 Peter 4: 11]. It will be a long time, however, before they can ever prove that the decrees of the councils are God's word. Still more foolish is it when they assert that kings, princes, and the mass of mankind believe thus and so. My dear man, we are not baptized into kings, or princes, or even into the mass of mankind, but into Christ and God himself. Neither are we called kings, princes, or common folk, but Christians. No one shall or can command the soul unless he is able to show it the way to heaven; but this no man can do, only God alone. Therefore, in matters which concern the salvation of souls nothing but God's word shall be taught and accepted.

Again, consummate fools though they are, they must confess that they have no power over souls. For no human being can kill a soul or give it life, or conduct it to heaven or hell. If they will not take our word for it, Christ himself will attend to it strongly enough where he says in the tenth chapter of Matthew [actually Luke 12: 4–5; cf. Matthew 10: 28], "Do not fear those who kill the body, and after that have nothing that they can do; rather fear him who after he has killed the body, has power to condemn to hell." I think it is clear enough here that the soul is taken out of all human hands and is placed under the authority of God alone.

Now tell me: How much wit must there be in the head of a person who imposes commands in an area where he has no authority whatsoever? Would you not judge the person insane who commanded the moon to shine whenever he wanted it to? How well would it go if the Leipzigers were to impose laws on us Wittenbergers, or if, conversely, we in Wittenberg were to legislate for the people of Leipzig! They would certainly send the lawmakers a thank-offering of hellebore to purge their brains and cure their sniffles. Yet our emperor and clever princes are doing just that today. They are allowing pope, bishop, and sophists to lead them on – one blind man leading the other – to command their subjects to believe, without God's word, whatever they please. And still they would be known as Christian princes, God forbid!

Besides, we cannot conceive how an authority could or should act in a situation except where it can see, know, judge, condemn, change, and modify. What would I think of a judge who should blindly decide cases which he neither hears nor sees? Tell me then: How can a mere man see, know, judge, condemn, and change hearts? That is reserved for God alone, as Psalm 7 [v. 9] says, "God tries the hearts and reins"; and [v. 8], "The Lord judges the peoples." And Acts 10 [1: 24; 15: 8] says, "God knows the hearts"; and Jeremiah 1 [17: 9–10], "Wicked and unsearchable is the human heart; who can understand it? I the Lord, who search the heart and reins." A court should and must be quite certain and clear about everything if it is to render judgment. But the thoughts and inclinations of the soul can be known to no one but God. Therefore, it is futile and impossible to command or compel anyone by force to believe this or that. The matter must be approached in a different way. Force will not accomplish it. And I am surprised at the big fools, for they themselves all say: *De occultis non judicat Ecclesia*, the church does not judge secret matters. If the spiritual rule of the church governs only public matters, how dare the mad temporal authority judge and control such a secret, spiritual, hidden matter as faith?

Furthermore, every man runs his own risk in believing as he does, and he must see to it himself that he believes rightly. As nobody else can go to heaven or hell for me, so nobody else can believe or disbelieve for me; as nobody else can open or close heaven or hell to me, so nobody else can drive me to belief or unbelief. How he believes or disbelieves is a matter for the conscience of each individual, and since this takes nothing away from the temporal authority the latter should be content to attend to its own affairs and let men believe this or that as they are able and willing, and constrain no one by force. For faith is a free act, to which no one can be forced. Indeed, it is a work of God in the spirit, not something which outward authority should compel or create. Hence arises the common saying, found also in Augustine, "No one can or ought to be forced to believe."

Moreover, the blind, wretched fellows fail to see how utterly hopeless and impossible a thing they are attempting. For no matter how harshly they lay down the law, or how violently they rage, they can do no more than force an outward compliance of the mouth and the hand; the heart they cannot compel, though they work themselves to a frazzle. For the proverb is true: "Thoughts are tax-free." Why do they persist in trying to force people to believe from the heart when they see that it is impossible? In so doing they only compel weak consciences to lie, to disavow, and to utter what is not in their hearts. They thereby load themselves down with dreadful alien sins, for all the lies and false confessions which such weak consciences utter fall back upon him who compels them. Even if their subjects were in error, it would be much easier simply to let them err than to compel them to lie and to utter what is not in their hearts. In addition, it is not right to prevent evil by something even worse.

Would you like to know why God ordains that the temporal princes must offend so frightfully? I will tell you. God has given them up to a base mind [Romans 1: 28] and will make an end of them just as he does of the spiritual nobility. For my ungracious lords, the pope and the bishops, are supposed to be bishops and preach God's word. This they leave undone, and have become temporal princes who govern with laws which concern only life and property. How completely they have turned things topsy-turvy! They are supposed to be ruling souls inwardly by God's word; so they rule castles, cities, lands, and people outwardly, torturing souls with unspeakable outrages.

Similarly, the temporal lords are supposed to govern lands and people outwardly. This they leave undone. They can do no more than strip and fleece, heap tax upon tax and tribute upon tribute, letting loose here a bear and there a wolf. Besides this, there is no justice, integrity, or truth to be found among them. They behave worse than any thief or scoundrel, and their temporal rule has sunk quite as low as that of the spiritual tyrants. For this reason God so perverts their minds also, that they rush on into the absurdity of trying to exercise a spiritual rule over the souls, just as their counterparts try to establish a temporal rule. They blithely heap alien sins upon themselves and incur the hatred of God and man, until they come to ruin together with bishops, popes, and monks, one scoundrel with the other. Then they lay all the blame on the gospel, and instead of confessing their sin they blaspheme God and say that our preaching has brought about that which their perverse wickedness has deserved – and still unceasingly deserves – just as the Romans did when they were destroyed. Here then you have God's decree concerning the high and mighty. They are not to believe it, however, lest this stern decree of God be hindered by their repentance.

But, you say: Paul said in Romans 13 [v. 1] that every soul should be subject to the governing authority; and Peter says that we should be subject to every human ordinance [1 Peter 2: 13]. Answer: Now you are on the right track, for these passages are in my favor. St Paul is speaking of the governing authority. Now you have just heard that no one but God can have authority over souls. Hence, St Paul cannot possibly be speaking of any obedience except where there can be corresponding authority. From this it follows that he is not speaking of faith, to the effect that temporal authority should have the right to command faith. He is speaking rather of external things, that they should be ordered and governed on earth. His words too make this perfectly clear, where he prescribes limits for both authority and obedience, saying, "Pay all of them their dues, taxes to whom taxes are due, revenue to whom revenue is due, honor to whom honor is due, respect to whom respect is due" [Romans 13: 7]. Temporal obedience and authority, you see, apply only externally to taxes, revenue, honor, and respect. Again, where he says, "The governing authority is not a terror to good conduct, but to bad" [Romans 13: 3], he again so limits the governing authority that it is not to have the mastery over faith or the word of God, but over evil works.

This is also what St Peter means by the phrase, "Human ordinance" [1 Peter 2: 13]. A human ordinance cannot possibly extend its authority into heaven and over souls; it is limited to the earth, to external dealings men have with one another, where they can see, know, judge, evaluate, punish, and acquit.

Christ himself made this distinction, and summed it all up very nicely when he said in Matthew 22 [v. 21], "Render to Caesar the things that are Caesar's and to God the things that are God's." Now, if the imperial power extended into God's kingdom and authority, and were not something separate, Christ would not have made this distinction. For, as has been said, the soul is not under the authority of Caesar; he can neither teach it nor guide it, neither kill it nor give it life, neither bind it nor loose it, neither judge it nor condemn it, neither hold it fast nor release it. All this he would have to do, had he the authority to command it and to impose laws upon it. But with respect to body, property, and honor he has indeed to do these things, for such matters are under his authority.

David, too, summarized all this long ago in an excellent brief passage, when he said in Psalm 113 [115: 16], "He has given heaven to the Lord of heaven, but the earth he has given to the sons of men." That is, over what is on earth and belongs to the temporal, earthly kingdom, man has authority from God; but whatever belongs to heaven and to the eternal kingdom is exclusively under the Lord of heaven. Neither did Moses forget this when he said in Genesis 1 [v. 26], "God said, 'Let us make man to have dominion over the beasts of the earth, the fish of the sea, and the birds of the air.'" There only external dominion is ascribed to man. In short, this is the meaning as St Peter says in Acts 4 [5: 29], "We must obey God rather than men." Thereby, he clearly sets a limit to the temporal authority, for if we had to do everything that the temporal authority wanted there would have been no point in saying, "We must obey God rather than men."

If your prince or temporal ruler commands you to side with the pope, to believe thus and so, or to get rid of certain books, you should say, "It is not fitting that Lucifer should sit at the side of God. Gracious sir, I owe you obedience in body and property; command me within the limits of your authority on earth, and I will obey. But if you command me to believe or to get rid of certain books, I will not obey; for then you are a tyrant and overreach yourself, commanding where you have neither the right nor the authority," etc. Should he seize your property on account of this and punish such disobedience, then blessed are you; thank God that you are worthy to suffer for the sake of the divine word. Let him rage, fool that he is; he will meet his judge. For I tell you, if you fail to withstand him, if you give in to him and let him take away your faith and your books, you have truly denied God.

Let me illustrate. In Meissen, Bavaria, the Mark, and other places, the tyrants have issued an order that all copies of the New Testament are everywhere to be turned in to the officials. This should be the response of their subjects: They should not turn in a single page, not even a letter, on pain of losing their salvation. Whoever does so is delivering Christ up into the hands of Herod, for these tyrants act as murderers of Christ just like Herod. If their homes are ordered searched and books or property taken by force, they should suffer it to be done. Outrage is not to be resisted but endured; yet we should not sanction it, or lift a little finger to conform, or obey. For such tyrants are acting as worldly princes are supposed to act, and worldly princes they surely are. But the world is God's enemy; hence, they too have to do what is antagonistic to God and agreeable to the world, that they may not be bereft of honor, but remain worldly princes. Do not wonder, therefore, that they rage and mock at the gospel; they have to live up to their name and title.

You must know that since the beginning of the world a wise prince is a mighty rare bird, and an upright prince even rarer. They are generally the biggest fools or the worst scoundrels on earth; therefore, one must constantly expect the worst from them and look for little good, especially in divine matters which concern the salvation of souls. They are God's executioners and hangmen; his divine wrath uses them to punish the wicked and to maintain outward peace. Our God is a great lord and ruler; this is why he must also have such noble, highborn, and rich hangmen and constables. He desires that everyone shall copiously accord them riches, honor, and fear in abundance. It pleases his divine will that we call his hangmen gracious lords, fall at their feet, and be subject to them in all humility, so long as they do not ply their trade too far and try to become shepherds instead of hangmen. If a prince should happen to be wise, upright, or a Christian, that is one of the great miracles, the most precious token of divine grace upon that land. Ordinarily the course of events is in accordance with the passage from Isaiah 3 [v. 4], "I will make boys their princes and gaping fools shall rule over them;" and in Hosea 13 [v. 11], "I will give you a king in my anger, and take away in my wrath." The world is too wicked, and does not deserve to have many wise and upright princes. Frogs must have their storks.

Again you say, "The temporal power is not forcing men to believe; it is simply seeing to it externally that no one deceives the people by false doctrine; how could heretics otherwise be restrained?" Answer: This the bishops should do; it is a function entrusted to them and not to the princes. Heresy can never be restrained by force. One will have to tackle the problem in some other way, for heresy must be opposed and dealt with otherwise than with the sword. Here God's word must do the fighting. If it does not succeed, certainly the temporal power will not succeed either, even if it were to drench the world in blood. Heresy is a spiritual matter which you cannot hack to pieces with iron, consume with fire, or drown in water. God's word alone avails here, as Paul says in 2 Corinthians 10 [vv. 4–5], "Our weapons are not carnal, but mighty in God to destroy every argument and proud obstacle that exalts itself against the knowledge of God, and to take every thought captive in the service of Christ."

Moreover, faith and heresy are never so strong as when men oppose them by sheer force, without God's word. For men count it certain that such force is for a wrong cause and is directed against the right, since it proceeds without God's word and knows not how to further its cause except by naked force, as brute beasts do. Even in temporal affairs force can be used only after the wrong has been legally condemned. How much less possible it is to act with force, without justice and God's word, in these lofty spiritual matters! See, therefore, what fine, clever nobles they are! They would drive out heresy, but set about it in such a way that they only strengthen the opposition, rousing suspicion against themselves and justifying the heretics. My friend, if you wish to drive out heresy, you must find some way to tear it first of all from the heart and completely turn men's wills away from it. With force you will not stop it, but only strengthen it. What do you gain by strengthening heresy in the heart, while weakening only its outward expression and forcing the tongue to lie? God's word, however, enlightens the heart, and so all heresies and errors vanish from the heart of their own accord.

This way of destroying heresy was proclaimed by Isaiah in his eleventh chapter [v. 4] where he says, "He shall smite the earth with the rod of his mouth, and with the breath of his lips he shall slay the wicked." There you see that if the wicked are to be slain and converted, it will be accomplished with the mouth. In short, these princes and tyrants do not realize that to fight against heresy is to fight against the devil, who fills men's hearts with error, as Paul says in Ephesians 6 [v. 12], "We are not contending against flesh and blood, but against spiritual wickedness, against the principalities which rule this present darkness," etc. Therefore, so long as the devil is not repelled and driven from the heart, it is agreeable to him that I destroy his vessels with fire or sword; it's as if I were to fight lightning with a straw. Job bore abundant witness to this when in his forty-first chapter he said that the devil counts iron as straw, and fears no power on earth. We learn it also from experience, for even if all Jews and heretics were forcibly burned no one ever has been or will be convinced or converted thereby.

Nevertheless, such a world as this deserves such princes, none of whom attends to his duties. The bishops are to leave God's word alone and not use it to rule souls; instead they are to turn over to the worldly princes the job of ruling souls with the sword. The worldly princes, in turn, are to permit usury, robbery, adultery, murder, and other evil deeds, and even commit these offenses themselves, and then allow the bishops to punish with letters of excommunication. Thus, they neatly put the shoe on the wrong foot: they rule the souls with iron and the bodies with letters, so that worldly princes rule in a spiritual way, and spiritual princes rule in a worldly way. What else does the devil have to do on earth than to masquerade and play the fool with his people? These are our Christian princes, who defend the faith and devour the Turk! Fine fellows, indeed, whom we may well trust to accomplish something by such refined wisdom, namely, to break their necks and plunge land and people into misery and want.

I would in all good faith advise these blind fellows to take heed to a little phrase that occurs in Psalm 107 [v. 40]: "*Effundit contemptum super principes.*" I swear to you by God that if you fail to see that this little text is applicable to you, then you are lost, even though each one of you be as mighty as the Turk; and your fuming and raging will avail you nothing. A goodly part of it has already come true. For there are very few princes who are not regarded as fools or scoundrels; that is because they show themselves to be so. The common man is learning to think, and the scourge of princes (that which God calls *contemptum*) is gathering force among the mob and with the common man. I fear there will be no way to avert it, unless the princes conduct themselves in a princely manner and begin again to rule decently and reasonably. Men will not, men cannot, men refuse to endure your tyranny and wantonness much longer. Dear princes and lords be wise and guide yourselves accordingly. God will no longer tolerate it. The world is no longer what it once was, when you hunted and drove the people like game. Abandon therefore your wicked use of force, give thought to dealing justly, and let God's word have its way, as it will anyway and must and shall; you cannot prevent it. If there is heresy somewhere, let it be overcome, as is proper, with God's word. But if you continue to brandish the sword, take heed lest someone come and compel you to sheathe it – and not in God's name!

But you might say, "Since there is to be no temporal sword among Christians, how then are they to be ruled outwardly? There certainly must be authority even among Christians." Answer: Among Christians there shall and can be no authority; rather all are alike subject to one another, as Paul says in Romans 12 [v. 10]: "Each shall consider the other his superior;" and Peter says in 1 Peter 5 [v. 5], "All of you be subject to one another." This is also what Christ means in Luke 14 [v. 10], "When you are invited to a wedding, go and sit in the lowest place." Among Christians there is no superior but Christ himself, and him alone. What kind of authority can there be where all are equal and have the same right, power, possession, and honor, and where no one desires to be the other's superior, but each the other's subordinate? Where there are such people, one could not establish authority even if he wanted to, since in the nature of things it is impossible to have superiors where no one is able or willing to be a superior. Where there are no such people, however, there are no real Christians either.

What, then, are the priests and bishops? Answer: Their government is not a matter of authority or power, but a service and an office, for they are neither higher nor better than other Christians. Therefore, they should impose no law or decree on others without their will and consent. Their ruling is rather nothing more than the inculcating of God's word, by which they guide Christians and overcome heresy. As we have said, Christians can be ruled by nothing except God's word, for Christians must be ruled in faith, not with outward works. Faith, however, can come through no word of man, but only through the word of God, as Paul says in Romans 10 [v. 17], "Faith comes through hearing, and hearing through the word of God." Those who do not believe are not Christians; they do not belong to Christ's kingdom, but to the worldly kingdom where they are constrained and governed by the sword and by outward rule. Christians do every good thing of their own accord and without constraint, and find God's word alone sufficient for them. Of this I have written frequently and at length elsewhere.

Balthasar Hübmaier, "Concerning Heretics and Those Who Burn Them" (1524)

Hübmaier (1481–1528) studied at Freiburg where he met John Eck whom he followed to Ingolstadt, in due course becoming co-rector of the university. Thereafter his renown as a preacher led him to the position of chief cathedral preacher at Regensburg. In 1521 he moved to Waldshut, from which vantage point he encountered the Swiss reformers and also descended into an ultimately fatal defiance of the Holy Roman Empire. By 1523 he became openly identified with reform, but went further than Zwingli in accepting believer's baptism in 1525. After suffering torture in Zürich, he moved on to Moravia but was surrendered to the imperial government and burned in Vienna in 1528. "But his behavior as an Anabaptist leader in Waldshut and Nikolsburg tends to indicate that he was not prepared to grant everyone the right of expressing a divergent religious conviction in a town or district" (Bergsten, *Balthasar Hübmaier*, p. 132).

SOURCE: Henry C. Vedder, *Balthasar Hübmaier: The Leader of the Anabaptists* (New York: G. P. Putnam's Sons, 1905), pp. 84–8.[3]
LITERATURE: George H. Williams, *The Radical Reformation*, 3rd edn (Kirksville, MO: Sixteenth-Century Studies Society, 1992); Torsten Bergsten, *Balthasar Hübmaier, Anabaptist Theologian and Martyr*, ed. W. R. Estep, Jr (Valley Forge: Judson, 1978 [1961]).

1 Heretics are those who wickedly oppose the Holy Scriptures, the first of whom was the devil, when he said to Eve, "Ye shall not surely die" [Genesis 3: 4], together with his followers.

2 Those also are heretics who cast a veil over the Scriptures and interpret them otherwise than the Holy Spirit demands; as those who everywhere proclaim a concubine as a benefice, pasturing and ruling the church at Rome, and compelling us to believe this talk.

3 Those who are such one should overcome with holy knowledge, not angrily but softly, although the Holy Scriptures contain wrath.

4 But this wrath of the Scriptures is truly a spiritual fire and zeal of love, not burning without the word of God.

5 If they will not be taught by strong proofs or evangelic reasons, then let them be, and leave them to rage and be mad [Titus 3: 2,3], that those who are filthy may become more filthy still [Revelation 22: 11].

6 The law that condemns heretics to the fire builds up both Zion in blood and Jerusalem in wickedness.

7 Therefore will they be taken away in sighs, for the judgments of God (whose right it is to judge) either convert or harden them, that the blind lead the blind and both the seduced and the seducer go from bad to worse.

8 This is the will of Christ who said, "Let both grow together till the harvest, lest while ye gather up the tares ye root up also the wheat with them" [Matthew 13: 29]. "For there must be also heresies among

you, that they that are approved may be made manifest among you"
[1 Corinthians 11: 19].

9   Though they indeed experience this, yet they are not put away until
Christ shall say to the reapers, "Gather first the tares and bind them
in bundles to burn them" [Matthew 13: 30].

10   This word does not teach us idleness but a strife; for we should
unceasingly contend, not with men but with their godless doctrine.

11   The unwatchful bishops are the cause of the heresies. "When men
slept, the enemy came" [Matthew 13: 25].

12   Again, "Blessed is the man who is a watcher at the door of the
bridegroom's chamber" [Proverbs 8: 34], and neither sleeps nor
"sits in the seat of the scornful" [Psalm 1: 1].

13   Hence it follows that the inquisitors are the greatest heretics of all,
since, against the doctrine and example of Christ, they condemn
heretics to fire, and before the time of harvest root up the wheat
with the tares.

14   For Christ did not come to butcher, destroy and burn, but that
those that live might live more abundantly [John 10: 10].

15   We should pray and hope for repentance, as long as man lives in
this misery.

16   A Turk or a heretic is not convinced by our act, either with the
sword or with fire, but only with patience and prayer; and so we
should await with patience the judgment of God.

17   If we do otherwise, God will treat our sword as stubble, and burning fire as mockery [Job 41].

18   So unholy and far off from evangelical doctrine is the whole order
of preaching friars (of which variegated birds our Antony is one),
that hitherto out of them alone the inquisitors have come.

19   If these only knew of what spirit they ought to be, they would not
so shamelessly pervert God's word, nor so often cry, "To the fire,
to the fire!" [Luke 9: 54–6].

20   It is no excuse (as they chatter) that they give over the wicked to the
secular power, for he who thus gives over sins more deeply [John
19: 11].

21   For each Christian has a sword against the wicked, which is the word
of God [Ephesians 6: 17], but not a sword against the malignant.

22   The secular power rightly and properly puts to death the criminals
who injure the bodies of the defenseless [Romans 13: 3,4]. But he
who is God's cannot injure any one, unless he first deserts the gospel.

23   Christ has shown us this clearly, saying, "Fear not them that kill the
body" [Matthew 10: 28].

24 The secular power judges criminals, but not the godless who cannot injure either body or soul, but rather are a benefit; therefore God can in wisdom draw good from evil.

25 Faith which flows from the gospel fountain, lives only in contests, and the rougher they become, so much the greater becomes faith.

26 That every one has not been taught the gospel truth, is due to the bishops no less than to the common people – these that they have not cared for a better shepherd, the former that they have not performed their office properly.

27 If the blind lead the blind, according to the just judgment of God, they both fall together into the ditch [Matthew 15: 14].

28 Hence to burn heretics is in appearance to profess Christ [Titus 1: 10,11], but in reality to deny him, and to be more monstrous than Jehoiakim, the king of Judah [Jeremiah 36: 23].

29 If it is blasphemy to destroy a heretic, how much more is it to burn to ashes a faithful herald of the word of God, unconvicted, not arraigned by the truth.

30 The greatest deception of the people is a zeal for God that is unscripturally expended, the salvation of the soul, honor of the church, love of truth, good intention, use or custom, episcopal decrees, and the teaching of the reason that come by the natural light. For they are deadly arrows where they are not led and directed by the Scriptures.

31 We should not presume, led away by the deception of our own purpose, to do better or more securely than God has spoken by his own mouth.

32 Those who rely on their good intention and think to do better, are like Uzziah and Peter. The latter was called Satan by Christ [Matthew 16: 23], but the former came to a wretched end [1 Chronicles 13: 10].

33 Elnathan, Delaiah and Gemariah acted wisely in withstanding Jehoiakim, the king of Judah, when he cast the book of Jehovah into the fire [Jeremiah 36: 25].

34 But in that, after one book was burnt, Baruch by the express direction of Jeremiah, wrote another much better [Jeremiah 36: 27–32], we see the just punishment of God on the unrighteous burning. For so it shall be that on those who fear the frost, a cold snow falls [Job 6: 16].

35 But we do not hold that it was unchristian to burn their numerous books of incantations, as the fact in the Acts of the Apostles shows [Acts 19: 19]. It is a small thing to burn innocent paper, but to point out an error and to disprove it by Scripture, that is art.

36   Now it is clear to every one, even the blind, that a law to burn her-
     etics is an invention of the devil. "Truth is immortal."

Dirk Philips, "The Church of God" (*c*. 1560)

There are many uncertainties about the life of Philips (1504?–68). It seems
that he was born in West Friesland; he may have been the son of a priest;
he may have been connected in some way with the Franciscans; he may
have attended a university. It appears that he was baptized around the end
of 1533 by a Münsterite apostle, but for the remainder of his career he
shied away from radical apocalyptic Anabaptism; rather, he devoted himself to the building of stable religious communities from his home province
to Danzig, though that effort was vitiated by growing conflict between
himself and other Anabaptist leaders. His statement against religious persecution was fairly typical of Anabaptist opinion.[4]

SOURCE: George H. Williams and Angel M. Mergal (eds), *Spiritual and Anabaptist Writers*
          (Philadelphia, PA: Westminster Press, 1957), pp. 251–4.
LITERATURE: William Keeney, "Dirk Philips' Life," *Mennonite Quarterly Review*, 32 (1958),
          pp. 171–91, 298–306.

The seventh ordinance is that all Christians must suffer and be persecuted,
as Christ has promised them and said thus [John 16: 33]: The world shall
have joy, but ye shall have tribulation: but be of good cheer, for your sorrow
shall be turned into joy; again [Matthew 24: 9]: Ye shall be hated by
everyone for my name's sake; again [John 16: 2]: The time cometh, that
whosoever killeth you will think that he doeth God service. Paul concurs
with this and says [Romans 8: 17]: If so be that we suffer with him, we shall
also be glorified together, and inherit our Heavenly Father's Kingdom;
again [2 Timothy 2: 12; 3: 12]: All that will live godly in Christ Jesus shall
suffer persecution. Again Paul and Barnabas testified [Acts 13: 50] in all
the congregation that they must through much persecution and suffering
enter the Kingdom of Heaven. In short, the entire Holy Scripture testifies
that the righteous must suffer and possess his soul through suffering [Luke
21: 19]. Where there is a pious Abel, there does not fail to be a wicked
Cain [Genesis 4: 1f.]; where there is a chosen David, there is also a rejected
Saul to persecute him [1 Samuel 18: 11]; where Christ is born, there is a
Herod who seeks his life [Matthew 2: 16]; where he openly preaches and
works, there Annas and Caiaphas, together with the bloodthirsty Jews,
gather together and hold counsel against him [Matthew 26: 3f.; Mark 14: 1;
Luke 22: 1; Acts 4: 6], nor can they cease until they have killed him and
force Pilate to do their will.

Thus must the true Christians here be persecuted for the sake of truth and righteousness, but the Christians persecute no one on account of his faith. For Christ sends his disciples as sheep in the midst of wolves [Matthew 10: 16]; but the sheep does not devour the wolf, but the wolf the sheep. Hence they can nevermore stand nor be counted as a congregation of the Lord who persecute others on account of their faith. For, in the first place, God, the Heavenly Father, has committed all judgment unto Jesus Christ [John 5: 22], to be a judge of the souls and consciences of men and to rule in his congregation with the scepter of his word forever. In the second place, it is the office or work of the Holy Spirit to reprove the world for the sin of unbelief [John 16: 8]. Now it is evident that the Holy Spirit through the apostles and all pious witnesses of the truth did not administer this reproof by violence nor with an outward sword, but by God's word and power. In the third place, the Lord Jesus Christ gave his congregation the power and established the ordinance that she should separate, avoid, and shun the false brethren, the disorderly and disobedient, contentious and heretical people, yea, all in the congregation who are found wicked, as has already been said [Romans 16: 17; 1 Corinthians 5: 10; 1 Thessalonians 5: 14; Titus 3: 10]; what is done over and above this is not Christian, evangelical, nor apostolic. In the fourth place, the parable of the Lord in the Gospel proves clearly to us that he does not permit his servants to pull up the tares lest the wheat be pulled up also; but they are to let the wheat and the tares grow together in the world until the Lord shall command his reapers, that is, his angels, to gather the wheat into his barn and cast the tares into the fire [Matthew 13: 29].

From this it is evident that no congregation of the Lord may exercise dominion over the consciences of men with the outward sword, nor seek by violence, to force unbelievers to believe, nor to kill the false prophets with sword and fire; but that she must with the Lord's Word judge and expel those in the congregation who are found wicked; and what is done over and above this is not Christian, nor evangelical, nor apostolic. And if someone ventures to assert that the powers that be have not received the sword in vain [Romans 13: 1], and that God through Moses commanded that the false prophets be put to death [Deuteronomy 13: 5], I will give this answer in brief: The higher power has received the sword from God, not that it shall judge therewith in spiritual matters (for these things must be judged by the spiritual, and only spiritually, 1 Corinthians 2: 13), but to maintain the subjects in good government and peace, to protect the pious and punish the evil. And that God commanded through Moses to kill the false prophets is a command of the Old, and not the New Testament. In contrast to this we have received another command from the Lord [Matthew 7: 15; John 10: 5; Titus 3: 10] that we are to beware of false prophets, that we are not

to give ear to them, that we are to shun a heretic, and thereby commit them
to the judgment of God. Now, if, according to the Old Testament command, false prophets were to be put to death, then this would have to be
carried out, first of all, with those who are looked upon as false prophets and
antichrists by the God-fearing and understanding persons, yea, by almost
the whole world. Likewise the higher powers would be obliged to put to
death not only the false prophets but also all image worshipers, and those
who serve idols, and who counsel other people to commit sacrilege [Exodus
22: 18], and all adulterers, and all who blaspheme the name of the Lord,
and who swear falsely by that name, all who curse father and mother and
profane the Sabbath [Exodus 20: 7; Deuteronomy 27: 16]; for they are all
alike condemned to death by the law as well as the false prophets are.

It is therefore nothing but an effort to sew fig leaves together to hide their
shame, on the part of those who would decorate their tyranny with Scripture and propose that they do not put Christians to death, but only heretics,
and that God thus commanded through Moses. Yea, the world even looks
upon the most pious Christians as the most wicked heretics, just as all good
prophets were always looked upon by the world as liars, agitators, demented
persons, and deceivers [Jeremiah 11: 21; Amos 2: 9; Matthew 5: 11; 23: 30;
Acts 6: 14], and Christ himself was numbered with the transgressors [Mark
15: 28]. And the apostles are set forth as the least, and as it were, appointed
unto death, made a curse of the world, and a purgatory sacrifice of the world
[Psalm 44: 13f.; 1 Corinthians 4: 9]. And this is still the case with all upright
Christians; but they are comforted herein. For they trust in the Lord their
God and comfort themselves with the glorious promises given them by
God, namely, that they are saved [Matthew 5: 10ff.], that theirs is the
Kingdom of Heaven and that the Spirit of God rests upon them when they
are persecuted for righteousness' sake, when men say all manner of evil
against them falsely and for the sake of the name of Christ, if they have
become partakers of the sufferings of Christ and for his sake are despised,
knowing that they shall also be made partakers of his glory [1 Peter 4: 14;
Romans 8: 17; 2 Timothy 2: 12].

Sebastian Castellio, *Advice to a Desolate France* (1562)

In 1554 Castellio published, anonymously, his *Concerning Heretics* which
was a response to Geneva's execution of the anti-trinitarian Michael Servetus.
Advice was written at the outset of the French wars of religion and points
the way toward later statements of the theory of religious liberty. Castellio
(1515–64), a Savoyard, had come to Geneva and headed the school in

that city, but fell out with Calvin and went to Basel where he taught Greek at the university. In the present work Castellio responded to the early signs of violence between religious factions in France, a conflict which would last for thirty years and fulfill his worst fears. He emphasized the priority and inviolability of conscience, and argued against the commonplace that heresy bred sedition; rather, he argued, suppression of heresy led to disaster. His argument was very biblical and pertained to a Christian society, however fragmented.

SOURCE: Sebastian Castellio, *Advice to a Desolate France: In the course of which the reason for the present war is outlined, as well as the possible remedy and, in the main, advice is given as to whether consciences should be forced*, tr. W. Valkhoff (Shepherdstown, West Virginia: Patmos Press, 1975), pp. 12–26, 39–41, 43, 45–6, 47–8. Reproduced with permission.

LITERATURE: Peter G. Bietenholz, *Basle and France in the Sixteenth Century* (Geneva: Droz, 1971), pp. 122–36; R. H. Bainton, "Sebastian Castellio and the Toleration Controversy of the Sixteenth Century," in J. Franklin Jameson (ed.), *Persecution and Liberty: Essays in Honour of George Lincoln Burr* (Freeport, NY: Books for Libraries Press, 1968 [1931]), pp. 183–209.

To the Catholics and the Evangelics, Concerning the Forcing of One Another's Consciences

It is a fact that when Jesus Christ argued with the Jews, he sometimes, however much they might be obstinate, convinced them so thoroughly with a single utterance of obvious truth that they were left quite speechless, not answering a single word. This happened when he said to them: "Render therefore unto Caesar the things which be Caesar's and unto God the things which are God's" [Luke 20: 25]. And also: "He that is without sin among you, let him first cast a stone . . ." [John 8: 7]. I wish the world were no more obstinate today than those people. I am quite persuaded that the matter which I am now discussing would then be resolved by a single utterance of obvious truth, and that there would then be no one who would dare to contradict, even in the slightest degree. For it would then but be necessary to say to those who force the consciences of others: "Would you like your own to be forced?" And their own conscience, which is worth more than a thousand witnesses, would then suddenly convince them so thoroughly, that they would be quite ashamed.

I would really like to take you up on these words and suppose that Jesus Christ ask you such a question (for the truth is also very much of Jesus Christ), would you, then, like your consciences to be forced? Answer in the name of Jesus Christ, answer me whether you would like your consciences to be forced. I am quite persuaded that your consciences answer no, and if this is the case, then why did you previously complain of the Catholics forcing yours, O Evangelics? And you, Catholics, why are you now beginning to complain of the Evangelics forcing yours? Are not your complaints condemning you, considering that you are doing those very things which you are finding fault with in others? Do you not know that Paul says: "Therefore thou are inexcusable, O man, whosoever thou are that judgest: for wherein thou judgest another, thou condemnest thyself. . . . Thou therefore which teachest another, teachest thou not thyself? Thou that preachest a man should not steal, dost thou steal?" [Romans 2: 1,21]. I ask you whether one cannot with the same reasoning say the following: "You are saying that one should not force consciences, but you are forcing those of others."

But do as you wish and seek everywhere in all diligence such scapegoats as you may, your own consciences will accuse you both at the day of Judgment, and in your own hearts will you carry your witnesses, witnesses which you will neither be able to despise nor reproach. And with you it will come to pass as with the Ephraimites of old, who were put to death by the Galaadites, because they were unable to pronounce the words Schibbolet, but pronounced it Sibbolet instead, from which pronunciation the Galaadites knew that they were Ephraimites. If you do not repent in time, you will thus be condemned at the judgment of the God of truth, for the reason that you will be unable to say that you have done to others as you would like others to do to you.

You should thus not excuse yourselves at this point, saying as a certain one once said: "If I were an adulterer, I would not like to be punished, but it does not follow from this, however, that if I were a judge, I should not punish an adulterer." For I would then answer as follows: "If you were an adulterer, and you were to be punished for it, you would have to admit that this would certainly not be an injustice." And a brigand or a thief, when punished, admits that he has indeed deserved it, or if he denies it with his mouth, his conscience will still contradict this and admit it in spite of himself. The invisible force of truth and righteousness which cannot be abolished from the heart of man, however evil he may be, is indeed clearly demonstrated through this. But this is not so with one whose conscience is forced, and who is persecuted because of his faith. For, however much one may force him to confess with his mouth that is not being treated unjustly, his heart will still always say: "You are doing me an injustice, and you would not like this to be done to you." This is such a true, just and natural rule, so much written into the hearts of all men by the law of God, that no one, however perverted and far-removed from all discipline and teaching he may be, would fail to admit its righteousness and reasonableness, as soon as it is put to him, from which it is fair to deduce that when the truth will judge us, it will do so in accordance with this rule. And Christ, who is truth, in fact confirms this when He not only forbids us to do something to someone else which we would not like to be done to us, but, what is more, commands us to do that to others which we would like to be done to us [Matthew 7: 12]. He furthermore says that we shall be measured with the same measure with which we shall have measured others [Matthew 7: 2].

At this point I could well end my argument, the matter being so obvious and so thoroughly inscribed into the conscience of everyone by the finger of God, that only a stubborn person or a fool might possibly contradict it. But as the same has been pointed out to you by the writings of certain others in the past, and as you have nevertheless persevered in your wrong ways, I now want to endeavor to draw you, finally, out of your stubbornness and to open your eyes somewhat, since you have both, for the same reason, come to suffer great anguish. It is generally said: "A fool only believes in as much as he receives." And Isaiah writes that only torment will cause his proposi- tions to be heard. Listen at least now, whilst you are being so horribly tormented, and do not follow the Jewish zealots of the time of Vespasian and Titus, emperors of Rome, which zealots were, I would say, not so much zealots, but rather fanatics. For they preferred to die rather than to turn over a new leaf, and in so doing caused the Jewish nation to be afflicted with grave ills, which are still continuing today. It is said better later than never. At least make amends now, in case the God of mercy may perhaps take pity on you. I can, indeed, assuredly tell you that you may otherwise but expect ills without number and, in the end, a terrible punishment by God, who will render to each in accordance with his works.

Thus, to revert to my argument, I am now, in view of your hard- headedness, forced to examine the subject in somewhat greater detail. I therefore ask you whether, when you thus force people's consciences, you are doing so by the commandment of God, by the example of certain holy persons, or by good intentions, thinking that you are doing well. For apart from these three points, I can see no reason for your doing it, unless, as I am inclined to believe, you are doing it out of pure malice.

About the Commandments of God

If you say that you are doing it in accordance with the commandments of God, I ask you where He has commanded it, for in the entire Bible I do not find a single word about it; even in the law of Moses which is otherwise rather rigorous, considering that in one place it goes so far as to command the murdering and massacring of the men, beasts and towns of idolaters, one nevertheless does not find a single word about one having to force

consciences. It does, however, permit strangers to be received into the
Israelite community if they are, of their own accord, prepared to be circumcised. But I find nothing written about one having to force them to do
so. Indeed, those very ones who have written books urging the persecution
and killing of heretics,[5] have been unable to quote a single passage to prove
that one should force consciences, although they were quite diligent enough
not to have forgotten it, would it have been possible to find one.

And certainly, if God had commanded the forcing of consciences, this
would, firstly, have been contrary to nature, of which He, Himself, is the
creator. And nature has, as mentioned above, so thoroughly impressed this
rule, namely: "Do not to another something which you would not like to be
done to you" into the heart of all nations, that no man, however perverted
and far-removed from all doctrine he may be, can fail to admit that it is
wrong to act against this rule. Secondly, it would be contrary to His own
commandment, considering that He has commanded this very thing through
Jesus Christ. Indeed, what is more, Saint Paul quite rigorously reprimands
someone who, through his example in eating flesh, causes another to do
likewise against his conscience, and comes to the following conclusion: "But
when ye sin so against the brethren, and wound their weak conscience, ye
sin against Christ" [1 Corinthians 8: 12]. Likewise, elsewhere: "All things
indeed are pure; but it is evil for that man who eateth with offense. For
meat destroy not the work of God" [Romans 14: 20]. And if he so earnestly
reprimands him who, by his example, causes another to sin against his conscience, without forcing him in any other way, indeed, without even telling
him to do it, what would he say today if he saw the enormous violations
which you are doing to consciences not by example, but as much by words as
by deeds, by censuring, condemning, vilifying, banishing, depriving of their
honor, their possessions and often of their body, those who cannot in good
conscience believe or do what you believe or do? For if that is not forcing,
then I do not know what forcing is. It is, indeed, impossible to commit
greater violence, and yet I really believe that if you could find a greater
one, you would commit it.

Now consider in what sort of position you are placing these poor people.
Here you have a man who has scruples about going to mass or about listening to the sermon of a preacher whom he considers to be a heretic, or
about helping either with money or with his person and arms a Church
which he considers heretical, against a Church which he considers catholic,
and you tell him that he will be banished, disinherited or dishonorably put
to death if he does not do it. What do you want him to do? Give him advice,
for he is in extreme anguish, much like a slice of bread which is being
toasted on a point of a knife, is burnt if it moves forwards and pricked if it
moves backwards. Thus this poor man, in acting against his conscience,

damns himself if he does as you want him to, and loses his possessions or his life, a weighty matter for every being, if he does not. What do you advise him here?

At least you, both old and new teachers and inquisitors of the faith, who are urging the princes to do this (for it is well known that it is you who are urging them, and I really do not think that you will deny it, considering that your actions and sermons and even your books are so obviously witnessing this), what advice do you give to such a man? Do you advise him to act against his conscience? His soul will perish. Do you recommend that he should act in accordance with his conscience? He will be put to death. The matter is such that he can indeed say what Susan said to those two old men who wanted to violate her: "I am anguished from all sides, for should I do it, I am dead, and should I refrain from it, I will also not escape from your hands" [Susanna 13: 22].

And I know well what some used to say here: "We would gladly teach them, but they are stubborn and they always persevere with their own ideas, whatever one says to them." To which I reply: "But then, you propose things to them which would cause astonishment were they accepted by a man of good conscience and which, not surprisingly, they do not accept. But let us assume that you are propounding the truth to them (as I believe you occasionally do) and that they do not accept it, what could one do about it? Would you make them accept it by force? If a sick person could not eat the good food which you might offer to him, would you force it down his throat by force? Or if a donkey does not want to drink, would you drown it to make it drink? Learn from Christ, and follow His example. When He came into contact with stubborn people He left them and said to His disciples: "Leave them" [cf. Luke 10: 10–12]. And so much for the commandment.

Examples

As far as examples are concerned, I find that there has neither in the Old nor in the New Testament ever been a holy man – what, holy? – a man who forced or wanted to force consciences like you are doing. Moreover I will, in this respect, say that even if there were any who might have done it, one should not draw conclusions from it, nor follow their example, considering that they would have acted against all reason and against the commandment of God. For examples do not make the commandment, but the commandment makes the examples, and should one not follow an example only in so far as it is in accordance with, or at least not against, the commandment of God? When it becomes necessary to decide what we should do, we should always look at the commandment of God and act accordingly.

Otherwise one could find plenty of examples (not of the forcing of consciences, for of this, as said, I cannot find any, but of other relevant matters), which examples it would be more than dangerous to follow. Dangerous
as it would be to follow the example of Moses, who killed an Egyptian
without any form of process, and of Phineas who did the same with two
sinners, and of Jacob who lied to his father, saying that he was Esau, and of
the Israelites, who pillaged the Egyptians in accordance with a particular
commandment of God, borrowing and carrying off their crockery; and
of David, who, in the service of Achish, king of Gath, waged campaigns
against the Geshurites and other enemies of the Israelites and butchered
everybody, sparing not a man or a woman, and then gave his master Achish
to understand that he had overrun the country of Judea. And, again, of the
same David, who, far from punishing the slanderer Siba, after he had
become aware of his slander, even went so far as to reward him with half of
his master's possessions, even though, according to law, he should have
punished and not rewarded him. These and other similar examples of holy
men, whether the Scriptures in so many words approve of them, or whether
they are there related without judgment being passed on them, should not,
when they are considered, be taken as a rule, nor should conclusions be
drawn from them, except as said.

Or else a dissolute person will find his excuse in Judas, who associated
with Thamare, thinking that she was a whore, a drunkard in Lot and Noah,
a liar in David, in the above example, and in Abraham who said that his wife
was his sister, a cruel person in the above-mentioned David, who made
the Ammonites go through a tile-baking furnace and tormented them with
saws, harrows and steel axes. Such examples, briefly, are too dangerous to
consider as matter for deliberation and have caused many to stumble. And
with this it often happens as with a child, who wishes to act like a man who
wields a sword and knows how to handle it, but hurts himself or another,
because he is a child and does not know how to handle it. And furthermore,
even if there were no danger, there are no examples concerning the forcing
of consciences to be found, and even if there were, one should still not
follow them, for the reasons set out above.

But the most important reason of all is that we owe allegiance to Christ,
whose doctrine and example we have to follow, irrespective of what the
others said or did, considering that the Father told us that He is His dear
Son, and that we should listen to Him and obey Him [Matthew 17: 5]. It is
this Son of God who forbade His disciples to follow Elias' example and to
call down the fires of Heaven, telling them that they did not know of which
spirit they were, and that He had not come to destroy men's lives, like Elias,
but to save them [Luke 9: 54–5]. It is this Son of God who told us that we
would go after Him, and that all those who go before Him, are thieves and

robbers [John 10: 7–8]. And go before Him is what those are doing who are forcing consciences without, and even against His commandment and example. For they cannot say that they are going after Christ. They are going very much before Him, through which they are proving themselves to be thieves and robbers. It is this Christ who has given us a perfect law which we should regard with at least the same degree of reverence as the law of Moses. This means that we should be careful that we do not add to it, or take away from it, considering that the Father has, as said, commanded us to obey it. He also said that the nations should have confidence in His law. It is this Son of God who says to us: "Learn of me; for I am meek and lowly in heart: and ye shall find rest unto your souls" [Matthew 11: 29]. If, therefore, we do not learn gentleness and humility from Him, let us not expect to find peace for our souls. And experience will indeed show you that people who thus force the consciences of others, never have peace in their hearts even in this life, let alone in the other. And so much for the examples from the Holy Scriptures.

And as far as other examples are concerned, not taken from the Holy Scriptures, I must admit that there have been some who have, in the past, forced consciences. One of these was Hyrcanus, pontiff of the Jews after the time of the Maccabees, who forced the Idumenians to circumcise themselves. The same applies to those who once forced the Saracens to be baptized. And to those who, in Spain, forced the Jews to do the same. But, for the reasons given above, such people are no more to be followed than you. I do not even want to mention that their forcing had no better results than ours; for neither did the Saracens ever become true Christians, as they have since shown when they reverted to their former religion, nor were the Jews of Spain, baptized by force, any more Christian than previously. They are, on the contrary, still preserving their old law and instructing their children in it, irrespective of what outward appearance they may, under duress, have to put up. It is for this reason that they are known by the infamous name Marrans, and one has in fact achieved nothing but the making of hypocrites and false Christians, through whom the name of Christ is blasphemed. I do not even wish to mention that even if some great benefit should result from such constraint, it would nonetheless still remain illicit, seeing that Saint Paul teaches that one should not do evil in order that good may result from it.

About the Good Intention

It but remains that what you are doing is being done by you as the result of a good intention, in the belief that you are doing well. But you know well, or you should at least know, that we must not follow our good intention, but the commandment of God, as He Himself says [Deuteronomy 12: 32]. For one is sometimes seriously mistaken in thinking that one is doing well. This is evident from King Saul who had kept back the fattest beast of the spoil to sacrifice them to God, and who was relieved of his reign for the reason that he had not done this because of the commandment of God, but only because of a good intention. Likewise, from the words of Christ, who speaks as follows to his disciples: "They shall put you out of the synagogues: Yea, the time cometh, that whosoever killeth you will think that he doeth God service" [John 16: 2]. And if, in fact, your servants would do what might seem right to them, and not what you command them, you obviously would not be pleased about it. Do not think, therefore, that God is satisfied with your thinking that you are doing well, if it is not done in accordance with His commandment. But know that your servants will judge you at the day of Judgment, seeing that, by allowing them to think that they are doing well, they are doing what you command them, and that it is you who are acting against your master.

The Fruits of Forcing Consciences

Let us now consider the fruits which result from your constraint. Firstly, if those whom you are forcing, are strong and persevering and prefer to die rather than to hurt their consciences, you kill them, and as the murderers of their bodies you will have to answer to God for this. Secondly, if they are so weak that they prefer to go back on their word and hurt their consciences, rather than to endure your torments and insufferable tortures, you are causing their souls to perish, which is still worse. And for this you will have to render account to God, with whom they are, and be punished in accordance with the law of the like, which is: "With what measure ye mete, it shall be measured to you again" [Matthew 7: 2]. Thirdly, you are causing enormous offense to all true Christians and children of God. These, having a spirit in Christ, who is the spirit of complete gentleness, goodness and kindness, are, not without cause, greatly offended by your enormous violence and are continuously wailing to God about it. And do not doubt that there are several amongst you who, fearing your violence, are effectively keeping quiet with their mouths, but whose heart cries to the Heavens and whose cry reaches up to the ears of Him who hears the sighs of the wrongly oppressed. Now consider whether it is a small sin to offend so many God-fearing people, considering that Christ says that it would be much better to be thrown into the middle of the sea with a millstone around your neck than to give the least offense to those who believe in Him. Think awhile, I pray you, about this millstone. Fourthly, you are the reason why the holy name and holy and blessed doctrine of Jesus Christ is found fault with and blasphemed amidst foreign nations, like the Jews and Turks who, seeing such wars and carnages amongst the Christians, think that these are due to the doctrine, which they therefore curse and with which they are daily becoming more disgusted. Fifthly, you are the reason why enmities, hatred and mortal and immortal grudges are being engendered amongst you, which might perchance go from father to son, as much because of the violence caused to the living as because of the blood of the dead which has already been shed, the memory of which for a long time remains fresh in the hearts of their relatives and friends. These, now, are the great ills which result from your violence.

There is only one benefit which the less bad amongst you are perhaps hoping for as the reward for all these evils, namely that through such violence some will be gained for Christ. To which I firstly answer that even if this were so, this benefit could in no way be compared to so many such great disadvantages as have already been mentioned. Furthermore, for you to commit so many wrongs for such a benefit, is just as great a madness as for someone to sow a hundred barrels of corn in order to harvest one, or for someone to burn his house in order to obtain ashes, or for one to kill a hundred men already advanced in age, in order to beget a child. But supposing that the good which follows from it were not only equal to the wrong, but incomparably greater, one should still not do it, considering that, as already said, the truth teaches us that one should not do wrong in order that good may result from it.

And what will we say if the good which you are seeking in it is not there? You want to make Christians by force, and so doing honor God, but you are greatly deluding yourselves in this, for if that could or should be done, Christ would have been the very first to have done and instructed it, seeing that He has been sent to honor God and to cause God to be honored, and that, to do this, He has the spirit of complete wisdom. But He acts quite differently, for He only wants voluntary disciples, without constraint, as symbolized and predicted in the Old Testament. Symbolized, in that the Tabernacle was made of gifts offered voluntarily by the people, and also in that God, when He teaches the people of Israel how to wage war, draws up a law for them to the effect that they shall, before entering into battle, make it known to all that he who is fearful, newly married, has built a new house of planted vines, should retire from the battlefield and return home, lest he cause others to lose courage in the battle. So much for the symbol. As far as the prediction is concerned, it appears in the Book of Psalms, there where God speaks the following words to Christ: "Thy people shall be willing in the day of thy power, in the beauties of holiness" [Psalm 110: 3]. These are the true soldiers of Christ, voluntary, cheerful and regretting nothing whatsoever worldly. And those who make or want to make soldiers by force, certainly neither understand corporal nor spiritual war, but, instead of making real champions of Christ, they make cowards, fearful, shamming and effeminate people, who are of greater advantage to the enemy than to Christ.

I say this with full conviction and without any doubt, for I know that it is definitely so, and have the experience which will not let me lie, as proof. For we manifestly see that those who are forced to accept the Christian religion, whether they are a people or individuals, never make good Christians. And I fear that they will be even less so than before, for they are disgusted by such constraint, sometimes even to the point where they plug their ears for fear that they might hear what is being preached to them, and where they pray to God that He will grant them the grace to let them leave the sermon in the same condition as they came to it. If someone, thus forced, comes to believe (which I strongly doubt, however), but if he does come to believe, it does not happen as the result of the constraint. If he had perhaps not been forced, he would have believed as soon or sooner than he has, for we see that there where none are forced, the number of believers generally grows more than there where constraint exists. I could quote many examples of this, were these not already well known to several, and did I not fear that some might be offended by them.

This is why I say that those who thus look to numbers and for that reason force people, gain nothing, but rather lose. They are like the fool who, possessing a large vat containing a small quantity of wine, fills it completely with water in order to have more, and so doing not only fails to increase his wine, but even spoils the good he had. Thus, such people wishing to augment the number of Christians, not only completely fail to do so, but even spoil whatever good there was. For this reason one should not be surprised that the wine of Christ is so minimal and so weak these days, considering that so much water is mixed with it. The Apostles did not act in this manner. They knew and adhered to the true way of making and receiving a Christian. Thus they rather asked the novice whether he believed, as Philip did with Queen Candace's eunuch: "If you believe with all your heart, you may be baptized" [Acts 8: 37]. But you who force consciences could not ask your novices this. For when you force someone to acknowledge the power of the Pope, mass or purgatory, or the doctrine or ceremonies which you observe, through fear of dishonor or the loss of possessions or life, it is already no longer necessary for you to ask him whether he believes with all his heart, that is to say truthfully and without any doubt. For you should know (if you are not more blind than moles) that, very far from believing with all his heart, he, on the contrary, disbelieves with all his heart. If he dared to say what his heart believes and thinks, he would say: "I believe with all my heart that you are proper tyrants and that that which you are forcing me into, is worthless; so much so, indeed, that if I had had some inclination towards it before, you have now deprived me of it, as the result of your coercion." For it must be said that wine is worth but little if people are forced to drink it, and it must equally be said that your doctrine is worth but little if you have to force it onto people.

In short, you are acting like your predecessors in the olden days, when they seized Burgundy and forced the inhabitants to say: "Long live the King." For the latter rather let themselves be killed than to say: "Long live the King." Or, if someone through fear said it with his mouth, his heart said exactly the opposite, and hated the king even more than ever. Those whom you are forcing are doing the same, so much so, that you are but engendering mortal hatreds, and making deceiving and hypocritical Christians who afterwards think of and strive for nothing but the destruction of that into which they have been forced. They also teach their children this and revolt at the first opportunity which presents itself to them.

These are the evils which, instead of good, result from your good intentions and coercions. It is amazing if you do not see these and fail to notice that, instead of advancing your religion, you are even retarding it. Consider the matter well, so that you may realize that this is so. Firstly, when Luther began to make himself heard, you, Catholics, began to persecute his sect and to burn its members in order to suppress it, and you have since never ceased to endeavor, in every possible manner, to uproot it. And what have you gained? You have rendered yourselves suspect and have caused people to want to investigate what it was, as the result of which the matter became so important that a hundred have come in the place of the one which you have burned. The result is that there are more thousands of them today than there were dozens of them previously, so much so that, as you see, they already dare to make war against you.

It is the same with you, Evangelics. When, hitherto, you fought with spiritual arms, which you learnt and took from Christ and His Apostles, namely faith, love, patience and others, God blessed you and strengthened you so much that your cause always progressed from good to better and that your numbers grew manifold, like the dewdrops of the dawn of day. But now that you have abandoned spiritual arms and taken up mortal ones, everything is going completely awry for you. For your violence renders you suspect and causes people to regard you in a very bad light and to withdraw instead of stepping forward. So that you may understand that this is not a matter of chance, but great wisdom and the will of God, who generally from such causes makes such results come forth, you should understand that that which is happening to you has even, to your recollection, happened

to others, namely to Zwingle and the Emperor Charles the Fifth. For while
Zwingle fought with doctrine and words, his cause advanced so much that
the whole country of Switzerland was moved to receive his doctrine. But
when he came to use violence and himself put his hand to the sword,
everything went awry, so much so that he himself and several others fell in
battle and that the Catholic cantons which had previously accepted the
doctrine, withdrew and confirmed their ancient faith to such a degree, even,
that they have since never deviated from it.

The same happened to the Emperor Charles. You know how he waged
war against the Protestants and how he achieved a total victory, to the point
even where he took and, for a long time, held their princes as prisoners. One
might therefore have thought that their doctrine and religion were done
with. But what finally happened? He was forced not by the Protestants, but
by those very ones who had helped him and especially by your own King,
O French, who was a mortal enemy of the Protestants' doctrine, to set the
prisoners free. And their Protestant religion remained so complete, thanks
to the assistance of its very enemies, that it still exists there today. It seems
that the God of armies clearly shows through such examples that He does
not want these aims to be achieved through violence. . . .

Whether One Should Put Heretics to Death

. . . There you have the ordinance of the Lord, concerning disputes which
are difficult to judge. Now the place of which He speaks and which He had
to choose, was, thereafter, the city of Jerusalem, where one had to go and
see the High Priest or Pontiff, for the settlement of any disputes which
might have arisen. But now that we are neither Israelites in the flesh, nor
subject to the law of Moses in the flesh, and that we have neither Jerusalem
nor the Pontiff, nor the High Priest in the flesh, we must address ourselves
to the heavenly and spiritual Jerusalem, namely the church, and to the
heavenly Pontiff, namely Christ, with our differences, as is evidenced by the
chapter in Hebrews [Hebrews 7–8, 9: 11ff]. Also, we should address ourselves to the prophet of whom Moses speaks, who is the same Christ, as is
evidenced by St. Stephen [Acts 7], and act in accordance with His judgment, on pain of God's indignation. And as Christ is no longer on this earth
in person (for if He were, one would have to go and look for Him), and as
we find ourselves in a period of famine with regard to God's word, that is
to say a period without prophets and oracles (for if there were any, it would
but be necessary to go to them, and the difference would be resolved), I can

find no way to ascertain His judgment, except from His written words, or from the example of His life, or from the nature of His Spirit, as manifested in His followers, or by some new revelation.

As far as His written word is concerned, it definitely does not say that one should kill a heretic. It does, however, say in general that if someone sins (which applies as much to a heretic as to someone else), he should be several times legitimately admonished and finally excommunicated, if he does not make amends, which duty belongs to the church and not to the magistrate. It particularly stresses that a heretic should be avoided after he has been admonished once or twice. But it says nothing about killing him. Now it is a fact that Moses says that the said prophet (who is Christ, as has been proved hereabove), will say whatever God shall have commanded Him to say. Even so, Christ definitely does not say that one should kill heretics, and God has therefore not commanded Him to say it. Or, at least, we find nothing in the Scriptures about it, and if we do not hold ourselves to and believe in these, I really think that we would not believe in Him either, should He speak to us in person. Similarly Abraham told Dives that if his brothers did not believe in Moses and the prophets, that is to say in their writings, they would not even believe in a resuscitated person either.

As far as the life of Christ is concerned, we see it to have been so noble, that to seek the example for the killing of a heretic by the sword in it, would be very much like seeking the example for the eating of a wolf, in a lamb. As far as His spirit, which is manifested in His followers is concerned, His disciples are such that they follow the Lamb wherever it goes, and that they have learned from Him who is noble and humble of heart. If someone does not have this spirit, though he may call himself a Christian as much as he likes, he is just as far from Christ as darkness is from light. And the persecutors themselves, indeed, finding nothing but complete gentleness in the New Testament, entirely contrary to their persecution, are forced to take recourse to the Old Testament, through which they clearly show that they do not know of which spirit they are, and that they do not possess the spirit of the new alliance.

As to the new revelation, those very ones who instruct the persecution of heretics, do not claim to have it, and if they did, one would have to think twice before believing it, considering that it would be contrary to the perfection both of the law of Moses and the law of Christ. For which reason, since neither Moses nor Christ commanded the killing of a heretic, I say in conclusion that the magistrate can, with a clear conscience, and without offending God, let him live, and speak as follows to the theologians who are urging him to kill him: "Show us the law under which God has commanded you to do it, and we shall do it." . . .

About Disadvantages

I am now going to talk about the disadvantages which could, it seems, come about if one should let the heretics live. These disadvantages could be twofold. The first, unrest and sedition, and the second, the false doctrine which the heretics might spread. To which I answer, firstly as far as the sedition is concerned, that the fools are bringing about that very evil which they think they are avoiding. For seditions are being caused by the fact that one wants to force and kill the heretics, rather than to let them live without constraint, for tyranny engenders sedition. It is for the moment certainly not necessary to quote old and remote examples to prove that this is so, for you are today carrying a more than adequate example of it in your bosom, O France. For it is certain that the sedition which torments you is the result of the tyrannizing and persecuting of those which are held for heretics. Had they not been tyrannized, they would perhaps not have revolted. Or, at worst, if they had revolted, it would have gone no worse with you than it already has, and the princes would then have had a more justifiable reason for countering force with force, not because of the religion, but because of the sedition. God, who grants victory to whom He pleases, would then have favored them more than He does, there where they are now in danger of falling into disgrace with Him. I do not even wish to mention that it would be better to be in danger of a future sedition than to use tyranny now, all the more so as tyranny is a far greater, certain and actual evil, which kills both the soul of the tyrant and the bodies and sometimes also the souls of the tyrannized, whilst sedition is an evil which may possibly not come about and which, if it does, can be repulsed or, at worst, will but affect the body.

As far as the false doctrine, which the heretics might sow, is concerned, I indeed admit that this is a disadvantage which it would be well to remedy. But one must take care (as I have just remarked, concerning the matter of sedition) that the remedy is not worse and more harmful to the patient than the ill which one desires to cure. Now it is a fact that the remedy which is being used, namely the tyrannizing and murdering of the heretics, is far worse and more harmful than the illness. . . .

In short, as the matter is such that Christianity encompasses so many sects today that one must be quite knowledgeable in order to be able to number them, each of which sects regards itself as Christian and the others as heretics, we are accepting a war such as the Midianites had [Judges 6–7], if we accept the law regarding the persecution of heretics. We shall then but gnaw and eat each other until such time as, as Saint Paul says, we consume each other, which is an incomparably greater disadvantage than the other one. Regarding this point, someone will say to me: "Do you then want the heretics to be left to do and say whatever they please, without resisting them in any way?" Most certainly not, I do not want this, but it is my desire that they should be resisted by good and becoming means, like the wise and godly resisted them in the past. For I ask you how Jesus Christ resisted the Pharisees and Sadducees? How did the Apostles resist Simon, the magician, and Bar-jesus and others? Was it not by means of divine and virtuous words, without putting the hand to the sword and without inciting anyone else, whether a public or private person, to do so? For they were wise warriors, who knew how to wage spiritual war with spiritual arms. They, therefore, who act differently and use violence, clearly show that they are not their followers. . . .

Conclusion and Advice

Consequently, all things well considered and examined, the advice which I am giving you, O France, is . . . that you should cease the forcing of consciences and stop persecution, not to mention the killing of a man because of his faith, and rather allow those who believe in Christ and who accept the Old and New Testament, to serve God in your country, not in accordance with the beliefs of others, but in accordance with their own. If you act in this manner, there is hope that the God of mercy will have pity on you, and you will find that, just as much as wrong advice and wrong remedies have hitherto been damaging to you, true advice and the true remedy will henceforth be of benefit to you.

Jacobus Acontius, *Stratagematum Satanae* (1565)

Acontius (c. 1500–c. 66) was born in Italy and practiced law; in 1557 he left Italy rather than face the danger entailed by his conversion to Protestantism. He visited Basel, Zürich, and Strasbourg, before going on to England in 1559. He was associated with Italian skeptics including Lelio Sozzini, and shared with them views on the trinity, liberty of conscience, and the need to simplify Christian teaching. Earlier, using the parable of the tares, he argued against magisterial imposition of religion, and in this later section went on to argue that diversity of opinion is actually a good thing in that it provokes investigation into the content of truth.

SOURCE: Jacobus Acontius, *Satan's Strategies, Books V–VIII*, intro. by Charles D. O'Malley (San Francisco, CA: California State Library, Sutro Branch, 1940), Book VI, pp. 132–3.

LITERATURE: Wilbur K. Jordan, *The Development of Religious Toleration in England*, 4 vols (London: George Allen & Unwin, 1932–40), vol. I, pp. 303–65; H. John McLachlan, *Socinianism in Seventeenth-Century England* (Oxford: Oxford University Press, 1951), pp. 55ff.

Book VI

. . . And the first thing we meet with is this: if every man is at liberty to cultivate and uphold whatever religion he most likes, since there is very great diversity of disposition and judgments, the result will be that there is considerable diversity of ideas and opinions also, and that there is no one who has not somebody who disagrees with and gainsays him; and since hardly any one is not gainsaid, it must needs be that many fall into doubt, what it is best to approve and follow. But he who doubts is stimulated to the investigation of what is true, and when many investigate, it is strange if none finds it; moreover if, when the truth is found, liberty of discussion is granted, when a comparison of opinions is made, that which is best must needs come to light. From this it follows that Satan's kingdom cannot long continue where there is liberty of opinions in regard to religion. But if liberty is not agreeable to him, it results that some established law to restrain and remove that liberty is agreeable to him. And since the very name of religion cannot be done away with and all men readily understand that not more than one can be true, what other will a law of that kind be than that whereby some particular religion, but one that is exceedingly wicked and abominable, is enjoined on men to be cultivated? And any one who dares so much as to whisper a word against it becomes liable to the very severest penalties? But whenever a law is to be promulgated, there must needs be some occasion for it. And it is by no means difficult to ascertain what things usually afford an occasion for doing away with liberty of opinion in regard to religion. For they are undoubtedly this excessively great multitude of discordant opinions, contentions, quarrels and brawlings, which Satan does not sow only when doctrine has already been perverted, but already when it is whole and undefiled – for contentions and brawlings are a way and means of perverting and weakening it. And although those institutions cannot be pleasing to Satan, which do not allow the doctrine, which is undefiled, to be perverted, yet those of a surety are pleasing to him, which, although they have been invented to that end, nevertheless rather confirm and propagate errors and give rise to sects, than hinder any of these things; and what they are has already been pointed out above. And since the more they are, who rebel against the received doctrine, and the more hasty, insolvent and peevish, and the more absurd the things they bring forward are, and the more influence those who preside over the churches have, and the more they are prone to wrath and indignation, the more passionately they seem likely to try any measures that may be taken against those who disturb the public tranquillity, you must be very careful that, while you think you are nobly resisting Satan, you are not really furthering Satan's cause beyond aught that he could himself hope for. . . . Moreover seeing that man has an innate desire to know things and has no little strength of judgment, wherewith he is often able to discern what is true – and this desire of knowing and this judgment may at one time be intenser and at another less active – it is beyond doubt to Satan's interest that these things should have as little force as possible. And since inquiry proceeds from a desire to know and inquiry is a means of arriving at a knowledge of what is true, on the one hand it is not expedient for Satan (as has been said) to allow freedom of inquiring in his kingdom, and on the other hand it even seems that harm will result, if it is suppressed. For what the poet says is quite true: "We always strive after what is forbidden and desire what is denied us." Moreover, if the desire is great and intense, we cannot rest till we have removed all obstacles in some way or other and satisfied it. Wherefore, if the desire of knowing is intensified when freedom of inquiring is suppressed, some method is needed whereby such desire can be held in check, or even, if it may be, altogether suppressed. Now all desire consists in thought; for no one can wish for aught save by thinking of it. Therefore if Satan can so contrive, that we do not even think about discovering the truth of religion, he will undoubtedly have made us cease to wish for it.

Juan de Mariana, "Not Fitting to Have Many Religions in One Province" (1599)

Mariana (1535–1624) was a leading Spanish Jesuit. He wrote a history of Spain, and in 1599 published his work on kingship especially for Philip III. Like other Spanish Thomists of his day, he upheld contractual notions of monarchy, and defended the ultimate sanction of tyrannicide. This selection about a solitary religion in a state lacks any dogmatic fervor, and does not state explicitly that the religion should necessarily be Roman Catholicism. Mariana's argument is rooted in notions of good government and in anxiety about the destructive potential of religious pluralism, based on historical study and his observations of European politics in the century of religious turmoil. He concluded that a good king would never conceive of granting religious toleration.

SOURCE: Juan de Mariana, *The King and the Education of the King*, tr. George Albert
    Moore (Washington, DC: Country Dollar Press, [1948]), pp. 361–75.
LITERATURE: Alan Soons, *Juan de Mariana* (Boston, MA: Twayne, [1982]), pp. 63–5;
    Guenter Lewy, *Constitutionalism and Statecraft during the Golden Age of Spain:
    A Study of the Political Philosophy of Juan de Mariana* (Geneva: Droz, 1960), ch. 6.

. . . the highest and very greatest duty of a wise Prince as well as his most
healthful maxim is to refer all his thoughts to peace and to guarantee the
Commonwealth from the ravages of war. For what is more beautiful than
peace? What is more ugly than war? Everybody wants peace and enjoys, as
it were, this fount of all blessings; they avoid war as the height of evil. We
are wont to signify with the word, war, all that is bad, with the term, peace,
a wealth of blessings. . . .

However, nothing is farther from peace than that in one city, state or
province there be several religions. But if the recent slaughters in many
cities and provinces which are right before our eyes and in our ears do
not teach how destructive this difference of religion is; if no examples
of this evil remained from ancient history, which, however, exist on every
side; the common sense of all and reason itself declare that nothing is more
destructive for the state than when worship is had not in accordance with
the religion of the fathers but of a foreign belief. For religion is the bond of
human society, by whose sanctity treaties, contracts, and alliances are sanc-
tified. Indeed, sprung from God, we return to God through religion, and in
Him we all find our peace; just as at the center of the earth all lines and radii
are joined. Moreover, what communion and society can there be among
men who do not recur to the same God of a certainty in a like ceremonial
and worship, since each turns away from the others as impious, and is
convinced that Heaven is served by injuring them? Wisely the parent of
Roman eloquence says, "Friendship is the harmony of the human and
divine through benevolence and charity." Therefore if they who agree on
earthly matters disagree on heavenly their friendship must limp of necessity; and among friends that have no agreement on divine concepts neither
will there be a full and real agreement on earthly affairs.

No blood relationship, no likeness of customs, type of life or country
binds wills together in well-wishing as much as difference of religion disturbs them; nor are any treaties capable of being hedged about with such
great sanctity that they are not easily frustrated, if diverse opinions of the
divinity are entertained. Nothing is more treacherous, nothing more violent
than when Heaven is given as a pretext in civil dissension; for part seem to
themselves to sin with impunity because their consciences excuse them.
The others do not dare to restrain their wantonness, in the first place, under
the fear that by merely avenging the treacheries some related divine law

may be violated. Then when dispositions are worn thin, and when the evil grows stronger, the very sons rise up against their parents; those born of the same parents show no milk of human kindness to their brothers. Necessarily all must swim in plots, blood, and murder of relatives. Discord, bathed in the blood of the citizens, makes men monstrous and despoils them of the very sense of nature. For the love for religion is more powerful than any affections. If some resist, the most serious uproars are set on foot with no respect for relationship, not even respect for the magistrates. For where a diverse opinion takes hold of the mind, we especially fear to lose the thing by which we hope for salvation, and those using force and busy in pressing their conviction we detest as impious and hated of heaven.

Since the evil spirit knew that nothing is equal to the difference in religion in destroying mutual charity and sowing discord among men, long ago he spread various sects throughout the world, lest mortals should come together further into the same society and grow together into one body, different from the other living beings which by a commonness of nature are friendly with each other. And now he does not cease to make anxious the quiet state of the individual cities and provinces with new opinions and with new sacred rites, and to rejoice in our ruin; with which hate he pursues our species. Long ago when the kingdom of the Jews was split, Jeroboam, having taken a great part of the country, being very anxious lest his subjects become weary of their new government, recall the blessings of David and Solomon, and bring their descendants back to power, brought in a new religion, in the form of two calves that were set up, and he made it so that the people would no longer agree, in his certainty that never on one form of rule would they agree when their minds and sentiments were disagreeing about religion. Likewise in Egypt it is clear that it happened, after King Seton died, the province separated into twelve districts or prefectures, and went under the same number of petty kings, and each one of these contrived different rites and new gods (whence the Egyptians have such a multitude of gods, so that they hold holy almost all living beings). They were taking care, of course, lest again the whole kingdom would come under one king and head. On the contrary, Moses, with his characteristic wisdom, to firmly establish the happiness of his people, and to make sacred their laws and courts, thought that among the first things it was pertinent to set up the sacred rites and ceremonies. This was common with him and the other law givers who followed him in the different parts of the world. Convinced that this could not be permanent and that concord could not last long if the people differed in matters of religion, before he wrote the laws, he set down what must be felt on all occasions and believed about God, concerning the nature of the world, about the happiness of mankind, and its fall through sin. He was, of course, taking prevision lest the public safety and tranquillity be disturbed by new beliefs being born, from which that people fell headlong into every misfortune.

But that we may consider this better we should look into the individual aspects of the Commonwealth. The interests of the kings, clergy, nobility, and people doubtless will be harmed if the old religion is changed by the birth of new religious ideas. Who would not see and confess that at least the kings would be involved in endless difficulties by this liberty? Imagine two religions in the same province, or flourishing in one city, armed with the favor of the nobles and with the people's support, and the number of the adherents of each sect not unequal. What will the Prince do? Whither will he turn? What plan of administering the Commonwealth will be set forth? Would he be able to rule the people with councils, to constrain them with laws, and to punish them by courts, if, as is almost a foregone conclusion, one, or both factions refuse to obey him? If he favors one party, he will feel the others alienated, and these, as suspects, and unfaithful, in my judgment at least, he will bar from the government and military duties, lest they abuse their privilege of arms, their authority, and favor overturning the Commonwealth; this precaution, though necessarily undertaken, will bring them to great trouble. To be barred from public honors in the state in which born, and this, on ground of their accepted religion, which they consider the truest, they will think a very real burden. But they will still conceal their hurt until they have the opportunity of pouring the concentrated virus of their indignation into the stream of public calamity; this they will do with the greater energy in proportion as they have lived for a relatively long time under restraint. And first they will conspire among themselves to protect their safety against the opposite faction's forces. When they will have the strength, they will extort freedom of religion from the Prince; they will add threats to their requests. If they attain this, elated in their pride, soon they will take up arms and make a fierce assault on the Commonwealth. If they win out, they will oppress their opponents, seize their possessions and drive them from the country. Then the King, bereft of his support, and brought back into their power, either they will convert to their own religion, or they will cast him from his position and deprive him of his kingdom and life. The calamities of our times teach us that all these things are related to each other and are accordingly tied one to the other, the second to the first and the last to the ones in the middle. If he will pretend to favor both sides, he will be suspected by both and remaining in the center, he will get the favor of neither, but he will engender the hate of all and their bitterness, like tepid water, because it is neither hot nor cold, but tempered by each, is unpleasing to the stomachs of all and is alike rejected by all; and trying to keep both seats, he will tumble to the ground from both. For how would he be able to satisfy both factions in such a great mixture of interests and wishes! Not even tyrants, for whom we have said above that it is advantageous that the people be divided would be able to lay out a plan for government and restraint of the people in a division because of religion. . . .

It could clearly come therefore that Christians would obey a Prince of a universal religion. But how could subjects of a foreign religion be ruled by a pious emperor in an empire which all look to and to whose sway the wills and desires of all should give way? Is it not rather likely that they would not obey laws which they will judge unworthy of that term? And yet the Christian flock while they lived under the Roman rule, if you consider human values, without glory, surmounted yet with no tumults in the cities, without taking up arms in the protection of their true religion, the conditions of the times, all the miseries and tortures with unconquered patience and with habits of the blameless life. But after that most happy day had dawned on the earth, when the Most High God overturned impiety and placed our people at the head of things, they turned their attention to destroying the impious worship of gods and strongly entrenching the peace of the Church. And so what Constantine Augustus, who was the first of the Roman emperors to acknowledge the majesty of Christ as God, began, and the fault of the following emperors, the neglect of Constantius and the malice of Julian threw into confusion, Theodosius the Emperor perfected, by publishing a law that no one would without penalty annoy the Christian religion with insults and calumnies. And rightly. If at Babylon, when the three young men had been snatched from the flames, a barbarian king put the death penalty against contumely of that God who had given such a glowing proof of his power and majesty, more rightly, indeed, it was that with such an emperor a like audacity should be suppressed.

Those who dispute this admit that in ancient times the impious worship of the gods was rooted out, but they deny that the sects springing up in the Christian people were cut out with the sword. They say that Constantine himself, with his probity, habits and power, winked at the opinions of Arius; that in the time of Theodosius the Great meetings of heretics were held in the suburbs. For in the time of Emperor Justinian, as has been said a little before, the privilege of private opinion was conceded to the sect of Eutyches. Now, of course, we do not look for what has been done, for we know that in the olden time many things were confused through the fault of times and men; it was not the privilege even of the good Emperors to root out all vices. We were thinking of seeking what by right and reason ought to be done, and what will be for the good of the Commonwealth. Varied and changeable is the tenor of different times, and many things, sometimes tolerated, would result in misfortune if they would be permitted in our times. . . .

But let us pass from the kings to the priests and other servants of the Church, which soundly Optatus and Epiphanius compared to the legal wife, because there is one Church in all the world, while they likened the meetings of the heretics, since they are countless, to concubines. But, if in the same house and family a wife lives with a mistress and possesses it with her on wholly equal terms, how great a confusion will there be in matters and what a great calamity it is unnecessary to say; everybody is able, as a matter of course, to imagine this debacle. In fact, what should the servants do when each of the two on her own wills and orders conflicting things? Which way should they turn? What scheme of obedience will they set about? A house beset with such great difficulty will divide into factions; it will flare up in hate, envy and ever present quarrels. Domestic duties will be neglected. The household, following the example of the master, will spend their time on their own pleasures; and as is said of the Trojan horse, the discord will extend even to the most vital issues, especially in the mistress, fortified with favor of the husband, has dared to enter into controversy with the wife about birth, modesty, and the very rights of marriage. Just like Arius and the other heretics against the true Church, each in his own time, claiming that they were really the Christians, and that his own was the Catholic Church, repudiated as heretics those who thought otherwise. According to the ancient Roman custom, the concubines were kept out of the temple of Juno, who presided over marriage; they judged, therefore, by this usage that nothing was more unhealthful to marriage than concubinage. Not even Abraham with the wisdom an authority that was his was able to keep Sarah at peace with Agar, and he was forced to put the maid-servant out of his house, as the legal wife was demanding. This case is an argument that never is it fitting for a wife to live in the same house with a concubine, nor in a city or province should a false religion be tolerated with the true one. It is unavoidable that they collide with each other, for their natures are contrary, and from long experience it has been learned that not without great misfortune to citizens and state has a new religion ever been put into any city. Cast the mind's eye around all the ages, unroll the old and recent histories; you will see at once wherever this evil flourishes honest rights are torn up, everything is in confusion from killings and brigandage, and those examples of cruelty stirred up against the adherents of the old religion and its ministers are such as never existed from the enemies of yester year.

. . . So, as soon as a leader presents himself to the rash crowd, especially when fortified with a show of religion, if there is an attack against the morals of the clergy, will fall as a prize to the mob, and they will take away from the churches the wealth and ornaments accumulated for many years.

This misfortune we know has happened in our time wherever religion has had vigorous dissensions. Further, when a people are divided and separated into two factions, it will be necessary to appoint two bishops in the same city, against all experience of the ages and the decrees. Every kind of evil will follow this calamity. How great a confusion of affairs there will be! For neither will with sufficient severity punish the offenses of his people, lest they will desert his sect and, as is the tendency in civil disorders, go into the camp of the opposition. From this lack of punishment the license of crime will be confirmed; a continuing nursery of discord and disagreement will exist. The destruction of the nobility will follow this disturbance of conditions and criminal license. For to what other end will this ungodly lack of restraint tend by which the mob is freed from all fear unless that, after the Church has been violated, the clergy prostrate, and the individual churches seized and burned, the blaze spreads like a serpent more widely and takes in the laying low of the nobles? Indeed the debacle does not stop at one class, but after the first are downed through them to the second and third strata it will successively make its way, and those who as spectators of the misfortunes of others seemed to be outside of the hazard of fortune are at once involved in the same destruction, the more that they are wont to rage with a greater hatred against the nobles than against the clergy. . . .

It is almost unavoidable that the status of the Commonwealth be changed along with the religion. Thus the more powerful and the very rich will be very near to the peril, and they fall a prey to the fury of the armed mob, which because of its own very greedy desire for revolution seeks to satisfy its want and thirst for having more things from the fortunes of others. But will they be held to their duty by the laws? This indeed would be the case, if in sedition and civil disorder the laws were not wont to be silent; everything resounds with the crash of arms, vanished and a nullity is the authority of the magistrates. And those laws are just and reasonable which provide that well ahead every occasion and every means of tumult be removed. Therefore just as the tops of the towers and the heights of the mountains are especially exposed to the blows of the sky and blasts of the winds, thus, when in a state a tempest arises, it first involves and lays low those who occupy the top positions of honor. Therefore, especially when religion has too little influence, the chiefs of state must be urged and exhorted – if they want to seek the advice of private citizens – to smother the wickedness of the heretics in their swaddling clothes before they get growing, lest they are forced later to lament in vain the earlier disregard.

Now to come to certain least important matters – what will be done if the power of this evil and the discord's fatal poison penetrates into the individual homes? What more abominable kind of state, what more disastrous condition of a people will be imaginable? Or what obedience, what love can there be among those who will differ in religious opinions? The wife will turn away from her own husband as impious. The husband will impute the crime of adultery to his wife who without consulting him goes to the meetings of another religion. For he will suspect, and not inconsiderately and not without examples, that there the chastity of religion does not flourish, but the impurity of lust rules. How many virgins are led away from their parents, how many wives are led away from their husbands under color of religion to the lustfulness of wicked men? There would be no end to these evils where entry is permitted to new religion. The day that gives freedom of worship puts an end to the happiness of the Commonwealth, and the name of liberty, bright in aspect and title, which in all history has seduced many a man, is found to be in fact false and empty. But unless it would seem superfluous in a matter by no means doubtful to offer examples, the tragedies, civil disturbances, and nefarious wars of our times, that came up rashly on account of religious causes and were carried on madly, we could mention – the many cities marred by the impact of internal trouble, the countless churches, venerated in the name of sanctity itself and for their grandeur, burned and destroyed, the sacred virgins violated, the many thousands of priests killed, the infinite number of men and troops delivered over to slaughter. . . .

But let these and other innumerable evils, born of religious dissension, be passed over; these are known to all and are available to posterity in the books of many people. It is not to the point to blame past events; it is vain to deplore and fruitless to offer no remedy except tears; at the same time the sails of my pen, sagging from the long discussion, must be furled, and some port must be made; even if first the arguments of our opponents must still be set forth.

For they object to us that think otherwise, that the empire of the Turks, which harbors several religions and various sects in its borders, is not agitated with any internal troubles and on the other hand daily grows and expands with every blessing of good fortune. They say that thus in Bohemia for a hundred fifty years two religions have been vigorous, and not long since a third has been officially allowed, composed out of the dictums of Martin Luther. The Swiss, a nation of warlike strength and renowned for their deeds, has admitted diverse religions into its Commonwealth; the Germans have done the same. But these people really do our Princes a grave injury, when they want to measure their empires according to the tyranny of the Turks and dispose Christian customs in accordance with the monstrousness of the laws of the Turks. For those on whom they impose their yoke they admit to no share of the government and do not permit them to bear arms, but rather they force them to be slaves, and they impose on them heavier taxes than on the others; to such a degree that they send their sons into slavery and shameful lewdness from the arms of their mothers; often their wives in the very sight of their husbands are violated without punishment.

But if the votaries of new sects would want to live under these conditions in a Christian commonwealth, so that they would bear rather heavy burdens, content with that liberty of conscience which they so much desire, perhaps this condition would be tolerable, and we could give them this freedom, bought at a great price, in our commonwealth. Now, when we see those who have left the religion of the fathers agitating for the chief positions and taking the highest office of authority, who would not call to mind the wickedness of those who want to protect freedom of religion after the example of the Turks? For, since they give the experience of the Bohemians and Germans, I wonder that they have cited neither the happenings in England nor at the Lake of Geneva, in which places not only do new sects flourish, but to the Catholics, of whom there is in both places a great number, the opportunity of practicing their religion is prohibited. Daily threats and terrors harry them more grievously. You see therefore that these very ones, who in other nations so impudently strive to get freedom of religion, and when it is denied they proclaim it an impious deed, a cruel tyranny, follow quite another method wherever they are in power. For they are not so imprudent as not to see that there is one way of retaining civil accord and protecting their own interests – if difference of religion is removed. Who is indeed so grossly ignorant that the strength of Germany has been weakened and great disasters encountered, in consequence of which it came to be agitated and torn with new opinions? And what was once a cause of fear for the Romans and not long since to the Turks, now as only a sick body and one afflicted with illnesses, not only is unable to help in the suffering of others, but is not even able to stand on its own feet without the help of somebody else.

Therefore what inconveniences come from the diversity of religion have been set forth in the last chapter herewith – that necessarily public and private affairs are disordered, if once the provincials begin to differ among themselves on religion. The establishments of the kings and clergy are upset; the happiness of the common people and the nobility cannot persist if this evil is vigorous. If all these matters are brought out into the light, if they are drawn from the very fountain-heads of nature, from the examples of antiquity and confirmed by recent history, if the whole discussion wins support and confidence to itself from reason and feeling, if it is strengthened by uncorrupted testimonies, if the voices of all orders grant that nothing in the old religion should be changed that people want to be saved; truly great gratitude must be felt toward those that cast out iniquity and prescribe that the institutions of the ancient religion be retained. Moreover, the authors of new sects are to be attacked, and rightly, and judged most worthy of the just hatred of posterity. And the Prince must be warned and exhorted that he must oppose himself to the very beginnings of the growing evil, and quench the initial flame, smothering it with his own body; lest if the contagion spread serpent-like more widely a remedy must be sought too late; and lest his own name be disparaged with the stains of stupidity and bad administration; and lest he himself – which is the most serious charge of all – after he has run his course, is considered a culprit for neglecting his duty and a criminal of the worst stripe on this account a perpetrator of great wrongs, for which he should pay most just penalties for holding the public and private safety of so little account.

Notes

1 Thomas More, "A Dialogue concerning Heresies," in *Complete Works*, vol. VI, ed. Thomas M. C. Lawler, Germain Marc'hadour and Richard C. Marius (New Haven, CT: Yale University Press, 1981), pp. 407, 416.
2 Sebastian Castellio, *Concerning Heretics* [1554], tr. R. H. Bainton (New York: Octagon, 1965 [1935]), pp. 141–53.
3 Another translation may be seen in H. Wayne Pipkin and John H. Yoder (eds), *Balthasar Hübmaier: Theologian of Anabaptism* (Scottdale, PA/Kitchener, Ont.: Herald Press, 1989), pp. 58–66.
4 See Harold S. Bender, "The Anabaptists and Religious Liberty in the 16th Century," *Mennonite Quarterly Review*, 29 (1955), pp. 83–100.
5 Theodore Beza, *De Haereticis* (1554).

4

THE SEVENTEENTH CENTURY

Arminius, "On Reconciling Religious Dissensions among Christians" (1606)

Arminius (c. 1559–1609) was a pastor in Amsterdam and later a professor of theology at Leiden. He started a major controversy by his advocacy of a doctrine of predestination which preserved some element of human freedom, if only in the capacity to resist grace. This, his Fifth Oration, dated 8 February 1606, spoke to the flaring debate. Arminius was not a skeptic; he believed that truth was not beyond hope of attainment, but he allowed that it was difficult to determine in some instances, that moderation in defense of one's beliefs was the best policy, and that one should emphasize points of agreement rather than divergence. He knew well the "Iliad of disasters" introduced into the Christian world by religious persecution. A synod was in fact held at Dort in 1618–9, but it did not conform to the pattern laid down in this speech; its outcome was predetermined, and dissenters (Remonstrants) were driven from their churches.

SOURCE: James Arminius, *Works*, 3 vols, trs. James and William Nichols (London, 1825–75), vol. I, pp. 407–12, 438–42, 451–64.
LITERATURE: Carl Bangs, *Arminius: A Study in the Dutch Reformation*, 2nd edn (Grand Rapids, MI: Francis Asbury Press, 1985 [1971]), pp. 275–83; Johannes Kühn, *Toleranz und Offenbarung: Eine Untersuchung der Motive und Motivformen der Toleranz im offenbarunggläubigen Protestantismus* (Leipzig: Felix Meiner, 1923), pp. 363–74.

These necessary concessions we shall obtain from our minds without much difficulty, if the following four considerations become the objects of our sedulous attention:

First. *How extremely difficult it is to discover the truth on all subjects, and to avoid error.* On this topic St Augustine most beautifully descants, when he thus addresses those worst of heretics, the Manichees: "Let those persons be enraged against you who are ignorant of the immense labor that is required for the discovery of truth, and how difficult it is to guard against error. Let those be enraged against you who know not how uncommon a circumstance and how arduous a toil it is to overcome carnal fantasies, when such a conquest is put in comparison with serenity of mind. Let those be enraged against you who are not aware of the great difficulty with which the eye of 'the inner man' is healed, so as to be able to look up to God as the sun of the system. Let those be enraged against you who are personally unconscious of the many sighs and groans which must be uttered before we are capable of understanding God in the slightest degree. And, lastly, let them be enraged against you who have never been deceived by an error of such a description as that under which they see you laboring. But how angry soever all these persons may be, I cannot be in the least enraged against you, whose weaknesses it is my duty to bear, as those who were near me at that period bore with mine; and I ought now to treat you with as much patience as that which was exercised towards me when, frantic and blind, I went astray in the errors of your doctrine."

Secondly. That those who hold erroneous opinions have been induced through *ignorance* to adopt them, is far more probable, than that *malice* has influenced them to contrive a method of consigning themselves and other people to eternal destruction.

Thirdly. It is possible that they who entertain these mistaken sentiments, are of the number of the elect, whom God, it is true, may have permitted to fall, but only with this design – that he may raise them up with the greater glory. How then can we indulge ourselves in any harsh or unmerciful resolutions against these persons, who have been destined to possess the heavenly inheritance, who are our brethren, the members of Christ, and not only the servants but the sons of the Lord Most High?

Lastly. Let us place ourselves in the circumstances of an adversary, and let him in return assume the character which we sustain; since it is as possible for us, as it is for him, to hold wrong principles. When we have made this experiment, we may be brought to think, that the very person whom we had previously thought to be in error, and whose mistakes in our eyes had a destructive tendency, may perhaps have been given to us by God, that out of his mouth we may learn the truth which has hitherto been unknown to us.

To these four reflections, let there be added, *a consideration of all those articles of religion respecting which there exists on both sides a perfect agreement.* These will perhaps be found to be so numerous and of such great importance, that when a comparison is instituted between them, and the others which may properly be made the subjects of controversy, the latter will be found to be few in number and of small consequence. This is the very method which a certain famous prince in France is reported to have adopted, when Cardinal Lorraine attempted to embroil the Lutherans, or those who adhered to the Augustan Confession, with the French Protestants, that he might interrupt and neutralize the salutary provisions of the Conference at Poissy, which had been instituted between the Protestants and the Papists.

But since it is customary after long and grievous wars, to enter into a truce, or a cessation from hostilities, prior to the conclusion of a treaty of peace and its final ratification; and, since, during the continuance of a truce, while every hostile attempt is laid aside, peaceful thoughts are naturally suggested, till at length a general solicitude is expressed with regard to the method in which a firm peace and lasting reconciliation may best be effected – it is my special wish, that there may now be among us a similar cessation from the asperities of religious warfare, and that both parties would abstain from writings full of bitterness, from sermons remarkable only for the invectives which they contain, and from the unchristian practice of mutual anathematizing and execration. Instead of these, let the controversialists substitute *writings full of moderation*, in which the matters of controversy may, without respect of persons, be clearly explained and proved by cogent arguments: let such sermons be preached as are calculated to excite the minds of the people to the love and study of truth, charity, mercy, long-suffering, and concord; which may inflame the minds both of Governors and people with a desire of concluding a pacification, and may make them willing to carry into effect such a remedy as is, of all others, the best accommodated to remove dissensions.

That remedy is, *an orderly and free convention of the parties that differ from each other*: In such an assembly (called by the Greeks a Synod, and by the Latins a Council) after the different sentiments have been compared together, and the various reasons of each have been weighed, in the fear of the Lord, and with calmness and accuracy, let the members deliberate, consult, and determine what the word of God declares concerning the matters in controversy, and afterwards let them by common consent promulge and declare the result to the Churches.

The Chief Magistrates, who profess the Christian religion, will summon and convene this Synod, in virtue of the Supreme official authority with which they are divinely invested, and according to the practice that formerly prevailed in the Jewish Church, and that was afterwards adopted by the Christian Church and continued nearly to the nine hundredth year after the birth of Christ, until the Roman Pontiff began through tyranny to arrogate this authority to himself. . . .

The presidency of that assembly belongs to Him alone who is the Head and the Husband of the Church – to Christ by his Holy Spirit. For He has promised to be present in a company that may consist only of two or three individuals gathered together in His name: His assistance therefore will be earnestly implored at the beginning and end of each of their sessions. But, for the sake of order, moderation, and good government, and to avoid confusion, it will be necessary to have presidents subordinate to Christ Jesus. It is my sincere wish that the magistrates would themselves undertake that office in the Council; and this might be obtained from them as a favor. But in case of their reluctance, either some members deputed from their body, or some persons chosen by the whole Synod, ought to act in that capacity. The duties of these Presidents will consist in convening the assembly, proposing the subjects of deliberation, putting questions to the vote, collecting the suffrages of each member by means of accredited secretaries, and in directing the whole of the proceedings. The course of action to be adopted in the Synod itself is this: (1) a regular and accurate debate on the matters in controversy, (2) mature consultation concerning them, and (3) complete liberty for every one to declare his opinion. . . .

And since nothing to the present period has proved to be a greater hindrance to the investigation of truth or to the conclusion of an agreement, than this circumstance – that those who have been convened were so restricted and confined to received opinions as to bring from home with them the declaration which they were to make on every subject in the Synod – it is therefore necessary that all the members assemble, should, prior to the commencement of any proceedings, take a solemn oath, not to indulge in prevarication or calumny. By this oath they ought to promise that every thing shall be transacted in the fear of the Lord, and according to a good conscience; the latter of which consists: in not asserting that which they consider to be false; in not concealing that which they think to be the truth (how much soever such truth may be opposed to them and their party); and in not pressing upon others for absolute certainties those points which seem, even to themselves, to be doubtful. By this oath they should also promise, that every thing shall be conducted according to the rule of the Word of God, without favor or affection, and without any partiality or respect of persons; that the whole of their attention in that assembly shall be solely directed to promote an enquiry after truth and to consolidate Christian concord; and that they will acquiesce in the sentence of the Synod on all those things of which they shall be convinced by the Word of God. On which account let them be absolved from all other oaths, either immediately or indirectly contrary to this, by which they have been bound either to Churches and their confessions, or to schools and their masters, or even to princes themselves, with an exception in favor of the right and jurisdiction which the latter have over their subjects. Constituted after this manner, such a Synod will truly be a free assembly, most suitable and appropriate for the investigation of truth and the establishment of concord. . . .

From a Synod thus constructed and managed, those who rely on the promise of God may expect most abundant profit and the greatest advantages. For, though Christ be provoked to anger by our manifold trespasses and offenses, yet the thought must not be once indulged, that his church will be neglected by him; or, when his faithful servants and teachable disciples are, with simplicity of heart, engaged in a search after truth and peace, and are devoutly imploring the grace of His Holy Spirit, that He will on any account suffer them to fall into such errors as are opposed to truths accounted fundamental, and to persevere in them when their tendency is injurious. From the decisions of a Synod that is influenced by such expectations, unanimity and agreement will be obtained on all the doctrines, or at least on the principal part of them, and especially on those which are supported by clear testimonies from the Scriptures.

But if it should happen, that a mutual consent and agreement cannot be obtained on some articles, then, it appears to me, one of these two courses must be pursued: First. It must become a matter of deep consideration, whether a fraternal concord in Christ, cannot exist between the two parties, and whether one cannot acknowledge the other for partakers of the same faith and fellow-heirs of the same salvation – although they may both hold different sentiments concerning the nature of faith and the manner of salvation. If either party refuse to extend to the other the right hand of fellowship, the party so offending shall, by the unanimous declaration of all the members, be commanded to prove from plain and obvious passages of scripture, that the importance attached to the controverted articles is so great as not to permit those who dissent from them to be one in Christ Jesus. Secondly. After having made every effort towards producing a Christian and fraternal union, if they find that this cannot be effected, in such a state of affairs the second plan must be adopted, which indeed the conscience of no man can under any pretext refuse: The right hand of friendship should be extended by both parties, and all of them should enter into a solemn engagement, by which they should bind themselves, as by oaths and under the most sacred obligations, to abstain in future from all bitterness, evil-speaking, and railing; to preach with gentleness and moderation, to the people entrusted to their care, that truth which they deem necessary; and to confute those falsities which they consider to be inimical to salvation and injurious to the glory of God – and, while engaged in such a confutation of error (however great their earnestness may be), to let their zeal be under the direction of knowledge and attempered with kindness. On him who shall resolve to adopt a course of conduct different to this, let the imprecations of an incensed God and his Christ be invoked, and let the magistrates not only threaten him with deserved punishment, but let it be actually inflicted.

But the Synod will not assume to itself the authority of obtruding upon others, by force, those resolutions which may have been passed by unanimous consent. For this reflection should always suggest itself: "Though this Synod appears to have done all things conscientiously, it is possible, that, after all, it has committed an error in judgment." Such a diffidence and moderation of mind will possess greater power, and will have more influence, than any immoderate or excessive rigor can have, on the consciences both of the contumacious dissidents, and of the whole body of the faithful. . . .[1]

Thomas Helwys, *The Mistery of Iniquity* (1612)

When John Smyth's separatist–baptist congregation broke up in Amsterdam, Helwys (c. 1550–c. 1616 or earlier) led his faction back to London in 1612 where it became the first baptist congregation in England. Not long before the return, this work was published in which Helwys expressed his emphases upon justification by faith, separation from ungodliness (including the Church of England), and complete religious freedom. His work also includes an early example of spiritualizing the Old Testament so that its notion of a king governing religion is subverted; now, under the New Testament, the only king of the church is Jesus Christ. James I was not convinced by either the correctness of the theology or the denial of subversive intent: Helwys apparently died in a London prison.

SOURCE: Thomas Helwys, *A Short Declaration of the Mistery of Iniquity* ([Amsterdam], 1612), pp. 73–6, 78–9, 81–2.
LITERATURE: Thomas Lyon, *The Theory of Religious Liberty in England, 1603–39* (Cambridge: Cambridge University Press, 1939), pp. 117–24.

Then judge, O King, for the case is all one and the same: for wee have Christ and his Appostles in their writings, and they do absolutely speake to our understandings, that in no wise there ought to be anie such hyrarchy of Archbishops and Lord Bishops in Christs Church. And the Lord Bishops say, that Christ and his Appostles, speakes to their understandings, that there power and names are not contrary to Christs words. Can our lord the King (that is accompted a most wise and just Prince in his judgment) judge, that wee are all bound to cast away our owne understandings of Christs speaking, and are to be compelled to beleeve and understand Christ to speake, as the Lord Bishops understand Christs speaking? Oh let our Lord the King with compassion, consider, whether ever since the heavens and earth were created, there was a more unequall extreame cruelty than this, that the Kings people should be compelled (in a cause that concernes the everlasting condemnation of their soules & bodyes to Hell) of force to submitt their soules and bodies to the understanding of the Lord Bishops that are not able to direct themselves from the waies of death, but are perished every man, that ever bare that Office with those names and power, if they repented not thereof, although they had no other sinne: and they also that do now beare that Office with those titles & power shall likewise all perish to everlasting destruction, if they do not repent thereof, and cast it away: the spirit of the Lord hath spoken it Revelation 19: 20: "the Beast was taken, and with him that false Prophet that wrought myracles before him, whereby he deceived them that received the Beasts marke, and them that worshipped his image, these both were cast alive into a lake of fire, burning with brimstone." And thus manifesting to our Lord the King that Jesus Christ is onely King of Israell, that sitts upon Davids throne, & therefore onely hath the power of the King of Israel, and none may partake with him in that kingdome and power, who had the Spirit without measure: and yet neither he, nor his Appostles that had the Spirit without error to deliver the Counsels of God, did ever by example, practice, nor by rule comaund nor give power that anie should be compelled by anie bodily punishment to obey their lawes and Ordinances, which were infalibly true, holy, and good: How much lesse ought our lord the King to comaund, or give a power to Archbishops & lord Bishops (men full of the spirit of error) to make lawes & Canons with aucthority from the King to compell by imprisonment & sharpe persecutions, the Kings true subjects, and people of God unto the obedience thereof: who for their religion to God (although they be contrary mynded to the King therein) ought not (seeing they deserve not) to be punished either with death or bonds: & this is confirmed to the King by the testimony of King Agrippa and noble Festus the governor, who adjudged Paul to have done nothing worthy of death or bonds, but that he might have bene loosed, if he had not appealed to Cesar: & yet Paul was contrary mynded to Cesar & to the jewes in his religion to God: But they judged him by the lawe of Nations: by the power of which law, the Kings of the nations are to rule & judge, according to their owne severall lawes, against which law, Paul had not transgressed for his cause was concerning the faith of Jesus Christ which could not be judged by that law.

And let our lord the King give his servants leave to comend this to the Kings best observation, which is worthy to be observed: that, wheresoever in the new testament throughout, the professors of the faith of Jesus, were adjudged by earthly rulers & Governors, for anie thinge that they did or held of conscience, to God, & of faith to Jesus Christ, if earthly Rulers and Governors tooke the cause in hand by their power, the judgment was alwaies wicked and abhominable. And if our lord the King will but begin his observation at the fore-runner of Christ, John Baptist, whome Herod put in prison and beheaded. And then let the King come to Jesus Christ, whome they judged and crucified, "finding no evil he had done." And so if it please the King to looke throughout the whole booke of the Acts there the King knowes how the disciples of Christ, were "imprisoned, threatned, beaten, stoned: Then made Saul havock" with his letters of Comission, "and entred into every house and drew out both men, & wemen and put them in prison." Then "Herod stretched furth his hand and vexed certen of the Church, and killed James the brother of John with the sword," and "Caught Peter and put him in prison." Then were Paul and Sylas taken at Philippi, by the Governors and people, and were "sore beaten & cast into prison, and the Jailer comaunded to kepe them surely, being charged to preach Ordinances which were not lawfull for the Romans to receive nor observe." Here may our lord the King see a true patterne, how the people of God are persecuted, when the Civill power doth judg their cause of their faith, and profession in their religion to God. Thus have worldly Governors delt with the Church of Christ, when the disciples fell under their censure for their faith to God. And all these sentences of death, bonds, and persecutions the King can judge to be unjust and unlawfull, in that these Rulers and Governors had no lawfull power nor aucthority to judge Christ, nor his disciples for matters of faith, they being in all other thinges obedient to their lawes. But men wil say all this is answered in one word. They were heathen Rulers. Now if our lord the King will challenge a Prerogative or power, because he professeth Christ, then let it be lawfull for the King's servants, to tell the King that if he will profess to be a disciple of Christ, that gives the King no power to do anie of all these thinges to imprison, to banish, to put to death, that belongs onely to his earthly kingdome: for Christ and Appostles had no such power given them: neither taught they the disciples to take upon them anie such power, and to execute it upon the contrary mynded, but taught them the contrary "to instruct them with meeknes," and by preaching the word seeke their conversion, with all long suffering, and not to destroy them by severe punishments: yea the disciples of Christ must wait and labor for "the grafting in againe of the Jewes," according to the prophesies of the scriptures. Romans 11: 24,27, and therefore the King knowes they may not be destroyed, although they be the greatest enimies of Christ that are upon the earth, and have, and yet do cast the greatest reproach and contempt upon Christ, with such words, as are most fearfull to utter: yet must the disciples of Christ wait for their conversion, and not worke their destruction. . . .

. . . whereby wee shew unto the King, that the King cannot have that power (in respect of Religion to God) in the kingdome and over the house and Israell or people of Christ now, that the Kings of Israell had in the old Testament, or in the time of the law. The ground wee repeat unto the King is this. That the kingdome of Israell was an earthly or worldly kingdome: an earthly or worldly Temple, Tabernacle, or house: an earthly or worldly people: and the King an earthly King, who in and over all that kingdome, Temple, and people could require onely earthly obedience. But the kingdome of Christ now, is an heavenly kingdome "not of this world": his Temple, Tabernacle, or house "an heavenly Temple, Tabernacle, or house," his people, a heavenly, or spirituall people, "not of this world": and the King Christ Jesus "a heavenly spirituall King," requiring spirituall obedience.

Therefore our lord the King can not as a King have anie power over this kingdome, Temple, Tabernacle, house and People of God in respect of the Religion of God: because our lord the King his kingdome is an earthly kingdome: and to our lord the King belongs onely all earthly obedience, service, and duty, which ought to suffice anie earthly man. And the God of all Grace, give our lord the King a gracious hart fully to be satisfied and contented with that great honor, power, and dignity that belongs unto the King and to give glory and honor to God for it, that it may go well with the King and his posterity for ever. . . .

And wee most humbly supplicate our Lord the King and all the honorable and worthy Governors under the king that they will not suffer themselves to be misled in judgment in condemning us as movers of Sedition, and our bookes for seditious bookes, because wee differ from the recieved profession of Religion in the land, but that they will according to that great gravity and wisedome that is upon them, wey what Sedition is, and they will easily find that to professe and teach a differing judgment in Religion to the State, cannot be proved Sedition: for then had our Savior Christ, and all his Disciples bene found seditious persons, which never could be proved against them: neither could Tertullus with all his Oratory prove Paul a mover of Sedition to Felix the Governor who was willing to pleasure the Jews in this matter [Acts 24], if he could have found anie advantage against Paul: but under all that excellent and mighty Goverment of Cesar, under whome there was so manie wise Kings and noble Governors, difference in Religion could never be proved Sedition against the State. Neither could it ever be proved Sedition in all or anie of those that differed from the profession of Religion established in Queen Maries daies although they taught and professed the same as even the Lord Bishops themselves will confesse.

And it is neither accounted nor found Sedition, in divers excellent well Governed Nations round about, to professe and teach a differing judgment in Religion from the profession generally established, as our Lord the King and all his worthy Governors see and knowe. It is but the false surmise and accusation of the Scribes and Phariseis, who feared their owne kingdome:

and of Demetrius the Silver-smith with the Craftsmen, whose Craft was in danger, whereby they gott their goods [Acts 19], they themselves raised tumults and moved Sedition, and ever laid the blame upon the Disciples: even so is it now and ever wilbe, that such as feare their owne kingdome and private gayne, do, and will falsly accuse the Disciples of Christ as movers of Sedition against the State. And if the lord Bishops will not be found false accusers herein, as their predecessors have bene, then lett them (if they can) forbeare to accuse before they have cause.

Roger Williams, *The Bloudy Tenet* (1644)

Though Williams (1603–83) was born in London and he published his works in England, his notoriety was gained in New England where he withstood the patriarchs of Massachusetts Bay and Plymouth, and established Rhode Island as a haven of religious liberty. One of the more striking features of his writing – apart from his prolixity – is his amalgamation of general baptist exegesis with calvinistic predestinarian theology. From the latter he drew the notion that the elect cannot be lost, they cannot finally fall into damnable error, hence there is no call for the magistrate to intervene so long as the security of persons and property is not compromised. From the baptists he borrowed a method of exegesis called typology (they were not its originators) whereby the Old Testament and its various institutions were regarded as types – not allegories, but foreshadowings of a greater, spiritualized reality to come in the future. Thus the kings of Israel were historical personages, but their power over the religious life of the nation was transferred to Christ, not to Constantine and later magistrates (i.e. any civil authority). "The state of the Land of Israel, the Kings and people thereof in Peace & War, is proved figurative and ceremoniall, and no patterne nor president [precedent] for any Kingdome or civill state in the world to follow."

SOURCE: [Roger Williams], *The Bloudy Tenent, of Persecution, for Cause of Conscience, Discussed, in a Conference Betweene Truth and Peace* ([London], 1644), pp. 52–9.
LITERATURE: Edwin S. Gaustad, *Liberty of Conscience: Roger Williams in America* (Grand Rapids, MI: William B. Eerdmans, 1991).

Chapter 28

[*Truth*]: I shall conclude this controversie about this Parable [Matthew 13: 24–30] in this briefe sum and recapitulation of what hath beene said. I hope by the evident demonstration of Gods Spirit to the conscience I have proved, Negatively,

First, that the Tares in this Parable cannot signifie Doctrines or Practices (as was affirmed) but Persons.

Secondly, the Tares cannot signifie Hypocrites in the Church either undiscovered or discovered.

Thirdly, the Tares here cannot signifie Scandalous Offenders in the Church.

Fourthly, nor scandalous offenders in life and conversation against the Civill state.

Fifthly, The field in which these Tares are sowne, is not the Church.

Againe affirmatively: First, the Field is properly the World, the Civill State or Common-wealth.

Secondly, The Tares here intended by the Lord Jesus, are Antichristian idolaters, opposite to the good seed of the Kingdome, true Christians.

Thirdly, the ministers or messengers of the Lord Jesus ought to let them alone to live in the world, and neither seeke by prayer or prophesie to pluck them up before the Harvest.

Fourthly, this permission or suffering of them in the field of the World, is not for hurt, but for common good, even for the good of the good Wheat, the people of God.

Lastly, the patience of God is, and the patience of Men ought to be exercised toward them, and yet notwithstanding their doome is fearfull at the harvest, even gathering, bundling, and everlasting burnings by the mighty hand of the Angels in the end of the World.

Chapter 29

Peace: The second Scripture brought against such persecution for cause of Conscience, is Matthew 15: 14 where the Disciples being troubled at the Pharises cariage toward the Lord Jesus and his doctrines, and relating how they were offended at him, the Lord Jesus commandeth his Disciples to let them alone, and gives this reason, that the blinde lead the blinde, and both should fall into the ditch.

Unto which, Answer is made, "That it makes nothing to the Cause, because it was spoken to his private Disciples, and not to publique Officers in Church or State: and also, because it was spoken in regard of not troubling themselves, or regarding the offense which the Pharises tooke."

Truth: I answer, (to passe by his assertion of the privacie of the Apostles) in that the Lord Jesus commanding to let them alone, that is, not onely not be offended themselves, but not to meddle with them; it appeares it was no ordinance of God nor Christ for the Disciples to have gone further, and have complained to, and excited the Civill Magistrate to his duty: which if it had beene an Ordinance of God and Christ, either for the vindicating of Christs doctrine, or the recovering of the Pharises, or the preserving of others from infection, the Lord Jesus would never have commanded them to omit that which should have tended to these holy ends.

Chapter 30

Peace: It may be said, that neither the Romane Caesar, nor Herod, nor Pilate knew ought of the true God, or of Christ; and it had been in vaine to have made complaint to them who were not fit and competent, but ignorant and opposite Judges.

Truth: I answer first, this removes (by the way) that stumbling block which many fall at, to wit, Pauls appealing to Caesar; which since he could not in common sense doe unto Caesar as a competent Judge in such cases, and wherein he should have also denied his own Apostleship or office, in which regard (to wit in matters of Christ) he was higher then Caesar himselfe: it must needs follow, that his appeale was meerly in respect of his Civill wrongs, and false accusations of sedition, &c.

Secondly, if it had been an Ordinance of God, that all Civill Magistrates were bound to judge in causes spirituall or Christian, as to suppresse heresies, defend the faith of Jesus; although that Caesar, Herod, Pilate were wicked, ignorant and opposite, yet the Disciples and the Lord Christ himselfe had been bound to have performed the duty of faithfull Subjects, for the preventing of further evill, and the clearing of themselves, and so to have left the matter upon the Magistrates care and conscience, by complaining unto the Magistrate against such evills; for every person is bound to goe so far as lies in his power for the preventing and the redressing of evill; and where it stops in any, and runs not cleere, there the guilt, like filth or mud, will lie.

Thirdly, had it been the holy purpose of God to have established the doctrine and kingdome of his Son this way, since his comming, he would have furnished Common-weales, Kingdomes, Cities, &c. then and since, with such temporall Powers and Magistrates as should have beene excellently fit and competent: for he that could have had legions of Angels, if he so pleased, could as easily have been, and still be furnished with legions of good and gracious Magistrates to this end and purpose.

Chapter 31

It is generally said, that God hath in former times, and doth still, and will hereafter stirre up Kings and Queenes, &c.

I answer, that place of Isaiah 49: 23 will appeare to be far from proving such Kings and Queenes Judges of Ecclesiastical causes: and if not Judges they may not punish.

In Spirituall things, themselves are subject to the Church, and censures of it, although in Civill respects superior. How shall those Kings and Queenes be supreme Governours of the Church, and yet lick the dust of the Churches feet? as it is there exprest.

Thirdly, Gods Israel of old were earnest with God for a King, for an Arme of Flesh, for a King to protect them, as other Nations had. Gods Israel still have ever been restlesse with God for an Arme of flesh.

God gave them Saul in his anger, and took him away in his wrath: And God hath given many a Saul in his Anger, that is, an Arm of Flesh in the way of his Providence, (though I judge not all persons whom Saul in his Calling typed out, to be of Sauls spirit) For I speake of a State and outward visible Power only.

I adde, God will take away such stayes on whom Gods people rest, in his wrath, that King David, that is, Christ Jesus the Antitype, in his own Spirituall power in the hands of the Saints, may spiritually and for ever be advanced.

And therefore I conclude, it was in one respect that the Lord Jesus said, Let them alone, because it was no Ordinance for any Disciple of Jesus to prosecute the Pharises at Caesars Bar.

Beside, let it be seriously considered by such as plead for present corporall punishment, as conceiving that such sinners (though they breake not Civill peace) should not escape unpunished, I say, let it be considered, though for the present their punishment is deferred, yet the punishment inflicted on them will be found to amount to an higher pitch, then any corporall punishment in the World beside, and that in these foure respects.

Chapter 32

First by just judgment from God, false teachers are starke blinde, Gods sword hath strucke out the right eye of their minde and spirituall understanding, ten thousand times a greater punishment then if the Magistrate should command both the right and left eye of their bodies to bee bored or pluckt out, and that in so many fearfull respects if the blindnesse of the soule and of the body were a little compared together, whether we looke at that want of guidance, or the want of joy and pleasure, which the light of the eye affordeth; or whether we looke at the damage, shame, deformity, and danger, which blindnesse brings to the outward man, and much more true in the want of the former, and miserie of the latter in spirituall and soule blindnesse to all eternity.

Secondly, how fearfull is that wound that no Balme in Gilead can cure? How dreadfull is that blindnesse which for ever to all eye-salve is incurable? For if persons be wilfully and desperately obstinate (after light shining forth) let them alone saith the Lord. So spake the Lord once of Ephraim, Ephraim is joyned to Idolls, let him alone, Hosea 7. What more lamentable condition then when the Lord hath given a poor sinner over as a hopelesse patient, incurable, which we are wont to account a sorer affliction, then if a man were torne and rack'd, &c.

And this I speake not that I conceive that all whom the Lord Jesus commands His servants to passe from, and let alone, to permit and tolerate (when it is in their power corporally to molest them) I say that all are thus incurable, yet that sometimes that word is spoken by Christ Jesus to His servants to be patient, for neither can corporall or spirituall Balme or Physicke ever heale or cure them.

Thirdly, their end is the Ditch, that bottomlesse pit of everlasting separation from the holy and sweet Presence of the Father of Lights Goodnesse and Mercy it selfe, endlesse, easelesse, in extremity, universality, and eternity of torments, which most direfull and lamentable downefall, should strike an holy fear &

trembling into all that see the Pit, whither these blinde Pharises are tumbling, and cause us to strive (so far as hope may be) by the spirituall eye-salve of the Word of God to heale and cure them of this their soule-destroying blindnesse.

Fourthly, of those that fall into this dreadfull Ditch, both leader and followers, how deplorable in more especiall manner is the leaders case, upon whose necke the followers tumble, the ruine not only of his owne soule, being horrible, but also the ruine of the followers soules eternally galling and tormenting.

Peace: Some will say these things are indeed full of horrour, yet such is the state of all sinners and of many Malefactours, whom yet the State is bound to punish, and sometimes by death it selfe.

Truth: I answer, The Civill Magistrate beareth not the sword in vaine, but to cut off Civill offenses, yea and the offendours too in case: But what is this to a blinde Pharisee, resisting the Doctrine of Christ, who happily may be as good a subject, and as peaceable and profitable to the Civill State as any, and for his spirituall offense against the Lord Jesus, in denying Him to be the true Christ, he suffereth the vengeance of a dreadfull judgment both present and eternall, as before.

Chapter 33

Peace: Yea but it is said that the blinde Pharises misguiding the subjects of a Civill State, greatly sinne against a Civill State, and therefore justly suffer civill punishment; for shall the Civill Magistrate take care of outsides only, to wit, of the bodies of men, and not of soules, in laboring to procure their everlasting welfare?

Truth: I answer, It is a truth, the mischiefe of a blinde Pharises blinde guidance is greater then if he acted Treasons, Murders, &c. and the losse of one soule by his seduction is a greater mischiefe then if he blew up Parliaments, and cuts the throats of Kings or Emperours, so pretious is that invaluable Jewell of a Soul, above all the present lives and bodies of all the men in the world! and therefore a firme Justice calling for eye for eye, tooth for tooth, life for life; calls also soule for soule, which the blind-guiding seducing Pharisee shall surely pay in that dreadfull Ditch, which the Lord Jesus speakes of, but this sentence against him the Lord Jesus only pronounceth in His Church, His spirituall judicature, and executes this sentence in part at present and hereafter to all eternity: Such a sentence no Civill Judge can passe, such a Death no Civill sword can inflict.

I answer secondly, Dead men cannot be infected, the civill state, the world, being in a naturall state dead in sin (what ever be the State Religion unto which persons are forced) it is impossible it should be infected: Indeed the living, the beleeving, the Church and spirituall state, that and that onely is capable of infection; for whose helpe we shall presently see what preservatives, and remedies the Lord Jesus hath appointed.

Moreover as we see in a common plague or infection the names are taken how many are to dye, and not one more shall be strucke, then the destroying Angel hath the names of. So here, what ever be the soule infection breathed out from they [the] lying lips of a plague-sicke Pharisee, yet the names are taken, not one elect or chosen of God shall perish, Gods sheep are safe in His eternall hand and counsell, and he that knowes his materiall, knows also his mysticall stars, their numbers, and calls them every one by name, none fall into the Ditch on the blinde Pharises backe, but such as were ordained to that condemnation, both guid and followers [1 Peter 2: 8; Jude 4]. The vessells of wrath shall breake and split, and only they to the praise of Gods eternall justice [Romans 9].

Chapter 34

Peace: But it is said, be it granted that in a common plague or infection none are smitten and dye but such as are appointed, yet it is not only every mans duty, but the common duty of the Magistrate to prevent infection, and to preserve the common health of the place; likewise though the number of the Elect be sure, and God knowes who are His, yet hath He appointed meanes for their preservation from perdition and from infection, and therefore the Angel is blamed for suffering Balaams doctrine, and Jesabel to seduce Christ Jesus His servants [Revelation 2; Titus 3: 10; Romans 16: 17].

Truth: I answer, Let that Scripture and that of Titus reject an Hereticke, and Romans 16: 17 avoid them that are contentious, &c. let them, and al of like nature be examined, and it will appeare that the great and good Physitian Christ Jesus, the Head of the Body, and King of the Church hath not been unfaithfull in providing spirituall antidotes and preservatives against the spirituall sicknesses, sores, weaknesses, dangers of his Church and people; but he never appointed the civill sword for either antidote or remedy, as an addition to those spiritualls, which he hath left with his wife, his Church or People.

Hence how great is the bondage, the captivity of Gods owne People to Babylonish or confused mixtures in Worship, and unto worldly and earthly policies to uphold State Religions or Worships, since that which is written to the Angel and Church at Pergamus, shall be interpreted as sent to the Governour and City of Pergamus, and that which is sent to Titus, and the Church of Christ at Creet must be delivered to the civill officers and City thereof.

But as the Civill Magistrate hath his charge of the bodies and goods of the subject: So have the spirituall Officers, Governours and overseers of Christs City or Kingdome, the charge of their souls, and soule safety: Hence that charge of Paul to Timothy [1 Timothy 5: 20]. Them that sinne rebuke before all, that others may learne to fear. This is in the Church of Christ a spirituall meanes for the healing of a soule that hath sinned, or taken infection, and for the preventing of the infecting of others, that others may learne to feare, &c.

Samuel Rutherford, "The State of the Question of Compulsion of Conscience, and Tolleration" (1649)

Bishop Reginald Heber wrote of this work that it "is perhaps the most elaborate defense of persecution which has ever appeared in a Protestant country."[2] Rutherford (1600–61) was the presbyterian minister of Anwoth in the south-west of Scotland before being exiled in 1637 on account of his non-conformity under the episcopalian regime. After the revolution of 1638 he was sent to St Andrews University as professor of divinity, and accompanied other leading covenanters to London in 1643. Here he defines the magisterial role in the compulsion of true religion, which cannot include tampering with the interior person; the magistrate can, however, protect the public integrity of religion and the sensibilities of true believers.

Rutherford's book production suffered from a lack of editorial precision, and readers who attempt to follow carefully his system of numbered points may quickly find themselves confused.

SOURCE: Samuel Rutherford, *A Free Disputation Against Pretended Liberty of Conscience* (London, 1649), pp. 46–58.

LITERATURE: Wilbur K. Jordan, *The Development of Religious Toleration in England*, 4 vols (London: George Allen & Unwin, 1932–40), vol. III, pp. 292–7; William M. Campbell, *The Triumph of Presbyterianism* (Edinburgh: St Andrew Press, 1958), ch. 9.

Chapter 4   The State of the Question of Compulsion of Conscience, and Tolleration

The question touching Libertie of conscience was never by us, nor any man, save Libertines themselves and ignorant Anabaptists both of old and late, moved concerning internall libertie remaining within the soule, as libertie to think, understand, judge, conclude, whether the Magistrate can force men with the sword to opinions and cudgell them out of some into other contrary judgments in the matters of God, for the Magistrate cannot take on him, yea nor the Church under the paine of censures, compell any to think well of Christ, or ill of Antichrist. Yet most of the senslesse arguments of the times are drawn from the immediate subjection of the conscience to God from the nature of conscience, Religion, faith, fear, and the elicit acts of the soul which cannot be compelled, yea in the meaning, we think God can neither offer violence to minde, understanding, will or affections of love, fear, joy, because all these elicit acts cannot flow from any principle, but the internall and vitall inclinations of the soul, though the devils be said to beleeve against their will, yet not against the inclination of the understanding or desiring facultie.

[1?] All the question is concerning the imperated acts and these externall, that is not touching opinions and acts of the minde, but that which is visible and audible in these opinions, to wit, the speaking, professed holding of them, publishing, teaching, printing, and known and externall perswading of others to be of our minde. So that the question will come to this, whether the Magistrates sword be to regulate our words that concern our neighbor, as that we lie not, we forsweare not, to the hurt of the life and credit of our neighbor, that we slander not, raile upon no man, farre lesse against the prince and ruler of the people, but whether the words we utter or publish of God though never such blasphemies, and lies, because they come from the conscience (as if truths or words we speak for or against our neighbor did not flow from a conscience either good or ill) be above or beyond all swords or coercive power of men. It is clear the question must be thus stated, for all the lawes of the old Testament (which we hold in their morall equitie to be perpetuall) that are touching blasphemies, heresies, solicitation to worship false Gods and the breach of which the Godly Magistrate was to punish, command or forbid onely such things as may be proved by two or three witnesses, and which husband and wife are not to conceale, and from which all Israel must abstain for fear of the like punishment [Deuteronomy 13: 8–11; 17: 5–6; Leviticus 20: 1–5]. But opinions in the minde, acts of the understanding, can never be proved by witnesses and such as neither Magistrate nor Church can censure.

Then we referre to all the Godly, if Libertines and Anabaptists deal brotherly in affirming that Presbiterians persecute them, because out of tendernesse of conscience, they cannot come up to the light and judgment of their brethren in all opinions.

(2)   There is a tolleration pollitick and Civil and spirituall or Ecclesiastick shame and fear in punishing heresies either by the Judge or the Church, whether in civil or Ecclesiasticall censures, rebukes, Excommunication is an evil of punishment in both, as is evident, if we compare Judges 18: 7, Where it is said, There was no Magistrate in the land that might put them to shame in anything. Deuteronomy 13: 11, with these places that speaketh of spirituall censures, in the feare and shame of them as 1 Timothy 5: 19, Receive not an accusation against an Elder, but before two or three witnesses, then an Elder that is scandalous may incur shame of being accused. And Matthew 18: 17, let him be to thee as a heathen and a Publicane. 1 Timothy 5: 20, Them that sinne, rebuke before all, that others also may fear. So the avoiding of Idolaters, and Hereticks, 1 Corinthians 9: 11; Titus 2: 1–2; John 10; Galatians 1: 8, brings publicke shame on them, 2 Thessalonians 3: 14. Then looke what forcing power the same Magistrates can put Hereticks to, and what compulsory influence it hath on the conscience and should not be inflicted on men for their conscience and holding of heresies, as Libertines say, the same compulsorie power hath concionall rebukes of Pastors or private Christians, and of admonition, excommunication, or the avoiding

of the societie of false teachers either by the whole Church or by private
Christians, and the arguments proving the Magistrate cannot punish for
conscience in his politick Spheare, doe also prove that hereticks should be
rebuked sharply that they may be found sound in the faith, contrary to
Titus 1: 13 and that we should neither admonish them nor avoid their
company which is absurd; so they be more ingenious Libertines who free
false teachers and hereticks from both civil and ecclesiasticall censures, than
these who free them from civil and subject them to Ecclesiasticall censures,
for Ecclesiasticall compulsion hath no more influence on the conscience by
way of teaching then politick or civil, and the arguments taken from the
nature of conscience is as strong to prove that the Church of Pergamus,
Ephesus, Thyatira should suffer lyars, false Apostles and seducers, such as
hold the doctrine of Balaam and Jezabel the deceiving Prophetesse, who
teach and professe according to their erroneous conscience contrary to
Revelation, chapters 1–3, 14, 20, as that the Godly Prince should suffer
them: nor can it be said that Church-censures are spirituall punishments
and so work on the spirit, and have instructing, rebuking and exhorting
going before, but the sword is a bodily punishment, and hath not instructing going before. For I answer, though these two punishments differ, yet
they agree that formally both are alike compulsory of the conscience, and
neither of them act upon the spirit by teaching and instructing as the word
doth, so as excommunication of a heretick should have instructing and
convincing going before, so should also the Magistrate presuppose, before
he strike with the sword, that the false teacher hath been instructed and
convinced, and so he doth formally punish him with the sword, for his
pertinacious perverting of souls.

(3)   Nor can it be replyed that men should not be punished for either
opinions, or for holding opinions that flow from meer conscience, when
they publish preach and print them from no principle, but meer conscience,
not for gain or a morsell of bread, or for preferment in the state or Armie.
To this I answer, lay aside opinions and answer me this, how the Judges
that are for libertie of conscience are not to punish some words except they
would be guilty of persecution, to wit, such as these, the Trinitie is but a
fiction, Christ is no more God then another holy man. Yea, Christ was but
an Imposter, and yet they punish words and deeds of the same kinde that
come from mere conscience. The answer must be, the former words are
from mere conscience and the publishers thereof will swear they hold them
as the mere inforcing light and judgment of their conscience. But these
other words and deeds which the Magistrate censures, are not from meere
conscience. But I beleeve these that acted in the late controverted Parliament and by vertue thereof, yea and many Godly men of them that are

punished by the Judges and many of the Godly that fled for fear act from meere conscience, and will sweare they did so act according to their sworn covenant, and to prevent a new warre: and that they did it neither for gain, not for preferment in State or Armie. And if it were referred to the consciences of most of the Armie why they disbanded not when the Parliament commanded them, but doe by their practices treat a warre to themselves and the land (a judgment of God of all others the saddest) when they have none to fight against but shadows and enemies of straw and hay; I judge they would swear that they judged the charge of the Houses against their conscience, and unjust, and that they hold up warres out of meere conscience, and to vindicate the oppressed subjects and for preventing of a new warre, and not for gaine or preferment. So the question is not yet answered; why some externall actions of words and deeds comming from meere conscience without any carnall pretext, as they will swear cannot be punished, but violence must be done to conscience, so the men persecuted, and others that doe the like and speak the like from no principle but pure conscience, without any carnall pretext, as they will sweare, are punished and yet neither violence is done to conscience nor the men persecuted, for acting according to conscience and a sworn Covenant. But they [are] justly punished: if acting from meere Conscience be the formall cause why men are not to be punished, it should hold in all such acts.

(4)   They seeme to me sick in the braine, who hold that it is an act of love and charity in the Magistrate to restrain Arrianisme, Socinianisme &c. and to discountenance such seducers, and yet bring arguments against all externall forces in matters of Religion or compulsion in generall: a discountenancing and a keeping of men from places, dignities, offices, is the highest compulsion of penaltie you can devise. What arguments fight against any compulsion of the Magistrate positive or negative doth fight against all. If it be lawfull for the Magistrate, as for all other men, to doe all hee can for the truth as some say, and the Magistrates invitations, recommendation, exemplarie profession, generall tuition, excluding coercing, are all nothing but words, these agree to all Christians as Christians and are nothing peculiar to the Magistrate, the Magistrate as a Magistrate cannot request, he must command as a Magistrate, and all his commands if disobeyed, are in order to the sword.

(5)   The question is not whether Religion can be inforced upon men by the Magistrate by the dint and violence of the sword, or onely perswaded by the power of the word. We hold with Lactantius that Religion cannot be compelled, nor can mercie and justice and love to our neighbor commanded in the second table, be more compelled then faith in Christ. Hence give

me leave to prove two things. (1) That Religion and faith cannot be forced
on men. (2) That this a vain consequence; Religion cannot be forced but
must be perswaded by the word and Spirit, *Ergo* the Magistrate can use no
coercive power in punishing Hereticks and false teachers.

For the first, we lay hold on all the arguments that prove the word
preached to be the onely means of converting the soule, begetting of faith
and that carnall weapons are not able, yea nor were they ever appointed of
God, to ding [knock] down strongholds, nor can they make a willing people:
and Lactantius said well, What is left to us, if anothers lust extort that by
force, which we must doe willingly? And that of Tertullian. It is of the law
or right of man and of his naturall power what every man worships, what he
thinks he should worship, nor doth the Religion of one either doe good or
doe evill to another man, nor is it religion to compell religion, which ought
to be received by will not by force: since sacrifices (of worship) are required
of a willing minde. In which I observe: (1) Tertullian speaks not of the true
Christian Religion which is now in question: but of Religion in generall as
it is comprehensive of both true and false Religion. Because he speakes of
that Religion which by the Law of nature a man chooseth, and is *humani
juris & naturalis potestatis*: but it is not of the law of man or naturall power,
nor in flesh and bloods power to chuse the true Christian Religion, that
election is Supernaturall saith Tertullian there and else where often, as also
the Scripture, John 6: 44; Matthew 16: 17; Matthew 11: 25–7; (2) Religion
is taken two wayes. . . . For the inward and outward acts of Religion as seen
both to God and man as Lactantius, Tertullian and others say, so it is most
true. Christians ought not with force of sword, compell Jews, nor Jews or
Pagans compell Christians to be of their Religion, because Religion is not
begotten in any, by perswasion of the minde, nor by forcing of the man.
Again Religion is taken for the externall profession and acting and performances of true Religion within the Church or by such as professe the
truth, that are obvious to the eyes of Magistrates and pastors, and thus the
sword is no meanes of God to force men positively to externall worship or
performances. But the sword is a means negatively to punish acts of false
worship in those that are under the Christian Magistrate and professe
Christian Religion, in so farre as these acts come out to the eyes of men and
are destructive to the souls of these in a Christian society; tis even so (& not
otherwise punishable by the Magistrate;) for he may punish omissions of
hearing the Doctrine of the Gospel and other externall performances of
worship, as these omissions by ill example or otherwise are offensive to the
souls of these that are to lead a quiet and peaceable life in all godlinesse and
honestie; nor does it follow that the sword is a kindly means to force
outward performances, for the Magistrate as the Magistrate does not command these outward performances as service to God, but rather forbids

the omissions of them as destructive to man, for example a Physician commands fasting, Pastors after the example of Jesus commands fasting when judgments are on us, the physician commands it, in so farre as eating troubles the common societie of humors, members and temper of the body, and the Physician forbids eating so as he will have no more to do with the patient, if he will disobey: and so trouble the temper of the bodie, which is the onely object the physician works on. Pastors command fasting to be in sincerity for afflicting and humbling the soul under the mightie hand of God. So the Magistrate forbids cutting of a veine or shedding of blood as a thing troubling the peace of humane societie, yet his command is not a direct means of preventing diseases in the bodie of a subject and for healthie living. But the Physician commands to cut a veine and to shed blood for health and to prevent a disease, and sinnes neither against the Magistrate nor God in so doing: so doth the Magistrate not directly command going to Church as a worship to God, so as his commands have influence on the conscience as the pastors commands have, but he commands going to Church and hearing so as the omission of hearing hurts the societie whereof God hath made him a civill and politick head: in this latter sense must Lactantius, Tertullian and others be taken, otherwise these words, the Religion of another does his neighbour neither good nor ill in rigor, are not true, the ill example of others in Idolatrie brings ill upon all the Church, Deuteronomy 13: 5, yea and the fierce anger of God, v. 17.

Again Lactantius saith "false Religion cannot be compelled," but he denyes not that Christians may punish blasphemies in true religion. (2) He denyes we may propagate the Gospel among Pagans with the sword: both which points we teach. "There is no need (saith he) of force and injurie, because Religion cannot be compelled, the businesse is to be transacted by words rather than blowes, that there may be willingnesse. Let them (enemies of the truth) draw the sword of sharpnesse of their wit: if their reason be good, let it be produced: we are ready to heare, if they teach (nothing more cleare then that he speaks of the Pagans that would force Pagans' worship on Christians): we believe nothing of their Religion while they are silent, as we cannot yeeld to them while they rage against us, let them imitate us, and declare the reason of the whole matter, for we (Christians) doe not allure, as they (Pagans) frequently object to us, but we teach, we prove, we demonstrate: therefore none by us are kept against their will, for he is unprofittable to God who wants devotion and faith: and yet no man departs from us when the truth detains him."

But saith Celsus,[3] fol. 84, "if in the time of Lactantius Christians killed men for their religion, no man can doubt but Lactantius in these same generall words inveighs against Christians who would compell men to their faith against their will, and that he abhorres the violence of ours against hereticks."

Answer   These are of a wide difference, to kill blasphemers, and false teachers for spreading hersies and blasphemies; and to compell them by warre, and fire and sword to be of our Christian Religion. As I hope to prove, for the former is lawfull, the latter unlawfull. Its true Lactantius speaks of all Religion true and false, that we are to compell none with the sword to any Religion, but he no where saith that the Magistrates may not kill open and pernicious seducers and false teachers who pervert others, for the Magistrate is not to compell yea nor to intend the conversion of a pernicious seducer, but to intend to take his head from him, for his destroying of souls. And Lactantius denyes Religion after it is begotten, can be defended, that is nourished and served in the hearts of people by the sword, but by the word and spirit. "Those are farre different, tormenting and pietie (saith he) nor can violence be conjoyned with veritie, nor justice with crueltie."

And again, "but as in Religion, so also in defending of Religion they are deceived; Religion is to be defended not by killing but admonishing, others read, by being killed, not by crueltie, but by patience, not by wickednesse, but by faith."

But here he speaks of defending in a hostile way, by killing those that will not be of our Religion, be it the Pagan religion and most devilish, not of defending the Christian professors from the infection of wolvish seducers, by the sword of the Nurse-father of the Church, who is to defend good men and to execute vengeance on evill doers. For in all this Lactantius speaks of such a violence as is without teaching, *parati sumus audire si doceant tacentibus certe nihil credimus.*[4] But suppose some fathers were in that errour (as Augustine was, but retracted it) though Augustine affirme we may compell men to the faith, yet he speaks of improper compassion, and of Donatists and such as are within the Church, whom he thinks the Magistrate ought to punish, which is not a compelling of the seducer to the sound faith, but an act of justice in punishing him for his spreading of heresies to the perverting of the faith of others. Upon these grounds Cyrillus[5] saith, Moses' Law is gone and the Kingdom of Christ is wholly heavenly, and spirituall, and therefore hath spirituall sacrifices and spirituall armour: "and therefore a spirituall not a carnal sword to punish the enemies of this Kingdom, becomes Christian men." But he speaks of enemies without the Church (who as I constantly hold) are not with warres and the sword to be compelled to embrace the Christian Religion and therefore aideth on the contrary. Israel did fight against Amorites, Canaanites and Jebusites with weapons of iron: but he speaks not of the Laws, Deuteronomy 13: 17; Leviticus 24, and such, in which death was decreed for the false Prophet within the visible Church. At sometimes the fathers have complyed with unsound Emperours who have tollerated, Naestorians, Arrians, and Jews, but that is no law for us.

But the other point is that though these that are without are not to be compelled to embrace the true Religion it followeth not that the Magistrate should not coerce false Prophets, or pernicious teachers, such as Baals Priests, who openly seduce the people of God to Idolatrie. (1) Because the Magistrate cannot, nor ought not to compell evildoers, murtherers, adulterers, robbers, lyars, to be internally peaceable, chaste, content with their own as well as they must be such externally, no more then he can compell them to inward fear, love, faith in God, and to the externall performances thereof. But it doth not follow that therefore the Magistrate cannot command externall acts of mercie, chastitie, selfe-contentednesse, and should not punish murther, adulterie, theft, robberie, perjurie, for to punish these makes many hypocritically peaceable, chast, content with their own, true in their word, as well as punishing false teachers and hereticks maketh many hypocritically sound in the faith. So Augustine contra Petilian, bk 3, ch. 32. (2) There is no ground in Scripture to say that because the Canaanites erred against the duties of the first table onely, that therefore Israel was to destroy them in warre. For Joshua 11: 26–8, the contrarie is clear, Joshua made warre with them, because God having hardened their heart they came out in battle against Israel: and so the cause of the warre was not Religion and their madnesse of Idolatrie (though on the Lords part it was a provoking cause) but violence in invading an harmelesse and innocent people, so Joshua and Israel compelled them not to embrace the true Religion, then from thence it cannot follow therefore no lawes were to be made against the false Prophets and blasphemer. And if that consequence was null then, it cannot be strong now. So we say under the new Testament: we cannot bring in to the faith the Heathen and pagans by violence and the sword, it follows not, *Ergo*, no blasphemer within the visible Church should be forced. (3) Violence and the sword is no means to work men to subjection to Christ, it follows not, *Ergo* because the weapons of our warfare are not carnall, but spirituall, 2 Corinthians 10: 5–6, the Apostle should not say "shall I come unto you with the rod or in love, or in the spirit of meeknesse," 1 Corinthians 4: 21, and therefore he should not deliver any to Sathan. (4) Nor is this a good consequence, because the fear of bodily death or punishment by the sword cannot convert, therefore it cannot terrifie men from externall blasphemie and tempting of others to false worship, for the externall man his words, solicitations, doe ill by teaching, and his actions, not the inward man or the conscience and the soule is the object the magistrate is to work on. For neither under Moses more then now, could the sword convert men to the true Religion, yet bodily death was to be inflicted on the seducer, then, as now, Deut. 13: 11, "And all Israell shall hear, and fear, and shall doe no more any such wickednesse as this is among you:" and afflictions work the same way now, Rom. 13: 3, "for rulers are not a terrour to good works but to the evil, wilt thou then not be afraid of the power? doe that which is good, and thou shalt have praise of the same."

There be five pull-backs that keep men even in heresie and in a false way, as may be collected out of Augustines writings from which by the terrour of just lawes, they may be affrighted from seducing of others as (1) fear of offending men especially those of their own way; (2) an hardning custome in a false way. (3) a wicked sluggishnesse in not searching the truth of God. (4) the wicked tongues of enemies that shall traduce them, if they leave heresies. (5) a vaine perswasion that men may be saved in any Religion . . . [1?] And so that which the Objector Mr John Goodwine long agoe objected is easily answered, that the "Magistrate cannot in justice punish that which is unavoydable and above the power of free-will to resist, but such are all heresies and errours of the minde." For this might well have been objected against that most just law, Deuteronomy 13, why should God command to stone to death a seducer that tempts any of his people to worship false Gods, because such a man is sick but of an errour in the minde, he beleeves he does service to his God, whom he beleeves to be the true God, in so doing, and had the heathen and Jews under Moses more strength of free-will and more grace to resist Apostacie, Blasphemie, wicked opinions against the true God, then we have now under the Gospel. And the Lord hath expressely said, Deuteronomy 13: 11, "Israel shall feare (bodily death) and doe such wickednesse no more:" now this was not Ceremoniall or typicall fear, but mere naturall feare sufficient to retract and withdraw men from externall acts of seducing and blaspheming, which is all that the Magistrate can doe. (2) This is the verie objection of Donatists and Augustine answers truely. By this answer the Magistrate should not punish murtherers and adulterers for they have not grace to resist temptation to murther, certainly the Spirit of Revenge, and of whoredoms must be as strong above free will as the Spirit of errour and lies. Achab then sinned not in beleeving the lying Prophets who deceived him: and it was not in his power to resist the efficacie of lying inflicted on him for his former sins. And what sinnes the Magistrate punisheth he doth punish as the formall Minister of God, Romans 13, and so this is the Pelagian, Arminian and Popish objection against God and free Grace, as much as against us. (3) The wickedest seducer is punished for his externall acts of false teaching and seducing which may, and must be proved by witnesse or confessed by the delinquent, before he can justly punish him, but not for any mind-error which is obvious neither to judge nor witnesse.

Then the true state of the question is not [1] whether the sword be a means of conversion of men to the true faith, not (2) whether heathen by fire and sword are to be compelled to embrace the truth, nor (3) whether violence without instruction and arguing from light of Scriptures, should be used against false teachers, nor (4) whether the Magistrate can punish the opinions of the mind, and straine internall liberty. But whether or no ought the Godly and Christian Prince restraine & punish with the sword false teachers, publishers of hereticall and pernicious doctrine, which may be proved by witnesse, and tends to the injuring of the souls of the people of God, in Christian societies, and are dishonorable to God, and contrary to sound doctrine; and so coerce men for externall misdemeanors flowing from a practicall conscience sinning aginst the second table, as well as from a speculative conscience (to borrow these tearmes here) when they professe and are ready to swear they performe these externalls meerely from and for conscience. For since false teachers and hereticks in regard of the spiritualnesse of their sinne are the worst of evill doers, and such as work abomination in the Israel of God, and there is no particular lawes in the New Testament for bodily coercing of Sorcerers, Adulterers, Thieves, Traitors, false witnesses, who but speakes against the good name of their neighbor, not against the name of God, nor against Sodomites, defilers of their bodies with beasts, perjured persons, Covenant breakers, liars &c. What reason in nature can there be to punish the one, and not the other? For it may with as good color of reason be said, that all the Lawes in the old Testament, for drawing of the sword against Sodomites, Adulterers and such like, were typicall and temporary, and are done away now in Christ, for Christ will have these converted in as spirituall a way by the onely power of the word of God as the other and no where in any expresse law in the New Testament doth God command to use the bloody sword against them, more then against blasphemers: And to remove these grosse sins out of Christian societies by the sword is no lesse a carnall and a bodily afflictive way of dealing with their consciences, as to to deal so with seducers; and tis enough to that negative argument, "that no where it is expressed as a dutie of the Magistrate, under the New Testament to use the sword against false teachers, nor does our Savior or the Apostles rebuke the Magistrate for omitting of their dutie in this." Yea Paul, 1 Corinthians 6: 9–11, when he shewes that some of the Corinthians abused their body with mankinde, were theevis, drunkards, extortioners, he no where saith that it was the Magistrates dutie to take away their head for Sodomie, which certainly it was, and that by the verie law of nature, but he was Gods instruments for their conversion by the power of the word, ver. 11 and 1 Corinthians 4: 15, as he labored to convert the Galathians who sometimes worshipped dumb Idols, and the Ephesians who worshipped the vaine Idol Diana, Acts 19, yea, nor is there any New Testament law for taking away the life of a murtherer, for that of our Saviors, Matthew 26: 52, "all they that take the sword shall perish with the sword," except we say it was so a Judiciall law among the Jews, as it was a law of nature, Genesis 9, before there was a Common wealth erected

among the Jews, cannot be called a new Testament law, to Peter and John
and the disciples who were obliged at that same verie time to keepe the
passeover and to be subject to all the Jewish laws.

John Milton, *Civil Power in Ecclesiastical Causes* (1659)

Milton (1608–74) had much in common with the sectarians of his time.
His theology wandered at times from orthodoxy, he repudiated both
bishops and presbyteries, he celebrated the Bible above all other religious
authorities, he acknowledged the necessity of religious commitment rooted
in conscience. But he drew back from some even more advanced positions (e.g., Williams'). He could find no place for Roman Catholics in his
tolerant state, and his "preoccupation with true religion" gave a role to the
Christian magistrate not seen amongst the most radical defenders of
religious liberty. Milton's more humanistic view of redemption meant that
if all were capable of it, then it might be necessary for the Christian as
magistrate to nudge his subjects in the right direction, though given the
latitude entailed by his Protestant principle, such action would be limited
to a few instances of scandalous behavior by those whose lives were not
at all directed by the sincere search for truth.

SOURCE: John Milton, *A Treatise of Civil Power in Ecclesiastical Causes*, in *The Prose
Works of John Milton*, 5 vols (London, 1848–53), vol. II, pp. 523–9, 544–5, 546.
LITERATURE: Don M. Wolfe, *Milton in the Puritan Revolution* (London: Cohen and West,
1963 [1941]), ch. 2; Arthur E. Barker, *Milton and the Puritan Dilemma, 1641–1660*
(Toronto: University of Toronto Press, 1976 [1942]), ch. 14.

It will require no great labor of exposition to unfold what is here meant by
matters of religion; being as soon apprehended as defined, such things as
belong chiefly to the knowledge and service of God; and are either above the
reach and light of nature without revelation from above, and therefore liable
to be variously understood by human reason, or such things as are enjoined
or forbidden by divine precept, which else by the light of reason would
seem indifferent to be done or not done; and so likewise must needs appear
to every man as the precept is understood. Whence I here mean by conscience or religion that full persuasion, whereby we are assured, that our
belief and practice, as far as we are able to apprehend and probably make
appear, is according to the will of God and his Holy Spirit within us, which
we ought to follow much rather than any law of man, as not only his word
everywhere bids us, but the very dictate of reason tells us [Acts 4: 19]:
"Whether it be right in the sight of God, to hearken to you more than to

God, judge ye." That for belief or practice in religion, according to this conscientious persuasion, no man ought to be punished or molested by any outward force on earth whatsoever, I distrust not, through God's implored assistance, to make plain by these following arguments.

First, it cannot be denied, being the main foundation of our protestant religion, that we of these ages, having no other divine rule or authority from without us, warrantable to one another as a common ground, but the holy scripture, and no other within us but the illumination of the Holy Spirit, so interpreting that scripture as warrantable only to ourselves, and to such whose consciences we can so persuade, can have no other ground in matters of religion but only from the scriptures. And these being not possible to be understood without this divine illumination, which no man can know at all times to be in himself, much less to be at any time for certain in any other, it follows clearly, that no man or body of men in these times can be the infallible judges or determiners in matters of religion to any other men's consciences but their own. And therefore those Bereans are commended [Acts 17: 11], who after the preaching even of St Paul, "searched the scriptures daily, whether those things were so." Nor did they more than what God himself in many places commands us by the same apostle, to search, to try, to judge of these things ourselves: and gives us reason also [Galatians 6: 4–5]: "Let every man prove his own work, and then shall he have rejoicing in himself alone, and not in another: for every man shall bear his own burden." If then we count it so ignorant and irreligious in the papist, to think himself discharged in God's account, believing only as the church believes, how much greater condemnation will it be to the protestant his condemner, to think himself justified, believing only as the state believes? With good cause, therefore, it is the general consent of all sound protestant writers, that neither traditions, councils, nor canons of any visible church, much less edicts of any magistrate or civil session, but the scripture only, can be the final judge or rule in matters of religion, and that only in the conscience of every Christian to himself. Which protestation made by the first public reformers of our religion against the imperial edicts of Charles the Fifth, imposing church traditions without scripture, gave first beginning to the name of Protestant; and with that name hath ever been received this doctrine, which prefers the scripture before the church, and acknowledges none but the scripture sole interpreter of itself to the conscience. For if the church be not sufficient to be implicitly believed, as we hold it is not, what can there else be named of more authority than the church but the conscience, than which God only is greater? [1 John 3: 20]. But if any man shall pretend that the scripture judges to his conscience for other men, he makes himself greater not only than the church, but also than the scripture, than the consciences of other men: a presumption too high for any mortal, since every true Christian able to give a reason of his faith, hath the word of God before him, the promised Holy Spirit, and the mind of Christ within him [1 Corinthians 2: 16], a much better and safer guide of conscience, which as far as concerns himself he may far more certainly know, than any outward rule imposed upon him by others, whom he inwardly neither knows nor can know; at least knows nothing of them more sure than this one thing, that they cannot be his judges in religion [1 Corinthians 2: 15]: "The spiritual man judgeth all things, but he himself is judged of no man." Chiefly for this cause do all true protestants account the pope antichrist, for that he assumes to himself this infallibility over both the conscience and the scripture; "sitting in the temple of God," as it were opposite to God, "and exalting himself above all that is called God, or is worshipped" [2 Thessalonians 2: 4]. That is to say, not only above all judges and magistrates, who though they be called gods, are far beneath infallible; but also above God himself, by giving law both to the scripture, to the conscience, and to the Spirit itself of God within us. Whenas we find [James 4: 12]: "There is one lawgiver, who is able to save and to destroy: Who art thou that judgest another?" That Christ is the only lawgiver of his church, and that it is here meant in religious matters, no well-grounded Christian will deny. Thus also St Paul [Romans 14: 4]: "Who art thou that judgest the servant of another? to his own lord he standeth or falleth: but he shall stand; for God is able to make him stand." As therefore of one beyond expression bold and presumptuous, both these apostles demand, "Who art thou," that presumest to impose other law or judgment in religion than the only lawgiver and judge Christ, who only can save and destroy, gives to the conscience? And the forecited place to the Thessalonians, by compared effects, resolves us, that be he or they who or wherever they be or can be, they are of far less authority than the church, whom in these things as protestants they receive not, and yet no less antichrist in this main point of antichristianism, no less a pope or popedom than he at Rome, if not much more, by setting up supreme interpreters of scripture either those doctors whom they follow, or, which is far worse, themselves as a civil papacy assuming unaccountable supremacy to themselves, not in civil only, but in ecclesiastical causes. Seeing then that in matters of religion, as hath been proved, none can judge or determine here on earth, no, not church governors themselves, against the consciences of other believers, my inference is, or rather not mine but our Savior's own, that in those matters they neither can command nor use constraint, lest they run rashly on a pernicious consequence, forewarned in that parable [Matthew 13: 29–30]: "Lest while ye gather up the tares, ye root up also the wheat with them. Let both grow together until the harvest: and in the time of harvest I will say to the reapers, Gather ye together first the tares," &c. Whereby he declares, that this work neither his own ministers nor any else can discerningly enough or judgingly perform without his own immediate direction, in his own fit season; and that they ought till then not to attempt it. Which is further confirmed [2 Corinthians 1: 24]: "Not that we have dominion over your faith, but are helpers of your joy." If apostles had no dominion or constraining power over faith or conscience, much less have ordinary ministers [1 Peter 5: 2–3]: "Feed the flock of God &c., not by constraint, neither as being lords over God's heritage." But some will object, that this overthrows all church discipline, all censure of errors, if no man can determine. My answer is, that what they hear is plain scripture, which forbids not church sentence or determining, but as it ends in violence upon the conscience unconvinced. Let whoso will interpret or determine, so it be according to true church discipline, which is exercised on them only who have willingly joined themselves in that covenant of union, and proceeds only to a separation from the rest, proceeds never to any corporal enforcement or forfeiture of money, which in all spiritual things are the two arms of Antichrist, not of the true church; the one being an inquisition, the other no better than a temporal indulgence of sin for money, whether by the church exacted or by the magistrate; both the one and the other a temporal satisfaction for what Christ hath satisfied eternally; a popish commuting of penalty, corporal for spiritual; a satisfaction to man, especially to the magistrate, for what and to whom we owe none: these and more are the injustices of force and fining in religion, besides what I most insist on, the violation of God's express commandment in the gospel, as hath been shown. Thus then, if church governors cannot use force in religion, though but for this reason, because they cannot infallibly determine to the conscience without convincement, much less have civil magistrates authority to use force where they can much less judge; unless they mean only to be the civil executioners of them who have no civil power to give them such commission, no, nor yet ecclesiastical, to any force or violence in religion. To sum up all in brief, if we must believe as the magistrate appoints, why not rather as the church? If not as either without convincement, how can force be lawful? But some are ready to cry out, what shall then be done to blasphemy? Them I would first exhort, not thus to terrify and pose the people with a Greek word; but to teach them better what it is, being a most usual and common word in that language to signify any slander, any malicious or evil speaking, whether against God or man, or anything to good belonging: blasphemy or evil speaking against God maliciously, is far from conscience in religion, according to that of Mark 9: 39, "There is none who doth a powerful work in my name, and can lightly speak evil of me." If this suffice not, I refer them to that prudent and well deliberated act, August 9, 1650, where the parliament defines blasphemy against God, as far as it is a crime belonging to civil judicature, *plenius ac melius Chrysippo et Crantore*; in plain English, more warily, more judiciously, more orthodoxally than twice their number of divines have done in many a prolix volume: although in all likelihood they whose whole study and profession these things are, should be most intelligent and authentic therein, as they are for the most part; yet neither they nor these unerring always, or infallible. But we shall not carry it thus; another Greek apparition stands in our way, Heresy and Heretic; in like manner also railed at to the people as in a tongue unknown. They should first interpret to them that heresy, by what it signifies in that language, is no word of evil note, meaning only the choice or following of any opinion good or bad, in religion, or any other learning; and thus not only in heathen authors, but in the New Testament itself, without censure or blame; Acts 15: 5, "Certain of the heresy of the pharisees which believed;" and 26: 5, "After the exactest heresy of our religion I lived a pharisee." In which sense presbyterian or independent may without reproach be called a heresy. Where it is mentioned with blame, it seems to differ little from schism [1 Corinthians 11: 18–19]: "I hear that there be schisms among you," &c. "for there must also heresies be among you," &c. Though some, who write of heresy after their own heads, would make it far worse then schism; whenas on the contrary, schism signifies division, and in the worst sense; heresy, choice only of one opinion before another, which may be without discord. In apostolic times, therefore, ere the scripture was written, heresy was a doctrine maintained against the doctrine by them delivered; which in these times can be no otherwise defined than a doctrine maintained against the light which we now only have of the scripture. Seeing, therefore, that no man, no synod, no session of men, though called the church, can judge definitely the sense of scripture to another man's conscience, which is well known to be a general maxim of the protestant religion; it follows plainly, that he who holds in religion that belief, or those opinions, which to his conscience and utmost understanding appear with most evidence or probability in the scripture, though to others he seem erroneous, can no more be justly censured for a heretic than his censurers; who do but the same thing themselves while they censure him for so doing. For ask them, or any protestant, which hath most authority, the church or the scripture? They will answer, doubtless, that the scripture: and what hath most authority, that no doubt but they will confess is to be followed. He then, who to his best apprehension follows the scripture, though against any point of doctrine by the whole church received, is not the heretic; but he who follows the church against his conscience and persuasion grounded on the scripture. To make this yet more undeniable, I shall only borrow a plain simile, the same which our own writers, when they would demonstrate plainest, that we rightly prefer the scripture before the church, use frequently against the papist in this manner. As the Samaritans believed Christ, first for the woman's word, but next and much rather for his own, so we the scripture: first on the church's word, but afterwards and much more for its own, as the word of God; yea, the church itself we believe then for the scripture. The inference of itself follows: If by the protestant doctrine we believe the scripture, not for the church's saying, but for its own, as the word of God, then ought we to believe what in our conscience we apprehend the scripture to say, though the visible church, with all her doctors, gainsay: and being taught to believe them only for the scripture, they who so do are not heretics, but the best protestants: and by their opinions, whatever they be, can hurt no protestant, whose rule is not to receive them but from the scripture: which to interpret convincingly to his own conscience, none is able but himself guided by the Holy Spirit; and not so guided, none than he to himself can be a worse deceiver. To protestants, therefore, whose common rule and touchstone is the scripture, nothing can with more conscience, more equity, nothing more protestantly can be permitted, than a free and lawful debate at all times by writing, conference, or disputation of what opinion soever, disputable by scripture: concluding that no man in religion is properly a heretic at this day, but he who maintains traditions or opinions not probable by scripture, who, for aught I know, is the papist only; he the only heretic, who counts all heretics but himself. Such as these, indeed, were capitally punished by the law of Moses, as the only true heretics, idolaters, plain and open deserters of God and his known law: but in the gospel such are punished by excommunion only. . . .

. . . To compel, therefore, the profane to things holy in his profaneness, is all one under the gospel, as to have compelled the unclean to sacrifice in his uncleanness under the law. And I add withal, that to compel the licentious in his licentiousness, and the conscientious against his conscience, comes all to one: tends not to the honor of God, but to the multiplying and the aggravating of sin to them both. We read not that Christ ever exercised force but once, and that was to drive profane ones out of his temple, not to force them in; and if their being there was an offense, we find by many other scriptures that their praying there was an abomination: and yet to the Jewish law, that nation, as a servant, was obliged; but to the gospel each person is left voluntary, called only, as a son, by the preaching of the word; not to be driven in by edicts and force of arms. For if by the apostle [Romans 12: 1] we are "beseeched as brethren by the mercies of God to present our bodies a living sacrifice, holy, acceptable to God, which is our reasonable service," or worship, then is no man to be forced by the compulsive laws of men to present his body a dead sacrifice; and so under the gospel most unholy and unacceptable, because it is his unreasonable service, that is to say, not only unwilling but unconscionable. But if profane and licentious persons may not omit the performance of holy duties, why may they not partake of holy things? Why are they prohibited the Lord's supper, since both the one and the other action may be outward; and outward performance of duty may attain at least an outward participation of benefit? The church denying them that communion of grace and thanksgiving, as it justly doth, why doth the magistrate compel them to the union of performing that which they neither truly can, being themselves unholy, and to do seemingly is both hateful to God, and perhaps no less dangerous to perform holy duties irreligiously, than to receive holy signs or sacraments unworthily? All profane and licentious men, so known, can be considered but either so without the church as never yet within it, or departed thence of their own accord, or excommunicate: if never yet within the church, whom the apostle, and so, consequently, the church have naught to do to judge, as he professes [1 Corinthians 5: 12] then by what authority doth the magistrate judge; or, which is worse, compel in relation to the church? If departed of his own accord, like that lost sheep [Luke 15: 4, &c.], the true church, either with her own or any borrowed force, worries him not in again, but rather in all charitable manner sends after him; and if she find him, lays him gently on her shoulders, bears him, yea, bears his burdens, his errors, his infirmities any way tolerable, "so fulfilling the law of Christ" [Galatians 6: 2]. If excommunicate, whom the church hath bid go out, in whose name doth the magistrate compel to go in? The church, indeed, hinders none from hearing in her public congregation, for the doors are open to all: nor excommunicates to destruction; but, as much as in her lies, to a final saving. Her meaning, therefore, must needs be, that as her driving out brings on no outward penalty, so no outward force or penalty of an improper and only a destructive power should drive in again her infectious sheep; therefore sent out because infectious, and not driven in but with the danger not only of the whole and sound, but also of his own utter perishing. Since force neither instructs in religion, nor begets repentance or amendment of life, but, on the contrary, hardness of heart, formality, hypocrisy, and, as I said before, every way increase of sin; more and more alienates the mind from a violent religion, expelling out and compelling in, and reduces it to a condition like that which the Britons complain of in our story, driven to and fro between the Picts and the sea. If, after excommunion, he be found intractable, incurable, and will not hear the church, he becomes as one never yet within her pale, "a heathen or a publican" [Matthew 18: 17], not further to be judged, no, not by the magistrate, unless for civil causes; but left to the final sentence of that Judge, whose coming shall be in flames of fire; . . . But grant it belonging any way to the magistrate, that profane and licentious persons omit not the performance of holy duties, which in them were odious to God even under the law, much more now under the gospel; yet ought his care both as a magistrate and a Christian, to be much more that conscience be not inwardly violated, than that license in these things be made outwardly conformable: since his part is undoubtedly as a Christian, which puts him upon this office much more than as a magistrate, in all respects to have more care of the conscientious than of the profane; and not for their sakes to take away (while they pretend to give) or to diminish the rightful liberty of religious consciences.

Henry More, "Of Liberty of Conscience" (1660[6])

More (1614–87) was one of a group of theologians and philosophers known as the Cambridge Platonists for their views about the immanence of truth; their preferred authorities included Plotinus and Origen, while they had little to say of Augustine and the Protestant reformers. More's theology was broad enough to embrace a variety of teachings about baptism. Still, he could be acerbic towards Roman Catholicism and certain forms of sectarianism, not least of all the Quakers, and he did not deny the magistrate's role in preserving national religious life, especially when reason was in danger of subversion by irrational enthusiasm.

SOURCE: Henry More, *An Explanation of the Grand Mystery of Godliness* (London, 1660), Book X, p. 10.
LITERATURE: Wilbur K. Jordan, *The Development of Religious Toleration in England*, 4 vols (London: George Allen & Unwin, 1932–40), vol. IV, pp. 94–137; C. A. Patrides (ed.), *The Cambridge Platonists* (Cambridge: Cambridge University Press, 1980), ch. 1.

Chapter 10

(1) Before we can well understand the Power of the Magistrate in matters of Religion, we must first consider the Common Right of mankind in this point, provided they be not degenerated into Atheisme and Profaneness. For he that believes there is no God, nor Reward, nor Punishment after this life, what plea can he have to Liberty of Conscience? or how improper is it to talk of his Right in matters of Religion, who professedly has no Religion at all, nor any tie of Conscience upon him to make that wicked profession? For Atheisme, as it is very coursely false in it self to any man that has the clear exercise of his Reason, so is it intolerably mischievous and destructive

even to the present Happiness of States and Kingdomes, and therefore to be shunned and repressed as the very plague and pest of humane Polities. But for those that seriously make profession of the Existence of God Creator of all things, and of his Providence, and acknowledging that there is a life to come wherein the wicked shall be punished and the vertuous rewarded; it seems to me that there does naturally accrew such a Right to these men of freedome in their Religion as is inviolable, and such as the power of the Magistrate ought not to invade, unless there be some perverse mixture in it that forfeits their Right.

In the mean time supposing there to be nothing but simple mistake, which they of the contrary Religion will call Superstition, yet the Conscience of the other party being bound up to this, it is his natural Right to have his Freedome therein; because his Conscience is necessarily subjected thereby to a greater power then any is on earth; and therefore not to give him the Liberty of his Religion is both a piece of Inhumanity and Injustice towards him, and a kind of Rebellion against God whose liege subject he is.

(2)   Nor can any thing that I know weaken the solidity of this Truth, unless you will say that no False Religion is the command of God, or at least that it is countermanded by the Promulgation of the True. To which I answer, That there is so much Truth in those Religions I speak of, that they contain a belief of the Existence of God & that there is a Life to come; which is a demonstration that the rest of their Religion, in the belief and exercise whereof they seriously and sincerely seek the favor of God and Eternal happiness, does bind their Conscience most severely and indispensably to obedience. Which immediate Dictate of Conscience in a soul that is sincere,[7] what is it but the Command of God? and before his voice be heard here, his will is not promulgated to that person. For nothing but Conviction of Conscience that this or that is the Will of God is properly the promulgation of his Will to every particular soul: Otherwise it is but as a recital of the Law in a language[8] the People understand not, and therefore can take no hold upon them.

Again, how can an Erroneous Conscience oblige to obedience, if its Dictate be but as from it self, and not the command of God? For it is improper to say a man is obliged to obey himself, especially in matters of Religion. Wherefore it is plain that the Obligation is to God, and from God, who has proclaimed in the heart of every man that is conscienciously and sincerely religious how he will be served and worshipped, and by inevitable trains of Providence has for a time fixt him to this or that perswasion. Which being the most express, the most complete and articulate way that God can promulgate his Law by, namely, the Conviction of mens Reason and Conscience (for I speak of such as are in their wits, not mad-men and

Fanaticks, nor yet such as embrace for Religious Precepts contrary to the Light and Law of Nature, which is the highest and most uncontrovertible Law of God, as being not Topical but Universal, and therefore there can be no perswasion against that, but it is to be imputed to the villany of man, not to the command of God, who in all Nations by the inward Light of Nature commands to the contrary, be their Topical Religion what it will); in these things, I say, whose falseness is not easily discoverable by the Light of Nature (such as are sundry matters of fact done many Ages ago, and Religious Precepts and Ceremonies thereupon depending) if there be this Conviction of Conscience concerning them, there is necessarily implied the command of God to that people so convicted. For when can God be said to command a person, if not then when he conveys a practical perswasion so unto him (be it by the intervention of what Providence it will) that there is no place left to doubt but that it is his Command? For if he spoke to him face to face (which he does not doe to one of infinite thousands, nor it may be properly to any) there could be no greater assurance of receiving a command from him. Wherefore a man being as fully assured that he has received a command from God as he can be assured, and this assurance being contrived into him by the Providence of God himself; it is evident that the command is truly from God. To which a man is still obliged till he does in as express a manner receive a Countermand from the same Soveraign Power.

(3)   Which Countermand, according to what I have already laid down, is not received nor promulgated till the Conscience be convinced, but is still as a Law repeated in a strange language; and therefore being not understood, is not obligatory. Nor does the great Law-giver of the Universe contradict himself in this variety, nay contrariety, if you will, of Religions. For he does not command them all to the same people at the same time; but every one according as his Conscience is convicted receives a new command, and where they are inconsistent, relinquishes the old. And truly there seems no harshnesse nor incongruity at all in admitting variety and contrariety of Religions in the world, and all commanded by God, if this Diversity and Opposition were discoverable only in several degrees of Perfection, or in the manner of Worship and Ceremony: but they being contradictory one to another in the very Articles of their Creeds, this seems an insuperable difficulty, how God should command them to believe Contradictions, of which one part must of necessity be false. As for example, It is impossible, That Christ died on the Crosse, and, That he died not on the Crosse, or, That he rose again from the dead, and, That he did not rise again from the dead, should both parts be true. In the former of which examples the Turks, in the latter the Jews Belief is opposite to ours.

(4)   This truly at first sight seems a very hard knot. But the difficulty will not prove so formidable, after we have considered wherein it lies and how it may be answered. And surely it lies mainly in this, Whether it be consistent with the Nature of God to conveigh a false Perswasion into the minde of man or no. This is the utmost of the intricacy. To which methinks the Answer is not difficult. I freely therefore do affirm, That it is not inconsistent with Gods nature so to do. For he is thereby neither the Authour of any sin committed by us, nor doth he commit any thing himself unworthy of his Divinity. He is not the Authour of Sin in us, in that invincible ignorance is no sin, nor any act that proceeds therefrom. There is indeed lesse perfection in these actions, but every imperfection is not sin; for they may be such imperfections as are utterly involuntary and unavoidable, as we suppose this false persuasion is and all the effects of it.

(5)   Nor does God do any thing unworthy of himself in introducing such an invincible or unavoidable perswasion, though it be false. For to cause another to think that which is not true, is not simply evil in it self. Otherwise it were unlawful to fence, and to use ordinary stratagems of warre, wherein the Enemy endeavors to deceive each other; which is not done but by bringing them into a false belief. And we are the worst kinde of Enemies against God, being Rebels and Apostates from him: And therefore though he needs insinuate no mistakes into us by way of stratagem, yet he may fix upon us the belief of such things as are false by way of punishment; and though he command homage from us as his Subjects, yet he may do it with several badges of disgrace, as some offended Prince might command a Rebel for a time to wear some sordid token of his Rebellion upon his outward garments whenever he went abroad, or an incensed High Priest for Penance adjudge some offender to do his devotions alwaies in some dark pit or dungeon, in stead of a convenient closet or well-adorned Church. Which things though they be but ugly in themselves, yet they being part of that duty they are tied up to by them that ought to command, they are free from the molestations of others that are inferiour to that Power that commanded them; nor are these Offenders the one to be drag'd into the Church to do his devotions there, nor is any one to pull off by violence from the other the badge of dishonor that he is commanded to wear.

Now the dishonorable badges of the Soul are those grosse Errours and Ignorances with which God may justly be deemed, by way of reproach and punishment, to command those to worship him that are convinced so to do, nor know yet any thing better. And the dark pit may be any blinde dispensation which Divine Providence has adjudged men to, till their conviction to the contrary. For Conviction is the immediate Command of God in the Conscience; as I have often repeated.

(6)   And as God by way of Punishment may introduce a false perswasion into the Minde of man, so also by way of Probation. For if to introduce a false perswasion in it self be not simply evil, how can it be evil when used for a good End, and by an unerring Wisedom, and from an infinite Goodness? Which powers if we were invested with, none could make any controversie of it, but that we might also take the liberty to do so too. And people hold it ordinarily very pardonable, if not allowable, to impose upon children and sick persons by false stories for their health, and to save the spilling of innocent bloud by concealing the pursued from the knowledge of him that would murther him. Nay, in smaller exigencies, as in the trial of a servants trust, no man would be much offended if one made his servants believe he trusted him further then he did, either to encourage his faithfulness or to detect his fraud; as if he should in his presence put up into a box some false Jewels that made a great show, but of small value, and should commit them unto his servants custody carefully sealed up as a most precious Treasure, thereby to try if he will run away with them; adding thereunto a sealed bag of Counters with an old inscription of so much in Gold. Such a Trial as this, which implies an introducing of a false opinion into the mind of the servant, few or none would hold culpable in his cautious Master. What injustice therefore can it be in God, if he try the Souls of men first in a false Religion, perswading them that it is true, and thereby commanding the practice thereof; since by this means their faithfulness is discovered, whether they will be sincere when that is committed to them which is wholly true indeed?

(7)   It is plain therefore that some falshoods in a Religion which has so much Truth in it as to engage a man in the exercise thereof in hope of Eternal life, doe not hinder but that this whole Religion that obliges the Conscience is the command of God to them whose Conscience it does oblige; and therefore that they are free from the commands of any external power, if some other things of another nature do not make them forfeit their liberty. For the simple falsities in Religion are not enough, that is, are not sufficient to detect that such a Religion is not commanded to such and such persons by God himself; who thought good to try Abraham's Faith by that false perswasion, that he was actually to sacrifice his son to him, whenas God intended no such matter. Which Example does prove that God has not only a power, but has put also into act this right that he has of causing men to think otherwise then what is really true. But what is that to thee? they must stand or fall to their own Master, nor hast thou any power to countermand them till they have a countermand from God by clear conviction that the way they are in is false: For then onely ceases it to be the Command of God to them.

(8)   But if thou wilt be so humorsome for all this as to deny that such a
Conviction of Conscience, so stated as I have stated it, is the real command
of God in every particular, namely, in the apprehensions which are false;
yet, though this were admitted, it will notwithstanding be evident that it is
a piece of Rudeness and Barbarity to incommodate a person thus perswaded
for the profession of his Religion. For first, his speaking and acting according to the unavoidable perswasions of his minde is not a sin, it arising
according to our hypothesis out of invincible Ignorance; nor is he supposed
to act any thing against the known laws of Nature; and therefore no just
right of any one is endamaged: but in the mean time the Soveraignty of
the Godhead is fully acknowledged, and the Loyalty and Sincerity of the
Religionist exercised therein.

Wherefore what reason can there be that any one for so good an action,
that is not exceptionable for any thing that is properly sinful, should be
rudely treated, punished, or any way disturbed or hindered? For whosoever
endeavors his forcible hindrance, does not only suppress an innocent and
laudable action, but he does necessarily perpetrate a foul and sinful one. For
such is the solicitation of others to the omission of that duty of Loyalty our
own Conscience tels us we owe to God. Wherefore he that hinders the
sincere Religionist from the Profession of his Religion, tempts him to a sin
against God: which no Powers in the World have a right to do, but are *ipso
facto* guilty of rebellion against their Maker, by corrupting his liege Subjects, and urging them to faithlessness and neglect of their duty. How
culpable are they then in forcing them and haling them to such actions as
they are perswaded God has severely forbid them? Verily if this be not
unjustly to command him who is under the power of another, I cannot
imagine what is; nor what can be deemed a sin against God, if urging others
to sin against him be not. So that again, even upon our Adversaries own
terms, it is plain the Soveraign power of God sets the sincere Religionist
free in matters of Religion from any external force or power whatsoever.

Now as this Position recommends it self sufficiently from its own native
concinnity and solidity; so will it also appear still more solid and more
consonous to Reason if we consider the absurdity of the contrary Position,
namely, That liberty of Conscience is by no means to be granted in Religion. For from hence it follows that every Religion may, nay ought to keep
out all other Religions with all care possible. For every mans Conscience
tels him His is the best, or else he would not be of it; nay, that there is none
true and saving but his own. For if they will say they may be saved in
others, then is our former argument a perfect demonstration against them,
that they are not only injurious to men but absolute rebels against God
indeed, in treating those ill that are his liege people, and whom he loves so
well that he intends to save them, and in persecuting them even for those
very actions wherein they do most seriously express their obedience to him.

But if there be but one true and saving Religion at once in the world, this is the greatest disinterest to it that can be imagined. For upon this Position it will be as carefully kept out and as forcibly as any of the rest; which in my apprehension is very foul play and therefore this is another evidence of the truth of our Thesis, viz. That the contrary is the greatest injury and disinterest to the True Religion that can be supposed, which nothing but external force hinders from spreading over all. For *magna est veritas, et praevalebit,*[9] I mean in the Mindes and Consciences of those men where she may have free audience, not in the noise and terrour of tyrannical impositions and obtrusions. Besides the frequent misery and calamity this Position brings upon Nations and Kingdoms, viz. Wars, bloud-shed, subversion of Families, deposing, stabbing or poisoning of Princes, perpetual enmity and hatred, and all the works and actions of the kingdom of Darkness. Of so mischievous consequence is this Opinion we do oppose. Whenas if it were acknowledged universally, *That Liberty of Religion is the natural right of mankinde,*[10] all these mischiefs would be prevented; The Prince could not pretend any quarrel against the People, nor the People against the Prince or against one another, but in Civil Rights that are more plain and intelligible.

Pierre Bayle, *Philosophical Commentary* (1686)

Bayle (1647–1706) was a Huguenot who observed first-hand the suffering of his co-religionists as Louis XIV moved toward the revocation of the Edict of Nantes. His brother, a pastor, died as the result of imprisonment, and he himself fled to the Netherlands. Bayle was a formative thinker of the pre-Enlightenment period, and left behind a difficult legacy for others to interpret. It is not entirely clear whether he was an atheist or a fideist, and his statements on religious toleration are muddied by the priority of always acting on conscience – might the conscientious persecutor be morally justified in racking the recalcitrant? Bayle's great work on persecution and toleration was the *Philosophical Commentary*. It was provoked specifically by the appearance of a work which compared the suppression of the Huguenots to that of the ancient Donatists,[11] and included some of Augustine's letters whose arguments Bayle proceeded to demolish. The contrary view was represented by Bishop Bossuet, Louis XIV's tutor and a court chaplain, in his *Politics Drawn from the Very Words of Holy Scripture* (1700).[12]

SOURCES: Pierre Bayle, *Pierre Bayle's "Philosophical Commentary": A Modern Translation and Critical Interpretation*, ed. Annie Godman Tannenbaum (New York: Peter Lang, 1987), pp. 39–43 [Part I]; Pierre Bayle, *A Philosophical Commentary*, 2 vols (London, 1708), vol. II, pp. 369–78 [Part III].

LITERATURE: Walter Rex, *Essays on Pierre Bayle and Religious Controversy* (The Hague: Martinus Nijhoff, 1965), esp. ch. 5; Edward John Kearns, *Ideas in Seventeenth-Century France* (Manchester: Manchester University Press, 1979), ch. 6; John Kilcullen, *Sincerity and Truth: Essays on Arnauld, Bayle, and Toleration* (Oxford: Clarendon, 1988).

Part I, Chapter III   Second Refutation of the Same Literal Sense for the Reason that It Is Contrary to the Spirit of the Gospel

Before proposing my second proof, I request my reader to remember what I said in the first chapter: (1) *that a positive law once verified on the basis of natural light acquires the force of rule and* criterium *in just the same manner as a proposition in geometry, demonstrated by incontestable principles, becomes itself a principle with regard to other propositions.* The reason why I am repeating this remark is that I want to prove in this chapter the falseness of the literal sense of these words, *Compel them to come in,* by showing it is contrary to the whole tenor and general spirit of the Gospel. If I were doing this *Commentary* as a theologian, I would not need to take the argument higher; I would rightfully suppose that the Gospel is the first rule of morality and that deviating from the Gospel-Morality is, without further proof, to be manifestly in a state of iniquity. But since I am acting as a philosopher, I am obliged to go back to the original and mother rule which is natural light or reason. I say then that the Gospel being a rule which has had its sanction from the purest ideas of right reason which are the primary and original of all truth and rectitude, to sin against this Gospel is sinning against the primary rule itself, or which is the same thing, against that inner and silent revelation through which God teaches all mankind the very first principles. I even add this consideration, that the Gospel having more fully developed the duties of morality, and being a more considerable extension of the idea of rectitude than God had originally revealed to us by natural religion, it follows that every Christian action which does not conform to the Gospel is more unjust and more enormous than if it were simply contrary to reason, because the more the rules of justice or principles of manners are developed, clarified and extended, the more inexcusable it is not to conform to them. So that if constraint in matters of religions be found opposite to the spirit of the Gospel, this will be a second and more forceful proof than the first to show this constraint unlawful and contrary to the primary and original rule of equity and reason.

But not to leave the least obstruction in our path, let us say a word about a difficulty which presents itself. I will be told that by the principle I established in the first chapter, the Gospel would never have been received as divine revelation because if one compares its precepts with my original rule, they will not conform; for nothing is more agreeable to natural light than defending oneself when assaulted, taking revenge on an enemy, caring for the body, etc., and nothing is more contradictory to the Gospel. If it were therefore necessary to judge that a doctrine, preached to us as given from heaven, was not divine unless conformable to natural light, to the primary, perpetual, and universal revelation of the divinity towards mankind, the doctrine of Jesus Christ would have to be rejected as false, and today the Gospel would not be able to pass for a second rule collated with the original, and consequently, I would be able to prove nothing by my method in proving here that compulsion is against the spirit of the Gospel-Morality.

I answer that all the moral teachings of Jesus Christ are such that being weighed in the balance of natural religion they will certainly be found to be sterling. Jesus Christ having moreover performed such a vast number of miracles, that only the opposition of his doctrine to some evident truths of natural revelation could give the least ground for doubting the divinity of His mission; one should be entirely at ease on this score. He performed miracles for the maintenance of a doctrine, which far from being opposite to the first notions of reason and to the purest principles of natural equity, extended them, clarified them, developed them and perfected them; He spoke, then, on the part of God. Does not natural light distinctly inform every soul which attentively consults it, that God is just, that He loves virtue, disapproves vice, merits our utmost respect and obedience; that He is the source of our felicity, and that it is to Him we ought to turn for all our necessities? Does this light not inform all who contemplate it with care and who raise themselves above the dark clouds which passions and the materiality of their habits form in their minds, that it is honest and praiseworthy to forgive enemies, to moderate our anger and subdue all our passions? From what source would all those shining maxims which abound in the writings of pagans come from were it not for a natural revelation of these things communicated to all persons? This being the case, it was easy to see that nothing could be more reasonable and more conformable to order than to command humility of men, forgiveness of offenses, mortification and charity. Our reason, clearly aware that God is the sovereign good, relishes and approves the maxims which unite us to Him. Now nothing is more capable of uniting us to God than contempt of this world and the mortification of the passions; thus, reason found the Gospel-Morality agreeable in every instance to order, and this morality, far from inclining it to doubt whether the miracles of Jesus Christ proved His divinity, became on the contrary a solid confirmation of it.

The same cannot be said of the morality one claims to find in the words *Compel them to come in.* If they were to signify, *employ prisons, tortures, duress to force the profession of Christianity upon those who will not willingly submit to it*, our reason, our natural religion would have had cause to become greatly mistrusted and to look upon Jesus Christ as an emissary of Satan, who came under the fairest appearances of an austere and well-spiritualized morality upheld by mighty prodigies to infuse the deadliest poison capable of ruining the human race and turning it into the horrendous and never-changing theater of blood and most execrable tragedy. But let us propose this second proof in form. Here is my reasoning:

An interpretation of Scripture completely contrary to the spirit of the Gospel can only be false; the literal sense of the words, *Compel them to come in*, is directly repugnant to the spirit of the Gospel; the literal sense, therefore, of these words can only be false.

I may reasonably presume that the *major* part of this argument needs no further proof. I will then only prove the *minor*.

To this end, I shall first observe that the superiority of the Gospel to the Law of Moses consists in this among other things, that it spiritualizes man, treats him more as a reasonable creature of a mature judgment and no longer as a child who needed to be amused by spectacles and grand ceremonies which would divert him from his penchant towards pagan idolatry. From here it follows that the Gospel most particularly requires us to follow it through reason, that its first and principal purpose is to enlighten the understanding by its truths, and afterwards attract our zeal and esteem; that it does not want either the fear of men or the apprehension of temporal misery to make us profess it outwardly without our heart being touched or our reason persuaded. Therefore, it does not want any one forced. This would be treating man as a slave, just like wanting to use him for servile manual operations or as a mere machine, where it matters little whether he work with good will or not, provided he works. But in the matter of religion, so far is it from being performed when gone about with an ill will, that it would be infinitely better to stay completely idle than to work by compulsion. Here the heart must get involved and with a thorough knowledge of cause. The more any religion requires the heart, goodwill, reasonable service, a thoroughly enlightened persuasion, as the Gospel does, the further it should be away from all constraint.

I observe in the second place that the principal personality traits of Jesus Christ, and so to speak, the dominant qualities of His person, were humility, meekness, and patience. "Learn from me," He said to his Disciples, "that I am meek and lowly in heart." He is compared to a lamb led to slaughter without protest or complaint. He says that the meek are blessed, as are the peacemakers and the merciful. When He was reviled, He reviled not again, but handed Himself over to Him who judges right. He wishes us to bless those who curse us and pray for those who persecute us; and far from permitting His followers to persecute infidels, He does not even want them to oppose their own persecutions with anything other than flight. "If they persecute you in one city," He says, "flee to another." He does not tell them to try and stir up the people against those who govern, call to their aid the cities which are on their side, lay formal seige to those who had persecuted them in order to compel them to believe. He says to them, "go out and take yourselves to another place." He does indeed, in another place, order them to protest in the streets against those who would not have heard them, but this is the utmost He allows them, and after that, commands them to withdraw. He likens Himself to a shepherd who goes before his sheep, "and they follow Him, for they know His voice." These words should be noted well; He does not say that He drives the flock before him with a whip as when one wants to constrain them from going in a place against their will. He says He puts Himself in front of them and they follow Him because they know Him, which signifies His leaving them at full liberty to follow as long as they know Him or to go astray if they come to know Him not and His accepting none other than voluntary obedience, preceded by and founded upon knowledge.

He puts His own mission in opposition to that of thieves and brigands who, like wolves, break into the fold to carry off by force the sheep who do not belong to them and who do not know their voice. When He sees Himself forsaken by the troops, He does not arm those legions of angels, which were as always in His debt, nor send them in pursuit of the deserters, to force them to come back. Far from it, He asks his very apostles, who had not yet forsaken Him, whether they had not a mind to do like the rest, "and will you also go away?" to let them know, as it were, that He did not want to retain any of them in His service against their inclination. When He ascends into heaven, He only commands His apostles to go and convert all nations by teaching, indoctrinating and by baptizing. His apostles followed the example of His meekness, and exhorted us to be imitators of them and of their Master. Almost the whole New Testament must be transcribed if one wishes to collect all the proofs it furnishes of that gentleness, goodness and long-suffering which constitute the distinguishing and essential character of the Gospel.

Let us now reason thusly: the literal sense of this Gospel text *Compel them to come in*, is not only contrary to the lights of natural religion, primary and original rule of equity, but also to the dominant and essential spirit of the Gospel itself, and of its author, because nothing can be more opposite to this spirit than dungeons, exiles, pillage, galleys, insolence by soldiers, torture and suffering. Therefore, this literal sense is false.

I do not think it possible to imagine anything more impious or more injurious to Jesus Christ, or more fatal in its consequence than to maintain that He has given Christians a general precept to make conversions by constraint, because not only could a maxim as opposite as that one to good sense, to reason, to the common principles of morality, be able to induce one to believe that he who sells it does not speak on behalf of the same God, who has already made another revelation quite different from this, by the oracles of natural light; on behalf of God, I say, who is incapable of contradicting Himself so grossly. Besides all this, what idea must we form of the Gospel if we find in it, on the one hand, so many precepts of gentleness and clemency, and on the other, a general order that enfolds within its territory all the crimes of craft and cruelty which hell can inspire? Who would not say it is a very odd medley of contradictory thoughts of a mind that did not know its lesson by heart or did not know itself too well? Or rather, who would not say that he knew his lesson too well and that the grand enemy of the human race having seduced him, used his organism to introduce into the world the most fearful deluge of misery and desolation that could be conceived, and that, the better to succeed, he had made him play his game under a fake and beguiling moderation, to let fly all of a sudden the terrible and dire sentence of constraining and forcing all nations to profess Christianity? Into such abysses the infamous defenders of the literal sense of the parable (who could better deserve the title of executioners and General Directors of the slaughterhouses than that of interpreters of Scripture) hurl themselves. A certain Oratorian father named Amelote, writing during the quarrels of the Jansenists, said that "if one had in the questions of fact concerning Jansenius, an evidence from nature as there is by sense or by the first principles of reason, they whose eyes were thus enlightened might reasonably take umbrage at the diligence and faithfulness of the Pope and Bishops who were opposed to them and justly demand an express revelation from those who would oblige them to sacrifice their opinion, and submit in spite of their knowledge." And that evidence which is founded on sense or on the first principles, he calls an *impregnable post*. From this principle of his, I conclude that the least a man should do to convince us of the literal sense of the words *Compel them to come in*, so opposite to the lights of reason and of the Gospel, is to prove to us by a new and most evident revelation, that he interprets this passage right. And yet it is my opinion that except in some special cases where God may make exception to His own laws, we ought never to trust a revelation of this kind, no matter how evident it is. My meaning is that if a prophet working miracles to maintain the literal sense of the text were to make it into a general precept unlimited by any particular circumstance as was, for example, the murder of Phineas, we would have the right to take him, with all his miracles, for an imposter.

Part III

As in the entrance of the first part of this *Commentary* I said, I would not dwell on any particular circumstances of the text which I designed to give a comment on, but confute the literal sense considered in itself, and attack it upon general principles: so in the entrance on this Third Part I think fit to signify, that I shall have no regard to any particular circumstances of St Augustine, of the Donatists of the century, or the country in which they lived; but endeavor, from the most general heads of proof, to show, that St Augustine's reasons, considered in themselves, and abstracted from all their disparaging circumstances, are nevertheless false. It is nothing to me if St Augustine was formerly of opinion, that no one ought to be constrained in matters of religion; or if he changed his opinion purely upon seeing the successes of the imperial laws in bringing in heretics, which is one of the wretchedest ways of reasoning that can be imagined; it being just the same as saying, such a man has heaped up much riches, therefore he has employed only lawful means. Nor does it concern me, that St Augustine was of such or such a spirit, of such or such a character; nor yet, that the Donatists were a ridiculous set of men who separated from the church upon mere trifles. My design is to examine St Augustine's reasons as if they were dropped from the clouds, without regard to persons or parties; though I should rather incline to defend so great a man against those who accuse him of insincerity and unfairness in this dispute. I am quite of another opinion, and believe verily he spoke as he thought; but being a well-meaning man, and carried away by an over-ardent zeal, he readily caught at anything that seemed to support his prejudices, and believed he did God good service by finding out arguments at any expense for what he believed to be the truth. He had a great share of knowledge, but he had more zeal; and so much as he indulged his zeal (now he indulged it very freely) so much he retrenched from solid reasoning, and from the purest lights of true philosophy. This is the real state of his case: a spirit of devotion and zeal is undoubtedly a great blessing, but it is sometimes at the expense of the reason and judgment; the party grows credulous, he takes up with the wretchedest sophisms, provided they advance his cause; he paints out the errors of his adversaries in the frightfullest colors: and if he be of a hot spirit withal, what ground can he stand upon, what efforts will he not make to wrest scripture, tradition, and all sort of principles? He would find his own account in all, he will strain all; in short, he will mar all. I do not think ever anyone made a juster judgment of St Augustine than one P. Adam a Jesuit, let P. Norris say what he please to the contrary in his *Vindiciae Augustinianae*. But as I said before, it is nothing to me, whether Augustine was this or that; my business is to examine his arguments abstractedly from all prejudices. Let us begin then and examine the two letters of this Father, lately printed by themselves, according to the last French version, by the archbishop of Paris' orders, with a preface at the head of them, part of which we have already confuted in the Preliminary Discourse; the whole is entitled *The Conformity of the*

Conduct of the Church of France for Reuniting the Protestants, with that of the Church of Africa for Reuniting the Donatists to the Catholic Church. The first of these two letters is the 93rd of the new edition, and the 48th of the old, written in the year 408 to Vincentius, a Donatist bishop in answer to one from him, expressing his surprise at the inconstancy of this Father; who having formerly been of opinion, that it was not lawful to employ the secular arm against heretics, nor any other means besides the word of God and sound reason, had changed from white to black on this important point. Let us hear St Augustine's first remark.

I   St Augustine's words

> I am even much more a Lover of Peace now than when you knew me in my younger days at Carthage; but the Donatists being so very restless as they are, I cannot but persuade myself, that it is fit to restrain them by the authority of the powers ordained by God.

Answer

Here is surely one of the scurviest leads that ever was seen, and the most capable of begetting a suspicion of St Augustine's honesty: for this plainly is talking like a man who had a mind to hide the true state of the question, who endeavored to change the dice upon his readers, who is loath to speak out; in fine, who would stick at no artifice to gain his point. Would not a body infer from the plain and obvious meaning of these words, that the reason upon which St Augustine believed it lawful to call in the secular arm against heretics, was the restlessness of their temper tending to disturb the public peace? If so, it was unreasonable applying to the prince against such of them as lived retired in their own houses, and gave no manner of disturbance; this is what might fairly be collected from the words before us; yet this was far from being St Augustine's true opinion: he was entirely for making laws against all heretics, even the most meek and inoffensive, in hopes the smart of temporal punishments might oblige them to come over into the unity of the church; and had he not been of this opinion, nothing would be more needless or more pitiful than the Reasons which he here lays out with so much pomp. It is plain he had made use of an artificial and fallacious preamble, or, which to me seems much more probable, fallen into a thought the wrongest, and the most opposite in the world to the justness of one who knows how to write and reason solidly.

For did ever any one doubt, that it was the duty of princes to enact wholesome laws against heretics who disturb the public peace, who are of a turbulent persecuting spirit, and so forth? Did ever anyone doubt, but the best men may and ought to exhort princes, who are slack in providing the proper remedies, to restrain such men by the sword which God has given into their hands? It is the duty of princes to repress not only heretics of a factious, turbulent and restless spirit, but those of the orthodox party too, who fall into the same irregularities. What does St Augustine mean then when he says, he thinks it very fitting to restrain by the authority of the higher powers, the boldness of heretics in forcing the world, and oppressing their neighbor? Was this the point in question? Could anyone have the least ground to wonder at this Father's being of such an opinion? Is there any need of writing apologies in defense of it? Nothing therefore could be more foreign than the laying down such a principle at the head of such a work, in which the business in hand was to justify, not any laws restraining the insolences of the Donatists, but those directly and immediately enacted against their errors; seeing they condemned them all indiscriminately to temporal punishments, in case they persisted in their opinions. . . .

. . . I say further, that had the emperors meant no more than just restraining the boldness of the Donatists and the fury of the Circumcellions, there had been no need of enacting new laws: there were laws enough ready made to hand, and known to every magistrate of the empire, against robbers, ruffians, against all in general who exercise any violence on their fellow citizens. . . .

But here it will be proper to obviate a difficulty; to wit, that by a disturber of the public peace we are not to understand those who are an accidental cause of mighty combustions and revolutions in the world: for in this case Jesus Christ and his apostles had been justly reputed disturbers of the state, as they attacked the established religion, and set up altar against altar, whence infinite disorders must of necessity have happened in human society. I mean then by disturbers of the public peace only those who scour the country, plunder villages and towns, and rob upon the highway; they who stir up seditions in a city; they who smite and buffet their neighbor, as soon as they have got an advantage of him; in a word, they who will not suffer the fellow citizens to live in the full and peaceable enjoyment of all their rights, privileges, and property. It is evident on this fact, that neither Jesus Christ nor his Apostles were disturbers of the public peace. . . .

The better to establish my opinion, I observe, that we must never render a doctrine odious which we believe false, by exposing it on such a side as is common to it, with that doctrine which we believe true. Seeing error therefore and truth have this in common, that when they make their first appearance in a country where people are settled in a contrary religion, they equally occasion stirs and disturbances; it were absurd to maintain, that they who come to preach an erroneous doctrine are punishable, for this reason only, that they endanger the peace resulting before from an uniformity of worship and opinion; because this peace and uniformity in a country which had slumbered in error, had been altogether as much endangered and disturbed by sending preachers of truth and righteousness among them: we must therefore equally acquit truth and error of the consequences which accidentally attend them. Whence it appears, that had the Donatists been guilty of no other mischief than the making a schism in the church, which before was perfectly united, the emperor's treating them as disturbers of the public peace had been very ill founded, and so had their compelling them by violent methods to return in to the bosom of the church. All the constraint these emperors could lawfully have exercised on the Donatists was the punishing very severely such of them as oppressed the Catholics, or who reducing them to beggary, extorted a feigned consent to receive a second baptism. If their penal laws had had no other view than the restraining attempts so opposite to the law of nature and nations, and destructive of the most sacred and inviolable rights of human society; St Augustine might not only have spared himself the trouble of an apology to justify his approbation of them, but would really have been very much to blame if he had not approved them. But as Mr Ferrand has fully proved, the laws of these emperors had quite another view, and aimed at constraining the Donatists to forsake their sect, from the apprehensions of leading a miserable and melancholy life. Now this is it, which is not only opposite to Christianity, but even to reason and humanity; insomuch as St Augustine's undertaking the defense of it is scandalous to the last degree. . . .

John Locke, *A Letter Concerning Toleration* (1685)

During the Restoration period Locke (1632–1704) was drawn into Whiggish political circles and was implicated in plotting directed against the succession of the Roman Catholic James II. For reasons of safety he spent some years in France and much of the 1680s in the Netherlands, returning to England only after the success of William of Orange. Thus Locke had opportunity to witness the effects of religious intolerance both in England and on the continent. His highly influential *Letter* was written in 1685 (though not published until 1689). It is not distinguished by innovation; his principal ideas on toleration can be located in earlier sources, especially Roger Williams and John Owen. Here one finds toleration as a *sine qua non* of authentic Christianity; the restriction of magisterial power to persons and property ("civil interests"); a church as a voluntary society whose regulations affect only those who choose to belong. Locke's toleration did not, however, embrace papists and atheists.

SOURCE: John Locke, *A Letter Concerning Toleration* (London, 1689), pp. 1–10, 12–13, 53–7.

LITERATURE: John Horton and Susan Mendus (eds), *John Locke: A Letter Concerning Toleration in Focus* (London and New York: Routledge, 1991); Winthrop S. Hudson, "John Locke: Preparing the Way for the Revolution," *Journal of Presbyterian History*, 42 (1964), pp. 19–38; J. Wayne Baker, "Church, State, and Toleration: John Locke and Calvin's Heirs in England, 1644–1689," in W. Fred Graham (ed.), *Later Calvinism: International Perspectives* (Kirksville, MO: Sixteenth-Century Essays and Studies, 1994), pp. 525–43.

Honored Sir,

Since you are pleased to inquire what are my Thoughts about the mutual Toleration of Christians in their different Professions of Religion, I must needs answer you freely, That I esteem that Toleration to be the chief Characteristical Mark of the True Church. For whatsoever some People boast of the Antiquity of Places and Names, or of the Pomp of their Outward Worship; Others, of the Reformation of their Discipline; All, of the Orthodoxy of their Faith; (for every one is Orthodox to himself:) These things, and all others of this nature, are much rather Marks of Men striving for Power and Empire over one another, than of the Church of Christ. Let any one have never so true a Claim to all these things, yet if he be destitute of Charity, Meekness, and Good-will in general towards all Mankind, even to those that are not Christians, he is certainly yet short of being a true Christian himself. "The Kings of the Gentiles exercise Lordship over them," said our Savior to his Disciples, "but ye shall not be so" [Luke 22: 25]. The Business of True Religion is quite another thing. It is not instituted in order to the erecting of an external Pomp, nor to the obtaining of Ecclesiastical Dominion, nor to the exercising of compulsive Force; but to the regulating of Mens Lives according to the Rules of Vertue and Piety. Whosoever will lift himself under the Banner of Christ, must in the first place, and above all things, make War upon his own Lusts and Vices. It is in vain for any Man to usurp the Name of Christian, without Holiness of Life, Purity of Manners, and Benignity and Meekness of Spirit. "Let every one that nameth the Name of Christ, depart from iniquity" [2 Timothy 2: 19]. "Thou, when thou art converted, strengthen thy Brethren," said our Lord to Peter [Luke 22: 32]. It would indeed be very hard for one that appears careless about his own Salvation, to persuade me that he were extreamly concern'd for mine. For it is impossible that those should sincerely and heartily apply themselves to make other People Christians, who have not really embraced the Christian Religion in their own Hearts. If the Gospel and the Apostles may be credited, no Man can be a Christian without Charity, and without that Faith which works, not by Force, but by Love. Now I appeal to the Consciences of those that persecute, torment, destroy, and kill other Men upon pretense of Religion, whether they do it out of Friendship and Kindness towards them, or no: And I shall then indeed, and not till then, believe they do so, when I shall see those fiery Zealots correcting, in the same manner, their Friends and familiar Acquaintance, for the manifest Sins they commit against the Precepts of the Gospel; when I shall see them prosecute with Fire and Sword the Members of their own Communion that are tainted with enormous vices, and without Amendment are in danger of eternal Perdition; and when I shall see them thus express their Love and Desire of the Salvation of their Souls, by the infliction of Torments, and exercise of all manner of Cruelties. For if it be out of a Principle of Charity, as they pretend, and Love to Mens Souls, that they deprive them of their Estates, maim them with corporal Punishments, starve and torment them in noisom Prisons, and in the end even take away their Lives; I say, if all this be done meerly to make Men Christians, and procure their Salvation, Why then do they suffer "Whoredom, Fraud, Malice, and such like enormities" [cf. Romans 1: 26–31], which (according to the Apostle) manifestly rellish of Heathenish Corruption, to predominate so much and abound amongst their Flocks and People? These, and such like things, are certainly more contrary to the Glory of God, to the Purity of the Church, and to the Salvation of Souls, than any conscientious Dissent from Ecclesiastical Decisions, or Separation from Publick Worship, whilst accompanied with Innocency of Life. Why then does this burning Zeal for God, for the Church, and for the Salvation of Souls; burning, I say, literally, with Fire and Faggot; pass by those moral Vices and Wickednesses, without any Chastisement, which are acknowledged by all Men to be diametrically opposite to the Profession of Christianity; and bend all its Nerves either to the introducing of Ceremonies, or to the establishment of Opinions, which for the most part are about nice and intricate Matters, that exceed the Capacity of ordinary Understandings? Which of the Parties contending about these things is in the right, which of them is guilty of Schism or Heresie, whether those that domineer or those that suffer, will then at last be manifest, when the Cause of their Separation comes to be judged of. He certainly that follows Christ, embraces his Doctrine, and bears his Yoke, tho' he forsake both Father and Mother, separate from the Publick Assemblies and Ceremonies of his Country, or whomsoever, or whatsoever else he relinquishes, will not then be judged an Heretick.

Now, tho' the Divisions that are amongst Sects should be allowed to be never so obstructive of the Salvation of Souls; yet nevertheless "Adultery, Fornication, Uncleanness, Lasciviousness, Idolatry, and such like things, cannot be denied to be Works of the Flesh"; concerning which the Apostle has expressly declared, that "they who do them shall not inherit the Kingdom of God" [Galatians 5: 19–21]. Whosoever therefore is sincerely sollicitous about the Kingdom of God, and thinks it his Duty to endeavor the Enlargement of it amongst Men, ought to apply himself with no less care and industry to the rooting out of these Immoralities, than to the Extirpation of Sects. But if any one do otherwise, and whilst he is cruel and implacable towards those that differ from him in Opinion, he be indulgent to such Iniquities and Immoralities as are unbecoming the Name of a Christian, let such a one talk never so much of the Church, he plainly demonstrates by his Actions, that 'tis another Kingdom he aims at, and not the Advancement of the Kingdom of God.

That any Man should think fit to cause another Man whose Salvation he heartily desires, to expire in Torments and that even in an unconverted estate, would, I confess, seem very strange to me, and, I think, to any other also. But no body, surely, will ever believe that such a Carriage can proceed from Charity, Love, or Good-will. If any one maintain that Men ought to be compelled by Fire and Sword to profess certain Doctrines, and conform to this or that exteriour Worship, without any regard had unto their Morals; if any one endeavor to convert those that are Erroneous unto the Faith, by forcing them to profess things that they do not believe, and allowing them to practice things that the Gospel does not permit; it cannot be doubted indeed but such a one is desirous to have a numerous Assembly joyned in the same Profession with himself; but that he principally intends by those means to compose a truly Christian Church, is altogether incredible. It is not therefore to be wondred at, if those who do not really contend for the Advancement of the true Religion, and of the Church of Christ, make use of Arms that do not belong to the Christian Warfare. If, like the Captain of our Salvation, they sincerely desired the Good of Souls, they would tread in the Steps, and follow the perfect Example of that Prince of Peace, who sent out his Soldiers to the subduing of Nations, and gathering them into his Church, not armed with Sword, or other Instruments of Force, but prepared with the Gospel of Peace, and with the Exemplary Holiness of their Conversation. This was his Method. Tho' if Infidels were to be converted by force, if those that are either blind or obstinate were to be drawn off from their Errors by Armed Soldiers, we know very well that it was much more easie for Him to do it with Armies of Heavenly Legions, than for any Son of the Church, how potent soever, with all his Dragoons.

The Toleration of those that differ from others in Matters of Religion, is so agreeable to the Gospel of Jesus Christ, and to the genuine Reason of Mankind, that it seems monstrous for Men to be so blind, as not to perceive the Necessity and Advantage of it, in so clear a Light. I will not here tax the Pride and Ambition of some, the Passion and uncharitable Zeal of others. These are Faults from which Humane Affairs can perhaps scarce ever be perfectly freed; but yet such as no body will bear the plain Imputation of, without covering them with some specious Color; and so pretend to Commendation, whilst they are carried away by their own irregular Passions. But however, that some may not color their Spirit of Persecution and unchristian Cruelty with a Pretense of Care of the Publick Weal, and Observation of the Laws; and that others, under pretense of Religion, may not seek Impunity for their Libertinism and Licentiousness; in a word, that none may impose either upon himself or others, by the Pretenses of Loyalty and Obedience to the Prince, or of Tenderness and Sincerity in the Worship of God; I esteem it above all things necessary to distinguish exactly the Business of Civil Government from that of Religion, and to settle the just Bounds that lie between the one and the other. If this be not done, there can be no end put to the Controversies that will be always arising, between those that have, or at least pretend to have, on the one side, a Concernment for the Interest of Mens Souls, and on the other side, a Care of the Commonwealth.

The Commonwealth seems to me to be a Society of Men constituted only for the procuring, preserving, and advancing of their own *Civil Interests*.

Civil Interests I call Life, Liberty, Health, and Indolency of Body; and the Possession of outward things, such as Money, Lands, Houses, Furniture, and the like.

It is the Duty of the Civil Magistrate, by the impartial Execution of equal Laws, to secure unto all the People in general, and to every one of his Subjects in particular, the just Possession of these things belonging to this Life. If any one presume to violate the Laws of Publick Justice and Equity, established for the Preservation of those things, his Presumption is to be check'd by the fear of Punishment, consisting of the Deprivation or Diminution of those Civil Interests, or Goods, which otherwise he might and ought to enjoy. But seeing no Man does willingly suffer himself to be punished by the Deprivation of any part of his Goods, and much less of his Liberty or Life, therefore is the Magistrate armed with the Force and Strength of all his Subjects, in order to the punishment of those that violate any other Man's Rights.

Now that the whole Jurisdiction of the Magistrate reaches only to these Civil Concernments; and that all Civil Power, Right and Dominion, is bounded and confined to the only care of promoting these things; and that it neither can nor ought in any manner to be extended to the Salvation of Souls, these following Considerations seem unto me abundantly to demonstrate.

First, because the Care of Souls is not committed to the Civil Magistrate, any more than to other Men. It is not committed unto him, I say, by God; because it appears not that God has ever given any such Authority to one Man over another, as to compell any one to his Religion. Nor can any such Power be vested in the Magistrate by the *consent of the People*; because no man can so far abandon the care of his own Salvation, as blindly to leave it to the choice of any other, whether Prince or Subject, to prescribe to him what Faith or Worship he shall embrace. For no Man can, if he would, conform his Faith to the Dictates of another. All the Life and Power of true Religion consists in the inward and full perswasion of the mind; and Faith is not Faith without believing. Whatever Profession we make, to whatever outward Worship we conform, if we are not fully satisfied in our own mind that the one is true, and the other well pleasing unto God, such Profession and such Practice, far from being any furtherance, are indeed great Obstacles to our Salvation. For in this manner, instead of expiating other Sins by the exercise of Religion, I say in offering thus unto God Almighty such a Worship as we esteem to be displeasing unto him, we add unto the number of our other sins, those also of Hypocrisie, and Contempt of his Divine Majesty.

In the second place. The care of Souls cannot belong to the Civil Magistrate, because his Power consists only in outward force; but true and saving Religion consists in the inward perswasion of the Mind, without which nothing can be acceptable to God. And such is the nature of the Understanding, that it cannot be compell'd to the belief of any thing by outward force. Confiscation of Estate, Imprisonment, Torments, nothing of that nature can have any such Efficacy as to make Men change the inward Judgment that they have framed of things.

It may indeed be alledged, that the Magistrate may make use of Arguments, and thereby draw the Heterodox into the way of Truth, and procure their Salvation. I grant it; but this is common to him with other Men. In teaching, instructing, and redressing the Erroneous by Reason, he may certainly do what becomes any good Man to do. Magistracy does not oblige him to put off either Humanity or Christianity. But it is one thing to perswade, another to command; one thing to press with Arguments, another with Penalties. This Civil Power alone has a right to do; to the other Good-will is Authority enough. Every Man has Commission to admonish, exhort, convince another of Error, and by reasoning to draw him into Truth: but to give Laws, receive Obedience, and compel with the Sword, belongs to none but the Magistrate. And upon this ground I affirm, that the Magistrate's Power extends not to the establishing of any Articles of Faith, or Forms of Worship, by the force of his Laws. For Laws are of no force at all without Penalties, and Penalties in this case are absolutely impertinent; because they are not proper to convince the mind. Neither the Profession of any Articles of Faith, nor the Conformity to any outward Form of Worship (as has already been said) can be available to the Salvation of Souls, unless the truth of the one, and the acceptableness of the other unto God, be thoroughly believed by those that so profess and practice. But Penalties

are no ways capable to produce such Belief. It is only Light and Evidence
that can work a change in Mens Opinions; which Light can in no manner
proceed from corporal Sufferings, or any other outward Penalties.

In the third place. The care of the Salvation of Mens Souls cannot belong
to the Magistrate; because, though the rigor of Laws and the force of
Penalties were capable to convince and change Mens minds, yet would not
that help at all to the Salvation of their Souls. For there being but one
Truth, one way to Heaven; what Hopes is there that more Men would be
led into it, if they had no Rule but the Religion of the Court, and were put
under a necessity to quit the Light of their own Reason, and oppose the
Dictates of their own Consciences, and blindly to resign up themselves to
the Will of their Governors, and to the Religion, which either Ignorance,
Ambition, or Superstition had chanced to establish in the Countries where
they were born? In the variety and contradiction of Opinions in Religion,
wherein the Princes of the World are as much divided as in their Secular
Interests, the narrow way would be much straitned; one Country alone
would be in the right, and all the rest of the World put under an obligation
of following their Princes in the ways that lead to Destruction; and that
which heightens the absurdity, and very ill suits the Notion of a Deity, Men
would owe their eternal Happiness or Misery to the places of their Nativity.

These Considerations, to omit many others that might have been urged
to the same purpose, seem unto me sufficient to conclude that all the Power
of Civil Government relates only to Mens Civil Interests, is confined to the
care of the things of this World, and hath nothing to do with the World
to come.

Let us now consider what a Church is. A Church then I take to be a voluntary Society of Men, joining themselves together of their own accord, in
order to the publick worshipping of God, in such a manner as they judge
acceptable to him, and effectual to the Salvation of their Souls.

I say it is a free and voluntary Society. No body is born a Member of any
Church; otherwise the Religion of Parents would descend unto Children, by
the same right of Inheritance as their Temporal Estates, and every one
would hold his Faith by the same Tenure he does his Lands; than which
nothing can be imagined more absurd. Thus therefore that matter stands.
No Man by nature is bound unto any particular Church or Sect, but every
one joins himself voluntarily to that Society in which he believes he has
found that Profession and Worship which is truly acceptable to God. The
hopes of Salvation, as it was the only cause of his entrance into that Communion, so it can be the only reason of his stay there. For if afterwards he
discover any thing either erroneous in the Doctrine, or incongruous in the
Worship of that Society to which he has join'd himself, Why should it not
be as free for him to go out as it was to enter? No Member of a Religious

Society can be tied with any other Bonds but what proceed from the certain expectation of eternal Life. A Church then is a Society of Members voluntarily uniting to this end. . . .

The End of a Religious Society (as has already been said) is the Publick Worship of God, and by means thereof the acquisition of Eternal Life. All Discipline ought therefore to tend to that End, and all Ecclesiastical Laws to be thereunto confined. Nothing ought, nor can be transacted in this Society, relating to the Possession of Civil and Worldly Goods. No Force is here to be made use of, upon any occasion whatsoever: For Force belongs wholly to the Civil Magistrate, and the Possession of all outward Goods is subject to his Jurisdiction.

But it may be asked, By what means then shall Ecclesiastical Laws be established, if they must be thus destitute of all Compulsive Power? I answer, They must be established by Means suitable to the Nature of such Things, whereof the external Profession and Observation, if not proceeding from a thorow Conviction and Approbation of the Mind, is altogether useless and unprofitable. The Arms by which the Members of this Society are to be kept within their Duty, are Exhortations, Admonitions, and Advices. If by these means the Offenders will not be reclaimed, and the Erroneous convinced, there remains nothing farther to be done, but that such stubborn and obstinate Persons, who give no ground to hope for their Reformation, should be cast out and separated from the Society. This is the last and utmost Force of Ecclesiastical Authority: No other Punishment can thereby be inflicted, than that, the Relation ceasing between the Body and the Member which is cut off, the Person so condemned ceases to be a Part of that Church. . . .

Ecclesiastical Assemblies, and Sermons, are justified by daily experience, and publick allowance. These are allowed to People of some one Perswasion: Why not to all? If any thing pass in a Religious Meeting seditiously, and contrary to the publick Peace, it is to be punished in the same manner, and no otherwise, than as if it had happened in a Fair or Market. These Meetings ought not to be Sanctuaries for Factious and Flagitious Fellows: Nor ought it to be less lawful for Men to meet in Churches than in Halls: Nor are one part of the Subjects to be esteemed more blameable, for their meeting together, than others. Every one is to be accountable for his own Actions; and no Man is to be laid under a Suspicion, or Odium, for the Fault of another. Those that are Seditious, Murderers, Thieves, Robbers, Adulterers, Slanderers, &c. of whatsoever Church, whether National or not, ought to be punished and suppressed. But those whose Doctrine is peaceable, and whose Manners are pure and blameless, ought to be upon equal Terms with their Fellow-Subjects. Thus if Solemn Assemblies, Observations of Festivals, publick Worship, be permitted to any one sort of Professors; all these things ought to be permitted to the *Presbyterians*, *Independents*, *Anabaptists*, *Arminians*, *Quakers*, and others, with the same Liberty. Nay, if we may openly speak the Truth, and as becomes one Man to another, neither *Pagan*, nor *Mahumetan*, nor *Jew*, ought to be excluded from the Civil Rights of the Commonwealth, because of his Religion. The Gospel commands no such thing. The Church, which "judges not those that are without" [1 Corinthians 5: 12–13], wants it not. And the Commonwealth, which embraces indifferently all Men that are honest, peaceable and industrious, requires it not. Shall we suffer a *Pagan* to deal and trade with us, and shall we not suffer him to pray unto and worship God? If we allow the *Jews* to have private Houses and Dwellings amongst us, Why should we not allow them to have Synagogues? Is their Doctrine more false, their Worship more abominable, or is the Civil Peace more endangered, by their meeting in publick than in their private Houses? But if these things may be granted to *Jews* and *Pagans*, surely the condition of any Christians ought not to be worse than theirs in a Christian Commonwealth.

You'll say, perhaps, Yes, it ought to be: Because they are more inclinable to Factions, Tumults, and Civil Wars. I answer: Is this the fault of the Christian Religion? If it be so, truly the Christian Religion is the worst of all Religions, and ought neither to be embraced by any particular Person, nor tolerated by any Commonwealth. For if this be the Genius, this the Nature of the Christian Religion, to be turbulent, and destructive to the Civil Peace, that Church it self which the Magistrate indulges will not always be innocent. But far be it from us to say any such thing of that Religion, which carries the greatest opposition to Covetousness, Ambition, Discord, Contention, and all manner of inordinate Desires; and is the most modest and peaceable Religion that ever was. We must therefore seek another Cause of those Evils that are charged upon Religion. And if we consider right, we shall find it to consist wholly in the Subject that I am treating of. It is not the diversity of Opinions, (which cannot be avoided) but the refusal of Toleration to those that are of different Opinions, (which might have been granted) that has produced all the Bustles and Wars, that have been in the Christian World, upon account of Religion. The Heads and Leaders of the Church, moved by Avarice and insatiable desire of Dominion, making use of the immoderate Ambition of Magistrates, and the credulous Superstition of the giddy Multitude, have incensed and animated them against those that dissent from themselves; by preaching unto them, contrary to the Laws of the Gospel and to the Precepts of Charity, That Schismaticks and Hereticks are to be outed of their Possessions, and destroyed. And thus have they mixed together and confounded two things that are in themselves most different, the Church and the Commonwealth. Now as it is very difficult for men patiently to suffer themselves to be stript of the Goods, which they have got by their honest Industry; and contrary to all the Laws of Equity, both Humane and Divine, to be delivered up for a Prey to other mens Violence and Rapine; especially when they are otherwise altogether blameless; and that the Occasion for which they are thus treated does not at all belong to the Jurisdiction of the Magistrate; but intirely to the Conscience of every particular man; for the Conduct of which he is accountable to God only; What else can be expected, but that these men, growing weary of the Evils under which they labor, should in the end think it lawful for them to resist Force with Force, and to defend their natural Rights (which are not forfeitable upon account of Religion) with Arms as well as they can? That this has been hitherto the ordinary Course of things, is abundantly evident in History: And that it will continue to be so hereafter, is but too apparent in Reason. It cannot indeed be otherwise, so long as the Principle of Persecution for Religion shall prevail, as it has done hitherto, with Magistrate and People; and so long as those that ought to be the Preachers of Peace and Concord, shall continue, with all their Art and Strength, to excite men to Arms, and sound the Trumpet of War. But that Magistrates should thus suffer these Incendiaries, and Disturbers of the Publick Peace, might justly be wondred at; if it did not appear that they have been invited by them unto a Participation of the Spoil, and have therefore thought fit to make use of their Covetousness and Pride as means whereby to increase their own Power. For who does not see that *these Good Men* are indeed more Ministers of the Government, than Ministers of the Gospel; and that by flattering the Ambition, and favoring the Dominion of Princes and men in Authority, they endeavor with all their might to promote that Tyranny in the Commonwealth, which otherwise they should not be able to establish in the Church? This is the unhappy Agreement that we see between the Church and State. Whereas if each of them would contain it self within its own Bounds, the one attending to the worldly Welfare of the Commonwealth, the other to the Salvation of Souls, it is impossible that any Discord should ever have hapned between them. *Sed, pudet haec approbria, &c.* God Almighty grant, I beseech him, that the Gospel of Peace may at length be preached, and that Civil Magistrates growing more careful to conform their own Consciences to the Law of God, and less sollicitous about the binding of other mens Consciences by Humane Laws, may, like Fathers of their Country, direct all their Counsels and Endeavors to promote universally the Civil Welfare of all their Children; except only of such as are arrogant, ungovernable, and injurious to their Brethren; and that all Ecclesiastical men, who boast themselves to be the Successors of the Apostles, walking peaceably and modestly in the Apostles steps, without intermedling with State-Affairs, may apply themselves wholly to promote the Salvation of Souls.

Farewell.

Notes

1 Here Arminius cites briefly both Lactantius and Tertullian.
2 In Jeremy Taylor, *Whole Works* (15 vols, London, 1822), I, cccxvii.
3 See Mino Celsi, *In haereticis coercendis quatenus progredi liceat*, ed. P. Bietenholz (Naples: Prism Editrice, 1982 [orig. 1577]).
4 "We are ready to listen if they should teach; certainly we believe nothing from those who keep silent."
5 Cyril of Alexandria, in his commentary on the Gospel of John, book 2, ch. 1.
6 This excerpt differs from that included in Gerald R. Cragg (ed.), *The Cambridge Platonists* (Oxford: Oxford University Press, 1968), pp. 313–21. Cragg's excerpt is taken from Henry More, *The Theological Works* (London, 1708), an English translation of a revised edition, in Latin, which was published in 1675.
7 [Note by Henry More]: Which qualification is all along supposed in this question, otherwise the falsities of a Religion cannot so rightly be conceived any commands of God, but a blindness and darkness the Religionist has brought upon or continues to himself through his own Hypocrisie and wickedness.
8 [Note by Henry More]: So it is to them that are sincere, but in those that are not it is like the stopping of the ears against the reading of the Law in a Known Language.
9 "For truth is great and it shall prevail."
10 Emphasis in original.
11 Philippe Dubois-Goibaud, *Conformité de la conduite de l'Église de France pour ramener les protestants avec celle de l'Église d'Afrique* (1685).
12 Jacques Bénigne Bossuet, *Politics Drawn from the Very Words of Holy Scripture*, tr. Patrick Riley (Cambridge: Cambridge University Press, 1990), pp. 195ff. See also E. K. Sanders, *Jacques Bénigne Bossuet: A Study* (London: SPCK, 1921).

5

THE EIGHTEENTH CENTURY

Jean Jacques Rousseau, "On Civil Religion" (1762)

Rousseau (1712–78), a Genevan-born philosopher who spent many years abroad, especially in France, discussed the foundations of the state, and in this chapter he turned his attention to the question of religion. He supplies a theory of the origins of religion and describes the various patterns by which religion has related to political life. Christianity comes in for the greatest attention, and is criticized for its exclusive concern with heavenly matters. Thus, "I am mistaken in speaking of a Christian republic; the terms are mutually exclusive." Still, a religion is needed for the *salus populi*. Clearly, Rousseau presented himself as a defender of tolerance in religion, but in suppressing inconvenient theological judgments and rendering religion socially and politically innocuous, his profession seems rather unconvincing.

SOURCE: Jean Jacques Rousseau, *The Social Contract and Discourses*, tr. G. D. H. Cole (London: J. M. Dent & Sons, 1913), pp. 113–15.
LITERATURE: R. A. Leigh, *Rousseau and the Problem of Tolerance in the Eighteenth Century* (Oxford: Clarendon Press, 1979).

Book IV

Chapter 8

But, setting aside political considerations, let us come back to what is right, and settle our principles on this important point. The right which the social compact gives the Sovereign over the subjects does not, we have seen, exceed the limits of public expediency. The subjects then owe the Sovereign an account of their opinions only to such an extent as they matter to the community. Now, it matters very much to the community that each citizen should have a religion. That will make him love his duty; but the dogmas of that religion concern the State and its members only so far as they have reference to morality and to the duties which he who professes them is bound to do to others. Each man may have, over and above, what opinions he pleases, without its being the Sovereign's business to take cognizance of them; for, as the Sovereign has no authority in the other world, whatever the lot of its subjects may be in the life to come, that is not its business, provided they are good citizens in this life.

There is therefore a purely civil profession of faith of which the Sovereign should fix the articles, not exactly as religious dogmas, but as social sentiments without which a man cannot be a good citizen or a faithful subject. While it can compel no one to believe them, it can banish from the State whoever does not believe them – it can banish him, not for impiety, but as an anti-social being, incapable of truly loving the laws and justice, and of sacrificing, at need, his life to his duty. If any one, after publicly recognizing these dogmas, behaves as if he does not believe them, let him be punished by death: he has committed the worst of all crimes, that of lying before the law.

The dogmas of civil religion ought to be few, simple, and exactly worded, without explanation or commentary. The existence of a mighty, intelligent, and beneficent Divinity, possessed of foresight and providence, the life to come, the happiness of the just, the punishment of the wicked, the sanctity of the social contract and the laws: these are its positive dogmas. Its negative dogmas I confine to one, intolerance, which is a part of the cults we have rejected.

Those who distinguish civil from theological intolerance are, to my mind, mistaken. The two forms are inseparable. It is impossible to live at peace with those we regard as damned; to love them would be to hate God who punishes them: we positively must either reclaim or torment them. Wherever theological intolerance is admitted, it must inevitably have some civil effect; and as soon as it has such an effect, the Sovereign is no longer Sovereign even in the temporal sphere: thenceforth priests are the real masters, and kings only their ministers.

Now that there is and can be no longer an exclusive national religion, tolerance should be given to all religions that tolerate others, so long as their dogmas contain nothing contrary to the duties of citizenship. But whoever dares to say: "Outside the Church is no salvation," ought to be driven from the State, unless the State is the Church, and the prince the pontiff. Such a dogma is good only in a theocratic government; in any other, it is fatal. The reason for which Henry IV is said to have embraced the Roman religion ought to make every honest man leave it, and still more any prince who knows how to reason.

Voltaire, *Philosophical Dictionary* (1764)

Voltaire's opinions on religion in general and Christianity in particular are not easy to ascertain. As Helvétius and others discovered, it was unwise to be too forthcoming about one's questionings of orthodox theological belief. However, Voltaire had no commitment to the Christianity of his time and place, and if not actually an atheist, was certainly an agnostic. This small book, published anonymously, was intended to purvey his free thought, and the reaction it aroused was furious. Here priests are subjected to criticism for inspiring intolerance, an attitude Voltaire insisted was far removed from the genuine spirit of Christianity, though he never advocated unlimited religious freedom. These sentiments followed hard on the heels of the Calas affair in which Voltaire had taken up the case of the Huguenot Jean Calas, brutally executed on a false charge of having murdered his son for religious reasons.[1]

SOURCE: Voltaire, *Philosophical Dictionary*, tr. Theodore Besterman (Harmondsworth: Penguin, 1972), pp. 332–4, 387–94.
LITERATURE: Theodore Besterman, *Voltaire* (London: Longman, 1970 [1969]).

Persecution

It is not Diocletian whom I would call a persecutor, for he protected the Christians for eighteen years; and if, in the last part of his reign, he did not rescue them from the resentment of Galerius, he was in that merely a prince, like so many others, seduced and drawn away by conspiracies from his true character.

Still less would I give the name of persecutors to Trajan and to Marcus Aurelius: I would feel like a blasphemer.

Who is a persecutor? It is he whose wounded pride and furious fanaticism irritate the prince or the magistrate against innocent men guilty only of the crime of holding different opinions. "Impudent fellow, you worship a god; you preach virtue, and practise it; you have served mankind, and consoled it; you have found the orphan girl a home, you have helped the poor; you have changed the deserts in which a few slaves dragged out a wretched existence into a fertile countryside peopled with happy families. But I have discovered that you despise me, and that you have never read my published disputation; you know that I am a rascal; that I have forged the handwriting of G——; that I have stolen——; you might well say so; I must forestall you. So I shall go to the prime minister's confessor, or the podesta. I'll demonstrate to them, inclining my head and twisting my mouth, that you had erroneous views about the cells in which the seventy[2] were locked up; that ten years ago you even talked about Tobias's dog in a manner by no means respectful, maintaining that it was a spaniel although I proved that it was a greyhound; I'll denounce you as the enemy of god and men." Such is the language of the persecutor; and if these words don't exactly leave his mouth, they're engraved in his heart with the burin of fanaticism dipped in the gall of envy.

Thus did the Jesuit Le Tellier persecute cardinal de Noailles, and Jurieu persecute Bayle.

When the persecution of the Protestants began in France, it was not Francis I nor Henry II nor Francis II who spied on these unfortunates, who took arms against them with deliberate fury, and who consigned them to the flames to wreak their vengeance on them. Francis I was too busy with the duchesse d'Etampes, Henry II with his old Diana, and Francis II was too young. Who started these persecutions? Jealous priests, who armed the prejudices of the magistrates and the politic manoeuvres of the ministers.

Had the kings not been deceived, had they foreseen that the persecution would cause fifty years of civil war, and that half the nation would be exterminated by the other half, their tears would have quenched the first pyres they allowed to be lit.

O god of mercy! if any man can resemble this malignant being who is depicted as ceaselessly busy in destroying your works, is it not the persecutor?

Toleration

I

What is toleration? It is the prerogative of humanity. We are all steeped in weaknesses and errors: let us forgive one another's follies, it is the first law of nature.

The Parsee, the Hindu, the Jew, the Mohammedan, the Chinese deist, the Brahman, the Greek Christian, the Roman Christian, the Protestant Christian, the Quaker Christian trade with each another in the stock exchanges of Amsterdam, London, Surat or Basra: they do not raise their daggers against one another to win souls for their religions. Why then have we butchered each other almost without interruption since the first council of Nicaea?

Constantine began by issuing an edict which permitted all religions, but he ended by persecuting. Before him the authorities acted against the Christians only because they started to form a party in the state. The Romans permitted all cults, even those of the Jews and Egyptians, for which they had so much contempt. Why did Rome tolerate these cults? It was because neither the Egyptians, nor even the Jews, tried to exterminate the ancient religion of the empire. They did not run up and down the earth to make proselytes: they thought only of making money. But the Christians unquestionably wanted their religion to predominate. The Jews did not want the statue of Jupiter in Jerusalem, but the Christians did not want it in the capitol. Saint Thomas had the honesty to admit that if the Christians did not dethrone the emperors it was because they could not. It was their opinion that the whole world should be Christian. So they were necessarily the enemies of the whole world until it was converted.

They were also each others enemies in every detail of their controversies. Should Jesus Christ be regarded above all as god? Those who denied it were anathematized by the name of Ebionites, who anathematized the worshippers of Jesus. Some of them wanted all property to be owned in common, as it is alleged it was in the time of the apostles. Their adversaries called them Nicolaitans, and accused them of the most infamous crimes. Others adhered to a mystical devotion. They were called gnostics, and they were attacked with fury. Marcion discussed the trinity, and he was called idolator.

Tertullian, Praxeas, Origen, Novatus, Novatian, Sabellius, Donatus were all persecuted by their brothers before Constantine; hardly had Constantine made the Christian religion prevail than the Athanasians and the Eusebians tore each other to pieces. Since then, and to this day, the Christian church has streamed with blood.

I admit that the Jewish people was very barbarous. It butchered without pity all the inhabitants of a wretched little country to which it had no more right than it has to Paris or London. Nevertheless when Naaman was cured of his leprosy by plunging seven times into the Jordan, when, as an acknowledgement to Elisha, who had taught him this secret, he told him that he would worship the god of the Jews out of gratitude, he reserved to himself the right to worship also his king's god, he asked Elisha's permission to do so, and the prophet did not hesitate to give it to him. The Jews worshipped their god, but they were never surprised that each people had its own. They thought it proper that Chemosh should give a certain district to the Moabites, provided that god gave them one also. Jacob did not hesitate to marry the daughter of an idolator. Laban had his god as Jacob had his. Here we have examples of toleration among the most intolerant and the most cruel people of all antiquity. We have imitated it in its absurd frenzies, and not in its forbearance.

It is clear that every individual who persecutes a man, his brother, because he does not agree with him, is a monster. This is obvious enough. But the government, the magistrates, the princes, how should they behave to those who have a different form of worship? If they are powerful foreigners it is certain that a prince will contract an alliance with them. François I, most Christian, joined with the Moslems against Charles V, most Catholic. François II gave money to the German Lutherans to help them in their rebellion against the emperor; but he started off according to custom by burning the Lutherans in his own country. He subsidized them in Saxony for political reasons, he burned them for political reasons in Paris. But what happened? Persecutions make proselytes: France was soon full of new Protestants. At first they submitted to being hanged, and then they took to hanging in their turn. Civil wars followed, then the saint Bartholomew, and this corner of the world was soon worse than everything the ancients and the moderns have ever said about hell.

Senseless people, who have never been able to offer up a pure worship to the god who made you! Wretches, who have never allowed yourselves to be guided by the examples of the Noachids, the educated Chinese, the Parsees, and all wise men! Monsters, who need superstitions as the gizzards of the ravens need carrion! I have already told you, and I have nothing else to tell you: if you have two religions in your midst they will cut each other's throats; if you have thirty, they will live in peace. Look at the Grand Turk: he governs Parsees, Hindus, Greek Christians, Nestorians, Roman Catholics. The first man who tried to make trouble is impaled, and everybody is peaceful.

II

Of all religions the Christian is undoubtedly that which should instill the greatest toleration, although so far the Christians have been the most intolerant of all men.

Jesus having deigned to be born in poverty and a low condition, like his brothers, never condescended to practice the art of writing. The Jews had a legal system written down in the greatest detail, and we do not have a single line from the hand of Jesus. The apostles disagreed on a number of points. Saint Peter and Saint Barnabas ate forbidden meat with new Christians who were foreigners, and abstained with Jewish Christians. Saint Paul reproached them for this conduct, and this same Pharisee Saint Paul, disciple of the Pharisee Gamaliel, this same Saint Paul who had furiously persecuted the Christians, and who, having broken with Gamaliel, himself became a Christian, nevertheless after that sacrificed in the temple of Jerusalem during his apostolate. For a week he publicly observed all the ceremonies of the Jewish law he had renounced. He even added super-fluous devotions and purifications. He judaized completely. For a week the greatest apostle of the Christians did the very things for which men are condemned to the stake by most Christian peoples.

Theodas and Judas had called themselves messiahs before Jesus. Dositheus, Simon, Menander called themselves messiahs after Jesus. A score of sects existed in Judea by the first century of the church, even before the name of Christian was known. The contemplative gnostics, the Dositheans, the Co-rinthians existed before the disciples of Jesus had taken the name of Chris-tians. There were soon thirty gospels, each of which belonged to a different community, and by the end of the first century thirty sects of Christians could be counted in Asia Minor, Syria, Alexandria, and even in Rome.

All these sects, despised by the Roman government and hidden by their obscurity, nevertheless persecuted each other, which is all they could do in their abject condition. They were nearly all composed of the scum of the people.

When at last a few Christians embraced the dogmas of Plato and injected a little philosophy into their religions, which they separated from Judaism, they gradually grew in importance, though still divided into several sects. There has never been a single moment when the Christian church was united. It had its birth in the midst of the divisions of the Jews, Samaritans, Pharisees, Sadducees, Essenes, Judaites, disciples of John, Therapeutes. It was divided in its cradle, it was divided even in the persecutions it occasion-ally suffered under the first emperors. A martyr was often regarded by his brothers as an apostate, and the Carpocratian Christian expired under the sword of the Roman executioner, excommunicated by the Ebionite Chris-tian, which Ebionite was anathematized by the Sabellian.

This horrible discord, which has lasted for so many centuries, is a most striking lesson that we should mutually forgive our errors. Dissension is the great evil of mankind, and toleration is its only remedy.

There is nobody who does not agree with this truth, whether he medit-ates calmly in his study, or whether he peacefully examines the truth with his friends. Why then do the same men who in private approve forbearance, beneficence, justice, so vehemently denounce these virtues in public? Why? Because self-interest is their god, because they sacrifice everything to this monster they worship.

I possess a rank and a power created by ignorance and credulity. I step on the heads of the men who are prostrate at my feet; if they get up and look me in the face, I am lost; I must therefore keep them fastened to the ground with chains of iron.

Thus have reasoned men made powerful by centuries of fanaticism. They have other powerful men under them, and these have still others, all of whom enrich themselves at the expense of the poor, fatten on their blood, and laugh at their stupidity. They all detest toleration, just as politicians enriched at the public's expense fear to submit their accounts, and just as tyrants dread the word liberty. Finally, to crown all, they bribe fanatics who loudly shout: "Respect my master's absurdities, tremble, pay, and be silent."

This was for long the practice in a large part of the world, but now that so many sects rival each others' power, what should be our attitude to them? We know that every sect is a guarantee of error. There are no sects of geometricians, algebraists, arithmeticians, because all the propositions of geometry, algebra, arithmetic are true. We can make mistakes in every other science. What Thomist or Scotist theologian would dare to say seriously that he is sure of what he says?

If there is any sect that recalls the times of the first Christians, it is undoubtedly that of the Quakers. Nothing more resembles the apostles. The apostles received the spirit, and the Quakers receive the spirit. Three or four of the apostles and disciples spoke at once in the assembly on the third floor; the Quakers do as much on the ground floor. According to Saint Paul women were allowed to preach, and according to the same Saint Paul they were forbidden to preach; female Quakers preach by virtue of the first permission.

The apostles and disciples swore by yes and by no, the Quakers do not swear otherwise.

No rank, no finery distinguished the disciples and apostles; the Quakers have sleeves without buttons; and all are dressed in the same way.

Jesus Christ did not baptize any of his apostles; the Quakers are not baptized.

It would be easy to press the parallel further. It would be still easier to show how the Christian religion of today differs from the religion practiced by Jesus. Jesus was a Jew, and we are not Jews. Jesus abstained from pork because it is unclean, and from rabbit because it ruminates and does not have a cloven foot; we boldly eat pork because to us it is not unclean, and we eat rabbit which has a cloven foot and does not ruminate.

Jesus was circumcised, and we keep our foreskins. Jesus ate the paschal lamb with lettuce, he kept the feast of tabernacles, and we do not. He observed the sabbath, and we have changed it. He sacrificed, and we do not sacrifice.

Jesus always concealed the mystery of his incarnation and his status. He did not say that he was god's equal. Saint Paul says expressly in his Epistle to the Hebrews that god created Jesus lower than the angels. And in spite of all the words of saint Paul the council of Nicaea acknowledged Jesus to be god.

Jesus gave the pope neither the marches of Ancona nor the duchy of Spoleto; and yet the pope possesses them by divine right.

Jesus did not make a sacrament of marriage and the diaconate; and with us the diaconate and marriage are sacraments.

If we look at the matter at all closely we see that the catholic, apostolic and roman religion is the opposite of the religion of Jesus in all its ceremonies and in all its dogmas.

But then must we all judaize because Jesus judaized all his life?

If it were permissible to reason consistently in matters of religion, it would be clear that we should all become Jews because our savior Jesus Christ was born a Jew, lived a Jew, and died a Jew, and because he said expressly that he accomplished, that he fulfilled the Jewish religion. But it is even clearer that we should tolerate each other because we are all weak, inconsistent, subject to mutability and to error. Would a reed laid into the mud by the wind say to a neighboring reed bent in the opposite direction: "Creep in my fashion, wretch, or I shall petition to have you torn up and burned?"

Joseph Priestley, *An Essay on the First Principles of Government* (1771)

Priestley (1733–1804) was an English materialist philosopher; his doctrine was unitarianism. Unlike other "old" dissenters, who strove to achieve emancipation for themselves, Priestley was also an advocate of a similar benefit for Roman Catholics; indeed he had no minimum creed for toleration or liberty. His thoughts on religious freedom were not really new, but he applied the notions he inherited to the conditions of his own time. With respect to government, he was a minimalist: societies are best when the ruling power does not meddle in religion. After all, religion is directed toward a final state where the institutions of this age have no influence. Furthermore, Priestley was full of the optimism of his time, tinged with a Christian millennial expectation. He believed that humankind was pressing onward and upward; thus to attempt to freeze humanity in its present state by means of, e.g., religious establishments was contrary to the Maker's design.

SOURCE: Joseph Priestley, *An Essay on the First Principles of Government*, in *Theological and Miscellaneous Works*, 25 vols (London, 1817–31), vol. XXII, pp. 54–9, 66–70, 119–27, 137–9, 142–3.

LITERATURE: Anthony Lincoln, *Some Political and Social Ideas of English Dissent, 1763–1800* (Cambridge: Cambridge University Press, 1938), pp. 151–81; Martin Fitzpatrick, "Joseph Priestley, and the Cause of Universal Toleration," *The Price–Priestley Newsletter*, 1 (1977), pp. 3–30.

[Section V]   The most important question concerning the extent of civil government is, whether the civil magistrate ought to extend his authority to matters of *religion*; and the only method of deciding this important question, as it appears to me, is to have recourse at once to first principles, and the ultimate rule concerning every thing that respects a society, viz. whether such interference of the civil magistrate appear to be for the public good. And as all arguments *a priori*, in matters of policy, are apt to be fallacious, *fact* and *experience* seem to be our only safe guides. Now these, as far as our knowledge of history extends, declare clearly for no interference in this case at all, or, at least, for as little as is possible. Those societies have ever enjoyed the most happiness, and have been, *caeteris paribus*, in the most flourishing state, where the civil magistrates have meddled the least with religion, and where they have the most closely confined their attention to what immediately affects the civil interests of their fellow citizens.

Civil and *religious* matters (taking the words in their usual acceptation) seem to be so distinct, that it can only be in very uncommon emergencies, where, for instance, religious quarrels among the members of the state rise very high, that the civil magistrate can have any call or pretence for interfering with religion.

It is, indeed, impossible to name any two things, about which men are concerned, so remote in their nature, but that they have some connections and mutual influences; but were I asked what two things I should think to be in the *least danger* of being confounded, and which even the ingenuity of man could find the *least pretense* for involving together, I should say, the things that relate to *this life*, and those that relate to the *life to come*. Defining the object of civil government, in the most extensive sense, to be the making provision for the secure and comfortable enjoyment of this life, by preventing one man from injuring another in his person or property; I should think the office of the civil magistrate to be in no great danger of being encroached upon, by the methods that men might think proper to take to provide for their happiness after death.

All the civil societies we enter into in this life will be dissolved by death. When this life is over, I shall not be able to claim any of the privileges of an Englishman; I shall not be bound by any of the laws of England, nor shall I owe any allegiance to its sovereign. When, therefore, my situation in a future life shall have no connection with my privileges or obligations as an Englishman, why should those persons who make laws for Englishmen interfere with my conduct with respect to a state to which their power does not extend? Besides, we know that infinite mischiefs have arisen from this interference of government in the business of religion; and we have yet seen no inconvenience to have arisen from the want or the relaxation of it.

The fine country of Flanders, the most flourishing and opulent then in Europe, was absolutely ruined, past recovery, by the mad attempt of Philip II to introduce the Popish Inquisition into that country. France was greatly hurt by the Revocation of the Edict of Nantes; whereas England was a great gainer on both occasions, by granting an asylum for those persecuted, industrious people; who repaid us for our kindness, by the introduction of many useful arts and manufactures, which were the foundation of our present commerce, riches, and power.

Pennsylvania flourished much more than New England, or than any other of the English settlements in North America, evidently in consequence of giving more liberty in matters of religion, at its first establishment. Holland has found its advantage in the indulgence she gives to a great variety of religious persuasions. England has also been much more flourishing and happy, since the *establishment*, as it may properly enough be styled, of the Dissenting method of worship, by what is commonly called the *Act of Toleration*. And all the sensible part of Europe concur in thinking, both that the Polish dissidents have a right to all the privileges of other Polish citizens; and that it would be much happier for that country if their claims were quietly admitted, and none but interested bigots opposed their demands.

If we look a little farther off from home, let it be said, what inconvenience did Jenghis Khan, Tamerlane, and other eastern conquerors, ever find from leaving religion to its natural course in the countries they subdued, and from having Christians, Mahometans, and a variety of Pagans under the same form of civil government? Are not both Christianity and Mohammedanism, in fact, established (the former, at least, fully tolerated) in Turkey; and what inconvenience, worth mentioning, has ever arisen from it?

Pity it is, then, that more and fairer experiments are not made; when, judging from what is past, the consequences of *unbounded liberty, in matters of religion*, promise to be so very favorable to the best interests of mankind.

I am aware that the connection between civil and religious affairs will be urged for the necessity of some interference of the legislature with religion; and, as I observed before, I do not deny the connection. But as this connection has always been found to be the greatest in barbarous nations and imperfect governments, to which it lends an useful aid; it may be presumed, that it is gradually growing less necessary; and that, in the present advanced state of human society, there is very little occasion for it. For my own part, I have no apprehension but that, at this day, the laws might be obeyed very well without any ecclesiastical sanctions, enforced by the civil magistrate.

Not that I think religion will ever be a matter of indifference in civil society; that is impossible, if the word be understood in its greatest latitude, and by religion we mean that principle whereby men are influenced by the dread of evil or the hope of reward from any unknown and invisible causes, whether the good or evil be expected to take place in this world or another; comprehending enthusiasm, superstition, and every species of false religion, as well as the true. Nor is such an event at all desirable; nay, the more just motives men have to the same good actions, the better; but religious motives may still operate in favor of the civil laws, without such a connection as has been formed between them in ecclesiastical establishments; and I think this end would be answered even better without that connection.

In all the modes of religion which subsist among mankind, however subversive of virtue they may be in theory, there is some *salvo* for good morals; so that, in fact, they enforce the more essential parts, at least, of that conduct, which the good order of society requires. Besides, it might be expected, that if all the modes of religion were equally protected by the civil magistrate, they would all vie with one another, which should best deserve that protection. This, however, is, in fact, all the alliance that can take place between religion and civil policy, each enforcing the same conduct by different motives. Any other "alliance between church and state"[3] is only the alliance of different sorts of worldly-minded men, for their temporal emolument.

If I be urged with the horrid excesses of the Anabaptists in Germany, about the time of the Reformation; of the Levellers in England, during the civil wars; and shocking practices of that people in Asia, from whom we borrow the term *assassin*; I answer, that, besides its being absolutely chimerical to apprehend any such extravagances at present, and that they can never subsist long, such outrages as these, against the peace of society, may be restrained by the civil magistrate, without his troubling himself about religious opinions. If a man commit murder, let him be punished as a murderer, and let no regard be paid to his plea of conscience for committing the action; but let not the opinions which led to the action be meddled with: for then it is probable that more harm will be done than good, and that for a small evident advantage, risk will be run of endless and unknown evils; or if the civil magistrate never interfere in religion but in such cases as those before-mentioned, the friends of liberty will have no great reason to complain. Considering what great encroachments have been made upon their rights in several countries of Europe, they will be satisfied if part of the load be removed. They will support themselves with the hope, that, as the state will certainly find a solid advantage in every relaxation of its claim upon men's consciences, it will relax more and more of its pretended rights; till, at last, religious opinions, and religious actions, be as free as the air we breathe, or the light of the common sun. . . .

[Section VI]   Besides, there is something in the nature of religion that makes it more than out of the proper sphere, or province of the civil magistrate to intermeddle with it. The duties of religion, properly understood, seem to be, in some measure, incompatible with the interference of the civil power. For the purpose and object of religion necessarily suppose the powers of individuals, and a responsibility, which is the consequence of those powers; so that the civil magistrate, by taking any of those powers from individuals, and assuming them to himself, doth so far incapacitate them for the duties of religion. If, for instance, I be commanded by divine authority to "search the scriptures," and the magistrate forbid me the use of them, how can I discharge my duty? And for the same reason, I must think the authority of the magistrates opposed to that of God, in every case in which human laws impede the use of my faculties in matters of religion.

As a being capable of immortal life, (which is a thing of infinitely more consequence to me than all the political considerations of this world,) I must endeavor to render myself acceptable to God, by such dispositions and such conduct as he has required, in order to fit me for future happiness. For this purpose, it is evidently requisite, that I diligently use my reason, in order to make myself acquainted with the will of God; and also that I have liberty to do whatever I believe he requires, provided I do not molest my fellow creatures by such assumed liberty. But all human establishments, as such, obstruct freedom of inquiry in matters of religion, by laying an undue bias upon the mind, if they be not such as, by their express constitutions, prevent all inquiry, and preclude every possible effect of it.

Christianity, by being a more spiritual and moral constitution than any other form of religion that ever appeared in the world, requires men to think and act for themselves more accurately than any other. But human establishments, by calling off men's attention from the commandments of God to those of men, tend to defeat the great ends of religion. They are, therefore, incompatible with the genius of Christianity.

[Section X]   All civil societies, and the whole science of civil government, on which they are founded, are yet in their infancy. Like other arts and sciences, this is gradually improving; but it improves more slowly, because opportunities for making experiments are fewer. Indeed, hardly any trials in legislation have ever been made by persons who had knowledge and ability to collect from history, and to compare the observations which might be of use for this purpose, or had leisure to digest them properly at the time. Taking it for granted, therefore, that our constitution and laws have not escaped the imperfections which we see to be incident to every thing human; by all means, let the closest attention be given to them, let their excellencies and defects be thoroughly laid open, and let improvements of every kind be made; but not such as would prevent all farther improvements: because it is not probable, that any improvements which the utmost sagacity of man could now suggest, would be an equivalent for the prevention of all that might be made hereafter. Were the best-formed state in the world to be fixed in its present condition, I make no doubt but that, in a course of time, it would be the worst.

History demonstrates this truth with respect to all the celebrated states of antiquity; and as all things (and particularly whatever depends upon science) have of late years been in a quicker progress towards perfection than ever; we may safely conclude the same with respect to any political state now in being. What advantage did Sparta (the constitution of whose government was so much admired by the ancients, and many moderns) reap from those institutions which contributed to its longevity, but the longer continuance of what I should not scruple to call the worst government we read of in the world; a government which secured to a man the fewest of his natural rights, and of which a man who had a taste for life would least of all choose to be a member. While the arts of life were improving in all the neighboring nations, Sparta derived this noble prerogative from her constitution, that she continued the nearest to her pristine barbarity; and in the space of near a thousand years (which includes the whole period in which letters and the arts were the most cultivated in the rest of Greece,) produced no one poet, orator, historian, or artist of any kind. The convulsions of Athens, where life was in some measure enjoyed, and the faculties of body and mind had their proper exercise and gratification, were, in my opinion, far preferable to the savage uniformity of Sparta.

The constitution of Egypt was similar to that of Sparta, and the advantages that country received from it were similar. Egypt was the mother of the arts to the states of Greece; but the rigid institutions of this mother of the arts kept them in their infancy; so that the states of Greece, being more favorably situated for improvements of all kinds, soon went beyond their instructress; and no improvements of any kind were ever made in Egypt, till it was subdued by a foreign power. What would have been the state of agriculture, ship-building, or war, if those arts had been fixed in England two or three centuries ago?

Dr Brown will urge me with the authority of Plutarch, who largely extols the regulations of Egypt and of Sparta, and censures the Roman legislators for adopting nothing similar to them. But I beg leave to appeal from the authority of Plutarch, and of all the ancients, as by no means competent judges in this case. Imperfect as the science of government is at present, it is certainly much more perfect than it was in their time. On the authority of the ancients, Dr Brown might as well contend for another institution of the famed Egyptians, viz. their obliging all persons to follow the occupations of their fathers; and perhaps this might be no bad auxiliary to his prescribed mode of education, and prevent the springing up of faction in a state. It would likewise favor another object, which the Doctor has professedly in view, viz. checking the growth of commerce.

Supposing this wise system of perpetuation had occurred to our ancestors in the feudal times, and that an assembly of old English Barons, with their heads full of their feudal rights and services, had imitated the wise Spartans, and perpetuated the severe feudal institutions; what would England at this day have been, (with the unrivalled reputation of uniformity and constancy in its laws,) but the most barbarous, the weakest and most distracted state in Europe? It is plain from fact, that Divine Providence had greater things in view in favor of these kingdoms; and has been conducting them through a series of gradual changes (arising from internal and external causes) which have brought us to our present happy condition; and which, if suffered to go on, may carry us to a pitch of happiness of which we can yet form no conception.

Had the religious system of our oldest forefathers been established on these wise and perpetual foundations, we had now been Pagans, and our priests Druids. Had our Saxon conquerors been endued with the same wisdom and foresight, we had been worshipping Thor and Woden; and had our ancestors, three centuries ago, persevered in this spirit, we had been blind and priest-ridden Papists. The greatest blessing that can befal a state, which is so rigid and inflexible in its institutions, is to be conquered by a people, who have a better government, and have made farther advances in the arts of life. And it is undoubtedly a great advantage which the Divine Being has provided for this world, that conquests and revolutions should give mankind those opportunities of reforming their systems of government, and of improving the science of it, which they would never have found themselves.

In the excellent constitution of nature, evils of all kinds, some way or other, find their proper remedy; and when government, religion, education, and every thing that is valuable in society seem to be in so fine a progress towards a more perfect state, is it not our wisdom to favor this progress; and to allow the remedies of all disorders to operate gradually and easily, rather than, by a violent system of perpetuation, to retain all disorders till they force a remedy? In the excellent constitution of the human body, a variety of outlets are provided for noxious humors, by means of which the system relieves itself when any slight disorders happen to it. But if these outlets be obstructed, the whole system is endangered by the convulsions which ensue.

Some things in civil society do, in their own nature, require to be established or fixed by law for a considerable time; but that part of the system, for the reasons mentioned above, will certainly be the most imperfect; and therefore it is the wisdom of the legislature to make that part as small as possible, and let the establishments which are necessary be as easy as is

consistent with the tolerable order of society. It is an universal maxim, that
the more liberty is given to every thing which is in a state of growth, the
more perfect it will become; and when it is grown to its full size, the more
amply will it repay its wise parent for the indulgence given to it in its infant
state. A judicious father will bear with the frowardness of his children, and
overlook many flights of youth, which can give him no pleasure, but from
the prospect they afford of his children becoming useful and valuable men,
when the fire of youth is abated.

I do not pretend to define what degree of establishment is necessary for
many things relating to civil society: but thus much I think is clear, that
every system of policy is too strict and violent, in which any thing that may
be the instrument of general happiness, is under so much restraint, that it
can never reform itself from the disorders which may be incident to it;
when it is so circumstanced, that it cannot improve as far as it is capable of
improvement, but that every reformation must necessarily be introduced
from some other quarter; in which case it must generally be brought about
by force. Is it not a standing argument that religion, in particular, has been
too much confined in all countries, that the body of the clergy have never
reformed themselves; and that all reformations have ever been forced upon
them, and have generally been attended with the most horrible persecutions,
and dangerous convulsions in the state? I cannot help thinking also, that
every system of government is violent and tyrannical, which incapacitates
men of the best abilities and of the greatest integrity, from rendering their
country any service in their power, while those who pay no regard to
conscience may have free access to all places of power and profit.

It seems to be the uniform intention of Divine Providence, to lead mankind to happiness in a progressive, which is the surest, though the slowest,
method. Evil always leads to good, and imperfect to perfect. The Divine
Being might, no doubt, have adopted a different plan, have made human
nature and human governments perfect from the beginning. He might have
formed the human mind with an intuitive knowledge of truth, without
leading men through so many labyrinths of error. He might have made man
perfectly virtuous, without giving so much exercise to his passions in his
struggles with the habits of vice. He might have sent an angel, or have
commissioned a man, to establish a perfect form of civil government; and,
a priori, this would seem to have been almost as essential to human happiness as any system of truth; at least, that it would have been a valuable
addition to a system of religious truth: but though it would be impiety in us
to pretend to fathom the depths of the Divine counsels, I think we may
fairly conclude, that if this method of proceeding had been the best for us,
he, whom we cannot conceive to be influenced by any thing but his desire

to promote the happiness of his creatures, would have pursued it. But a contrary method has been adopted in every thing relating to us.

How many falls does a child get before it learns to walk secure! How many inarticulate sounds precede those which are articulate! How often are we imposed upon by all our senses before we learn to form a right judgment of the proper objects of them! How often do our passions mislead us, and involve us in difficulties, before we reap the advantage they were intended to bring us in our pursuit of happiness; and how many false judgments do we make, in the investigation of all kinds of truth, before we come to a right conclusion! How many ages do errors and prejudices of all kinds prevail, before they are dissipated by the light of truth; and how general and how long was the reign of false religion before the propagation of the true! How late was Christianity, that great remedy of vice and ignorance, introduced! How slow and how confined its progress!

In short, it seems to have been the intention of Divine Providence, that mankind should be, as far as possible, self-taught; that we should attain to every thing excellent and useful, as the result of our own experience and observation; that our judgments should be formed by the appearances which are presented to them, and our hearts instructed by their own feelings. But by the unnatural system of rigid, unalterable establishments, we put it out of our power to instruct ourselves, or to derive any advantage from the lights we acquire from experience and observation; and thereby, as far as is in our power, we counteract the kind intentions of the Deity in the constitution of the world, and in providing for a state of constant though slow improvement in every thing.

A variety of useful lessons may be learned from our attention to the conduct of Divine Providence respecting us. When history and experience demonstrate the uniform method of Divine Providence to have been what has been above represented, let us learn from it to be content with the natural though slow progress we are in to a more perfect state. But let us always endeavor to keep things in this progress. Let us, however, beware, lest, by attempting to accelerate, we in fact retard our progress in happiness. But more especially, let us take heed, lest, by endeavoring to secure and perpetuate the great ends of society, we in fact defeat those ends. We shall have a thousand times more enjoyment of a happy and perfect form of government, when we can see in history the long progress of our constitution through barbarous and imperfect systems of policy; as we are more confirmed in the truth, and have more enjoyment of it, by reviewing the many errors by which we were misled in our pursuit of it. If the Divine Being saw that the best form of government that even he could have prescribed for us, would not have answered the end of its institution, if it had been imposed by himself; much less can we imagine it could answer any valuable purpose, to have the crude systems (for they can be nothing more) of short-sighted men for ever imposed upon us.

Establishments, be they ever so excellent, still fix things somewhere; and this circumstance, which is all that is pleaded for them amounts to, is with me the greatest objection to them. I wish to see things in a progress to a better state, and no obstructions thrown in the way of reformation.

In spite of all the fetters we can lay upon the human mind, notwithstanding all possible discouragements in the way of free inquiry, knowledge of all kinds, and religious knowledge among the rest, will increase. The wisdom of one generation will ever be folly in the next. And yet, though we have seen this verified in the history of near two thousand years, we persist in the absurd maxim of making a preceding generation dictate to a succeeding one, which is the same thing as making the foolish instruct the wise; for, what is a lower degree of wisdom but comparative folly?

Had even Locke, Clarke, Hoadley, and others, who have gained immortal reputation by their freedom of thinking, but about half a century ago been appointed to draw up a creed, they would have inserted in it such articles of faith as myself, and hundreds more, should now think unscriptural and absurd: nay, articles, which they would have thought of great importance, we should think conveyed a reflection upon the moral government of God, and were injurious to virtue among men. And can we think that wisdom will die with us? No: our creeds, could we be so inconsistent with ourselves as to draw up any, would, I make no doubt, be rejected with equal disdain by our posterity.

That ecclesiastical establishments have really retarded the reformation from Popery, is evident from the face of things in Europe. Can it be thought that all the errors and abuses which had been accumulating in the space of fifteen hundred years, should be rectified in less than fifty, by men educated with strong prejudices in favor of them all? And yet the Augsburg Confession, I believe, stands unrepealed; the Church of England is the same now that it was in the reign of Queen Elizabeth, and the Church of Scotland is to this day in that imperfect and crude state in which John Knox left it.

Little did those great Reformers, whose memory I revere, think what burdens they, who had boldly shaken off the load from their own shoulders, were laying on those of others; and that the moment they had nobly freed themselves from the yoke of servitude, they were signing an act to enslave all that should come after them; forgetting the golden rule of the gospel, to do to others as we would that they should do to us.

Could religious knowledge have remained in the state in which the first Reformers left it; could the stone they had once moved from its seat, on the top of a precipice, have been stopped in its course, their provisions for perpetuation would have been wise and excellent; but their eyes were hardly closed, before their children found that their fathers had been too precipitate. They found their own hands tied up by their unthinking parents, and the knots too many, and too tight for them to unloose. . . .

Hitherto, indeed, few of the friends of free inquiry among Christians have been more than partial advocates for it. If they find themselves under any difficulty with respect to their own sentiments, they complain, and plead strongly for the rights of conscience, of private judgment, and of free inquiry; but when they have gotten room enough for themselves, they are quite easy, and in no pain for others. The Papist must have liberty to write against Pagans, Mohammedans, and Jews; but he cannot bear with Protestants. Writers in defence of the Church of England justify their separation from the Church of Rome, but, with the most glaring inconsistency, call the Protestant Dissenters, Schismatics; and many Dissenters, forgetting the fundamental principles of their dissent, which are the same that are asserted by all Christians and Protestants in similar circumstances, discourage every degree of liberty greater than they themselves have taken, and have as great an aversion to those whom they are pleased to call heretics, as Papists have for Protestants, or as Laud had for old Puritans.

But why should we confine our neighbor, who may want more room, in the same narrow limits with ourselves? The wider we make the common circle of liberty, the more its friends will it receive, and the stronger will be the common interest. Whatever be the particular views of the numerous tribes of searchers after truth, under whatever denomination we may be ranked; whether we be called, or call ourselves, Christian, Papists, Protestants, Dissenters, Heretics, or even Deists (for all are equal here, all are actuated by the same spirit, and all engaged in the same cause,) we stand in need of the same liberty of thinking, debating, and publishing. Let us, then, as far as our interest is the same, with one heart and voice, stand up for it. Not one of us can hurt his neighbor without using a weapon which, in the hand of power, might as well serve to chastise himself. The present state of the English government (including both the laws and the administration, which often corrects the rigor of the law) may, perhaps, bear my own opinions without taking much umbrage; but I could wish to congratulate many of my brother free-thinkers, on the greater indulgence which their more heretical sentiments may require.

To the honor of the Quakers be it spoken, that they are the only body of Christians who have uniformly maintained the principles of Christian liberty, and toleration [in Pennsylvania, where established]. . . . For this reason, if I were to pray for the general prevalence of any one sect of Christians (which I should not think it for the interest of Christianity to take place, even though I should settle the articles of it myself) it should be that of the Quakers; because, different as my opinions are from theirs, I have so much confidence in their moderation, that I believe they would let me live, write, and publish what I pleased unmolested among them. And this I own is more than I could promise myself from any other body of Christians whatever; the Presbyterians by no means excepted.

The object of this forced uniformity is narrow and illiberal, unworthy of human nature. Supposing it accomplished, what is it possible to gain by it, but, perhaps, a more obstinate and blind belief in the vulgar; while men of sense, seeing themselves debarred the very means of conviction, must of course be infidels? In those circumstances, it would really be an argument of a man's want of spirit, of sense, and even of virtue, to be a believer, because he would believe without sufficient evidence. Who would not, with every appearance of justice, suspect any cause, when he was not allowed to examine the arguments against it, and was only pressed with those in its favor? What sensible and upright judge would decide a cause, where all the witnesses on one side were by violence prevented from giving their evidence? Those who converse with Deists well know, that one of their strongest objections to Christianity arises from hence, that none of the early writings against it are preserved. How much stronger, and even unanswerable, would that objection have been, if Christianity had been, from the beginning, so effectually protected by civil magistrate, that no person had dared to write against it at all! Such friends to the evidence and true interests of Christianity, are all those who would suppress deistical writings at this day!

Suppose any article in a system of faith, so established and guarded, to be wrong, which is certainly a very modest supposition; let any of the advocates of this scheme say, how it is possible it should ever be rectified; or that if the truth should insinuate itself, by any avenue which they had not sufficiently guarded, how it could bring its evidence along with it, so as to command the attention and acceptance which it deserved. . . .

This seems to be the time, when the minds of men are opening to large and generous views of things. Politics are more extended in practice, and better understood in theory. Religious knowledge is greatly advanced, and the principle of universal toleration is gaining ground apace. Schemes of ecclesiastical policy, which, in times of barbarity, ignorance, and superstition, were intimately interwoven with schemes of civil policy, and which, in fact, made the greatest part of the old political mixed constitution, have been gradually excluded; till, at present, though ecclesiastical power be looked upon as an useful support and auxiliary of civil government, it is pretty much detached from it. And the more sensible part of humankind are evidently in a progress to the belief, that ecclesiastical and civil jurisdiction, being things of a totally different nature, ought, if possible, to be wholly disengaged from one another. Religious sentiments, with respect to their influence on civil society, will perhaps be regarded, in time, as a theory of morals, only of a higher and more perfect kind, excellent to enforce a regard to magistracy and the political duties, but improperly adopted into the same system, and enforced by the same penalties. Till we know whether this work, which seems to be going forward in several parts of Europe, be of God, or not, let us not take, at least any rigid and violent methods to oppose it, but patiently wait the issue; unless, in the mean time, the disorders of the state absolutely force us into violent measures. At present, notwithstanding some trifling alarm, perhaps artfully raised and propagated, may seem to give a handle to the friends of arbitrary power to make use of some degree of coercion, more gentle measures seem better adapted to ensure tranquillity. . . .

Claude Adrien Helvétius, *A Treatise on Man* (1772)

Helvétius (1715–71) was a successful tax farmer until he retired in 1751 to devote himself to philosophy. He opposed himself vigorously both to the organized religion of Roman Catholic France and to the vestiges of feudalism as continued under the *ancien régime*. His *De l'esprit* was condemned in 1758–9 on account of its thoroughgoing sensationalism which rendered the soul unnecessary, since matter was now deemed to be capable of thought. Along with the soul went immortality, salvation, the moral imperatives deduced from such beliefs, and the church as the guardian of all these notions. This selection exudes the writer's bitterness toward those who would silence the voice of a new world.

SOURCE: Claude Adrien Helvétius, *A Treatise on Man, his Intellectual Faculties and his Education*, 2 vols, tr. W. Hooper (New York: Burt Franklin, 1969 [repr. 1810 ed.]), vol. I, pp. 341–59; vol. II, pp. 358–9.
LITERATURE: D. W. Smith, *Helvétius: A Study in Persecution* (Oxford: Clarendon Press, 1965).

Section IV

Chapter 18   Of religious intolerance

This is the most dangerous of all intolerance; its motive is the love of power, religion its pretense. What is it they would punish in a heretic or unbeliever? The audacity of the man who would think for himself; who would believe his own reason before that of the priest, and thereby declare himself their equal. The pretense of avenging Heaven is nothing but that of his offended pride. Priests of almost all religions are the same.

In the sight of the mufti, as in that of a bonze, an infidel is an impious wretch that ought to be destroyed by fire from heaven; a man so destructive to society as to deserve to be burnt alive.

In the eyes of a wise man, however, this same infidel is a man who does not believe the tale of mother Goose: for what is there wanting to make that tale a religion? A number of people to maintain its veracity.

Whence comes it that men covered with the rags of penitence and the mask of charity have been at all times the most atrocious? How can it be possible that the light of toleration has not yet broken forth? What! must honest men hate and persecute each other without remorse for disputes about a word, frequently about the choice of errors, and because they are distinguished by the different names of Lutherans, Calvinists, Catholics, Mahometans, &c.

When in a convocation the monk anathematizes the dervise, can he be ignorant that in the sight of the dervise the truly impious, the real infidel, is the Christian, pope, or monk who does not believe in Mahomet? Can each sect, eternally condemned to stupidity, approve in itself what it detests in others?

Let them sometimes recollect the ingenious parable of a celebrated painter. Transported in a dream to the gates of heaven, says he, the first object that struck me was a venerable old man; by his keys, his bald head, and his long beard, I knew him to be St Peter. The apostle sat on the threshold of the celestial gates; a crowd of people advanced towards him; the first who presented himself was a papist; I have, said he, all my life been a religious man, and yet honest enough. Go in, replies the saint, and place yourself upon the bench for catholics. The next was a protestant, who gave a like account of himself; the saint said in the like manner, place yourself among the reformed. Then came merchants of Bagdat, Bassora, &c. these were all musulmans who had been constantly virtuous; St Peter made them sit down among the musulmans. At last came an infidel; What is thy sect? said the apostle. I am of no sect, he replied, but I have always been honest. Then you may go in. But where shall I seat myself? Next to those who appear to you most rational.

Would to heaven that, enlightened by this fable, men would no longer pretend to command the opinions of others! God has decreed that truth should be the recompense of inquiry. The most efficacious prayers for obtaining it are, it is said, study and application. O stupid monks! have you ever offered up those prayers?

What is truth? You do not know: yet you persecute him who, you say, knows it not, and have canonized the dragoons of Cevennes, and elevated to the dignity of a saint one Dominic, a barbarian, who founded the tribunal of the inquisition, and massacred the Albigenses. Under Charles IX you made it the duty of the catholics to murder the protestants; and even in this age, so enlightened and philosophic, when the toleration recommended in the gospel ought to be the virtue of all men, there are Caveiracs who treat toleration as a crime and an indifference to religion, and who would again fain behold that day of blood and massacre, that horrid day of St Bartholomew, when sacerdotal pride stalked through the streets commanding the death of Frenchmen; like the sultan who passed through the streets of Constantinople, followed by an executioner, demanding the blood of the Christian, who wore red breeches. More barbarous than the sultan, you put swords into the hands of Christians to cut the throats of each other.

O religions, (I speak here of the false), you have ever been palpably ridiculous! and even if you were merely ridiculous, the man of understanding would not expose your absurdities. If he thinks himself obliged to do it, it is because those absurdities in men armed with the sword of intolerance are one of the most cruel scourges of humanity.

Among the diversity of religions, which are those that bear the greatest hatred to others? The Catholic and the Jewish. Is this hatred the effect of ambition in their ministers, or that of a stupid and ill-advised zeal? The difference between true and false zeal is remarkable; they cannot be mistaken. The first is all gentleness, humanity, and charity; it pardons all, and offends none. Such at least is the idea we must form of it from the words and actions of the Son of God.

Chapter 19   Intolerance and persecution are not of divine commandment

To whom gave Jesus the appellation of a race of vipers? Was it to the Pagans, the Essenes, or Sadducees, who denied the immortality of the soul, and even the existence of the Divinity? No: it was to the Pharisees and Jewish priests.

Will the Catholic priests by the fury of their intolerance continue to merit the same appellation? By what right do they persecute a heretic? He does not think as we do, they will say: but to desire to unite all men precisely in the same belief, is to require them all to have the same eyes and the same complexion; a desire contrary to nature. Heresy is a name which those in power give to opinions commonly various, but contradictory to their own. Heresy, like orthodoxy, is local. The heretic belongs to a sect not predominant in the country where he lives: this man having less protection, and being consequently weaker than others, may be insulted with impunity. But why is he insulted? Because the strong persecute the weak even in their opinions.

If the ministers of Neufchatel, the accusers of M. Rousseau, had been born Athenians or Jews, they would, by virtue of being the strongest, in like manner have persecuted Socrates or Jesus. Oh, eloquent Rousseau! regard the favor of the great prince who protects you against such fanatics as a full recompense for their insults! you must have blushed at the approbation of those wretches; it would have inferred some analogy between your ideas and theirs, and have stained your talents. You were persecuted in the name of the Divinity, but not by him.

Who more forcibly opposed intolerance than the Son of God? His apostles would have had him call down fire from heaven on the Samaritans; he reproved them sharply. The apostles, still animated with the spirit of the world, had not then received that of God; scarcely were they enlightened when they became proscribed, not proscribers.

Heaven has given to no one the power to massacre a heretic. John does not command the Christians to arm themselves against the Pagans: "Love one another," he repeats incessantly, "for such is the will of God; by observing this precept you fulfill the law."

Nero, I know, persecuted among the first Christians men of a different opinion from his own; but Nero was a tyrant, horrible to humanity. They who commit the same barbarities, who violate without remorse the natural and divine laws, which command us "to do unto others as we would they should do unto us," ought equally to be accursed of God and man.

They who tolerate intolerants render themselves guilty of their crimes. If a church complain of being persecuted, when its right to persecute is opposed, the prince should be deaf to its complaints. The church ought to regulate its conduct by that of the Son of God. But Jesus and his apostles left to men the free exercise of reason. Why then does the church forbid them the use of it? No man has authority over the noble function of my mind, that of judging for myself, any more than over the air I breathe. Shall I abandon to others the care of thinking for me? I have my own conscience, reason, and religion, and do not desire to have the conscience, reason, or religion of the pope. I will not model my belief after that of another, said an archbishop of Canterbury. Each one is to answer for his own soul; it therefore belongs to each one to examine,

What he believes;
On what motive he believes:
What is the belief that appears to him the most rational.

What! said John Gerson, chancellor of the university of Paris, has heaven given me a soul, a faculty of judging, and shall I submit it to that of others; and shall they guide me in my manner of living and dying?

But ought a man to prefer his own reason to that of a nation? Is such a presumption lawful? Why not? If Jupiter should again take in hand the balance with which he formerly weighed the destiny of heroes; if in one scale he should put the opinion of Locke, Fontenelle, Bayle, &c. and in the other that of the Italian, French, and Spanish nations, the last scale would rise up, as if loaded with no weight. The diversity and absurdity of different forms of worship shew in how little esteem we ought to hold the opinion of the people. The divine wisdom itself appeared, says the scripture, a stumbling-block to the Jews, and to the Gentiles foolishness; *Judaeis scandalum, gentibus stultitiam*. In matters of religion I owe no respect to the opinion of a people; it is to myself alone that I owe an account of my belief; all that immediately relates to God, should have no judge but him. The magistrate himself, solely charged with the temporal happiness of men, has no right to punish any crimes not committed against society: no prince or priest has a right to persecute in me the pretended crime of not thinking as he does.

From what principle does the law forbid my neighbor to dispose of my property, and permit him to dispose of my reason and my soul? My soul is my property. It is from nature that I hold the right of thinking, and of speaking what I think. When the first Christians laid before the nations of the earth their belief, and the motives for that belief, when they permitted the Gentiles to judge between the Christian religion and their own, and to make use of the reason given to man to distinguish between vice and virtue, truth and falsehood; the exposition of their sentiments had certainly nothing criminal in it. At what period did the Christians deserve the hatred and contempt of the world? When by burning the temples of the idols, they would have forced the pagans to relinquish the religion they thought the best. What was the design of that violence? Force imposes silence on reason; it can proscribe any worship rendered to the Divinity. But what power has it over belief? To believe supposes a motive to believe. Force is no motive. Now without motive we cannot really believe; the most we can do is to think we believe.

There can be no pretence for admitting an intolerance condemned by reason and the law of nature: that law is holy; it is from God; it cannot be disannulled; on the contrary, God has confirmed it by his gospel.

Every priest, who under the name of an angel of peace excites men to persecution, is not, as is imagined, the dupe of a stupid and ill-informed zeal; it is not by his zeal but by his ambition that he is directed.

Chapter 20   Intolerance is the foundation of the grandeur of the clergy

The doctrine and practice of the priest both prove his love of power. What does he protect? Ignorance. Why? Because the ignorant and credulous, make little use of their reason, think after others, are easy to be deceived, and are the dupes of the grossest sophistry.

What does the priest persecute? Learning. Why? Because a man of learning will not believe without examination; he will see with his own eyes, and is hard to be deceived. The enemies of learning are the bonze, the dervise, the bramin, in short, every priest of every religion. In Europe the priests rose up against Galileo; excommunicated Polydore Virgil and Scheiner for the discovery which the one made of the antipodes, and the other of the spots in the sun. They have proscribed sound logic in Bayle, and in Descartes the only method of acquiring knowledge; they forced that philosopher to leave his country; they formerly accused all great men of magic; and now magic is no longer in fashion, they accuse those of atheism and materialism, whom they formerly burned as sorcerers.

The care of the priest has ever been to keep men at a distance from the truth: all instructive study is forbidden. The priest shuts himself up with them in a dark chamber, and carefully stops up every crevice by which the light might enter. He hates, and ever will hate, the philosopher: he is in continual fear lest men of science should overthrow an empire founded on error and intellectual darkness.

Without love for talents, the priest is a secret enemy to the virtues of humanity; he frequently denies their very existence. There are, in his opinion, no virtuous actions but what are conformable to his doctrines, that is, to his interest. The first of virtues with him are faith, and a submission to sacerdotal power: it is to slaves only that he gives the name of saints and virtuous men.

What, however, are more distinct than the ideas of virtue and sanctity? He is virtuous who promotes the prosperity of his fellow-citizens: the word virtue always includes the idea of some public utility. It is not the same with sanctity. A hermit or monk imposes on himself the law of silence, flogs himself every night, lives on pulse and water, sleeps on straw, offers to God his nastiness and his ignorance, and thinks by virtue of maceration to make a fortune in heaven. He may be decorated with a glory; but if he do no good on earth, he is not honest. A villain is converted at the hour of death; he is saved, and is happy: but he is not virtuous. That title is not to be obtained but by a conduct habitually just and noble.

It is from the cloister that saints are commonly taken: but what are monks in general? Idle and litigious men, dangerous to society, and whose vicinity is to be dreaded. Their conduct proves that there is nothing in common between religion and virtue. To obtain a just idea of it, we must substitute a new morality in the place of that theological morality, which, always indulgent to the perfidious arts practiced by the different sects, sanctifies to this day the atrocious crimes with which the Jansenists and Molinists reciprocally charge each other, and which, in short, commands them to plunder their fellow-citizens of their property and their liberty.

An Asiatic tyrant would have his subjects promote his pleasures with all their power, and lay down at his feet their homage and their riches: the popish priests exact in like manner the homage and the riches of the catholics.

Are there any means of increasing their power and wealth that they have not employed? When it was necessary for that purpose to have recourse to barbarity and cruelty, they became cruel and barbarous.

From the moment the priests, instructed by experience, found that men paid more regard to fear than to love, that more offerings were presented to Ariman than Oromaza, to the cruel Molva than the gentle Jesus, it was on terror that they founded their empire. They sought to have it in their power to burn the Jew, imprison the Jansenist and Deist; and notwithstanding the horror with which the tribunal of the inquisition fills every sensible and humane soul, they then conceived the project of its establishment. It was by dint of intrigues that they accomplished this design in Spain, Italy, Portugal, &c.

The more arbitrary the proceedings of this tribunal became, the more it was dreaded. The priests, perceiving that the sacerdotal power increased by the terrors with which it struck the imagination of mankind, soon became obdurate. The monks, deaf with impunity to the cry of compassion, to the tears of misery, and the groans of tortures, spared neither virtue nor talents; it was by confiscation of property, by the aid of tortures and butcheries that they at last usurped over the people an authority superior to that of the magistrates, and frequently even to that of kings. The bold hand of sacerdotal ambition dared in a Christian country to lay the foundation of such a tribunal; and the stupidity of the people, and of princes, suffered it to be completed.

Are there no longer in the Catholic church a Fenelon or a Fitzjames, who, touched with the misfortunes of their brethren, behold this tribunal with horror? There are still Jansenists virtuous enough to detest the inquisition, even though it should burn a Jesuit; but in general men are not at once religious and tolerant: humanity supposes intelligence.

A man of an enlightened mind knows that force makes hypocrites, and persuasion Christians; that a heretic is a brother, who does not think as he does on certain metaphysical dogmas: that this brother, deprived of the gift of faith, is to be pitied, not persecuted; and that if no one can believe that to be true, which appears to him to be false, no human power can command belief.

The consequence of religious intolerance is the misery of nations. What sanctifies intolerance? Sacerdotal ambition. The excessive love of the monk for power produces his excessive barbarity. The monk, cruel by system, is

still more so by education. Weak, hypocritical, cowardly by situation, every
Catholic priest in general must be atrocious; so that in countries subject to
his power he exercises perpetually all that the most refined cruelty and
injustice can imagine. If, while professing a religion instituted to inspire
gentleness and charity, he became the instrument of persecutions and mas-
sacres; if, reeking with the blood spilt at an *auto da fé*, he ventures at the
altar to raise his murderous hands to Heaven, let no one wonder: the monk
is as he ought to be. Covered with the blood of a heretic, he regards himself as the avenger of the divine wrath. But can he at such a time implore
the clemency of Heaven? Can his hands be pure because the church has
declared them so? What community has not legitimated the most abominable crimes, when they served to increase its power?

The approbation of the church is sufficient to sanctify any crime. I have
regarded the different religions, and have seen their several followers snatch
the torch from each other's hands to burn their brethren; I have seen the
several superstitions serve as footstools to ecclesiastical pride. Who is then,
I have said to myself, the truly impious? Is it the infidel? No: the ambi-
tious fanatic. It is he who persecutes and murders his brethren; it is he
who, wishing to execute the vengeance of Heaven on the infernal regions,
anticipates that horrid function on earth; who, regarding an infidel as a
damned soul, is desirous by a violent death to hasten his perdition, and by
an unheard-of progression of cruelty, to cause his brother to be at the same
instant arrested, imprisoned, judged, condemned, burned and damned.

*Chapter 21   The impossibility of suppressing in man the sentiment of
intolerance – means of counteracting its effects*

The leaven of intolerance is indestructible. It is only practicable to suppress
its increase and action. Severe laws ought therefore to be employed in
restraining it, as they do robbery.

Does it regard personal interest? The magistrate, by preventing its action,
will bind the hands of intolerance; and why should they be unbound, when,
under the mask of religion, intolerance will exercise the greatest cruelties?

Man is by nature intolerant. If the sun of reason enlighten him for a
moment, he should seize the opportunity to bind himself down by wise
laws, and put himself in a happy state of impotency, that he may not injure
others if he should be again seized with the rage of intolerance.

Good laws can equally restrain the furious devotee, and the perfidious
priest. England, Holland, and a part of Germany are proofs of this truth.
Multiplied crimes and miseries have opened the eyes of the people on this
subject: they have perceived that liberty of thought is a natural right; that

thinking produces a desire of communicating our thoughts, and that in a people, as an individual, indifference in this matter is a sign of stupidity.

He who does not feel the want of thought never thinks. It is with the body as with the mind; if the faculties of the one or the other are not exerted they become impotent. When intolerance has weighed down the minds of men, and has broken their spring, they then become stupid, and darkness is spread over a nation.

The touch of Midas, the poets say, turned every thing into gold; the head of Medusa transformed every thing into stone: intolerance, in like manner, transforms into hypocrites, fools, and idiots, all that it finds within the sphere of its attraction. It was intolerance that scattered in the East the first seeds of stupidity, which since the institution of despotism have there sprung up. It is intolerance that has condemned to the contempt of the present and future ages all those superstitious countries whose inhabitants in fact appear to belong rather to the class of brutes than of men.

There is only one case in which toleration can be detrimental to a people, and that is when it tolerates a religion that is intolerant, such as the Catholic. This religion, becoming the most powerful in a state, will always shed the blood of its stupid protectors; it is the serpent that stings the bosom which has warmed it. Let Germany beware! its princes have an interest in embracing popery; it affords them respectable establishments for their brothers, children, &c. These princes becoming Catholics would force the belief of their subjects, and if they found it necessary, would again make human blood to stream; the torch of superstition and intolerance would again blaze. A light breath would kindle it, and set all Europe in flames. Where would the conflagration stop? I know not. Would Holland escape? Would the Briton himself, from the height of his rocks, for any long time brave the Catholic fury? The straits of the sea would prove an impotent barrier against the rage of fanaticism. What could hinder the preaching up of a new crusade, and the arming of all Europe against England, the invasion of that country, by the Catholics and their treating the Britons as they formerly treated the Albigenses!

Let not the insinuating manner of the Catholics impose on the Protestants. The same priest who in Prussia regards intolerance as an abomination, and an infraction of the natural and divine law, looks on toleration in France as a crime and a heresy. What renders the same man so different in different countries? His weakness in Prussia, and his power in France.

When we consider the conduct of Catholic Christians, they at first, when feeble, appear to be lambs; but when strong, they are tigers.

Will the nations, instructed by past misfortunes, never see the necessity of restraining fanaticism, and of banishing from every religion the monstrous doctrine of intolerance? What is it at this hour that shakes the throne of Turkey, and ravages Poland? Fanaticism. It is this that prevents the Catholic Poles from admitting the Dissenters to a participation of their privileges, and makes them prefer war to toleration. In vain do they impute the present miseries of those countries merely to the pride of the nobility; without religion the great could never have armed the nation, and the impotence of their pride would have preserved peace in their country. Popery has been the secret cause of the miseries of Poland.

At Constantinople it is the fanaticism of the Mussulmans, that by loading the Greek Christians with ignominy, has armed them in secret against the empire which they ought to have defended.

Would to heaven that these two examples now before us, and glaring with the evils produced by religious intolerance, may be the last of the kind; and that hereafter, indifferent to all modes of worship, governments may judge men by their actions, and not by their opinions; that they may regard virtue and genius as the only recommendations to public favor; and be convinced that it is not of a Romish, Turkish, or Lutheran mechanic, but of the most skillful workman that we should purchase a watch: in short, that it is not to extensive faith, but to superior talents, that offices ought to be intrusted.

As long as the doctrine of intolerance subsists, the moral world will contain within its bosom the seeds of new calamities. it is a volcano half extinguished, that may one day blaze forth with greater violence, and produce fresh conflagrations and destruction.

Such are the fears of a citizen, who, the sincere friend of mankind, earnestly wishes their happiness.

I think I have sufficiently proved in this section, that in general all the factitious passions, and civil and religious intolerance in particular, are nothing more in man than a disguised love of power. The long detail into which the proofs of this truth have led me, has doubtless made the reader forget the motives that forced me into this discussion.

My object was to show, that if in man all the passions above cited be factitious, all men are in consequence susceptible of them. To make this truth still more evident, I shall here [sect. 4, ch. 22] present him with the genealogy of the passions.

Section IX

Chapter 23 Interest makes man daily contradict this maxim; do not to others what thou wouldst not they should do unto thee

The Catholic priest, persecuted by the Calvinist or the Mussulman, denounces persecution to be an infraction of the law of nature; but when this priest becomes a persecutor, persecution appears to him legitimate: it is in him the effect of a holy zeal, and a love of his neighbor. Thus the same action becomes either just or unjust according as the priest is executioner or malefactor.

If we read the history of the different sects among the Christians, we find that as long as they were weak they employed no other arms in their theological disputes than those of argument and entreaty. But when those sects became strong, from the persecuted, as I have already said, they became the persecutors. Calvin burned Servetus. The Jesuit persecutes the Jansenist, and the Jansenist would burn the Deist. Into what a labyrinth of errors and contradictions does interest lead us! It obscures in us even self-evident truths.

What in fact does the theatre of this world present to us? Nothing but the various and perpetual movements of interest. The more we meditate on this principle, the more we perceive its extent and fecundity. It is an inexhaustible mine of subtle and powerful ideas.

Moses Mendelssohn, *Jerusalem* (1783)

Mendelssohn (1729–86) was a German Jew whose work became "the first attempt at a philosophy of Judaism in the modern period" (Altmann, "Introduction," p. 3). In *Jerusalem*, he distinguished between the roles of state and religion: "the state gives orders and coerces, religion teaches and persuades." Hence he denied any coercion in religion, including the use of excommunication within a religious community. He argued that variety in religion was part of the Maker's design, and any attempt at fusion of religions was a risky adventure and one likely to return to religious persecution, for every orthodoxy will find its heretics. If there is a problem with Mendelssohn's impassioned plea, it arises from his own commitment to observant Judaism, grafted somewhat uneasily onto a Deistic approach to religious belief. The latter tended to level all religions in terms of their expression of certain moral truths known naturally; therefore, one may wonder about the substantive basis for an appeal for the full freedom of the non-essential historical accidents of the various religions.

Mendelssohn was a friend of the German playwright and essayist Gotthold Ephraim Lessing, and supplied Lessing with the model for his Nathan the Wise in the play (1779) of the same name.[4]

SOURCE: Moses Mendelssohn, *Jerusalem: A Treatise on Religious Power and Judaism*, tr. Isaac Leeser (Philadelphia, [1853]), pp. 110–15.

LITERATURE: Alexander Altmann, "Introduction" to Moses Mendelssohn, *Jerusalem, or on Religious Power and Judaism,* tr. Allan Arkush (Hanover: University Press of New England, 1983); Ze'ev Levy, "On Spinoza's and Mendelssohn's Conceptions of the Relationship between Religion and State," in C. de Deugd (ed.), *Spinoza's Political and Theological Thought* (Amsterdam: North-Holland, 1984), pp. 107–16.

. . . On the contrary, from his [Jesus'] whole demeanor, as also from the demeanor of his disciples in the first period, one may evidently derive the rabbinical principle: "Whoever is not born under the law, need not bind himself by the law; but whoever is born under the law, must live according to the law, and die according to the law." If his followers, in later times, have thought differently, and believed themselves enabled to absolve those Jews likewise who adopted their doctrines, they did so, most assuredly, without his authority.

And you, beloved brothers and fellow-men, who are followers of the doctrine of Jesus! can you blame us if we do that which the founder of your religion did himself, and sanctioned by his authority? Can you seriously believe, that you dare not return our love as citizens, and unite with us as citizens, so long as we are outwardly distinguished by the ceremonial law; eat not with you, intermarry not with you, which, as far as we can discover, the founder of your religion would neither have done himself, nor permitted us to do? If this is and must ever remain your real sentiment, which we cannot suppose of men endowed with a Christian spirit; if a civil union is not to be obtained under any other condition than our departing from the law, which we still esteem as binding on us: we are heartily sorry that we find it necessary to declare, that we had rather renounce our claim to a civil union; the philanthropic Dohm[5] will, in that case, have written to no purpose, and everything must remain in the intolerable condition in which it now is, or in which your philanthropy may find it good to place it. It is not in our power to yield in this matter; but it nevertheless is in our power, if we are honest men, to love you as brothers, and to entreat you as brothers, to make our burdens as supportable as you possibly can. Look upon us, if not as brothers and fellow-citizens, at least as fellow-men and co-inhabitants of the land. Show us ways and furnish us with the means, how we can become (*better* men and) *better* fellow-residents, and permit us also to enjoy the rights of humanity as much as time and circumstances will allow. We cannot depart from the law with a clear conscience, and what use can fellow-citizens be to you, if they are without a conscience?

"But how can, in this manner, the prophecy be brought to fulfillment, that, at some future time, there shall be but *one shepherd and one flock?*"

You, beloved brothers! who are well inclined towards mankind, suffer yourselves not to be deceived! To belong to this omnipresent Shepherd, it neither is necessary for the entire flock to feed on one pasture, nor to go in and out in the Lord's house through but one door. Neither is this in accordance with the Shepherd's wish, nor compatible with the prosperity of the flock. Do not some people confound the ideas, or endeavor purposely to produce a confusion of them? They represent to you, that union of religions is the nearest way to that brotherly love and brotherly toleration, which the kind-hearted among you so earnestly desire. If all of us have but one belief (some of you may imagine), then can we no longer hate each other, for the sake of belief and the difference of opinions; then will religious hatred and the rage for persecution be seized hold of by the root and exterminated; then will the scourge be snatched from the hand of hypocrisy, and fanaticism be bereft of the sword, and the happy days commence: "When the wolf will dwell with the lamb, and the leopard lie down with the goat," &c. The benevolent at heart, who, propose such a union, are ready to apply their hands to the laboring oar forthwith; they wish to meet as negotiators, and undertake the philanthropic task, to bring about a *religious compact*; to treat for *truths* as for *rights*, as for merchandise that is offered for sale; and they wish to make demands, offer, haggle, obtain concessions through threats or petition, surprise, overreach, until the parties have shaken hands, and the agreement for the promotion of the happiness of the human race is progressed so far that it can be committed to writing. Many, who reject such a scheme as chimerical and impracticable, nevertheless speak of the union of religions as a very desirable condition of society, and pity in sadness the human family, that this acmé of happiness cannot, probably, be reached by human means. But take great heed, ye friends of men! how you give ear to such sentiments without the most careful scrutiny. It is possible that they are but snares, which fanaticism, now become powerless, endeavors to lay to entrap the liberty of conscience. *You* know that this enemy of all that is good, possesses many shapes and forms: the lion's rage and lamb's meekness, the dove's simplicity and the serpent's cunning; no attribute is so foreign to it, which it either does not possess or knows how to assume, to gain its bloodthirsty designs. Since, through your beneficent exertion, open violence is no longer within its reach, it takes perhaps the mask of meekness, in order to circumvent you; it feigns brotherly love, makes pretensions to toleration, whilst it secretly forges the chains with which it purposes to fetter our reason, to cast it again unawares into the slough of barbarism, from which you have commenced to drag it forth.[6]

Let it not be thought, that this is nothing but an imaginary fear, the legitimate offspring of hypochondria. For, in truth, a religious union, if ever it should be brought about, can have no other than the unhappiest consequences for reason and liberty of conscience. For, admitted that men shall have agreed concerning the form of belief which they intend to introduce and establish; that symbols should be hit upon against which none of the religious parties now dominant in Europe can find anything to allege: still what is gained thereby? will this have caused you all to think just alike concerning religious truths? Whoever has the least conception of the nature of the human mind, cannot suffer himself to be persuaded of this. In words only, therefore, in the form simply can the conformity be at all expected, and for this end the uniters of religions will coalesce; therefore they wish to clip off, here and there, a little of our notions; to enlarge, here and there, the meshes of words so widely, to render these so uncertain and latitudinarian, that the different ideas, despite of their internal variations, may be squeezed into them in case of necessity. If this should be the case, everybody would, in point of fact, attach to the same words a different meaning, peculiarly his own; and could you thus boast to have united mankind in faith, to have brought the flock under but one Shepherd? Alas! if this universal dissimulation shall have any object whatever, I fear greatly that it is intended as a first step again to confine within narrow bounds the now liberated spirit of mankind! The shy animals will then allow themselves to be caught, and permit the bridle to be forced into their mouths. Bind the belief but once to symbols, the interpretation to words, be ye ever so meek and indulgent; only once for all lay down unalterably your articles of faith: and woe to the unfortunate who comes one day too late, or who dares to find the least fault with these *modest, purified* words! He is a disturber of the peace, and all of you will exclaim, "To the stake with him!"

Brothers! if you are solicitors for true happiness, then let us not falsely dissemble a conformity, where diversity is the evident plan and intention of Providence. Not one of us thinks and feels just exactly as his fellow-man; why then shall we cheat each other by deceptive words? If even we do this, unfortunately, in our daily intercourse, in our conversations, which are of no particular importance: why should this be done, I ask, in matters which concern our temporal and permanent happiness, our whole destiny? Why shall we render ourselves unknown to each other in the most important concerns of life by a sort of masquerade, whereas, God has impressed upon each, not without cause, his own peculiar features? Would this not be, as far as could be in our power, an opposing of Providence; to nullify, if it be possible, the end of creation; to counteract purposely our calling, our appointment in this and the future life? Rulers of the earth! if an unimportant fellow-inhabitant of the same may be permitted to raise his voice in order to reach you, do not trust those advisers, who wish to mislead you by smooth words to so pernicious an attempt. They are either blinded themselves, and see not the enemy of mankind, who waits in ambush, or they seek to blind you. Our most precious ornament, the liberty to think, is lost, if you give an ear to them! For the sake of your own and the happiness of us all, believe me, that a *union of beliefs is not toleration*, and is diametrically opposed to real toleration! For the sake of your own and our happiness, lend not your very powerful countenance to transform any one *eternal truth*, without which civil happiness can be sustained, into a law, – or any one *religious opinion*, which is a matter of indifference to the state, into an *enactment of the land*! Keep a watchful eye over the *doings* and *omissions* of men; bring these before the judgment-seat of wise laws, and leave to us the right of *thinking* and *speaking*, just as the Father of us all has ordained it for an inalienable inheritance, instituted it for an unchangeable right. Should, however, the connection between *privileged right* and *opinions* be too *antiquated*, and the period be not yet arrived, that it could be entirely abolished without serious injury: then seek, at least, to diminish, as much as you can, its pernicious influence, and to set wise limits to the prejudice, which has become gray with age. At least level for your more fortunate posterity the way to that summit of civilization, to that universal toleration of all mankind, for which our reason has still to sigh in vain! Reward and punish no doctrine, entice and bribe no one to adopt any religious opinion! Whoever disturbs not the public happiness, whoever acts honorably toward the civil laws, toward you and his fellow-citizens, permit to speak as he thinks, to call on God after his own manner, or that of his fathers, and to seek his everlasting salvation where he believes he can find it. Let no one in your states be a censor of the heart or a judge of thoughts; let no one assume a right which the Omniscient has reserved to himself alone! If we *give unto the emperor what is the emperor's*, then do you yourselves *give to God what is God's! Love ye the truth! Love ye peace!*

Thomas Jefferson, *Notes on the State of Virginia* (1781–2)

Jefferson (1743–1826) was a tireless promoter of religious liberty, engaging, with his friend and collaborator James Madison, in a decade-long struggle to ensure its implementation in Virginia. In fact, other options were available, and, if successful, American history might have been profoundly altered: "The United States of America would not be what it has become, would have a different moral meaning and a different composition, had the original arrangements been other than they were" (Miller, *The First Liberty*, p. 69). Here, Jefferson describes, during the War of Independence, the historical situation in Virginia. He had earlier attempted to push a bill through the legislature. An Act for Establishing Religious Freedom was originally proposed in October 1776 in the context of a general revision of the newly independent state's laws. It was finally made law on January 16, 1786 when Jefferson was in Paris and became the basis for the First Amendment in the American Constitution.

SOURCE: Thomas Jefferson, *Notes on the State of Virginia*, in *The Writings of Thomas Jefferson*, ed. Andrew A. Lipscombe, 9 vols (Washington, DC: Thomas Jefferson Memorial Association, 1903), vol. II, pp. 217–25.
LITERATURE: Leonard W. Levy, *Jefferson and Civil Liberties: The Darker Side* (New York: Quadrangle/New York Times Book Co., 1973 [1963]); William Lee Miller, *The First Liberty: Religion and the American Republic* (New York: Paragon House, 1988 [1986]).

Query XVII   The Different Religions Received into That State?

The first settlers in this country were emigrants from England, of the English Church, just at a point of time when it was flushed with complete victory over the religious of all other persuasions. Possessed, as they became, of the powers of making, administering, and executing the laws, they showed equal intolerance in this country with their Presbyterian brethren, who had emigrated to the northern government. The poor Quakers were flying from persecution in England. They cast their eyes on these new countries as asylums of civil and religious freedom; but they found them free only for the reigning sect. Several acts of the Virginia assembly of 1659, 1662, and 1693, had made it penal in parents to refuse to have their children baptized; had prohibited the unlawful assembling of Quakers; had made it penal for any master of a vessel to bring a Quaker into the State; had ordered those already here, and such as should come thereafter, to be imprisoned till they should abjure the country; provided a milder punishment for their first and second return, but death for their third; had inhibited all persons from suffering their meetings in or near their houses, entertaining them individually, or disposing of books which supported their tenets. If no execution took place here, as did in New England, it was not owing to the moderation of the church, or spirit of the legislature, as may be inferred from the law itself; but to historical circumstances which have not been handed down to us. The Anglicans retained full possession of the country about a century. Other opinions began then to creep in, and the great care of the government to support their own church, having begotten an equal degree of indolence in its clergy, two-thirds of the people had become dissenters at the commencement of the present revolution. The laws, indeed, were still oppressive on them, but the spirit of the one party had subsided into moderation, and of the other had risen to a degree of determination which commanded respect.

The present state of our laws on the subject of religion is this. The convention of May 1776, in their declaration of rights, declared it to be a truth, and a natural right, that the exercise of religion should be free; but when they proceeded to form on that declaration the ordinance of government, instead of taking up every principle declared in the bill of rights, and guarding it by legislative sanction, they passed over that which asserted our religious rights, leaving them as they found them. The same convention, however, when they met as a member of the general assembly in October, 1776, repealed all *acts of Parliament* which had rendered criminal the maintaining any opinions in matters of religion, the forbearing to repair to church, and the exercising any mode of worship; and suspended the laws giving salaries to the clergy, which suspension was made perpetual in October 1779. Statutory oppressions in religion being thus wiped away, we remain at present under those only imposed by the common law, or by our own acts of assembly. At the common law, *heresy* was a capital offense, punishable by burning. Its definition was left to the ecclesiastical judges, before whom the conviction was, till the statute of the I Elizabeth *c.* 1 circumscribed it, by declaring, that nothing should be deemed heresy, but what had been so determined by authority of the canonical scriptures, or by one of the four first general councils, or by other council, having for the grounds of their declaration the express and plain words of the scriptures. Heresy, thus circumscribed, being an offense against the common law, our act of assembly of October 1777, *c.* 17, gives cognizance of it to the general court, by declaring that the jurisdiction of that court shall be general in all matters at the common law. The execution is by the writ *De haeretico comburendo* [1401]. By our own act of assembly of 1705, *c.* 30, if a person brought up in the Christian religion denies the being of a God, or the Trinity, or asserts there are more gods than one, or denies the Christian religion to be true, or the scriptures to be of divine authority, he is punishable on the first offense by incapacity to hold any office or employment ecclesiastical, civil, or military; on the second by disability to sue, to take any gift or legacy, to be guardian, executor, or administrator, and by three years' imprisonment without bail. A father's right to the custody of his own children being founded in law on his right of guardianship, this being taken away, they may of course be severed from him, and put by the authority of a court into more orthodox hands. This is a summary view of that religious slavery under which a people have been willing to remain, who have lavished their lives and fortunes for the establishment of their civil freedom. The error seems not sufficiently eradicated, that the operations of the mind, as well as the acts of the body, are subject to the coercion of the laws. But our rulers can have no authority over such natural rights, only as we have submitted to them. The rights of conscience we never submitted, we could not submit. We are answerable for them to our God. The legitimate powers of government extend to such acts only as are injurious to others. But it does me no injury for my neighbor to say there are twenty gods, or no God. It neither picks my pocket nor breaks my leg. If it be said, his testimony in a court of justice cannot be relied on, reject it then, and be the stigma on him. Constraint may make him worse by making him a hypocrite, but it will never make him a truer man. It may fix him obstinately in his errors, but will not cure them. Reason and free inquiry are the only effectual agents against error. Give a loose to them, they will support the true religion by bringing every false one to their tribunal, to the test of their investigation. They are the natural enemies of error, and of error only. Had not the Roman government permitted free inquiry, Christianity could never have been introduced. Had not free inquiry been indulged at the era of the Reformation, the corruptions of Christianity could not have been purged away. If it be restrained now, the present corruptions will be protected, and new ones encouraged. Was the government to prescribe to us our medicine and diet, our bodies would be in such keeping as our souls are now. Thus in France the emetic was once forbidden as a medicine, and the potato as an article of food. Government is just as infallible, too, when it fixes systems in physics. Galileo was sent to the Inquisition for affirming that the earth was a sphere; the government had declared it to be as flat as a trencher, and Galileo was obliged to abjure his error. This error, however, at length prevailed, the earth became a globe, and Descartes declared it was whirled round its axis by a vortex. The government in which he lived was wise enough to see that this was no question of civil jurisdiction, or we should all have been involved by authority in vortices. In fact, the vortices have been exploded, and the Newtonian principle of gravitation is now more firmly established, on the basis of reason, than it would be were the government to step in, and to make it an article of necessary faith. Reason and experiment have been indulged, and error has fled before them. It is error alone which needs the support of government. Truth can stand by itself. Subject opinion to coercion: whom will you make your inquisitors? Fallible men; men governed by bad passions, by private as well as public reasons. And why subject it to coercion? To produce uniformity. But is uniformity of opinion desirable? No more than of face and stature. Introduce the bed of Procrustes then, and as there is danger that the large men may beat the small, make us all of a size, by lopping the former and stretching the latter. Difference of opinion is advantageous in religion. The several sects perform the office of a *censor morum* over such other. Is uniformity attainable? Millions of innocent men, women, and children, since the introduction of Christianity, have been burnt, tortured, fined, imprisoned; yet we have not advanced one inch towards uniformity. What has been the effect of coercion? To make one half the world fools, and the other half hypocrites. To support roguery and error all over the earth. Let us reflect that it is inhabited by a thousand millions of people. That these profess probably a thousand different systems of religion. That ours is but one of that thousand. That if there be but one right, and ours that one, we should wish to see the nine hundred and ninety-nine wandering sects gathered into the fold of truth. But against such a majority we cannot effect this by force. Reason and persuasion are the only practicable instruments. To make way for these, free inquiry must be indulged; and how can we wish others to indulge it while we refuse it ourselves. But every State, says an inquisitor, has established some religion. No two, say I, have established the same. Is this a proof of the infallibility of establishments? Our sister States of Pennsylvania and New York, however, have long subsisted without any establishment at all. The experiment was new and doubtful when they made it. It has answered beyond conception. They flourish infinitely. Religion is well supported; of various kinds, indeed, but all good enough; all sufficient to preserve peace and order; or if a sect arises, whose tenets would subvert morals, good sense has fair play, and reasons and laughs it out of doors, without suffering the State to be troubled with it. They do not hang more malefactors than we do. They are not more disturbed with religious dissensions. On the contrary, their harmony is unparalleled, and can be ascribed to nothing but their unbounded tolerance, because there is no other circumstance in which they differ from every nation on earth. They have made the happy discovery, that the way to silence religious disputes, is to take no notice of them. Let us too give this experiment fair play, and get rid, while we may, of those tyrannical laws. It is true, we are as yet secured against them by the spirit of the times. I doubt whether the people of this country would suffer an execution for heresy, or a three years' imprisonment for not comprehending the mysteries of the Trinity. But is the spirit of the people an infallible, a permanent reliance? Is it government? Is this the kind of protection we receive in return for the rights we give up? Besides, the spirit of the times may alter, will alter. Our rulers will become corrupt, our people careless. A single zealot may commence persecutor, and better men be his victims. It can never be too often repeated, that the time for fixing every essential right on a legal basis is while our rulers are honest, and ourselves united. From the conclusion of this war we shall be going down hill. It will not then be necessary to resort every moment to the people for support. They will be forgotten, therefore, and their rights disregarded. They will forget themselves, but in the sole faculty of making money, and will never think of uniting to effect a due respect for their rights. The shackles, therefore, which shall not be knocked off at the conclusion of this war, will remain on us long, will be made heavier and heavier, till our rights shall revive or expire in a convulsion.

Notes

1   See his *A Brief Account of the Death of Jean Calas* (1763) in *Voltaire, Candide and Other Writings*, ed. Haskell M. Block (New York: Modern Library, 1956) pp. 357–66. The affair is discussed in David D. Bien, *The Calas Affair: Persecution, Toleration, and Heresy in Eighteenth-Century Toulouse* (Princeton, NJ: Princeton University Press, 1960); Edna Nixon, *Voltaire and the Calas Affair* (London: Victor Gollancz, 1961); and Geoffrey Adams, *The Huguenots and French Opinion, 1685–1787: The Enlightenment Debate on Toleration* (Waterloo, Ont.: Wilfrid Laurier University Press, 1991), ch. 15.

2   The reference is to the 70 translators of the Septuagint, the ancient Greek version of the Hebrew scriptures.

3   A reference to William Warburton's book of that name, first published in 1736.

4   On the significance of the play for the theme of religious pluralism, see Jay Newman, *Competition in Religious Life* (Waterloo: Wilfrid Laurier University Press, 1989), pp. 130–40, and Jo-Jacqueline Eckardt, *Lessing's "Nathan the Wise" and the Critics: 1779–1991* (Columbia, SC: Camden House, 1993).

5   Christian Wilhelm Dohm, *On the Civil Improvement of the Jews* (Berlin, 1781).

6   [Note by Moses Mendelssohn]: even atheism has its fanaticism, as sad experience teaches. Perhaps it may be averred that fanaticism never could have displayed its rage without an admixture of an inward (atheism) ungodliness. But that outward, evident atheism could also become fanatical, is as undeniable as difficult to be comprehended. Although the atheist, to be consistent, must do everything from selfishness, and inconsonant as it may appear with this feeling for the atheist to endeavor forming a party and not to keep the secret to himself: it is nevertheless true, that he has been heard preaching his doctrines with the most ardent enthusiasm, nay, been seen to rave, even to persecute, if his preaching did not meet with a favorable reception. And zeal is frightful if it animates a declared atheist; if innocence falls into the hands of a raving tyrant, who fears all things but a God.

6

THE NINETEENTH CENTURY

John Brownlow, *Liberty of Conscience* (*c.* 1826)

John Thomas Brownlow (1795–1888) was born near Lincoln, England, to Methodist parents. He converted to Roman Catholicism as a teenager and was ordained in 1820. From 1824 to 1875 he served with a mission based at Harvington near Kidderminster, Worcs. The opinions expressed in this tract were hardly representative of his church's leadership in the nineteenth century, but were symptomatic of changes effected in a religion by the conditions of oppression. As early as 1788 the Catholic Committee had attempted to allay public fears about the intentions of English Catholics by asserting, among other points, individual religious freedom. Here one sees a wide variety of dissenters joining forces against the established Church of England. Many of the ideas presented by Brownlow were commonplaces, but it is interesting to note both his use of the term "separated brethren" (Peter Canisius) and his recognition of the problem of doctrinal change in the Roman Catholic Church, which he solves by distinguishing between doctrine and opinion.

SOURCE: John Brownlow, *Liberty of Conscience; or a Dialogue between a Catholic Priest and his Separated Brethren, to Explain the Nature and Make Known the Worth of Religious Liberty* (London, *c.* 1826).

LITERATURE: For general historical background, see G. I. T. Machin, *The Catholic Question in English Politics, 1820 to 1830* (Oxford: Clarendon Press, 1964).

To the people of all religions this little work is most respectfully inscribed by the author.

Priest: *Liberty of Conscience* is to be the subject of this conversation. Hence we are
not going to speak on the merits or demerits of any religious system; nor to say

which is right, or which is wrong; which is true, or which is false; which is best, or which is worst: we are to confine our talk to a thing which concerns us all, without interfering in the least with any of our religious tenets or practices. This thing is a matter of very great importance to all people of every religion all over the world. Let us endeavor to discuss it impartially for the general good. All men may perfectly agree in their notions of LIBERTY OF CONSCIENCE, notwithstanding their living in a thousand nations, and adopting ten hundred thousand different religious creeds.

Quaker: The topic of discussion not being *Religion*, but *Religious Liberty*, shall certainly engage my most serious attention. It has very frequently occupied my mind, and I do seriously think it is far too little considered in theory and exhibited in practice among the children of Adam. The page of history presents us with awful narratives of the dreadful sufferings which thousands have been made to undergo on account of their respective religions. There is perhaps no country, especially no Christian country, whose soil has not been literally soaked and steeped in the blood of innumerable human victims, sacrificed by the brutal force of barbarous power, merely because their consciences told them to adopt a certain faith.

Priest: I believe you are right.

Lutheran: How are such things to be prevented? If they have always been, will they not always necessarily continue to be?

Priest: I can tell you how such things might be prevented. Let every man, more especially every man in power, attend to the maxim, *Do as you would be done by*; let him learn the proposition, *It is the natural right of every man to worship God according to the dictates of his conscience, without being subject, on that account, to civil penalties and disabilities*; let him learn this lesson of reason, and act consistently with it, and the horrors of persecution will cease: no more Peters shall be crucified, Pauls beheaded, nor Lawrences roasted; nor more virgins racked, confessors imprisoned, nor martyrs burnt.

Methodist: That proposition must be sound and correct, otherwise all the world is in error when it condemns the violent acts of numbers of barbarians, and reprobates the perpetrators under the opprobrious name of persecutors. How could a bloodthirsty Dioclesian be condemned, or a cruel Mary, or Elizabeth, if violence might properly be resorted to for the purpose of preserving or propagating religion? For, in that case, they only acted upon a right principle, namely the principle of using CIVIL FORCE in religion. I do not see why all religions, as far as civil laws are concerned, should not be equally free, in every country.

Calvinist: Every man in the state, for his own soul's sake, should be a good religious man; but every state, as such, ought to be blind to the difference of religious tenets, and every statesman, as such, namely in his public capacity of a state officer, ought not to give a preference to one creed above another. *Render to Caesar the things that are Caesar's; and to God the things that are God's.* Distinguished between temporals and spirituals; between religion and the state; between Caesar's kingdom and God's kingdom. The one is of this world, the other is not of this world. They are two distinct powers, the one temporal, the other spiritual; and should go side by side, like two parallel lines, without ever touching. Hence, when the temporal government goes beyond its own boundaries and interferes in the province of religion, there is usurpation, there is persecution, there is barbarism; and all the consequent train of evils, discontent, murmuring, quarrelling, seditions, murders, wars. Usurpation, too, on the other side, is sure to be attended with lamentable effects.

Unitarian: Had the principle of religious liberty been known and attended to by the nations of the earth, there would have been no wars, no bloodshed, no racking, no burning, no imprisonment, on account of faith; but for want of its being known and adopted, the whole world has been deluged with the blood of martyrs, and every country cries to the God of Justice for vengeance on the head of persecutors.

Quaker: When people are wronged, it is natural they should complain; should be discontented; and should use means to remove the cause of their dissatisfaction. No one but a fool, or a knave, or a savage can reproach them for so doing. Yet I have read that such have been reproached for thus listening to the voice of reason!

Presbyterian: If one pig eats his own breakfast, and robs another pig of half his, can the robber wonder if the robbed is dissatisfied and squeals? And who but a pig could think of reproaching the oppressed in such a case?

Lutheran: The records of every country would almost impress on the mind of a superficial reader the idea that persecution has been a feather in the wing of almost every religion.

Priest: The evil was not in the system, but in the heart and judgment of the professor. The creed itself, in general, deserves not the blame; but the people. Persecution is the darling child of *ignorance* and *barbarism*, fostered for the most part on the lap of *worldly interest*. Now this ignorance, barbarism, and interest, may exist in any country, in any government, be its religion what it may, Pagan, Jewish, Catholic, Mahometan, Calvinistic, or any thing else. The religion should not, therefore, be blamed for these brutalities, but the persons who entertain and cherish them. Persecution often tenders the hand of friendship to religion; but is never greeted by religion with an offer of the same kind. Religion knows her to be of too beastly a character to adopt her as a sister or a friend. They sometimes go together accidentally, but never through mutual choice. If you should see them together in the same house, condemn not both for the fault of one. Distinguish between them. See the club-foot of the one, and the beauty of the other. What says the Book of Job? *On a certain day when the sons of God came to stand before the Lord, Satan also was present among them.* Condemn not the sons of God for the works of Satan.

Quaker: I see very clearly that a king may persecute, and yet not be taught to persecute by his religion; and that the same may be said of any individual, or any body of individuals, in power.

All: That is evident enough.

Priest: It must be equally evident that, in such a case, the religion deserves no part of the blame; and that the members of that religion, who do not persecute, ought not to be punished for the fault of those who do persecute. Can any thing be more clear?

Methodist: Hence how unjust has it been, how cruel and barbarous, to punish all
the Catholics of this kingdom for more than two hundred years, for the alleged
fault of some of their predecessors, ages ago!

Lutheran: Have the Catholics been persecuted?

Unitarian: Persecuted! they have been most dreadfully persecuted. Look into the
English law-books, and you will see and blush! They are even now more unjustly
dealt with on account of religion than any other of his Majesty's subjects. Oh!
look into Ireland, if you wish to see what persecution can effect! Their property
taken from them! their ditches filled with the blood of the slain! their churches
taken from them! the support of the ministers and the poor taken from them!
their Pastors driven from them! and banished! or murdered! their schools taken
from them, and forbidden to found others! &c. &c. It requires a heart of stone
to read the history of Ireland. No country has suffered so much for religion.
Even now, whilst the land is filled with plenty, and the parsons are in affluence,
the poor catholic people are dying by thousands for want; being nevertheless
obliged to give about two millions a year to support Pastors who are not their
own. Think of seven millions of people treated thus! and then, if your indignation will permit your mouth to open, hoot Barbarism!!

Presbyterian: Your society is also persecuted in some degree, and so is every
dissenting community. I have seen some countries; I have read of many; and I
do declare that it is my sincere conviction that in England and Ireland more
people suffer more losses, privations and punishments on account of religion,
than in any other kingdom. Two thirds suffer, to feed and pamper one third. In
other lands a few are scourged by the many; but here the minority are made to
feast on the rights of the majority.

Quaker: Pity that all the people of all religions do not unite together in their
efforts to obtain universal Liberty of Conscience! One great, general, national
outcry for relief from unmerited suffering might shake the castle of intolerance,
as the trumpets and the shouts of the sons of Israel, around the walls of Jericho,
tumbled them down to the ground.

Calvinist: Oh! that every man in every nation, may breathe the pure air of religious liberty! The whole world will then rejoice! and every mountain and every
valley will be clothed with gladness! Liberty forbids that any man should be
forced into any religion, or forced out of it; or forced to support any other
religion than his own; or forced to pay to any other Clergyman than his own; or
forced to contribute towards any other place of worship than his own. Who, that
attends to reason, disputes this? who, but a blind zealot, or a money loving tool
[sic], can assert the contrary? Liberty hates *force*, as light hates darkness. If force
look at liberty, it is like a devil looking at an angel.

Priest: In our conversation we consider LIBERTY as a *natural* RIGHT, and persecution, as its opposite, *natural* WRONG; and when we speak of liberty, we mean
religious, not *civil* liberty. Most certainly! I think myself as truly persecuted if a
man, of a different religion from my own, seizes my estate and keeps it to
support his religion, as if he seized my body and imprisoned it for the same
purpose. I am severely punished in both cases, though to a different extent.
Should I be forced to pay part of my property away, under the name of tithes,

or under any other name, to a parson or priest, when I do not believe in the doctrine of that parson or priest, I consider and feel myself persecuted; because *violence is done to my conscience*, and I am robbed of my money to support a religious system which I look upon as false, and which my soul consequently abhors.

Methodist: Now the name of tithes is mentioned, let us consider them a little. Several able writers, of different creeds, have proved beyond the possibility of a doubt, that there is no divine command to pay tithes, or the tenth of our property, to support any religion of its Ministers. Among the Jews, hundreds and hundreds of years ago, tithes were paid by God's command; but remember he was then their *temporal Ruler*; he gave them the land of Canaan, he divided nearly the whole of the land among the eleven tribes; to the twelfth tribe he gave no adequate portion, and to compensate their loss, he commanded the other tribes to pay tithes to them. As God also appointed this portionless tribe to minister to the others in spirituals, the tithe regulation was well calculated to spur them on to the performance of their duties. This slight glance at the tribe of Levi in Canaan, shows clearly that it was not in the circumstances of any tribe in England or Europe; and that there is no probability that any such very extraordinary circumstances will ever occur again; and that, therefore, nothing can be argued from them in favor of present corruption.

Lutheran: All countries paid tithes to the Catholic Priests before the event, called by Protestants, the Reformation; and may we not infer from hence that the obligation of paying tithes should be considered as forming part and parcel of the Christian religion?

Priest: If you would draw that inference, you must also, for precisely the same reason, draw this too: that the chief part of them strictly belongs to the poor and to deeds of charity, as was taught by Catholics. This inference, you are aware, would not please the stomachs of the Parsons, which are able to digest the whole of the tithes themselves.

Unitarian: All Catholic countries have done away the tithe system; and this shows that Catholics themselves do not, and never did, consider it as an essential part of their religion. It was looked upon, among them, as a regulation made by the *temporal power* for the relief of the Poor, the support of the priest, the repairs of the Church, &c. The power which made the regulation could of course suppress it when it pleased; and, accordingly, has suppressed it among *them*.

Priest: The Catholic Church never *could* enact a law obligating all Catholics, or any Catholics, to pay tithes. This would be stepping out of its own spiritual bounds, and usurping the temporal dominion. All that the Church can say, on the subject of the support of its ministers, is what our Savior said: "*The labourer is worthy of his hire*;" that is, *it is the duty of the flock to support their pastor*. He spends his time and strength in their service, and cannot, therefore, labor to support himself like other men. If Catholic Prelates have seemed to make a law in some countries to go farther than this, they meant merely to declare, that it was the duty of all Catholic subjects to obey the *just temporal laws of their country*, relative to the support of their Clergy and the poor. If they meant more than this; namely, if they meant, as *bishops*, to lay a command upon the *civil power* to enact tithe laws, and see them put in execution, they stretched their authority beyond its spiritual limits, invaded the temporal right, and deserved to be resisted and contemned. The fact just mentioned by our UNITARIAN Friend speaks volumes. In Catholic times, the countries were so completely Catholic that the tithe laws were seldom found to be oppressive to people of other creeds. But I freely and voluntarily condemn them whenever they were made to extract a single farthing from the pocket of a person not a Catholic, to support the Catholic PRIEST. In those days, there were no paupers, no poor's levies, and the PRIEST was considered by the *temporal powers* to be the most likely person to know the wants of his parishioners, and the most fit to proportion relief to their necessities: he was, therefore pressed into a *civil office* in addition to his *spiritual one*. Great must have been the *burden* of distributing this charity-money properly, and happy the removal of that burden afterwards from the Minister's shoulders!

Methodist: How different this application of the tithes from that which we now witness! Methinks one might almost bear with the system now, if it were managed in that manner. But NOW we have both tithes and poor-rates!!! Goodness! what were the people of the Reformation doing, to reform in this manner!

Quaker: Liberty would not allow the system of tithes *now*, even if they were managed as of old; because now we are divided into a great number of classes, of different religions; so that to levy contributions by force upon all religionists, to support the ministers of but one creed, would be real violence upon conscience.

Lutheran: If England and Spain had attended to the rights of religious liberty, we evidently should not have heard of Star Chambers and Inquisitions. These and such odious and iniquitous institutions, would never have been permitted to find way into their borders. But are there not some Catholics of opinion that these measures have been attended with happy effects in Spain? Have they not preserved *one religion* there? *one faith*? But for these measures, might not that country have been, like England, split into a thousand jarring creeds? I once heard an ignorant Catholic say: "The Inquisition has served to prop up our holy religion in Spain."

Priest: Since the *Star Chamber* has not united England in one faith, I am inclined to think the Inquisition has not preserved Spain in one faith; and if Spain really is in one faith, I am tempted to imagine there may be some other cause for this unity; especially when I look at the faith of Ireland, a faith firm and durable, without the aid of Inquisitions, and even in spite of all the malice, craft, and violence executed against it unceasingly.

In my opinion no nation ought to be kept in one faith, by the use of Inquisitions or any violence. Faith is to be propagated and preserved by instruction, by teaching, by preaching, by good example: these are the proper means to extend and keep up the faith. Prayer may join them; the invisible grace of God may co-operate. *The weapons of our warfare*, says St Paul, *are not carnal, but spiritual*. Jesus Christ never used force to make known or keep up his doctrine; he never taught his disciples to use force for that purpose; and we cannot find that they ever did use it. Whence, then, has this brutal means come into the world? Not from Christianity, not from Catholicity, not from religion, but from the dark abyss of barbarism.

Now to your questions. I do not believe that the Catholic religion, or any other religion, has received any real good from persecuting laws enacted to "prop it up." The very idea is disgusting! What! "prop up" the religion of God! Cannot God rule his own kingdom? Must he have the aid of human passion, of racks, swords and prisons? Prop up the sublime religion of the Deity! Though MILDNESS ITSELF, prop it up with coarse rude violence! How revolting the thought! As well might you talk of propping up the heavens with a rotten hedge-stake.

The sins of Spain might have been fewer, and less enormous, and I think they even would have been so, if the consequences of true liberty had been permitted to take place; yea, even if one of those consequences had been a sprinkling of false religions. Do not men naturally take more care of their corporal health, and use more vigilance to preserve it, when they are under the vivid conviction that it is in danger? Do not tradesmen manage their affairs better when they see the prospect of a rival? Do not coaches run the faster when there is an opposition? Does not experience teach us that the Clergy are naturally more vigilant, active, zealous and exemplary, where the Clergy and people of another system are looking on and watching the favorable opportunities for proselytizing? Then, if the Clergy are prompted to be better, more given up to the spirit and practice of their calling, are not the people likely to be thereby induced to be better too? Does not the piety of the flock mainly depend upon the piety of the Pastor? Where the officer is idle and careless, the soldiers are in danger of being remiss and undisciplined.

Through these and similar reflections, I am of opinion that Spain would have possessed a more zealous Clergy and a more devout people, if full *religious liberty* had always blessed the land.

Presbyterian: I believe the God of heaven can and will carry on the religion of heaven without the paltry aid of man's brutish violence. To force down a persons's throat a religion which he disbelieves, or to force him to support such a one, is a monstrous absurdity. Whence, but from such barbarism, could originate the first seedlings of infidelity in the wild mind of a deluded Blanco?

Quaker: Whenever I hear the word *persecution*, my blood is chilled with horror: and I immediately fancy I see before me swords, racks, prisons, fires, melted lead, boiling oil, chains, gibbets, famine, fires of Smithfield, the gallows of Tyburn, Star Chambers, Inquisitions, tithe exactors, and all the thousands of terrific instruments used by the fierce enemies of freedom.

Lutheran: Have we not observed that persecution comes not from the faith or religion of the persecutor, but from his passions? One difficulty strikes me: we all know that the Priests of Spain and Italy (not excepting the Pope)[,] the Calvinist preachers of France, and the Established Clergy of England, have had, at different times, a finger in the pie; I mean, have aided or abetted persecution in one shape or other. Now when Popes, and Priests, and Parsons, and Preachers did so, was it not true that then their respective religions were to be justly blamed?

Priest: You think, when priests teach or encourage any thing, their religion must necessarily do the same; but in this you are greatly mistaken. When they teach a thing, and, at the same time, declare it to form a part of their religious doctrine, then you might think it to be so; but there are thousands of opinions political, religious, and philosophical, which form no part of the doctrine of the Church, and which any person may therefore use his judgment in adopting or rejecting without involving religion in the least blame. The church *doctrine* is fixed and unalterable; *opinion* is unsettled and wavering. *Doctrine* is a firm rock, assailed in vain by waves and storms; *opinion*, a heap of sand, moved here and there by the billows of the ocean. *Doctrine* is the determined property of the *body of people* to whom it belongs, and adds honor or attaches disgrace to *all the body*, collectively and individually; opinion is the exclusive property of the individual who holds it, and he alone has any right to its advantages and honor, or its disadvantages and opprobrium. Doctrine is one thing, opinion quite another: the former is included within certain sure bounds; the latter comes not within them. The doctrine of the Catholic church belongs to *every Catholic without a single exception*; opinion belongs to the individual who adopts it, whatever may be his religion. To punish all Catholics, therefore, because any individual Catholic holds, or has held, a certain opinion, is as foolish, as unjust, and as barbarous, as to punish all blue-coated men, because one blue-coated man was guilty of murder. The Catholic religion has no more to do with the opinion, than the blue-coat had to do with the murder; and all other Catholics are no more involved in the opinion, than all other blue-coated men are implicated in the murder. Hence how unjust to punish all the millions of Catholics of this empire, for hundreds of years, by most cruel laws, for the faults of some Catholics of past ages in *matters of opinion*! faults over which the other Catholics could not possibly have the slightest control. When I am reading of these things in the British Statute Book, I cannot help exclaiming, Barbarism! barbarism! barbarism!

Lutheran: But if all Catholics formerly held the "*deposing doctrine*," as it is sometimes called, does it not follow that their Church held that doctrine? and, since the Church never changes its doctrines, does it not also follow that the Church still holds that tenet, and that of course all Catholics are involved in the guilt and deserve the consequent punishment?

Priest: First, it was not a *doctrine*, but only an *opinion*: it never was taught as a *doctrine*. It is *now* universally rejected even as an *opinion*, much more as a *doctrine*; and therefore, to use your own argument, "since the Church never changes her doctrine, does it not follow that this never was her doctrine?"

Calvinist: If she does not hold it NOW, and yet never CHANGES, she of course *never did hold it*. That she does not hold it now, every little child well knows.

Priest: Secondly, that *opinion* was not held by all Catholics as every impartial history will declare. Thirdly, if that *opinion* had been held by all Catholics of those days, it does not by any means follow that it must be held by all, or by any, Catholics of these days. Opinions are opinions, and not articles of faith, as water is water, and not a rock. Think again of what has been already said of them.

Unitarian: All Catholics, Clergy and Laity, may hold the opinion that a limited monarch is preferable; and yet none of them think this to be part of their church doctrine. They may hold this opinion to day; and, since it is but an opinion, they may reject it tomorrow, like the people of any other religion. For my part, I think this so evident, that nothing more need be said upon it.

Methodist: The Catholics have certainly been most unchristianly dealt with. Henceforward I shall wish them perfect liberty of conscience as well as every other class of his Majesty's subjects. They have been punished to the third, fourth, and fifth generation, for the opinion of some of those of their religion ages ago, on the weak and worthless pretense that the children must necessarily inherit and possess all the notions of their fathers.

Lutheran: "But," says Hob, "what this blue-coated man *has* done, another blue-coated man *may* do; and therefore it is right to punish them all by anticipation. If this blue-coat has murdered, all the others *may* do so; to prevent it, let's hang them all!!"

Presbyterian: Hob might have carried his argument farther, and said: "Some men *have* been rogues, therefore all *may* be; to prevent it, let's stab them all!!"

Priest: Very true! and then what would become of Hob?

Unitarian: What a horrible blindness it is in many persons to forge bad doctrines and palm them upon the Catholics! doctrines which the Catholics disavow and disclaim, and which they hate as truly as any other people! and then, more horrible is it to persecute them on the strength of these forgeries! Yet how common this is! When *we ourselves* disclaim a tenet, we expect to be believed; but when *they* disclaim one, for which they have long unjustly suffered, we immediately lose sight of the maxim, DO AS YOU WOULD BE DONE BY, and disregard all their fervent protestations, their deliberate declarations, their solemn oaths, and all the other means that man can make use of to man, to correct his error and avert his suspicion. We forget that the only bar to the possession of their rights is their regard for the sacredness of an oath.

Quaker: Are we not somewhat rambling from our subject?

Calvinist: We began about Liberty of Conscience, and lately we have been inquiring whether Catholics are justly deprived of it, at least in part, by being made to pay dear for it. But does not the late turn of our conversation seem to admit that there may be cases in which this kind of deprivation may be just, prudent, and desirable?

Priest: There may be such cases, and I think there often are such. LIBERTY, though MILD and KIND and AMIABLE in all her features and all works, even Liberty may justly *defend her own life*, and may consequently make use of such means as are necessary for that purpose. Numbers of people are enemies to the existence of Liberty, both in their principles and practice: such people should be so managed as not to have it in their power to carry into execution their illiberal designs. This is clearly the voice of reason.

Lutheran: In what class of religionists are these anti-liberty men to be found? and by what means is their sting to be deprived of its venom?

Unitarian: They are scattered in all nations and climes, and in all sects and persuasions. We have nothing to do but use our eyes to be convinced that these oppressors are to be found wherever ignorance, bigotry, or avarice choose to introduce them. Hence, some are of course Catholics, some Unitarians, some

Methodists, some Calvinists, some Jews, some Pagans, and if I might particularly allude to any description of men rather than another, I should point out our established clergy, who are forever using all the means in their power to keep a third part, or rather a two-third part, of his Majesty's subjects in spiritual bondage. For proof, see their yearly petitions to Parliament by hundreds, their sermons, and their tracts. Since these anti-liberty men are to be found in all classes of religionists, any law, made to fetter their efforts, should be perfectly *general*, should mention no sect or party, should be levelled only at the offending individuals, whatever may be their religious creed. No just law punishes the innocent for the faults of the guilty. No just law loves to be partial and capricious, picking out the culprits of one name and screening those of another.

Presbyterian: A law, to grant *full liberty of conscience to all*, is certainly a most desirable thing; and another law, to restrain the malice of those whose principles and practice are opposed to this liberty, is certainly equally desirable. Should civilization come to such perfection in England, as to introduce these laws, what numbers that are first would be last!

Quaker: What sort of law might the latter be?

Calvinist: Do you know what laws at present exist against Catholics? I think these ought to be repealed, as being unjust and full of persecution; and then, what could be done better than make the same, or such, *general*, that is, against *all persons who are opposed to universal liberty of conscience*, in whatever religion they may be?

Methodist: Certainly, that would be quite fair, quite just, and could not possibly excite complaint or dissatisfaction in any reasonable mind. All men have an equal right to the blessing of religious liberty, who themselves do not hold principles subversive of that right in others; and those who do hold these illiberal principles should be *equally* liable to be punished, *without any reference to their religious creeds*. I like that expression – "Liberty may defend her own life." It speaks home; and requires no support from argument. Its truth flashes conviction the moment the words are uttered.

Quaker: The newspapers told us, some time ago, that the Pope had made a law in his own temporal dominions, that his Jewish subjects should wear the badge of a yellow ribbon. I know we none of us like this law.

Priest: If this law really does exist, and is *on account of religion*, I not only do not like it, but hate and abominate it, as being unjust. For, if the Italian Jews do even hold principles contrary to religious liberty, why make a law to punish ONLY THEM, when it must be probable that some *other Italians* are equally guilty? The law should not have mentioned *Jews*, but *all people*. It should have been general and impartial; then all anti-liberty men, of every religion, would have been equally punished.

Unitarian: There have been persons whose religions have strangely descended to an interference with temporal concerns, so as to be dangerous to the right of property, and the tranquillity and safety of the state in which they have existed; pray, should such as these be allowed full liberty of conscience?

Methodist: You allude to the Lollards and Waldenses. If such were to be allowed unrestricted religious liberty, the state would be in danger of confusion and ruin!

Priest: You know, early in our talk, it was observed and agreed to, that there is a *natural and distinct difference between things religious and things civil*, between spirituals and temporals. Now, with this truth before us, your question is easily answered. The state always can and will make civil laws to regulate civil affairs, to preserve temporal rights and to secure the temporal dominion; so that, when any one's tenets have passed the line of separation, they fall under the civil law, and may be treated accordingly.

Presbyterian: Yes; in that case, they are not so properly called *religious tenets as political dogmas*. Any danger, to be apprehended from them, may certainly be easily averted by the laws of the land.

Methodist: I am now satisfied! Undoubtedly the civil power may easily secure all civil rights.

Lutheran: Whilst I think of it, let me ask, whether an Atheist ought to have Liberty of Conscience?

Quaker: An Atheist is a man of no religion; and, since you cannot thrust religion down his throat, he must be managed entirely by the temporal laws as the makers and administrators of those laws think proper. He is a civil thing completely, and not at all religious; what then can rule him but the civil power?

Lutheran: You have observed again and again, that there is a clear distinction between religion and the state, "between things religious and things civil." Now, a difficulty occurs to me, which is this: we daily see *chapels, churches* and *burial grounds; tithes, glebes,* and *parsonages;* pray, what are these? which side of the line do they come? are they civil or religious?

Priest: Your difficulty is not a great one. These things are used for religious purposes; but they are temporal concerns, and, like all other temporal affairs, they are to be managed in justice and equity by the temporal laws. All property, whether money, land, or goods, in any nation, is subject to the just laws of that nation; but perhaps there is no property in any country more unjustly affected by iniquitous laws than that which is termed ECCLESIASTICAL. We need not go out of our own land to be convinced of this.

Lutheran: If Catholics were allowed by the laws of this country to give or bequeath property to their Church, would not the Pope, who is chief bishop, acquire temporal power in this kingdom?

Priest: When, by the permission of the laws of any land, a Catholic in that land gives property to *the Church*, he means he gives it according to the tenor of those laws; so that if they forbid any foreigner to have temporal right or power within that land, then no gift to the Catholic church gives any foreigner temporal influence there, be he Pope, Bishop, or Priest. A gift to *the Church*, in such case, is a gift to the Church of *that nation only*.

Methodist: I never knew so much in my life, respecting religious liberty! What a pity its nature and rights are not more generally known and appreciated, and laws framed in every country accordingly! Numbers of oppressions and wrongs would then be done away, and buried for ever in the dark abyss out of which barbarism has produced them. The tithe system would no longer weigh down England and Ireland, and thousands of other grievances would be heard of no more.

Lutheran: What could be done with the tithes?

Presbyterian: Tithes, glebes, parsonages, churches, and church appendages – the whole mass of *national property of this description* might, at this time of national distress, be well applied by the legislature, towards paying off part of the national debt. Could the legislature, do you think, do better than let the whole of the property be sold and the amount applied as already said? Great would that amount be, as the mere yearly interest is perhaps not less than ten or twelve millions of pounds. Then consider what an immense difference would be made in taxes! Every farmer and every landlord would feel his burden exceedingly lightened; and so would every tradesman, laborer, and artisan. Ten millions a year! this less to pay! what a happy difference would it make, even to all the nation! At present, the parsons alone of one church feel the good of all this money; but, then, all people of all religions would each participate in the wealth; because each would have a considerably less yearly load of taxation. No nation is so weighed down with taxes and levies as England and Ireland. The established clergy of these two little islands receive more money yearly than all the clergy together of all the nations of Europe! This has been proved.

Calvinist: After this disposal of the church property, then might all religions be made equally free, equally independent, and be equally blessed with all the enjoyments attending religious liberty. Then would England and her dependencies cease to hear the dismal howl of religious oppression, cease to feel the voracious gnawnings [sic] of internal discontent, cease to be in danger of splitting to pieces on the rock of party violence. Oh, yes! then, would be a happy union of hearts, of wishes, of efforts and of powers: all the exertions of hostile strength and energy could not move, nor touch, nor appal a nation thus standing on a rock of lasting concord, and fortified all round with a rampart of invincible power.

Lutheran: After the measure of granting all religions in the kingdom equal freedom and removing persecution from all, I think a law should be made, as in France, to provide out of the taxes a *moderate yearly salary* for each clergyman, of every religion alike. There could be nothing unjust in such a law; because all people would be treated exactly alike: all would feel the burden alike; and all would equally taste the advantage. All would be placed upon an equal footing, in the eye of the law, and none could feel persecution.

Priest: I think a *more excellent* way would be to allow all classes of religionists to support their clergy as they please, by *voluntary contribution*. Does it not strike you that this would be more according to the nature and views of *liberty*? Besides, among the endless variety of new religions which are perpetually popping into existence, it is possible a man may differ from the rest of the world, and be attached to no persuasion which has had time to choose and possess a minister; and would it not be hard that such a man should be forced by law to give his part towards the *general support* of clergymen, when he himself has no clergyman?

   The *very making* of the law you speak of, would be attended with most bewildering difficulties. The number of the flock must be a condition, or else the nation's money might be demanded by many clergy *without flocks*. On the other hand, if the number must be limited as to its minority, there will be clergy *without support*, and small flocks without assistance, who have a right to assistance, since they give their proportion to the tax-fund. How, then, could persecutions be avoided?

Also, consider the trouble and expense the nation must undergo to distribute the tax-salaries to so many clergy, so widely scattered and so undetermined in number.

Methodist: One very great good evidently would arise from the practice of providing the income by *voluntary contribution*; the pastor would thereby be spurred on to the performance of his duty, since he would feel conscious, that if he neglected the flock, he might be deprived of the fleece: the people might deny him their money, if he neglected their service.

Quaker: The other method would have one great evil in it, besides those already mentioned. It would excite an apprehension, in the minds of the ignorant and thoughtless, that the total amount of the tax-salaries of all the clergy of every religion would swell up to a fourth part of that enormous mass of wealth given at present to the established clergy. Thousands of considerations, justly calculated to remove their uneasiness, would never once enter their brains.

Presbyterian: All things being considered, I give the preference by far to the *voluntary contribution method*.

Methodist: However full of injustice and persecution the existence of *the establishment* is, numbers of great people would be very loth to part with it, because their sons and daughters feast plentifully upon its riches; and to preserve this source of their fatness and abundance, they would not fail to use their most strenuous endeavors to excite in the minds of the populace an idea that the established *religion* would utterly fall away.

Quaker: In that case, I should hope the populace would remember, that, if it is a *religion*, it would stand the same chance as *all other religions*, and that, if it is not a *religion*, but a *trade*, they would have many reasons to rejoice in its extinction.

Lutheran: Certainly! for that trade brings the populace no profit, but loss to their pockets.

Let me ask another question. If all people were permitted by law to support their different ministers as they please, would there not be great reason to fear that, in time, most of the land and wealth of the nation would get into the hands of the clergy; and that, since the clergy would be of course, chiefly employed in spirituals, the temporals would be neglected, and consequently the whole nation gradually droop, sink, and decay, and lose her positive and relative honor, greatness and power?

Priest: All these evils might be prevented by a law forbidding any and every clergyman to receive a yearly benefice of a value higher than a certain specified and fixed amount.

Calvinist: Great good would come from such a law; as by it would be lessened the temptation to enter the ministry from the unworthy and corrupt motive of SORDID GAIN. The shepherd, not being a hireling, would desire an endeavor to promote the comfort and secure the lives of his flock.

Quaker: In our conversation on religious liberty, we none of us means to be understood to think that *in the sight of God*, all religion[s] are equally good, and equally safe, and equally true; but that no difference should be made or discovered in them by *the law of the land*, and no force or violence should be used to protect one, and to oppress another; in short that religion should be *free from force*. God is able to rule and protect his kingdom, which is not of this world, by means suitable to its own spiritual nature, without calling aloud from the portals of heaven to the kings of the earth, to lend him their words, racks, fires, gallowses, and prisons. I do not fear that God's kingdom will fall away for want of the support of civil laws, any more than I fear that the kingdoms of the moon will fall away for want of the support of the laws of the earth. We have all agreed that, *force in religion* is *persecution*.

Methodist: A Jonathan the other day observed that, in his opinion, the *true religion*, might carry itself on by force. It was easy to see what was his object, though he did not openly point it out. No doubt, he wished to justify the tithe-system, in which he knew is a system of violence and persecution upon all those persons who do not believe in the tithe religion. My reply was this: "If force may be used by the members of the true religion, why did not Christ use force? why in fact, did the apostles never use it? And if these questions are not sufficient, let me put another or two. If members of the true religion may use force, will not the members of all religions use it in self defense, and believing themselves to be true? And if all religions should use it, where will be an end to wars, bloodshed, and all the horrors of cruel violence?" He was silent and withdrew.

Unitarian: I once heard a sermon maintaining and defending *the use of force* in religion, and never was so disgusted with any pulpit eloquence in my life. I could have imagined I was in Turkey instead of England; in a barbarian's temple, rather than a British cathedral; in a butcher's slaughter-house, rather than in the house of God. All his sermon amounted to this: "*By God's command*, the Jews used force in acquiring and keeping possession of the *land of promise*; therefore, *without God's command*, the established church may use force in acquiring and keeping possession of *the milk and honey of tithes*." Oh! to what sophistry will not men resort, to what deception will they not have recourse, *to swell their purses, and to keep them swelled!* He beautifully expatiated upon the miraculous theocracy of the children of Israel, the wonderful manna from heaven, the dividing of the sea and the river, the march of the pillars of fire and cloud, the ten Egyptian plagues, and the other astonishing prodigies, which proved beyond doubt the protection and the *will* of the Deity, in the case of the Jews; but when he came to his own case, to the other side of the comparison, to that part of his argument, which should have carried him safe to his conclusion, lo! and behold! to prove the extraordinary protection and *will* of heaven in his favor, he spoke, not of prodigious miracles, but of prodigious *purses!!!* I heard, was ashamed, laughed, and ran away.

Quaker: Whenever you hear a man of the establishment arguing in favor of persecution; look at his belly! you will always see an argument kicking there, much more powerful than any which may drop from his lips.

Presbyterian: I wonder how any Christian can argue in support of tithes from the ancient practice of the Jews! Do we receive from the Almighty daily astonishing interference, daily commands, and daily miracles, as the Jews did? Are *we* bound to do everything which the Jews did? Are *we* to sacrifice bulls and goats, because *they* did? Are *we* to circumcise, because *they* did? Are *we* to abstain from certain kinds of meats, as unclean, under penalties, because *they* did? Are we allowed to have many wives, because they were? Are our ministers to be of the tribe of Levi, because those of the Jews were? Is the Jewish religion obligatory, or is it not? If it is, Sir, insist upon *it all*; urge the necessity of observing all its ancient rites and ceremonies. But if it is not, then sophisticate no longer about it.

Methodist: I know of one argument which is frequently adduced in favor of persecution, and which deceives many weak and thoughtless people. It is this: A *king* is the same to his *subjects*, as a *father* is to his *family*. Now a father may force his children, in matters of religion; therefore a *king* may force his *subjects*.

Priest: The assertion, which forms the basis of this argument, is perfectly gratuitous and assumed, and not proved, nay even false, as a little consideration will demonstrate, and therefore the reasoning is unsound and deceitful. Bob says "a king is the same to his subjects, as a father to his children." This is his foundation, if this be undermined, his whole building will fall. As long as a child has not arrived at the age of reason and judgment, his deficiency is to be supplied by the wisdom and discretion of the parent. Reason and religion teach this. All people of all nations allow it. At that age, the parent may use force, may use the rod, and may and ought to proportion his severity to the exigencies of the case. All allow this too. His correction may relate to temporals or spirituals. But when the child has arrived at the age of discretion, the father can no longer use *force in spirituals*. Liberty of conscience forbids it. What *then* must the father do? He must reason, explain, argue, advise, exhort, intreat; must pray to God, the master of the heart of man; and must preach by example: if he call for the assistance of force, he becomes a persecutor.

Now, Bob! to come to close quarters. Why may a father exercise *force*, in ruling his children in spirituals, for a time? Because, during that time, they are *wanting in sense*. To put your argument in a clear point of view, look here!

A *father* may	therefore	A king may
force his children		*force* his subjects
for a while		always(!)
in *spirituals*; because		in *spirituals*; because
they are wanting		they are wanting
in sense;		in sense!!!!

Here you are too lame to walk any farther. Your foundation has been undermined, and the superstructure has therefore fallen down. Your comparison between the king and the father has turned out to be absurd; since it supposes that the sense of the king is as superior to that of his subjects, as the sense of the father is superior to that of his little children. The worthless argument, resting on this comparison, is worthy only of a barbarous country and a weak and tyrannical mind.

Lutheran: Did not Peter use *force* against those who came to seize the Redeemer? did he not cut off the high priest's servant's ear with his sword? and does not this fact prove that the followers of Christ may defend him and his doctrine by force?

Quaker: That scripture fact is most unlucky for the gentleman who uses it in favor of persecution; for, if it proves any thing, it proves that persecution is unchristian. This action of Peter's took place before his conversion, and, so far from pleasing Christ, greatly offended him, as appears from the severe reprimand which immediately followed it: "Put up thy sword into the sheath; for *all they that take the sword shall perish with the sword.*" And he instantly healed the servant. What could more truly and loudly proclaim that his kingdom was not of this world, was not a kingdom of violence? and what fact could more strikingly confirm all we have attempted to prove relative to religious liberty? Does it not, in other words, declare, that *all those* of Christ's disciples, who *make use of persecution* against others, may naturally expect, in turn, *to suffer persecution* from others? And, unfortunately, this has been perfectly realized in thousands of instances mentioned in church history.

Presbyterian: There is another remarkable fact, recorded in one of the gospels, to teach us the same lesson. Two disciples of Christ, being angry with certain people, because "*they did not receive him,*" said, "*Lord, wilt thou that we command fire to come down from heaven, and consume them?*" "But he turned, and *rebuked* them, and said, Ye know not what manner of spirit ye are of!" Hereby giving them to understand that *mildness, kindness, goodness* and *forbearance* should be the character of himself, his followers, and his doctrine.

Calvinist: I have read over the New Testament again and again, and I am quite confident, our Savior never taught that it was proper or wise, or expedient to propagate or preserve religion *by force*. He knew well that religion could preserve itself by teaching, preaching, prayer, and the divine assistance; and that force is as foreign to its nature, as barbarism is to the nature of civilization.

Unitarian: We are compelled by the laws to be married by the Clergy of the establishment, and this compulsion is most severely felt, by hundreds of thousands, as an infringement on the right of conscience. Are not such laws barbarous and cruel? but, I know I need not ask the question, since we have sufficiently expressed our opinion.

Priest: The state should have nothing to do with the *religious part* of the ceremony of marriage; but since matrimony is also a *civil contract*, involving many most important civil interests, it should come under the inspection of the civil law, one way or other.

Presbyterian: Then there should be two marryings, the one *religious* and the other *civil*; the one performed, according to the *dictates of conscience*, by the religious Minister; the other by the civil Magistrate. If this were the case, there would be no persecution; because each one would be left to perform the RELIGIOUS PART of the ceremony according to the practice of his own religion; and the CIVIL PART would be that alone which would ever be referred to by the civil law, or for any state purpose. This regulation would be possible in England, because it is actual in France.

Quaker: It seems to me a relic of barbarism to make the possession of *property* and *civil rights* depend on the *religious ceremony of baptism*, since the religion of many will not permit them to use that ceremony at all, and, especially, according to the laws.

Priest: I have always looked upon the laws, to which you allude, as barbarous and
cruel; and, never was able to see why a man unbaptized, had not as much *natural
right* and *natural capacity* to inherit and manage his father's estate, as a man
baptized. Who ever discovered that baptism makes any difference in the nature,
situation, and use of the eyes, mouth, hands, belly, legs and feet? And if it makes
no difference in these, and the other parts of the human frame, why should it be
called in as an indispensable qualification for natural performances and civil rights?

Lutheran: In some law-cases, what could be done without *a register*?

Quaker: Can no one write a *register* but a Clergyman? Could not the time, when
any child is born, be recorded in a book by the neighboring Magistrate? and
could not this Magistrate's book be referred to, as easily as the Parson's, for the
purpose of discovering any one's age or tracing his pedigree? Here, again, France
has outstripped us! We English are for ever mixing religion and the state, for
ever making one muddled jumble or another. Can *we* consistently ridicule *those*
who think that without their religion no one can be fitted *for heaven*; when *we*
ourselves are so scrupulously precise, as to think that, without *one ceremony* of
our religion, no one can be fitted even for THE EARTH?

Methodist: Blind, fiery zeal has been the mother of many persecutions, as daily
experience teaches us. A hot-headed zealot becomes thoroughly convinced that
his own religion is the only true one, and he immediately, of his own accord, by
his own authority, and according to the suggestions of his narrow will and
corrupt heart, begins to devise means by fire and sword, laws, jails and gibbets,
and every violent expedient, to propagate and defend his system. Obstinate as a
bull, and unfeeling as a bloodthirsty cannibal, he asks not what was the mildness
of his Redeemer, what were the sweetness and kindness and charity and goodness of his doctrine and practice; he asks not how the apostles and first disciples
conducted themselves towards unbelievers; he asks not what are the dictates of
wisdom, prudence, and experience; but rushes headlong into all the wretched
suggestions of his own self-will, passion, and depravity; and renders himself an
object of contempt to some, of pity to others, and of disgust to all. I have made
my observations very carefully, and I do sincerely believe there are more than a
few of this description of bigots among all classes of religionists; though, in all
cases, I do think they are more to be pitied as ignorant barbarians, than contemned as natural brute beasts. They are a blot in the body to which they belong.
Their extravagance eclipses their judgment.

Quaker: *A zeal not according to wisdom* has undoubtedly been the unhappy mother
of many persecution; yet I think THE LOVE OF MONEY has been a more prolific
source of these scourges. Why did the Jews persecute Christ and his apostles?
For fear of losing their "place and nation." Why did Judas help to murder Jesus?
For the "thirty pieces of silver." Why have Clergymen generally, or at least
often, been the foremost in aiding and encouraging violent measures and unjust
laws against religious liberty? The shepherds were afraid of losing part of the
fleece. Why do the Clergy of the establishment exert themselves so very much
in every city, town, and village, to support and keep up the present oppressive, unjust, and degrading laws against liberty of conscience to Catholics and
others? For fear of losing their immense incomes. Why do many noblemen and

gentlemen join them in their selfish and illiberal endeavors? Because their sons or daughters, their brothers or sisters, partake, or are likely to partake, of the fat booty. *"The love of money,"* says St Paul, *"is the root of all evil."*

Presbyterian: For my part, I must candidly own, that when I hear the established Clergy hooting out; *"The Church is in danger!"* I always understand it to mean nothing more than *The* TITHES *are in danger!*

Lutheran: They cannot possibly mean any thing else! For why should *their* Church be in any more danger than the Churches of *other people*, if, by *Church*, they do not mean the TEMPORALITIES *of the Church*?

Quaker: These Clergy of the establishment know very well that a great part of their fat livings are *forced* out of the pockets of the people of other religions; they know this could not be, if full liberty of conscience existed in the land; and, therefore, are they always under an alarm when the sound of religious freedom approaches their dwellings; always posted upon their castles with their Spanish guns and bayonets, ready to ward off the slightest attack of English justice upon their profitable and most beloved inquisition. Oh! CURSED LOVE OF MONEY! to what dreadful lengths of injustice and cruelty hast thou not often led thy deluded votaries!!

Unitarian: Do we not all wish that no man in the whole world may ever again suffer religious persecution?

All: We do.

Unitarian: Then, I am sure we all heartily wish universal religious liberty; and hence, freely and sincerely subscribe to the truth of the proposition, with which we began our talk: *It is the natural right of every man to worship God according to the dictates of his conscience, without being subject, on that account, to civil penalties and disabilities.*

Priest: After death, God will judge all thieves and robbers, and all the partakers of their ill-gotten goods; and, will he not equally judge all persecutors and religious plunderers, and all the partakers of their iniquitous spoils?

Methodist: Undoubtedly. But, alas! there is reason to fear that those, whose money is their god on earth, care very little for the God of heaven. *"Covetousness,"* says St Paul, *"is idolatry"*; and where men are so abandoned to vice as to set up false gods or idols, they generally lose all sight of the true God, and of his righteous judgment.

FINIS

Felicité de Lamennais, *Words of a Believer* [*Paroles d'un Croyant*] (1834)

Lamennais (1782–1854), priest, journalist, philosopher, was a major contributor to liberal Catholicism in France in the 1820s and 1830s. This work appeared in April 1834, and was an attempt to restate his political and social views; it was condemned in a papal encyclical, *Singulari nos.* Written in a pithy, aphoristic style, and imbued with the spirit of biblical prophecy and apocalyptic, *Words* articulates a vision of a liberated humanity. With the papacy's rejection of his social and political liberalism, Lamennais gradually retreated from the church and his once vigorous defense of its teachings.

SOURCE: Felicité de Lamennais, *Words of a Believer and the Past and Future of the People*, tr. L. E. Martineau (London, 1891), pp. 85–7.
LITERATURE: Alec R. Vidler, *Prophecy and Papacy: A Study of Lamennais, the Church, and the Revolution* (London: SCM Press, 1954).

XXVIII

There have been times when men, in slaying those whose faith differed from their own, persuaded themselves that they were offering a pleasing sacrifice to God.

Hold in horror these execrable murders.

How should the slaughter of men be pleasing unto God, who has said to man: Thou shalt not kill.

When man's blood flows upon the ground, as an offering to God, the demons hasten thither to drink it, and they enter into him who hath shed it.

Men only begin to persecute when they despair of convincing, and he who despairs of convincing, either blasphemes in himself the power of truth, or lacks confidence in the truth of the doctrine which he preaches.

Can anything be more senseless than to say to men: Believe or die?

Faith is the daughter of the Word: she pierceth hearts with speech, and not with a dagger.

Jesus went about doing good, drawing the hardest hearts unto him by his goodness, and touching them by his gentleness.

His divine lips blessed, and cursed not, save the hypocrites. He chose not executioners for his apostles.

He said to his disciples: Let them grow together, until the harvest, the good grain with the bad, the householder shall separate them upon the threshing-floor.

And to those who urged him to bring down fire from heaven upon an unbelieving city, He said: Ye know not what spirit ye are of.

The spirit of Jesus is a spirit of peace, of mercy, and of love.

Those who persecute in his name, who try consciences with the sword, who torture the body in order to convert the soul, who cause tears to flow instead of drying them; such have not the spirit of Jesus.

Woe unto him who profaneth the Gospel by making it a terror unto men!
Woe unto him who writeth the good news upon a blood-stained page!

Remember the catacombs.

In those days you Christians were dragged to the scaffold, you were
delivered unto savage beasts in the amphitheatre for the amusement of the
populace, you were thrown by thousands into the depths of mines and
prisons, your goods were confiscated, you were trodden under foot like the
mud of the public streets; you had no refuge save the bowels of the earth
wherein to celebrate your proscribed mysteries.

What said your persecutors? They said that you propagated dangerous
doctrines; that your sect, as they called it, disturbed the public peace and
order; that, violators of the laws and enemies of the human race, you shook
the empire in shaking the religion of the empire.

And in this distress, beneath this oppression, what was it that you asked?
Liberty. You claimed the right to obey God alone, to serve and worship
Him according to your conscience.

When others, even though misguided in their faith, shall claim from you
this sacred right, respect it in them, even as you asked that the pagans
should respect it in you.

Respect it, that you may not tarnish the memory of your confessors, nor
sully the ashes of your martyrs.

Persecution is a two-edged sword: it wounds right and left.

If you no longer remember the teachings of Christ, remember at least
the catacombs.

John Stuart Mill, *On Liberty* (1859)

While working for thirty-five years for the East India Company, Mill (1806–
73) gained for himself a reputation as one of the most influential English
philosophers of the nineteenth century. He was an exponent of the modern philosophy of liberalism, emphasizing the need for individual autonomy
and self-realization. He feared not only the threat to his ideal from the
actions of persecuting states, but also from societal pressures. Like a
number of humanistic thinkers before him, he was prepared to see the
virtues of diversity: "the Christian system is no exception to the rule, that
in an imperfect state of the human mind, the interests of truth require a
diversity of opinions" (p. 92), though he himself was not a Christian. Not
all his contemporaries welcomed the assault on traditional patterns. His
contemporary James Fitzjames Stephen did not intend to ban diversity,
but he thought social intolerance had its place in defending the good of

the status quo and he warned those who would attack the basic institutions of British life to expect a battle: an assault such as Mill's "should be done sword in hand, and a man who does it has no more right to be surprised at being fiercely resisted than a soldier who attacks a breach."[1]

SOURCE: John Stuart Mill, *On Liberty* (London, 1859), pp. 17–19, 32–3, 51–4, 57–62, 64, 74–8.
LITERATURE: James Fitzjames Stephen, *Liberty, Equality, Fraternity*, ed. R. J. White (Cambridge: Cambridge University Press, 1967 [orig. 1873]); Susan Mendus, *Toleration and the Limits of Liberalism* (Atlantic Highlands, NJ: Humanities Press, 1989).

The likings and dislikings of society, or of some powerful portion of it, are thus the main thing which has practically determined the rules laid down for general observance, under the penalties of law or opinion. And in general, those who have been in advance of society in thought and feeling, have left this condition of things unassailed in principle, however they may have come into conflict with it in some of its details. They have occupied themselves rather in inquiring what things society ought to like or dislike, than in questioning whether its likings or dislikings should be a law to individuals. They preferred endeavoring to alter the feelings of mankind on the particular points on which they were themselves heretical, rather than make common cause in defense of freedom, with heretics generally. The only case in which the higher ground has been taken on principle and maintained with consistency, by any but an individual here and there, is that of religious belief: a case instructive in many ways, and not least so as forming a most striking instance of the fallibility of what is called the moral sense: for the *odium theologicum*, in a sincere bigot, is one of the most unequivocal cases of moral feeling. Those who first broke the yoke of what called itself the Universal Church, were in general as little willing to permit difference of religious opinion as that church itself. But when the heat of the conflict was over, without giving a complete victory to any party, and each church or sect was reduced to limit its hopes to retaining possession of the ground it already occupied; minorities, seeing that they had no chance of becoming majorities, were under the necessity of pleading to those whom they could not convert, for permission to differ. It is accordingly on this battle field, almost solely, that the rights of the individual against society have been asserted on broad grounds of principle, and the claim of society to exercise authority over dissentients, openly controverted. The great writers to whom the world owes what religious liberty it possesses, have mostly asserted freedom of conscience as an indefeasible right, and denied absolutely that a human being is accountable to others for his religious belief. Yet so natural to mankind is intolerance in whatever they really care about, that religious freedom has hardly anywhere been practically realized, except where religious indifference, which dislikes to have its peace disturbed by theological quarrels, has added its weight to the scale. In the minds of almost all religious persons, even in the most tolerant countries, the duty of toleration is admitted with tacit reserves. One person will bear with dissent in matters of church government, but not of dogma; another can tolerate everybody, short of a Papist or an Unitarian; another, every one who believes in revealed religion; a few extend their charity a little further, but stop at the belief in a God and in a future state. Wherever the sentiment of the majority is still genuine and intense, it is found to have abated little of its claim to be obeyed.

. . . Let us suppose, therefore, that the government is entirely at one with the people, and never thinks of exerting any power of coercion unless in agreement with what it conceives to be their voice. But I deny the right of the people to exercise such coercion, either by themselves or by their government. The power itself is illegitimate. The best government has no more title to it than the worst. It is as noxious, or more noxious, when exerted in accordance with public opinion, than when in opposition to it. If all mankind minus one, were of one opinion, and only one person were of the contrary opinion, mankind would be no more justified in silencing that one person, than he, if he had the power, would be justified in silencing mankind. Were an opinion a personal possession of no value except to the owner; if to be obstructed in the enjoyment of it were simply a private injury, it would make some difference whether the injury was inflicted only on a few persons or on many. But the peculiar evil of silencing the expression of an opinion is that it is robbing the human race; posterity as well as the existing generation; those who dissent from the opinion, still more than those who hold it. If the opinion is right, they are deprived of the opportunity of exchanging error for truth: if wrong, they lose, what is almost as great a benefit, the clearer perception and livelier impression of truth, produced by its collision with error.

Aware of the impossibility of defending the use of punishment for restraining irreligious opinions, by any argument which will not justify Marcus Antoninus, the enemies of religious freedom, when hard pressed, occasionally accept this consequence, and say, with Dr Johnson,[2] that the persecutors of Christianity were in the right; that persecution is an ordeal through which truth ought to pass, and always passes successfully, legal penalties being, in the end, powerless against truth, though sometimes beneficially effective against mischievous errors. This is a form of the argument for religious intolerance, sufficiently remarkable not to be passed without notice.

A theory which maintains that truth may justifiably be persecuted because persecution cannot possibly do it any harm, cannot be charged with being intentionally hostile to the reception of new truths; but we cannot commend the generosity of its dealing with the persons to whom mankind are indebted for them. To discover to the world something which deeply concerns it, and of which it was previously ignorant; to prove to it that it had been mistaken on some vital point of temporal or spiritual interest, is as important a service as a human being can render to his fellow-creatures, and in certain cases, as in those of the early Christians and of the Reformers, those who think with Dr Johnson believe it to have been the most precious gift which could be bestowed on mankind. That the authors of such splendid benefits should be requited by martyrdom; that their reward should be to be dealt with as the vilest of criminals, is not, upon this theory, a deplorable error and misfortune, for which humanity should mourn in sackcloth and ashes, but the normal and justifiable state of things. The propounder of a new truth, according to this doctrine, should stand, as stood, in the legislation of the Locrians, the proposer of a new law, with a halter round his neck, to be instantly tightened if the public assembly did not, on hearing his reasons, then and there adopt his proposition. People who defend this mode of treating benefactors, cannot be supposed to set much value on the benefit; and I believe this view of the subject is mostly confined to the sort of persons who think that new truths may have been desirable once, but that we have had enough of them now.

But, indeed, the dictum that truth always triumphs over persecution is one of those pleasant falsehoods which men repeat after one another till they pass into commonplaces, but which all experience refutes. History teems with instances of truth put down by persecution. If not suppressed for ever, it may be thrown back for centuries. To speak only of religious opinions; the Reformation broke out at least twenty times before Luther, and was put down. Arnold of Brescia was put down. Fra Dolcino was put down. Savonarola was put down. The Albigeois were put down. The Vaudois were put down. The Lollards were put down. The Hussites were put down. Even after the era of Luther, wherever persecution was persisted in, it was successful. In Spain, Italy, Flanders, the Austrian empire, Protestantism was rooted out; and, most likely, would have been so in England, had Queen Mary lived, or Queen Elizabeth died. Persecution has always succeeded, save where the heretics were too strong a party to be effectually persecuted. No reasonable person can doubt that Christianity might have been extirpated in the Roman Empire. It spread, and became predominant, because the persecutions were only occasional, lasting but a short time, and separated by long intervals of almost undisturbed propagandism. It is a piece of idle sentimentality that truth, merely as truth, has any inherent power denied to error, of prevailing against the dungeon and the stake. Men are not more zealous for truth than they often are for error, and a sufficient application of legal or even of social penalties will generally succeed in stopping the propagation of either. The real advantage which truth has, consists in this, that when an opinion is true, it may be extinguished once, twice, or many times, but in the course of ages there will generally be found persons to rediscover it, until some one of its reappearances falls on a time when from favorable circumstances it escapes persecution until it has made such head as to withstand all subsequent attempts to suppress it.

. . . What is boasted of at the present time as the revival of religion, is always, in narrow and uncultivated minds, at least as much the revival of bigotry; and where there is the strong permanent leaven of intolerance in the feelings of a people, which at all times abides in the middle classes of this country, it needs but little to provoke them into actively persecuting those whom they have never ceased to think proper objects of persecution.[3] For it is this – it is the opinions men entertain, and the feelings they cherish, respecting those who disown the beliefs they deem important, which makes this country not a place of mental freedom. For a long time past, the chief mischief of the legal penalties is that they strengthen the social stigma. It is that stigma which is really effective, and so effective is it, that the profession of opinions which are under the ban of society is much less common in England, than is, in many other countries, the avowal of those which incur risk of judicial punishment. In respect to all persons but those whose pecuniary circumstances make them independent of the good will of other people, opinion, on this subject, is as efficacious as law; men might as well be imprisoned, as excluded from the means of earning their bread. Those whose bread is already secured, and who desire no favors from men in power, or from bodies of men, or from the public, have nothing to fear from the open avowal of any opinions, but to be ill-thought of and ill-spoken of, and this it ought not to require a very heroic mold to enable them to bear. There is no room for any appeal *ad misericordiam* in behalf of such persons. But though we do not now inflict so much evil on those who think differently from us, as it was formerly our custom to do, it may be that we do ourselves as much evil as ever by our treatment of them. Socrates was put to death, but the Socratic philosophy rose like the sun in heaven, and spread its illumination over the whole intellectual firmament. Christians were cast to the lions, but the Christian church grew up a stately and spreading tree, overtopping the older and less vigorous growths, and stifling them by its shade. Our merely social intolerance kills no one, roots out no opinions, but induces men to disguise them, or to abstain from any active effort for their diffusion. With us, heretical opinions do not perceptibly gain, or even lose, ground in each decade or generation; they never blaze out far and wide, but continue to smoulder in the narrow circles of thinking and studious persons among whom they originate, without ever lighting up the general affairs of mankind with either a true or a deceptive light. And thus is kept up a state of things very satisfactory to some minds, because, without the unpleasant process of fining or imprisoning anybody, it maintains all prevailing opinions outwardly undisturbed, while it does not absolutely interdict the exercise of reason by dissentients afflicted with the malady of thought. A convenient plan for having peace in the intellectual world, and keeping all things going on therein very much as they do already. But the price paid for this sort of intellectual pacification, is the sacrifice of the entire moral courage of the human mind. A state of things in which a large portion of the most active and inquiring intellects find it advisable to keep the genuine principles and grounds of their convictions within their own breasts, and attempt, in what they address to the public, to fit as much as they can of their own conclusions to premises which they have internally renounced, cannot send forth the open, fearless characters, and logical, consistent intellects who once adorned the thinking world. The sort of men who can be looked for under it, are either mere conformers to common-place, or time-servers for truth, whose arguments on all great subjects are meant for their hearers, and are not those which have convinced them-selves. Those who avoid this alternative, do so by narrowing their thoughts and interest to things which can be spoken of without venturing within the region of principles, that is, to small practical matters, which would come right of themselves, if but the minds of mankind were strengthened and enlarged, and which will never be made effectually right until then: while that which would strengthen and enlarge men's minds, free and daring speculation on the highest subjects, is abandoned.

Those in whose eyes this reticence on the part of heretics is no evil, should consider in the first place, that in consequence of it there is never any fair and thorough discussion of heretical opinions; and that such of them as could not stand such a discussion, though they may be prevented from spreading, do not disappear. But it is not the minds of heretics that are deteriorated most, by the ban placed on all inquiry which does not end in the orthodox conclusions. The greatest harm done is to those who are not heretics, and whose whole mental development is cramped, and their reason cowed, by the fear of heresy. Who can compute what the world loses in the multitude of promising intellects combined with timid characters, who dare not follow out any bold, vigorous, independent train of thought, lest it should land them in something which would admit of being considered irreligious or immoral? Among them we may occasionally see some man of deep conscientiousness, and subtle and refined understanding, who spends a life in sophisticating with an intellect which he cannot silence, and exhausts the resources of ingenuity in attempting to reconcile the promptings of his conscience and reason with orthodoxy, which yet he does not, perhaps, to the end succeed in doing. No one can be a great thinker who does not recognize, that as a thinker it is his first duty to follow his intellect to whatever conclusions it may lead. Truth gains more even by the errors of one who, with due study and preparation, thinks for himself, than by the true opinions of those who only hold them because they do not suffer themselves to think. Not that it is solely, or chiefly, to form great thinkers, that freedom of thinking is required. On the contrary, it is as much, and even more indispensable, to enable average human beings to attain the mental stature which they are capable of. . . .

. . . However unwillingly a person who has a strong opinion may admit the possibility that his opinion may be false, he ought to be moved by the consideration that however true it may be, if it is not fully, frequently, and fearlessly discussed, it will be held as a dead dogma, not a living truth. . . .

To what an extent doctrines intrinsically fitted to make the deepest impression upon the mind may remain in it as dead beliefs, without being ever realized in the imagination, the feelings, or the understanding, is exemplified by the manner in which the majority of believers hold the doctrines of Christianity. By Christianity I here mean what is accounted such by all churches and sects – the maxims and precepts contained in the New Testament. These are considered sacred, and accepted as laws, by all professing Christians. Yet it is scarcely too much to say that not one Christian in a thousand guides or tests his individual conduct by reference to those laws. The standard to which he does refer it, is the custom of his nation, his class, or his religious profession. He has thus, on the one hand, a collection of ethical maxims, which he believes to have been vouchsafed to him by infallible wisdom as rules for his government; and on the other, a set of every-day judgments and practices, which go a certain length with some of those maxims, not so great a length with others, stand in direct opposition to some, and are, on the whole, a compromise between the Christian creed and the interests and suggestions of worldly life. To the first of these standards he gives his homage; to the other his real allegiance. All Christians believe that the blessed are the poor and humble, and those who are ill-used by the world; that it is easier for a camel to pass through the eye of a needle than for a rich man to enter the kingdom of heaven; that they should judge not, lest they be judged; that they should swear not at all; that they should love their neighbor as themselves; that if one take their cloak, they should give him their coat also; that they should take no thought for the morrow; that if they would be perfect, they should sell all that they have and give it to the poor. They are not insincere when they say that they believe these things. They do believe them, as people believe what they have always heard lauded and never discussed. But in the sense of that living belief which regulates conduct, they believe these doctrines just up to the point to which it is usual to act upon them. The doctrines in their integrity are serviceable to pelt adversaries with; and it is understood that they are to be put forward (when possible) as the reasons for whatever people do that they think laudable. But any one who reminded them that the maxims require an infinity of things which they never even think of doing, would gain nothing but to be classed among those very unpopular characters who affect to be better than other people. The doctrines have no hold on ordinary believers – are not a power in their minds. They have an habitual respect for the sound of them, but no feeling which spreads from the words to the things signified, and forces the mind to take *them* in, and make them conform to the formula. Whenever conduct is concerned, they look round for Mr A and B to direct them how far to go in obeying Christ.

Now we may be well assured that the case was not thus, but far otherwise, with the early Christians. Had it been thus, Christianity never would have expanded from an obscure sect of the despised Hebrews into the religion of the Roman empire. When their enemies said, "See how these Christians love one another" (a remark not likely to be made by anybody now), they assuredly had a much livelier feeling of the meaning of their creed than they have ever had since. And to this cause, probably, it is chiefly owing that Christianity now makes so little progress in extending its domain, and after eighteen centuries, is still nearly confined to Europeans and the descendants of Europeans. Even with the strictly religious, who are much in earnest about their doctrines, and attach a greater amount of meaning to many of them than people in general, it commonly happens that the part which is thus comparatively active in their minds is that which was made by Calvin, or Knox, or some such person much nearer in character to themselves. The sayings of Christ coexist passively in their minds, producing hardly any effect beyond what is caused by mere listening to words so amiable and bland. There are many reasons, doubtless, why doctrines which are the badge of a sect retain more of their vitality than those common to all recognized sects, and why more pains are taken by teachers to keep their meaning alive; but one reason certainly is, that the peculiar doctrines are more questioned, and have to be oftener defended against open gainsayers. Both teachers and learners go to sleep at their post, as soon as there is no enemy in the field.

The same thing holds true, generally speaking, of all traditional doctrines – those of prudence and knowledge of life, as well as of morals or religion.

All languages and literatures are full of general observations on life, both as to what it is, and how to conduct oneself in it; observations which everybody knows, which everybody repeats, or hears with acquiescence, which are received as truisms, yet of which most people first truly learn the meaning, when experience, generally of a painful kind, has made it a reality to them. How often, when smarting under some unforeseen misfortune or disappointment, does a person call to mind some proverb or common saying, familiar to him all his life, the meaning of which, if he had ever before felt it as he does now, would have saved him from the calamity. There are indeed reasons for this, other than the absence of discussion; there are many truths of which the full meaning *cannot* be realized, until personal experience has brought it home. But much more of the meaning even of these would have been understood, and what was understood would have been far more deeply impressed on the mind, if the man had been accustomed to hear it argued *pro* and *con* by people who did understand it. The fatal tendency of mankind to leave off thinking about a thing when it is no longer doubtful, is the cause of half their errors. A contemporary author has well spoken of "the deep slumber of a decided opinion."

Anonymous, *The Ultimate Principle of Religious Liberty* (1860)

This anonymous document was published at the end of a decade which had witnessed a continued struggle by some dissenters to gain implementation of the principle of voluntaryism, hence disestablishment of the Church of England. The author was apparently a dissenter and a strenuous opponent of the continuing establishment, and sought to ground his objection upon an "ultimate principle" which had eluded no less a thinker than John Locke. This principle was the priority of the human relationship with God as anterior to structures of civil rule.

SOURCE: [Anonymous], *The Ultimate Principle of Religious Liberty* (London, 1860), pp. 7, 21, 22–5, 28–30, 198–9.
LITERATURE: General historical background may be gained from G. I. T. Machin, *Politics and the Churches in Great Britain, 1832 to 1868* (Oxford: Clarendon Press, 1977), chs 8 and 9.

. . . In so far as the distinct *origins* of civil authority and of moral authority determine their respective provinces and limits, they separate the two, and place the subjects of each beyond the jurisdiction of the other. Springing from relationships quite distinct and essentially different, morals, whether viewed as comprehending religion or not, are wholly beyond the legitimate interference of civil authority. . . .

The true religion to every man, is that which he conscientiously believes to be true; and no circumstances in the present conditions of man's being insure uniformity of belief. Men are so situated in the present imperfect state that their beliefs may and do differ. Two men may severally hold most opposite creeds to be the truth. It is therefore absurd to assume that what we believe must also be believed by others. This assumption, however, is necessarily involved in imposing upon others our own belief. . . .

These cannot but be regarded as insuperable objections to such an authority as is implied in the State establishment of religion, involving as it does the double assumption that the civil ruler is capable of attaining to an infallible judgment, and that he is commissioned to enforce his belief upon others; neither of which pretensions is there the slightest reason to admit. If this enforcement of religious belief and obedience be the right and duty of civil governments, as such, the consideration that the form to be established is, or is alleged to be, the true religion, is entitled to no consideration at all. But, if the civil magistrate possesses no inherent authority to take charge of religious education and observance, except only of the *Christian* religion, then, it is clear, the higher ground of a general right of governments ought to be abandoned; for there are heathen as well as Christian governors, and such a right may be predicated as justly of the one as of the other. Thus the principle on which the supporters of establishments would give to the Christian ruler a jurisdiction over morals and religion, would give it to the superstitious or idolatrous heathen also. Nay, the objection would hold good even against the establishment of the Bible as a whole, could such a proposal be intelligibly explained.

This "material consideration," then, turns out to be only what may be put forward by the sincere believer of any other religion, or any modification of the same one. The plea that the religion proposed to be established is the true religion, when advanced in vindication of constraint of conscience in those who dissent, is nothing else than an absurd assumption.

We may, however, infer from this specification, that a certain class of advocates would not have the false religion established. Still, this is merely saying in other words that they would approve of their own religious system being established, but object to the establishment of every other. But the conscientious and enlightened Dissenter would not endow his own religion; and he would thus avoid the injustice and inconsistency involved in such an abuse of temporal power.

Under the influence of the fundamental mistake which we have pointed out respecting the principle on which the Governor of the world will administer reward or punishment, the advocates of establishments proceed to determine what is true and obligatory, and to enforce the support of their own belief and practice upon others. Such a principle of judgment could only obtain under an economy where the subjects of government each possessed the means of absolutely perfect knowledge. So long as the circumstances of man's condition remain what they are, the exercise of such a judgment and authority by one man over his fellows would be, not merely illegitimate, but impossible.

But our principle makes it equally illegitimate and unjust to require the profession of certain prescribed opinions in religion, in order to the assumption of official authority by any civil functionary, or to exact such profession from the private subject of the State under a penalty of distraint, incarceration, or any other form of civil disability.

If such be the limits of civil power, it is *unjust* to employ it coercively in matters wherein all are entitled to equal liberty.

In concluding the present chapter, we may reply to the question proposed at the commencement of the inquiry, viz., What is justice in the matter of religious belief and practice? We answer, that nothing short of the absence of any creed or worship prescribed by civil authority, or of any pecuniary exaction for religious purposes, can leave intact the individual rights of every citizen. Even a simple official declaration in favor of certain views of forms would be an unfair use of the *préstige* of civil authority and influence, not to be tolerated by those members of the community who may dissent from the doctrine and worship proclaimed. Not even the majority of a civil community have any right to set at a disadvantage the creed and worship of any other members of the commonwealth, however few in number. To do anything whatever, beyond such employment of civil power as may be necessary for insuring (and *this* by main force, if need be) to each member of the community such liberty and privilege in the exercise of his religious convictions and performance of his religious duties, as may be consistent with the enjoyment of the same privilege and protection by every other subject of the government, is an unjust use of governmental power. To prevent one person from interfering with another's religious observances, is a legitimate exercise of power; but this is a very different thing from using civil force to favor the system of one to the disadvantage of that of another, or even to favor all alike (if such were possible) by positive *propagation*. Propagation or support government has no business to attempt: even-handed protection is a purely civil affair; and this alone is within its legitimate range. The civil relations authorize nothing more; the moral relations interdict anything beyond. This is our notion of justice in the matter.

The *disposition of mind* to admit this, is true liberality; for liberality is not so properly affirmed of acts as of dispositions, or sentiments and motives. Liberality, carried into outward acts or regulations, is justice. *Toleration*, in the proper sense of the word, can have no place, in the absence of rightful power and patronage; and, as civil government possesses neither, the term toleration cannot apply to simple and proper neutrality. Toleration, in the vocabulary of those who uphold the establishment of religion means the simple absence of molestation. It has no place at all in the vocabulary of true religious liberty; unless, indeed, it be that the Dissenter tolerates the Churchman in the violation of his own indubitable rights. There can be no toleration elsewhere in such a case; for, where an establishment exists, something very far short of justice must be the lot of those who dissent from the views and modes of worship happening to be endowed. The grand sin of the civil patronage of religion is, doubtless, the presumptuous usurpation of the exclusive prerogative of the Divine Ruler of the world; and the violation of the conscientious rights of man is an evil only second in enormity to the offense against his God. The "vested interests" enjoyed by those who may have profited by the establishment of religion, can alone be the objects of toleration in the matter. There cannot, in such a case be any mutuality. It is a "reciprocity all on one side," and can never be otherwise so long as a fragment of the advantage, direct or derived, continues to accrue to the adherents of such an institution from the appropriation of national property. So long as the ministrations of religion are supported at the public expense, the Dissenter must be constrained in one form or another to contribute to the maintenance of the Churchman's religious system of worship; and, even if he were not, his highest moral rights would continue to be infringed so long as any State-patronage of religion should be upheld.

The substance of what Locke here advances is just this: – first, we have the assertion of the absence of authority, then the proofs of this proposition: – (1) the people cannot give it – (2) no man can devolve his salvation on another – (3) or conform his faith to that of another – (4) conviction is the life of religion – (5) an insincere profession would be an offense against the Divine Majesty.

Here are five excellent objections to the employment of coercive power; but they may be resolved into the *impossibility* of effectually accomplishing the religious object by civil force, and the wrong of pretending its accomplishment by a false profession.

Now, we are not content with this: we want what we might almost designate the *à priori*, or at least the *antecedent*, ground of proof that the magistrate *cannot* have the authority in question. We are not content with stating the *obstacles* which lie in the way of his doing the thing that he aims at: we wish to show, on higher and ultimate grounds, that he is forestalled and interdicted, and has no right or liberty to *try* to do it. And this reason we desire to see reduced to its primary form of definition as a postulate. Locke ought to have done this; and then all the rest would have fitly followed. But this is just what he has not done, and what we cannot afford to dispense with when discussing this subject on the general ground of reason and expediency. Give to this primary reason its due place and supremacy; and we may then follow it up with the additional argument, that there are no circumstances in the present state of things which render everyone's belief necessarily the same. Man's present condition, and the rule of judgment under which he shall be judged, being such as to admit difference in religious conviction, it must be wrong to exact *uniformity of profession and practice*.[4]

Since uniformity cannot be secured, and since religious belief and the discharge of religious duty upon the conviction and command of our fellow-creature are impossible, and, if possible, would not be acceptable, God cannot have intended religion to be under the legislative direction of man at all; but He must have designed, that, under His own perfect moral government, and to himself alone, every man, as a moral agent and subject of religion, should be accountable. The Divine Ruler reserves all authority and control in this matter to Himself; purposing that all apparent inequalities and discrepancies should be adjusted by His own infallible hand, in a state beyond the present, a state to the destinies of which the conduct and experience of this life are subservient and probationary.

These, we say, are excellent and powerful reasons against investing the political ruler with any authority in religion; but we regard it as a reply of a much more definite and satisfactory character to say, that the nature of relationship always determines the nature of authority possessed. The religious duties of men are antecedent to and independent of civil society, and must therefore attach to and arise out of the *antecedent moral relations* of man to God, and to his fellow-man as man. It would not satisfy us to reply simply, that coercive power, *from its very nature*, would probably fail, and was manifestly improper as a constraining influence where perfect liberty should be ordained. We want to see to what relation the function has been ordained to attach; and that will show us where and to what it *cannot* belong, and thus, by disproving the natural authority to employ coercion, exclude it entirely from the region of religion.

If we have completed our argument on grounds which any man, statesman or philosopher, might adopt independently of the supposed testimony of

Scripture, we need not be denied a momentary glance, in the light of such revelations, at the aspect of the system we oppose. The ambition and cupidity of the priest, the policy of the statesman, or both combined, may appear to the philosophical student of history to furnish an exhaustive solution of the origin of this great and monstrous evil alike to the Church and to the State. Be it so to him; we pronounce only for ourselves. If, however, the Bible is anything more than a mythical imposture, encroachment on the sovereign prerogative and authority of God began before man existed, to become either the ally or the victim of a soaring ambition. From that dark and fateful hour when the spirit of rebellious usurpation first raised its head against the right and rule of sovereign power, the pride and counsel of the demon have never ceased to wage the unequal and presumptuous strife. The impious war-cry of non-allegiance hushed through the realm of government by the sweep of Almighty vengeance, the enemy of heaven and earth has nevertheless not ceased by lure and strategy to prosecute his dark rebellious vow. Baffled and despoiled in the open war of defiance and usurpation, the archangelic foe, still in the inscrutable purpose of the Most High left in the undiminished might and scope of his spiritual power, pursues his malignant ends while liberty and resources remain to him. The Prince of the powers of the air bides his time till the conscious treachery and infatuation of the priest, or the godless hypocrisy and ambition of the politician, may subserve his purpose. The league between the rulers of this world and the visible framework of the "spiritual kingdom" on earth, discloses to us the master-strategy of the common adversary of God and man. Albeit many godly dupes be found upholding the supreme delusion, the original of the "idea" of this alliance is not of Hooker, nor of Coleridge, nor of Gladstone; and the man who, whether by the enginery of philosophical logic or by the invincible weapons of revealed truth, seeks to bring to an end this adulterous connection, is the true friend of God, and labors in the holy service of the universal kingship of the Redeemer.

Mandell Creighton, *Persecution and Tolerance* (1895)

Creighton (1843–1901) was an Anglican priest, professor of ecclesiastical history at Cambridge, and later bishop of Peterborough and then London. It was from Peterborough that he returned to the university to deliver the Hulsean Lectures for 1893–4, which he described as "a trifling contribution to a great subject." Creighton was a self-described "enthusiastic and fanatical Anglican," and a strong English nationalist, the two finding a ready union in his mind. By nature broad-minded and conciliatory, he was promoted to the episcopate in a time of great stress in the church, and eventually his health would succumb to the burden of office. While favoring strong authority in both church and state, he was utterly convinced that coercion could not be used to further the interests of the church, and this selection embodies a profound sense of contrition about the church's past. His view of humanity was not optimistic; he thought persecution "a natural impulse to man" (p. 120).

SOURCE: Mandell Creighton, *Persecution and Tolerance* (London, 1895), pp. 131–40.
LITERATURE: Louise Creighton, *Life and Letters of Mandell Creighton*, 2 vols (London: Longmans, Green, 1913), esp. vol. II, pp. 90–2; John Neville Figgis, *Churches in the Modern State*, 2nd edn (London: Longmans, Green, 1914), pp. 231–40; W. G. Fallows, *Mandell Creighton and the English Church* (London: Oxford University Press, 1964).

I have spoken of tolerance in its outward aspect and have attempted to disentangle it from some qualities with which it is often compared. It does not rest upon indifference, or complacency, or abandonment of principles in deference to popular opinion; but it rests upon respect for human nature, of which our own individual nature, however enlightened, intellectually or spiritually, still forms a part. If toleration, as a principle of civil policy, is the result of the discovery that a community is bound together by moral principles which underlie and survive differences of opinion, so tolerance as an individual virtue is the recognition of the great truth about human nature on which that discovery rests. To the pious mind it was no new discovery. The earliest message that we have on record respecting man's estate was: "God said, Let us make man in Our image, after Our likeness." In Christ Jesus the dignity of man was revealed in its fulness. Men were created that they might become both seers and prophets of God's truth, which each man who perceived it was to help in making known to his fellows. "The true light lighteth every man, coming into the world" [John 1: 9]. Every man is capable of becoming the home of God's Spirit. Every man is charged with a message which none but he can hear and deliver, for which he is solely responsible. Hence the first practical application which St Peter drew from the Incarnation was not, "Love the brotherhood," but, "Honor all men." How could it be otherwise to one who had himself experienced the infinite tenderness of Jesus? What, he must ask himself, had prompted such condescension? what save God's inexplicable respect for the creature of His hand? "Honor all men": had not God honored them in a way which passed understanding and so penetrated the soul? "Honor all men": had not Jesus endured what was more intolerable even than the pangs of death, endured man's ignorance, and arrogance, and triviality, and vulgarity? Had He not listened patiently to their superficial smartness, and been the object of their paltry intrigues? He bore the sins of the world, and we think sometimes that we can examine and classify the contents of His overpowering burden.

"The sins of the world," they defy the power of man's analysis; our crude categories can only take account of acts which disturb society; we condone the wilful ignorance, the selfishness, the jealousies, the harsh judgment, the deliberate misrepresentation by which many of the noblest causes are marred. It is not the wickedness of bad men, but the failings of good men which reveal the dominion of sin. It was not only the jeers of the soldiers, or the bloodthirsty cries of the mob which rent the heart of Jesus; but the curses and the denial of Peter. So the apostle felt and knew that for him too Christ died. To him the Cross of Christ was the manifestation of man's baseness and man's dignity alike. Strengthened by the knowledge which he gained from gazing on it, he could steadily face the actual facts of life, and say: "So is the will of God that by well-doing ye should put to shame the ignorance of foolish men. Honor all men."

This then is the basis of tolerance; and its further contents are expressed in the words of my text: "Let your forbearance be known unto all men. The Lord is at hand." *To epieikes humon*, the reflex in you of that *epieikeia* which was so manifested in Christ. "Forbearance" is a poor word to express its meaning. It is the quick sympathy with another, by which you unconsciously put yourself in his place and appraise not his actual words or deeds, but their origin and their intent. It is the quality by which you throw away the rude measures and standard of the world, and trust yourself to the surer guidance of that "spirit of man" which is in you. It is a splendidly human virtue, known and valued by those who contemplated man's excellence. Listen to Aristotle's penetrating description: "It is *epieikeia* to pardon human failings, and to look to the lawgiver not to the law; to the spirit and not to the letter; to the intention not to the action; to the whole and not to the part; to the character of the actor in the long run and not in the present moment; to remember good, rather than evil, and good that one has received rather than good one has done; to bear being injured; to wish to settle a matter by words rather than by deeds" [*Rhet.*, I, p. xiii].

The forbearance, the equitableness, the fairmindedness of Christ, – surely this should be the spirit of the Christian life, and this is what the Christian means by tolerance. It comes from the confidence of an assured hope, from the outlook on a vast horizon. The kingdom of heaven was to begin on earth; it has its place here and now, and before its contemplation the petty activities of actual life fall into due proportion. "The Lord is at hand"; that is the great motive for forbearance. Before His judgment all things will be tried, our aims among the rest. That thought is a mighty call to effort, but is a warning that more valuable than the thing done is the spirit in which it is done, and the motive from which it springs.

It is for us to see that our motive is pure; then, though we fail to accomplish what we aim at, in the exact form in which we set it before ourselves, still a result remains, grander it may be than any we could fancy. "In nothing be anxious; but in everything let your requests be made known unto God. And the peace of God which passeth all understanding shall guard your hearts and your thoughts in Christ Jesus." This is the secret of true tolerance, a genuine faith in God which rises above the temptation to identify God's will with our own will –

                                                       None
                    Could trace God's will so plain as you, while yours
                    Remained implied in it.

Success may be well; but the peace of God is better. He who has gained it for Himself has assuredly shed it on others, and that is a greater boon than any outward organization can bestow. Success is not worth having, unless it be fairly won; for force may coerce, and fraud may beguile, but only persuasion and conviction can bring lasting benefits. "The ignorance of foolish men": it is always with us. We cannot escape it; but we are not to trample it down, and think that so we have got rid of it. It is a nobler work to make the foolish wise, and turn their ignorance into knowledge. This is a long task, but meanwhile "it is the will of God that we put them to silence by well-doing." There is an eloquence beyond that of speech. There is the persuasive significance of a devoted life, whose silence is indeed golden. It knows not misrepresentation, and uses no unsound arguments, and avoids clap-trap, and sows its seed for eternity.

Tolerance is not merely a negative virtue. It is needful on the part of the Church, as an organized body; for only by its liberal exercise can the sincerity of its individual members be preserved. No educator can discharge his task unless he encourages frankness, outspokenness, and sincerity amongst those whom he undertakes to teach. The Church, as the divinely appointed educator of mankind, must cherish these qualities. Tolerance is needful to the individual; for it is the expression of that reverence for others, which forms a great part of the lesson which Christ came to teach him. It is the means whereby he learns to curb self-conceit, and submit to the penetrating discipline imposed by Christian love.

I have traversed a large field. Let me point out one conclusion which I would leave with you. The fatal policy of persecution in the past has brought its own punishment, and the present divisions of Christendom owe their origin to that cause. Man's claim to freedom of thought has been asserted unmistakably, even wilfully. The Church has been taught afresh truths which she really knew, but which she overlooked concerning her organization and its uses. Shall we not frankly accept the lesson, and put away any root of bitterness which remains? The day is past when any organization can claim to do God's work by the exercise of power; and the attempt so to do has left its heritage of disaster. Ecclesiastical power will never be revived; but any lingering desire after it prevents the growth of ecclesiastical influence. God has taught us that He works by influence, not by power. He taught it by His own dealings with man; He declared it in the Incarnation. But men would not entirely learn God's lesson, and chose their own way instead of His. He has written His condemnation of their error on the record of history. He has put His Church to shame at the bar of human judgment. In the place of that uniformity which she strove to enforce on Christendom He has afflicted her with discord and schism. Why? Because unity is undesirable or impossible? Not so. It was the subject of our Lord's last prayer for His Church: its restoration is an aim which can never be absent from the mind of any one who calls himself by Christ's name. Why, then, I ask again? Because in times past that uniformity was enforced by carnal means, when the Church grasped the weapons of the world. The hope of the future lies in the entire abandonment of those weapons. The Church will affect society as it shows its capacity to persuade, rebuke, exhort in its Master's name, not as it claims to command. The reunion of Christendom will be possible, when Christians have abandoned those prejudices which are the legacy of the days of persecution, and recognize that unity of the spirit which alone can make controversy profitable.

Meanwhile I do not know that the tolerance which is now praised by the world is very firmly established. It rests at present mainly on an equilibrium of forces which might easily be upset. There is always a temptation to the possessors of power – be they an individual, an institution, or a class – to use it selfishly or harshly. Liberty is a tender plant and needs jealous watching. It is always unsafe in the world, and is only secure under the guardianship of the Church; for the Church possesses the knowledge of man's eternal destiny – which alone can justify his claim to freedom.

Notes

1   James Fitzjames Stephen, *Liberty, Equality, Fraternity*, 2nd edn (London, 1874), p. 84.
2   James Boswell, *Boswell's "Life of Johnson,"* ed. George B. Hill, 6 vols (Oxford: Clarendon Press, 1934–64), vol. II, pp. 249–53; May 7, 1773. Johnson is reported to have said:

> Sir, the only method by which religious truth can be established is by martyrdom. The magistrate has a right to enforce what he thinks; and he who is conscious of the truth has a right to suffer. I am afraid there is no other way of ascertaining the truth, but by persecution on the one hand and enduring it on the other.

On Johnson, see Chester F. Chapin, *The Religious Thought of Samuel Johnson* (Ann Arbor, MI: University of Michigan Press, 1968), esp. ch. 8.

3   [Note by J. S. Mill]: Ample warning may be drawn from the large infusion of the passions of a persecutor, which mingled with the general display of the worst parts of our national character on the occasion of the Sepoy insurrection. The ravings of fanatics or charlatans from the pulpit may be unworthy of notice; but the heads of the Evangelical party have announced us their principle, for the government of Hindoos and Mahomedans, that no schools be supported by public money in which the Bible is not taught, and by necessary consequence that no public employment be given to any but real or pretended Christians. An Under-Secretary of State, in a speech delivered to his constituents on 12 November 1857, is reported to have said: "Toleration of their faith" (the faith of a hundred millions of British subjects), "the superstition which they called religion, by the British Government, had had the effect of retarding the ascendancy of the British name, and preventing the salutary growth of Christianity. . . . Toleration was the great corner-stone of the religious liberties of this country; but do not let them abuse that precious word toleration. As he understood it, it meant the complete liberty to all, freedom of worship, *among Christians, who worshipped upon the same foundation.* It meant toleration of all sects and denominations of *Christian who believed in the one mediation.*" I desire to call attention to the fact, that a man who has been deemed fit to fill a high office in the government of this country, under a liberal Ministry, maintains the doctrine that all who do not believe in the divinity of Christ are beyond the pale of toleration. Who, after this imbecile display, can indulge the illusion that religious persecution has passed away, never to return?

4   [Note by J. S. Mill]: Locke appears to lay much stress on the *impossibility* of religious belief and practice by proxy; which, of course, we admit. But this argument, in the form in which he states it, we cannot regard as worthy of unqualified adoption; for it might be replied, that the object sought to be attained by the use of coercive power is, not the impossible one of substituting another's faith, but simply to bring the man himself to a right belief and practice; or, in other words, to make it his own faith; which, to say the least, does not appear to be an *impossible* result of thus enforcing the consideration and claims of an established religion. This argument of Locke, therefore, misses its aim.

7

THE TWENTIETH CENTURY

Arthur Vermeersch, *Tolerance* (1912)

A Belgian Jesuit, Vermeersch (1858–1936) was a moral theologian and canon lawyer. He taught at Louvain and at the Gregorian University. *Tolerance* was first published in 1912. It represents a moderate restatement of the Roman Catholic position, that the Roman Church, as the repository of truth, cannot be an intrinsically tolerant institution. His historical perspective is that of defending the Roman communion against charges of cruelty, while accusing heretics of subversion of the entire social order. But while modern Catholics would embrace religious unity, "We have no absurd dream of a return to the past. The true Catholic is not the reactionary that he is represented to be; . . . would Catholics in power suppress a single one of the liberties which are so dear to the present generation? A categorical negative is the answer given by their acts, their words, and their very principles" (pp. 347, 348–9).

SOURCE: Arthur Vermeersch, *Tolerance*, tr. W. Humphrey Page (London: R. & T. Washbourne, 1913), pp. 314–28, 330–3.

LITERATURE: George G. Coulton, *The Death Penalty for Heresy from 1184 to 1921* (London, 1924), esp. pp. 80–5.

The Genesis of Civil Tolerance

Tolerance exists as a *fact*, more or less extended, but real; as a *right*, recorded in codes of law and even in constitutions; and as a popular *ideal*. It will, then, be convenient to investigate its origin, or, rather, to put it in evidence, for the preceding pages, in describing doctrines and events and the order of their succession, have already given a substantial account of it.

In the New World, as in the Old World, treaties of tolerance have been concluded, edicts have been published, and laws enacted, as an inevitable consequence of the divisions which have separated the peoples into different Christian bodies, and have necessitated the recognition and regulation of various forms of worship on the same territory. Christians have had to live with Jews; henceforth Christians of different denominations must live in peace together. Material interests, too, the voice of which is almost always listened to, plead the cause of tolerance. We must also add political considerations. Merchants of different nationalities and beliefs must be enabled to meet in the same markets; and in North America it became necessary for the different religious bodies, established side by side on the same territory, to come to an understanding, in order to obtain political unity, and finally complete independence. For the Old World we may mention, as an example, the secret treaties admitting heretical merchants into the Spanish Netherlands; for the New World it will be enough to quote the testimony of Hägerman. In a study specially intended to show the influence of the religious factor on the libertarian movement in America, that learned writer comes to the distinct conclusion that decrees of toleration have often had economic or political circumstances as their first cause.

Considered as satisfying a right of man, civil tolerance does not originate from any desire to promote peace, or any process of intellectual reasoning. It was only in 1776 that America proclaimed the right to religious liberty; but this liberty had already found its way into public life, as a means of settling disputes entirely unconnected with religion. Thus we sum up the observations of M. Adalbert Wacht.

We must not, however, neglect to make allowance for the rise of new ideas on the subject of religion, or underrate their influence. When supernatural faith and life grow weaker, concepts of religion are formed which contain the germ of a more radical tolerantist doctrine, and the exigencies of facts at the same time become more and more pressing.

From our point of view we can thus distinguish three periods or stages, corresponding to medieval Catholicism, the modern Renaissance, and the contemporary Revolution.

For ages after the triumph of Christianity, all education was given and all edification perfected on the basis of Revelation. Only one religion was known – the religion given by God. It reigned in undisputed sovereignty, and sciences and politics alike took their inspiration from it.

As long as this faith was supreme in men's minds, it was impossible to speak against religion without offering an outrageous insult to God; and the idea of putting human error and Divine truth on an equality was rejected as blasphemous. Faith would have incited even the believer to violence and fanaticism if the meekness of Christ had not intervened, as it always does in true Christianity, to forbid hatred, to moderate anger, and to prevent violent excesses.

In the second period of pagan renaissance, cultivated minds took their stand on human reason rather than on faith, moulded their style on classic models, and sought to establish on the principles of natural law the rules of political government, and the rights and duties of Sovereigns and subjects. Without precisely denying revealed religion, they compared its claims with those of natural religion; they endeavored to define the authority in religious matters that the Sovereign would have exercised if it had not been for the institution of the Church, and to show the influence of that institution on the juridical position of Governments.

Natural religion is no longer Divine, except in its object. It is human in its developments; and the mind, in taking natural religion for its base, by degrees becomes accustomed to consider different religions as so many human constructions springing from the religious foundation laid in our hearts. The idea of giving equal treatment to different forms of worship meets with less resistance, and soon the religion which asks for favors or privileges, or a monopoly, will be looked upon as giving way to jealousy and setting up an unjust claim.

On the other hand, the duties of the Sovereign with regard to religion are no longer estimated according to revealed commandments, but according to the indications of Nature. He protects religion less for God or for its own sake than for the sake of society; and thence it begins to be discussed how far a single religion – that is, a State religion – is necessary. Men write on the mutual rights of the conscience and the Sovereign, and easily end by restricting the authority of the latter to outward and public worship. Men no longer trouble themselves so much about truth or about social unity, and so heretics come to be defined as "Christians who obstinately refuse to join in the profession of faith officially received and approved in the State."

This indifference shown to the various forms of religion – at least, to those which are called "Christian" – is, in fact, a mild form of skepticism; and partial skepticism bears within it the germ of more complete skepticism, which degenerates from diluted Christianity into philosophic Deism, only to end in simple atheism.

Political tolerance is obliged to enlarge the scope of its concessions, for men are not agreed even as to the existence of God. Atheists claim to be recognized, and even those who are not atheists desire to establish society on a purely human foundation. That was the spirit of the French Revolution. With it all reason for intolerance had disappeared. By that we mean the intolerance which was exercised in favor of religion; but a new form of intolerance remained possible, and its first edicts were signed by the French Revolution. This is the intolerance which persecutes religion, and specially the Catholic Church, in the name of a vague secular dogma, which is sometimes dignified by the honorable name of "progress."

Such, in short, it seems to us, is the genesis of civil tolerance. An unfortunate event made it necessary, and an increasing contempt for religion made an idol of it. Its history, or three-fourths of it, is the history of religious decay.

The tolerance which is admitted and professed by Catholics is a matter of necessity; but it is, nevertheless, sincere and loyal and constant.

And what of Protestantism, it will be asked? The leaders of the Reformation were certainly anything but tolerant. They persecuted wherever they had the power. Some of them, like Zwingli and Calvin, hankered after a pitiless theocracy modelled on that of the Old Testament, and all the more terrible because it gave up everything to the head of the State. As late as the second half of the seventeenth century, Thomasius continually taxed the Protestant ministers with continuing the traditions of Popery.

They certainly can take no credit for the spread of tolerance; but did they not help it unconsciously? Was not civil tolerance a necessary result of Protestant teaching?

Opinions on this point are divided; and in the Catholic camp, as in the Protestant, some persons admit and others deny that tolerance is a logical postulate of Protestantism.

It is not, say some; and they appeal to the theocratic concept of the Reformers and their acts. Others say that it is and point to the principle of private judgment, which Protestantism substituted for the principle of authority, even in religion.

There is something to be said on both sides. Nothing in orthodox Protestantism, which retained a belief in Christ and Holy Scripture, logically contained a dogma of absolute tolerance; but a limited tolerance seems necessarily to follow from the individualist principle of private judgment. This principle inevitably led to the disruption of Christianity into rival sects, no one of which had any claim to supremacy over the others. It produced a diversity of opinions, which was afterwards, with great inconsistency, denounced and condemned. Thus we soon see Protestant writers rising against the oppression of one sect by another, and showing that they are of one mind on essential points.

This tolerance, which was limited to Christian sects without being extended even to all of them, was opposed by reasons of State, the rights of the Sovereign, and that alienation of personal rights which was implied by a theory much in favor with the jurists of the Reformation – the theory of the *social contract*.

But complete tolerance is not by any means the result of Protestantism. Friedberg expresses himself in these terms: "In tolerance, as we understand it, we must, before all things, recognize a product of the school of natural law, of the period of the *Aufklärung*, and to some extent, of religious indifference in general." In short, it is rooted in humanism, rationalism, and irreligion. Döllinger wrote in 1861: "Historically there is no greater mistake than to consider the Reformation as a movement in favor of liberty of conscience. The exact opposite is the truth."

What Agreement is Possible?

"No one shall be molested on account of his opinions, even his religious opinions, and no one shall incur any incapacity or disability on that account. Everyone is at liberty to express and spread his opinions, even his religious opinions, and to associate himself with others, provided that they conform to the laws relating to associations, and do not disturb the public peace."

Do these provisions, which are found in many laws and constitutions, prove the existence of that radical antagonism between the political principles of Catholics and those of the modern State which is alleged by many persons, and to which they even appeal as a reason for excluding Catholics from power and official position, or for inducing them to withdraw voluntarily?

Our study of doctrines and facts since the French Revolution has shown us that they do not. If these formulae are intended to indicate a new policy, they should be derived from a principle both absolute and new, which we cannot find anywhere – certainly not in the conscience, the inviolability of which has always existed without any such declaration of liberty, for throughout the ages no one has defended it more eloquently than the Church by the blood of her martyrs and the voice of her most illustrious doctors; not in the Declaration of the Rights of Man, "which no one has ever applied, which its authors were the first to contravene, and which on the least pretext is put aside altogether."

In more than one country Catholics are left to hope that some day they will see a more liberal and more equitable application of these provisions in their favor; and they learn to their cost the unsubstantial character of the sacrosanct principle that gives liberty to every opinion. There are other significant exceptions to the rule. The idea which suggests the commission of a crime is an opinion, but who will justify the propagation of that opinion? And what are we to think of the attacks made upon principles considered as essential to existing society? Ought the civil power to disregard them? "The question remains open, and in practice is not susceptible of any but temporary solutions." Such is the astonishing but instructive reply of an authorized representative of contemporary rationalistic politics, M. Bouché-Leclercq. Ten lines earlier the same author had written that the State "condemned nothing but acts!" The question remains open, in spite of the natural rights of man and their immortal Declaration, in spite of the much-vaunted abolition of the crime of opinion. And would not many vote against liberty of discussion of the general policy of laicization and of laws proclaimed unalterable? To prove this, see the discourses of French Members of Parliament. And what would become of liberty of opinions and their public expression in days of revolutionary effervescence, when tribunals are set up to search for suspected persons? Is not the fact that a palpable material interest is in danger enough to make the rationalist Press and the accredited organs of modern politics complain of mischievous and dangerous theories; to make them use the language of former days, and show themselves ready to ratify the most violent measures of proscription? If anyone ventured to express astonishment, they would reply by appealing to social necessities.

And now they come round to the Catholic point of view, which considers civil liberties valuable in proportion as they conduce to the public good. Men have varied in the idea of what is good, but all honest policy is directed to the attainment of that end. Modern philosophers and politicians, on the one hand, considering religion as a thing of no value to the community, and, on the other hand, intoxicated with evolutionism and relativist opinions, were led to look for the principles of a new order in ideas now considered subversive of all order, and to make free discussion an essential condition of progress; and they naturally declared for liberty of opinions and their expression, and the most absolute religious tolerance. But for what reason? For the sake of some right of man or some new philosophy? It would seem so at first sight, but this is not the case really. The true reason was that they looked upon all religious tolerance as socially inoffensive, and the tolerance of opinions as socially useful. Thus, when facts speak too loudly, and an opinion seems to endanger social order as they imagine it, their declarations are ignored, and their dogma of absolute tolerance is entirely forgotten.

The policy of the modern State, then, has no supreme positive principle peculiar to itself, for the principle of the rights of man is neither supreme nor even effective. Society may be deceived as to its foundations and its essential principles; but it remains true that "every society is intolerant in regard to what attacks its foundation," and absolute liberty in religious and philosophical matters is "a system of anarchy which never has existed, and never will exist anywhere." "Absolute liberalism is a sociological heresy, for it misunderstands the essential conditions of social life; and for that very reason it is an impossible and purely Utopian idea." M. L. de la Vallée-Poussin thus concludes the reflections suggested by M. Goblet d'Aviella's work on the congresses of religion.

Between believers and unbelievers the discord is not political, but religious. If unbelievers were converted tomorrow, if they looked upon religion as we look upon it, the dogma of religious tolerance would have no more adherents, and all men would understand tolerance as we do.

But while we are waiting for this conversion to take place, will not the irreconcilable religious conflict necessarily put citizens on a footing of mutual hostility? How can we imagine civic peace among people who, while disagreeing as to the foundations of social order, are, nevertheless, agreed on the necessity of defending them? If the first disagreement were complete, peace and fraternity could not exist at all. At present they are only rendered more difficult of attainment. A more fragile and more superficial peace may be established on a basis of ideas remaining common to both parties, and on a certain natural sense of honor and morality, which are admitted by all persons to be necessary, provided that Catholics do not seek to force upon others their ideas on religion, nor unbelievers their evolutionist doctrine, and consequently their dogma of tolerance, which is the fruit of that doctrine. This peace admits, and, indeed, peremptorily demands, a practical rule of tolerance, but a tolerance founded upon a principle of charity, and not upon a religious theory, which would be the negation of Catholicism. Still less does it demand the recognition of an absolute dogmatic tolerance, which is a myth, an idol without worshippers. Such a peace, immediately made and loyally observed, may ultimately lead to the restoration of religious unity.

Catholics have always been willing to conclude such a peace, and to observe its conditions, and so were the Liberals of the Belgian Constitution. But the death-knell of that Liberalism has sounded, and radical extremists claim to monopolize the idea of true progress, to set the pace for society, and so to proceed methodically and pitilessly, even by way of confiscation and banishment, to the elimination of the religious idea. Liberalism has passed away. False in principle, it has fallen into ruin, dragging with it its bigoted followers into the mire of irreligious demagoguism. But, like all error, it has left its portion of truth as a heritage to the Church and to Catholics.

God, indeed, who protects His Church, does not exempt it from the conditions of human life and progress, nor does He preserve it from all liability to failure. Infallible in her teaching authority, but not in her practical politics (at least, there is nothing to prove it), she learns from experience, which is sometimes happy and sometimes painful, how best to direct her steps towards her glorious end. And thus all ages, even the worst, have been fruitful in teaching for the Church.

Born on Calvary, hunted down and persecuted for more than three hundred years, the Church has retained from the first period of her history that aversion to bloodshed that we claim as her chief honor; and she has proclaimed in the face of the whole world that faith must proceed from the will moved by the grace of God.

A second period showed her the lawfulness and expediency of outward coercion – not to produce convictions, but to preserve them, and sometimes to give them liberty; less to force than to permit people to believe. Public authorities, under the pressure of circumstances, proceeded to measures of extreme severity, which received the approval of the heads of the Church. Then appeared the uselessness and impotence of severity. Neither wars nor courts of justice were able to prevent a disruption, but for which a wholly Catholic Europe would have formed a Christian universe. The Church had to pay very dearly for the services of the secular arm; and, however lawful and necessary its intervention may have been, it has left behind it a prejudice and distrust from which we are still suffering. St Augustine wrote in 412: "In times of turbulence and danger, moderation is looked upon as a sign of weakness or indifference; but when once the excitement has passed away, the beauty of mercy is recognized, and men take pleasure in reading the annals in which it is recorded." Noxious germs are always swarming in the air that surrounds our globe, and cause to feeble organisms harm that sometimes requires heroic remedies, while healthy bodies are able to resist their influence. If the reforming Council of Trent had been assembled a century earlier, it might have saved Christianity from that religious disaster which is still the greatest misfortune of the world.

A third period thus begins in the midst of rebellions and apostasies, in the course of which the Church devotes her attention to herself, applies herself with all her power to beautify and strengthen her inward position, and displays the immense resources that she possesses in the purity of her doctrine, the exemplary life of her ministers, the virtues of her faithful children, the enlightenment of her preaching, and the sweet unction of her sacraments. When outward help fails, she feels her own inward vigor increase; when civil Governments refuse to stand by her, she pursues her own course unaided; and what she loses in the prestige of physical force, she gains in a prestige of moral force more sublime, more impressive, more successful in winning hearts that long for enlightenment and peace.

Formed thus in the school of twenty centuries, that Church is now preparing, by the gentleness and virtues of her mature age, to win back from anarchy that same world, now made with license, which, by the gentleness and the virtues of her infancy, she delivered from the degrading despotism of Caesar.

The Past: General Conclusions

... To sum up the results of our inquiry. No preconceived idea impelled the Church to demand the punishment of heretics, or to have recourse to any but ecclesiastical penalties; but little by little the violent conduct of certain sects, and the force used by them to retain their disciples, led to special repressions which prepared the way for a more general proscription.

Heresy in our Western countries did not present itself merely as a platonic or speculative contradiction of doctrine; it set up a revolutionary principle in opposition to the Church. Theoretical discussion, if there was any, was a secondary weapon, which served it to support a movement subversive of ecclesiastical authority and often of social order. We need not, then, imagine a new theological controversy, cut short by the sword; the retraction of error was insisted upon less for its own sake than as an indication of submission to lawful authority. The Church did not desire so much to attack men's convictions as to organize her own defense.

Laws of exceptional severity may be meant simply to terrify, and the most elementary honesty obliges us to judge of legislation, not only by the text of the laws, but also by their application. As we have seen, this was the object of the terrible laws of Theodosius; and M. Pirenne, speaking of the cruel proclamations of Charles V, tells us that "most of them [the échevins] regarded the proclamations as mere bugbears designed to frighten the people, but that they were applied with discretion, the punishment being made proportionate to the crime"; and, according to the testimony of Lea, the Inquisition did not take proceedings against all persons who were liable to prosecution under the laws then in force.

In short, the repression of heresy was not signalized by any increase of judicial severity, but, on the contrary, its influence on the penal system was rather favorable than otherwise. In occupying itself with the reformation of the criminal, it drew an attention to one object of punishment which was at that time very little considered; and in introducing the practice of imprisonment, it made possible all the humanitarian reforms of criminal legislation.

But, for all that, we cannot reconcile the institutions of the past with our present ideas: these ideas require to be enlarged. In order to understand thoroughly the severe punishments prescribed and sometimes inflicted for heresy, we need to have the lively faith of the Middle Ages, and to attach the same importance as the men of that time to religious unity for the good of civil society. We need to take careful account, on the one hand, of the revolutionary conduct and language of many heretics, and, on the other hand, of the disorder and agitation produced by heresy in the whole community. In short, we need to put ourselves in the place of men whose thoughts and sentiments and judgments were suggested by a civilization ruder than our own, and, above all, infinitely more cruel in its measures of repression.

Francesco Ruffini, *Religious Liberty* (1912)

Ruffini (1863–1934) taught ecclesiastical law at the University of Turin, after earlier positions at Pavia and Genoa. He was committed to the liberal tradition in Italy, and as a senator (from 1914) withstood the Fascists' concordat with the Roman Catholic Church which hindered the freedom of religious bodies. He had to resign from the university in 1931 for his refusal to swear the Fascist oath. *Religious Liberty* (*La Liberta Religiosa*, Turin, 1901) remains alone in the field for its scope. The excerpt which follows defines important issues and also describes different approaches to religious liberty in Europe and in the United States, namely jurisdictionalism and separatism.

SOURCE: Francesco Ruffini, *Religious Liberty*, tr. J. Parker Heyes (London: Williams & Norgate, 1912), pp. 1–17.

LITERATURE: Historical context may be gained from D. A. Binchy, *Church and State in Fascist Italy* (London: Oxford University Press, 1941); A. C. Jemolo, *Church and State in Italy, 1850–1950*, tr. David Moore (Oxford: Basil Blackwell, 1960). His life is reviewed briefly in *Enciclopedia Italiana di Scienze, Lettere ed arti*, 36 vols (Rome, 1929–39), vol. 30, p. 219.

Chapter I

(1) It not infrequently happens that the expression *religious liberty* is used both in lectures and writings to signify things differing widely from each other and all very far removed from the precise and technical meaning which science has assigned to that expression for some time past.

There are, in fact, many who understand it in too wise a sense, and make use of it as the equivalent of *liberty of thought*. They employ the term to indicate the emancipation of the human mind from all dogmatic preconceptions, from all the shackles of religious faith. Heretics, schismatics and apostates, sorcerers and necromancers, skeptics, freethinkers, and the *esprits forts* of all times and all places, are the standard-bearers, the champions, the martyrs of this idea; illuminism, deism, rationalism, Voltairianism, naturalism, materialism, etc. etc., are its equivalents.

On the other hand, there are many who fall into precisely the opposite exaggeration and understand the expression in too restricted a sense, that is to say, as being the equivalent of *ecclesiastical liberty*. And for them it indicates the privilege conceded, or, rather, to be conceded, to the members of a particular Church to bring all the acts not only of their private but also of their public life into the fullest conformity with the precepts of that Church, and in such a manner as to have the State entirely and supinely subjected to demands of a religious character.

But it is very easy to see that this privilege, which is invoked in the name of the unlimited liberty of conscience and worship for a single religious confession, is at variance with the true idea of liberty, inasmuch as the latter can only exist where identical concessions are made to all religions, and where the free exercise of one finds a restraint and regulation in the equally free exercise of the others. And when it is considered that this privilege is demanded principally by the most zealous defenders of the Catholic Church, which has laid down and, as we shall see, even to this day maintains among its fundamental principles, that the State cannot concede, we will not say equal liberty and identical privileges except to herself, but not even simple toleration to other religions, then everybody must agree that this so-called religious liberty is as opposed as anything can possibly be to the true liberty of religion. It is almost needless to add that none of the Churches will hear a word about any kind of liberty for atheists or, in general, for freethinkers.

The latter, for their part, do not make it their supreme object to obtain the same liberty for those who do not believe as for those who do, but they aim, one and all, at undermining the foundations both of traditional and imposed beliefs. For them the principle that thought must be left free and that opinion must not be coerced, is not an end in itself, but merely the indispensable means of prosecuting, demonstrating, and causing the ultimate triumph of their anti-religious speculations. That the liberty of religion in its technical significance is not confused with the more generic liberty of thought, and is not even a part or an aspect of it, is shown by this very significant fact better than by any argument, namely, that there have been most fervent believers who have been in every possible way favorable to religious liberty, as well as utterly prejudiced freethinkers who have been absolutely against it. Who, indeed, could doubt the piety, I do not say of the most ancient Fathers of the Church, but of those communities of Socinians, Unitarians, and Baptists who first fought for the principle of religious liberty in the very bosom of the Reformation? And what soul was ever more ardently pious than that of Alexander Vinet, who, at the same time, was one of the most strenuous champions of religious liberty in the last century? Yet, on the other hand, it is part almost of the nature of unenlightened and unreasonable disbelief to endeavor even to compel the State to restrain the free exercise of those opinions and religious rites which it believes to be harmful to human progress and well-being. Have we not, indeed, seen the French Revolution giving to the world the supremely significant spectacle of disbelief becoming in its turn intolerant and persecuting? But there is also another reason for which religious skepticism may involve the negation of all religious liberty. The English freethinkers of the beginning of last century, not believing in religion, but holding it to be the best means of government, maintained that no liberty should be accorded to dissidents. And Jean Jacques Rousseau, after having outlined the dogmas of his civil religion, did not hesitate in assigning to the State the duty of imposing it upon everybody, even by violence.

We certainly do not wish to deny that the progress made by the idea of religious liberty has not been usually accompanied by progress in freedom of thought, and that such progress has not usually met with its greatest obstacles in the excesses of pious fervor; but this does not alter the fact that religious liberty is an idea quite different from, and a principle entirely independent of, those which have so far been considered.

(2)   Religious liberty takes sides neither with faith nor with disbelief; but in that ceaseless struggle which has been waged between them since man first existed, and which will be continued, perhaps, as long as man exists, it stands absolutely apart. I do not say it stands above the conflict, since its aim is not so high; its object is not, as with faith, eternal salvation, nor, as with freethought, scientific truth. Its purpose is subordinate to those, and it is much more modest and far more practical. It consists in creating and maintaining in society such a condition of things that each individual may be able to pursue and in time to reach those two supreme ends, without other men, either separately or grouped in associations, or even personified in that supreme collectivity known as the State, being able to offer him the least impediment in pursuing those ends, or cause him the least damage on their account.

From all this it appears that religious liberty is not, like freethought, a *philosophical* idea or principle, that it is not, like ecclesiastical liberty, a *theological* idea or principle; but that it is an idea and a principle essentially *juridical*.

(3)   Yet on first hearing of religious liberty, the majority of people think only of its negative aspect. Persecutions and pyres, the Holy Inquisition and Index of Prohibited Books, all the excesses and rusty arms of religious intolerance, rise immediately in their minds and encumber them in such a manner as to hide the positive aspect of the question.

Anyone, however, who reflects for a moment will easily understand that it is not the negative aspect which interests us here, and that it is not in that direction our investigation has been made; since, apart from every other consideration, we should only have done over again what has already been done by others in an exhaustive manner.

It has been our aim, on the contrary, to trace the rise in the most remote antiquity, the development in modern times, and the definitive triumph in our century, of the idea that nobody ought, for religious motives, to be persecuted or deprived of full juridical capacity. Hence we have studied only the positive side of this great question, and this has not been done hitherto in an adequate manner.

The literature of religious liberty, in fact, is composed almost entirely of occasional writings, polemics and apologetics, propaganda and protest, few of them, especially among the more recent, being purely scientific in aim. Moreover, in the latter, even in the best of them, two points have been neglected more than they deserved, namely, the historical development and the literary elaboration of the idea. But both of these aspects appear to us to be of vital importance; the first because in a dispute in which party passion is predominant it is only wise to endeavor to secure the intervention of that dispassionate judge, history; and the second because every step in the progress of religious toleration has been prepared by a wide literary movement, and also because nothing better than literature can give an exact idea of the real conditions of liberty at a given time and in a given environment where the bare letter of the law is an incomplete and uncertain document.

Chapter II

(1)   The idea of *religious liberty* is susceptible of a still more precise determination, since it presents different stages in its historical evolution and different aspects even in its actual configuration. In past ages, and in many countries right down to the second half of the nineteenth century, it has always been a question of simple *toleration*, rather than of real liberty.

Toleration, or rather, in order to explain our idea more easily, intolerance, may be simply religious; and it consists in the exclusivist notion that a definite religion must be the only true one, the only one instituted by the divinity, and therefore the only one capable of procuring eternal salvation. So long as this intolerance, availing itself of purely spiritual arms, confines itself to fighting and repelling everything and everybody that opposes or disputes its fundamental dogmas, it cannot be regarded as unjustified, and certainly cannot be opposed except by purely spiritual arms. For to wish to impede it otherwise would be to do a grave injury to the principle of liberty of conscience.

But it happens that the public power places its means of external coercion at the service of this same religious intolerance, adopts its cause, and fights and repels with material arms everything and everybody that disputes the dogmas of the religion which it has recognized as being the only one. Thus we get a new form of intolerance which should be qualified as civil-religious, but which, for the sake of brevity, is called simply civil intolerance. The latter, in contrast to the other, far from having any sort of foundation in the principle of liberty of conscience, becomes the most unjustifiable violation of it; and it is precisely against this that the earliest appeals for toleration have been made.

Toleration, moreover, is among the most elastic of ideas. There may be a purely *de facto* toleration which might be restricted only to the persons of the dissidents, in so far as they are permitted to live in the territory of the

State but not to carry on religious worship there; or it may be extended to the religion itself.

But this form of toleration, in order that it may be stable and in order that the fanaticism of intolerant individuals may not disturb it, requires a legal sanction. Hence comes a very limited governmental protection of the dissidents which, however, is always liable to be capriciously revoked and which must be paid for, as witness the case of the Jews, by a thousand humiliations, all duly set forth in the laws, and is not infrequently to be purchased by hard cash.

This rudimentary form of *de jure* toleration, however, which is substituted for *de facto* toleration, starting with the simple concession of a few of the most essential civil rights and from the privilege of religious worship in private, can with the progress of time rise by degrees, and does in fact rise very slowly, to the full conferment of all civil and political rights, and finally to the granting of the faculty of exercising the religion with all the outward signs and privileges of publicity.

Having reached this point, toleration aims at real liberty; and it will eventually be compelled to make way for it.

For, on the one hand, the voice of the most strenuous defenders of liberty will be raised against it, and Mirabeau will protest in the National Assembly: "The word toleration seems to me to be in a certain measure tyrannical, since the authority which tolerates could also not tolerate"; while Lord Stanhope will warn the House of Lords: "There was a time when the dissenters begged for toleration as a grace; now they ask for it as a right; but a day will come when they will scorn it as an insult."

And, on the other hand, the popular conscience will of itself eliminate from social intercourse a word which has become too full of mournful memories. Thus it will happen that the expression *culti tollerati* (tolerated denominations), which in Article I of the Italian Statute was used to designate the non-Catholic religions and which was really the last act of intolerance of a régime which was deprived by the statute of all its power, will gradually and tacitly be replaced by the expression *culti ammessi* (admitted denominations), in which that same Catholic religion will be comprised, without any distinction from the non-Catholic.

Toleration, indeed, which is an admirable private virtue, has in public relationships an odious sound, and not the last cause of this is certainly the technical meaning, which it still preserves in Catholic ecclesiastical law, as a forced and opportunistic recognition of things which, nevertheless, the Church must not be understood absolutely to approve. *Tolerari posse*, e.g., is the formula adopted both in regard to the military service in the Italian provinces of which the Roman curia does not recognize the legitimate annexation, and in regard to the non-religious schools of America, etc.

The word toleration presupposes the existence of a religious State, that is to say, of a State which believes it necessary for itself to make, as a collective person, profession of a certain religion, just as if, like its individual members, it had a soul to be saved. Hence the religion professed by it will be called, as was said at one time, and as our statute says to-day, the *only religion*, or the *official religion*, the *dominant religion*, the *established religion*, or the *religion of the State*. And the latter, compelled by necessity to admit other religions within its territory, will not be able to do so without disapproving them and regarding them with a certain pious aversion; in other words, it will *tolerate* them.

Now, this is no longer suitable for a modern State, which may have the utmost respect for religious feelings, but cannot profess itself a particular religion. The modern State can, and eventually must, bow to some of the demands of that which is the religion of the great majority of its subjects, adopting, for example, its calendar as official. But from this it must not by any means be inferred that the State should regard all the other religions of the minority with less respect and sympathy. Therefore the French Government was absolutely right when, during the negotiations for the Concordat of 1801, it would not agree to the demand of the Roman Curia that in the proemium it should be stated that the Catholic religion was the dominant and exclusive religion of France; but insisted on the simple statement that it was the religion of the majority of the people of France. And it is precisely towards the same interpretation that Italian publicists are endeavoring to bend the letter – somewhat intractable, truth to tell – of Article I of the Italian Statute, which declares that the Catholic religion is "the only religion of the State," and that other denominations are "tolerated in conformity with the laws."

To sum up: the modern State can no longer have cognizance of *toleration*, but only of *liberty*, because the former means a gracious concession made by the State to the individual; while the latter, on the contrary, is a duty of the citizen towards the State. Religion is now a domain in which the State can give nothing, but in which the citizen can claim all.

(2) Religious liberty presents, as we have said, different aspects in its actual configuration.

(a) First and foremost, it can be considered in relation to single individuals, and it should then be more properly called *liberty of conscience*, or of *faith*, or of *worship*.

Although it is usual to define this form of religious liberty generically as the privilege of the individual to believe in what religion he pleases, or, if he prefers, to believe in none, it does not, however, come within the juridical field under this aspect of an essentially internal privilege. As such, of course, it may be the object of pure psychological and philosophical inquiry, and therefore it would be just as superfluous and ridiculous to sanction it in the laws of liberty, as, adopting the illustration of a French writer, to proclaim the liberty of the circulation of the blood. It comes within the juridical field only in so far as it gives rise to external, and therefore legally important, demonstrations.

Under this aspect, either for the purpose of removing ancient obstacles which were at one time placed in the way of such external manifestations, or for that of ensuring their ordered liberty in the present, a threefold series of dispositions was necessary in all civil legislation.

Some are negative; and they consist in removing entirely all penalties, disabilities, and legal inequalities which were imposed for religious motives, so that the names, and the very ideas, of heresy, apostasy, and schism shall be deprived of all significance in the eyes of the law.

Others, on the contrary, are simply indirect, and they consist in arranging the relations between the State and individuals in such a manner that the life of the latter, in the picturesque phrase of Friedberg, can run its course from the cradle to the grave without receiving from the State any disturbance or impulse of a religious character. This will be obtained by a series of measures which, starting from the registration of civil status, proceed gradually to non-religious public education, the institution of civil marriage, the abolition or transformation of the political and legal oath, the secularization of *assistance publique*, and finally, the creation of communal cemeteries.

Others, again, are positive and direct; and they consist, in the first place, of those articles of some Constitutions wherein, in spite of the stupidity already mentioned of such proclamations, the right to liberty of conscience is expressly recognized; and secondly, in those special measures which various legislatures have deemed it necessary to pass in order directly to guarantee the manifestation, propaganda, and exercise of religious convictions, in addition to those generic measures which protect every other form of individual liberty.

Liberty of conscience cannot be subject to exclusions and limitations except such as imposed by the common law.

(b) Religion, however, is certainly the field in which the social character of man expresses itself most imperiously; hence religious liberty will not be complete where there is no concession of the privilege of collective as well as individual manifestation, propaganda, and exercise of a religious belief, whether the collectivity is limited to the assumption of the transitory aspect of a meeting, or becomes fixed in the stable and continuous aspect of an association. Hence the necessity of taking a step upwards on the ladder of religious liberty with the recognition and assuring of the so-called *liberty of worship*, which Vinet once well defined as the liberty of conscience of associations.

Here also there would be no difficulty in the principle of the State contenting itself with the regulation, both by guarantees and limitations, of this liberty to a share in the common right of meeting and association. All States, indeed, have regarded it as practically necessary to assign such special guarantees and limitations.

But their application has afterwards shown that in every law it must be clearly determined what is to be understood by *worship* in the juridical sense; because in the case of religions which were historically, numerically, or socially insignificant, it would neither be opportune, nor perhaps possible, to apply a special law, made for the purpose, instead of the common law of which we have spoken. Thus, to give an example, any three or four friends who had associated themselves together for the purpose of founding a new form of worship, and who had assigned to one member of their small association the quality of a minister, could evidently neither be subjected nor make an appeal to those penal dispositions against the abuses of ministers of religion on the one hand, or those, on the other, by which offenses or injuries done to ministers of religion in the exercise of their functions are punished in a particularly severe manner.

Granted, however, that the small association, which we may call a *sect* (but divesting this word of its former odious meaning), should enjoy, under the protection of the common law of meeting and association, the same amount of privilege, and perhaps even a greater one, than the *religion* which is explicitly recognized under the special law – which is particularly protective, it is true, but also particularly limitative – can it also be said that its different legal position implies a diversity in the recognition of religious liberty in regard to the citizens belonging to the *sect* as compared with those belonging to the *religion*? In most instances this does not seem to be the case, and rightly so, in our opinion.

(c) But this smooths our way in approaching another point, still more important and much more controversial, that, namely, of the *equality*, or *parity of religions*.

This idea has so far not been clearly defined except in German law, which derives from it the principle of so-called *Parität*. Historically, however, this principle of "parity" does not appear in Germany as connected with that of religious liberty, because at one time, by the Treaty of Westphalia, for example, only a few religions were placed in a condition of absolute *parity*; these were the Catholic, the Lutheran, and the Reformed; the others were not even tolerated.

Religious associations can enter into relations with the State not only in so far as the latter protects their religious liberty, but also, and principally, in so far as they, like all other associations, are organized and governed by virtue of statutes which do not merely concern faith and discipline, but also matters of a very different and entirely mundane character, such, for example, as the acquisition of property and its administration.

Hence arises the question: Since religious liberty is truly equal for all and therefore complete in one State, is it necessary that the State should treat all religious associations in a precisely identical manner, even those which conform to a purely temporal régime?

As, however, such absolute equality of treatment does not appear – theoretically – to be possible when the State claims to maintain its ancient interference in the government of ecclesiastical affairs – since an imposing body like the Catholic church and one of those small associations of friends of which we have already spoken cannot be governed by the same standards – and as, on the other hand, such absolute equality will undoubtedly exist when the State permits all religious associations the same unlimited power of governing themselves, ignores them all, both small and great, and declares its incompetence in regard to all – in other words, separates itself absolutely from Church or Churches, so that question is changed into this other: Since there is true and complete religious liberty in a State, must the State renounce the jurisdictional and adopt the separatist régime?

Formulated thus, the question dates back to the rise of the modern idea of religious liberty. We shall see, in fact, that the first champions of liberty, the Socinians, were in favor of a large measure of State interference in ecclesiastical affairs, and that, on the contrary those who first learned the doctrine from the Socinians, namely, the Anabaptists and all their numerous affiliations, immediately began to oppose such interference in the most precise manner.

It was by these latter sects that the principle of liberty was transplanted to North America; and it is principally because of this fact that it made progress and became imposed as a principle connected with that of separatism. It is easy, therefore, to understand why the American writers are unable to conceive the idea of true liberty apart from separatism. And thus it is that *religious liberty* and *separatism* have become in America two terms which, ideally, historically, and practically, are inseparable. Such is the theory which is defended by those European writers who took upon themselves to extol the American system of *separatism* as against the European system of *jurisdictionalism* or *Erastianism*.

But of the latter, supporters have not been and are not now lacking. They have observed that not a few European states (typical example, Prussia) although remaining purely jurisdictional precisely, indeed, because they understood how to keep in check the most powerful and intolerant Churches, have succeeded in past centuries in bringing into effect a régime of religious liberty much more complete and wider than that which prevailed at the same period in the United States of America. It has also become apparent that if most advantage has been derived in recent years from the separatist régime by those Churches in America which are most strongly organized and carry on the most active propaganda, as much cannot be said of the religious liberty of the individual, especially if it assumes the form of unbelief. For rationalism in general, and scientific freethought in particular, precisely because they are lacking in any kind of organization, not only do not profit by separatism, but also remain isolated from and without any defense against the different organized religious associations, which under the guardianship of the separatist régime have too much freedom to display their spirit of intolerance.

And then, to that principle of justice which was solemnly invoked in favor of equality at all costs, was opposed this other principle, namely, that to regulate unequal juridical relationships in an equal manner is every bit as unjust as to regulate equal juridical relationships in an unequal manner. Hence there can be, it is said, a parity in the false sense, which is that of absolute, abstract, mathematical equality, and a parity in the right sense, which is that of relative, concrete, juridical equality, since, as Kahl writes, "The true principle of parity does not say: 'to each *the same*,' but 'to each *his own*.'"

By all means let the perfect equality in America, where it exists as between the various denominations, be extolled; but let us in Europe, where ancient historical differences and tremendous social inequalities even yet divide the various Churches, hold firm to the system which measures out the regulating action of the public authority for each one in proportion.

Reinhold Niebuhr, "The Test of Tolerance" (1943)

Niebuhr (1892–1971) was the American-born son of German immigrants. Following study at Yale he accepted a call to a church in Detroit where he turned toward a liberal Christian activism in the political and social issues of his time. In 1928 he moved to the Union Theological Seminary in New York where he taught social ethics until his retirement in 1960. Niebuhr's Protestant view of grace – the paradox of having and not having – necessitates the practice of tolerance, for one cannot have certainty of the possession of truth. Thus the reformers contradicted their own theology in succumbing to the temptation to persecute those who would not follow.

SOURCE: Reinhold Niebuhr, *The Nature and Destiny of Man*, 2 vols (New York: Charles Scribner's Sons, 1963 [1941, 1943]), vol. II, ch. 8.3, pp. 220–43.

LITERATURE: Philip Wogaman, *Protestant Faith and Religious Liberty* (Nashville, TN: Abingdon, 1967), pp. 100–4; Richard Wightman Fox, *Reinhold Niebuhr: A Biography* (New York: Pantheon, 1985), ch. 9; Niels H. Søe, "The Theological Basis of Religious Liberty," *Ecumenical Review*, 11 (1958), pp. 36–42.

If we apply the test of toleration to the various versions of the Christian faith, in order to determine how closely they approximate to the wisdom of the gospel, we meet with some obvious results and with others which will seem surprising until they are more fully explored. The foregone conclusion is that the Catholic version of the Christian faith is intolerant in principle. This is not surprising because the Catholic idea of sanctification in regard to the problem of truth is consistent with its general theories of grace. The more surprising result of such an historical investigation is that Reformation theology has not, in fact, brought forth fruits of the contrite spirit and the broken heart in the field of intellectual controversy which would be consonant with its theory of grace and its doctrine of justification. The reason for this failure has been partially anticipated in our general survey but must be considered in the light of the test of toleration. The chief source of toleration in modern history has been in the various forces of the Renaissance movement, both sectarian and secular. But it is necessary to inquire whether the tolerant attitude of the "liberal" spirit meets both, or only one, of the two aspects of the test of toleration. Does it also maintain a vital and organic relation between thought and action while it achieves forbearance of contrary and contradictory views and opinions?

1   Catholicism and Toleration

Catholicism is impelled by its whole history and by its peculiar doctrine of grace to claim unconditioned possession of the truth. In this claim in the realm of culture it obviously destroys the Biblical paradox of grace. It pretends to have as a simple possession, what cannot be so possessed. It may vary its attitude slightly towards other versions of the Christian faith from time to time, but it is completely consistent and unyielding in its conviction that it alone possesses the truth and the whole truth.

One of the ablest exponents of Augustinian thought in contemporary Catholicism, Erich Przywara, writes about the Inquisition:

> The Dominican order had become, willy-nilly, the servants of the Inquisition, not on account of a sort of fanaticism (the great Dominicans were all men of child-like humility and even tender sensitiveness) but on account of an utter abandonment of all individualism to the service of the everlasting truth. . . . God is just *the* Truth (a genuine Augustinian phrase) and so service

to the Truth is service to God. . . . The Dominican type regards itself as entrusted by an inscrutable providence with the sacred guardianship of the one Truth in the midst of the world. It is of the type which stands in the world . . . but yet while in the world it stands there with the single task of subjecting the world . . . to the dominion of this one everlasting truth. Truth remote from all fluctuations due to individuality and existence.

The difficulty with this essentially high-minded justification of the Inquisition is that it does not understand that the one everlasting truth of the gospel contains the insight that mere men cannot have this truth "remote from all fluctuations due to individuality and existence." This error is the root of all Inquisitions.

Catholics may indeed be individually humble and contrite, as Przywara avers; and may therefore compare favorably with Protestant individualists who have a fanatic zeal for their own individual interpretation of truth. But Catholicism is collectively and officially intolerant. Its intolerance expresses itself not only in blindness towards possible facets of truth contained in other than its own interpretations of the truth; but also in efforts to suppress the profession of other religions, including the profession of other versions of the Christian religion.

The Jesuit protagonist of intolerance in Elizabethan England, Robert Parsons, defined the logic of the Catholic position with rigorous consistency:

If every man which hath any religion and is resolved therein must needs suppose this only truth to be in his own religion, then it followeth necessarily that he must likewise persuade himself that all religions beside his own are false and erroneous; and consequently all assemblies, conventicles, and public acts of the same are wicked and dishonorable to God.

Parsons carried this logic to the point of asserting that even if the other religions were really true, "yet would I be condemned for going among them, for that in my sight and judgment and conscience, by which only I must be judged, they must need seem enemies to God."

The Catholic doctrine, which forces the church to seek for the monopoly of the public profession of religion in a state, is officially defined in the encyclical *Immortale Dei* of Pope Leo XIII:

Since no one is allowed to be remiss in the service due to God, and since the chief duty of all men is to cling to religion in both its teaching and practice . . . not such religion as they may have preference for but the religion which God enjoins, and which certain and most clear marks show to be the only true religion . . . it is a public crime to act as if there were no God. So too it is a sin in the state not to have care of religion . . . or out of the many forms of religion to adopt that one which chimes in with the fancy, for we are bound absolutely to worship God in that way which He has shown to be His will.

A modern Catholic theologian, commenting on these official words, underscores them as follows:

> If the state is under moral compulsion to profess and promote religion it is obviously obliged to promote and profess only the religion that is true; for no individual, no group of individuals, no society, no State is justified in supporting error or in according to error the same recognition as to truth.

The simple distinction between "truth" and "error," consonant with similar simple distinctions in Catholic teachings between "justice" and "injustice" is a convenient tool of the terrible and pathetic illusion that "our" truth must use every instrument of coercion, as well as persuasion, to destroy and suppress the "falsehood" of an opposing belief. For the distinction ignores the ambiguous character of all knowledge in history and obscures the residual error in even the purest truth, and the saving truth in even the most obvious error. It supports Catholicism in its fury against the "enemies of God" and the "enemies of Christ." The church does not understand that rebellions and revolutions against its authority may be prompted not by hatred of God or Christ, but by resentment against the unjustified use of Christ as a "cover" for the historical relativities of culture and civilization in which it happens to be involved. It is not the Christ but "my" Christ who arouses this fury.

The Greek Orthodox version of this Catholic error differs slightly from the Roman one. The difference is in the more mystical conception of "grace" which, in Eastern thought, is regarded as the triumph of eternity over time and finiteness. Thus an Orthodox theologian defines the unconditioned truth possessed by the church as the achievement of the eternal in time: "The Catholic nature of the church is seen most vividly in the fact," he writes,

> that the experience of the church belongs to all times. In the life and existence of the church time is mysteriously overcome and mastered. Time so to speak stands still. It stands still because of the power of grace which gathers together in catholic unity of life that which has become separated by walls built by the course of time.

Anglo-Catholicism has been saved, by the lack of such actual historical universality as the Roman church can boast, from making as consistent pretensions as the Roman church. But it has the same difficulty in recognizing the contingent and sinful elements in the truth which the Church possesses. Due to this error it has introduced confusion into the ecumenical movement of the non-Roman churches by insisting that the basis of ecumenical unity must include both a common faith and a common "order." But the "order" of a church, its rites and its polity, belong clearly to the realm of the historically contingent. Failure to recognize this fact naturally leads the Catholic wing of the non-Roman churches to insist that its order is the only possible one for an ecumenical church. The logic of this sinful spiritual imperialism conforms to the logic of sin generally. It is the unconscious ignorance, and the conscious denial, of the finiteness of its own perspective. Anglo-Catholicism is not alone in displaying this sin, but it has been particularly blind to the finite perspectives in the realm of "grace" and therefore especially prone to refute its sanctificationist interpretations of the Church by its own actions.

2 The Reformation and Toleration

We have maintained that the Reformation doctrine of "justification by faith" in its relation to the doctrine of sanctification represents the final recognition within the Christian faith of the twofold aspect of grace in Biblical religion. Logically the paradox of grace, that it is a having and not having, applies to the realm of culture and truth with the same validity as to any other realm of life. But the Reformation failed to apply it to this realm. Its fanaticisms disturbed the peace of both the church and civil society no less than did Catholic intolerance. In its treatment of those who differed from its interpretation of the Gospel it was singularly barren of the "fruits meet for repentance," of the humility which betrays the "broken spirit and the contrite heart." It gave little indication of any consciousness that error might be mixed with the truth which it possessed; though the truth which it possessed contained the recognition of this very paradox.

Martin Luther had some misgivings about the use of the death penalty for heretics as late as 1526 and declared: "I can in no wise admit that false teachers ought to be put to death. It is sufficient to banish them." But only a year later the lust of battle against the Anabaptists had dissipated these scruples and he was urging the use of the sword to suppress them. In dealing with both the mystic and the radical-apocalyptic forms of sectarianism, Luther and Calvin were equally pitiless; and the Swiss reformer Zwingli had a similar attitude towards them. Calvin, writing to the Duke of Somerset (Protector during Edward VI's minority), demanded the suppression of heresy by the civil arm: "There are two kinds of rebels who have arisen against the king," he declared.

The one is a fanatical sort of people who under the color of the gospel would put everything to confusion. The other are those who persist in the super-stitions of the papal Antichrist. Both alike deserve to be repressed by the sword, which is committed to you, since they not only attack the king but strive with God, who has placed him on his throne.

In the long history of religious controversy in England from the reign of Elizabeth to that of Cromwell, Presbyterianism pursued a policy very similar to that of Catholicism. It pled for liberty of conscience when it was itself in danger of persecution; and threatened all other denominations with suppression when it had the authority to do so. A contemporary Anglican critic of Presbyterianism charged that,

> these men cried out for liberty of conscience and boasted that the oppression which was levied against them was the hallmark of their own sainthood. But directly they gained even partial authority, they instantly renounced their former tenderness of conscience and accomplished the destruction of the church with every instrument that a persecuting zeal could recommend.

An impartial historian summarizes the position of both Catholics and Puritans in this long controversy:

> It has been said that Puritans and Catholics were contending for liberty of conscience. To put it so seems misleading, if not altogether untrue. They were contending for the liberty of their own consciences, not for those of other people. . . . What they both claimed was freedom to dominate. So far as they were concerned it was merely an accident in the vast process of things, that their efforts to free themselves helped to enlarge human freedom.

The intolerance of theologians of the orthodox Reformation was the more reprehensible because the sectaries, against which their fanaticism was particu-larly directed, emphasized the very truths which supplemented the insights of the Reformation. While it would be wrong to give a purely economic inter-pretation of the differences between the Reformation and sectarianism, it cannot be denied that the theological differences were partly occasioned by, and the expressions of, social and economic conflicts. Sectarianism was on the whole the religion of the poor; and their insistence that religious ideals were socially relevant was occasioned by the pressure of their economic and social disabilities. Meanwhile the orthodox Reformation frequently became the religious screen for higher middle class economic interests, as generally as Catholicism was involved politically and economically with the older feudal classes. The mixture of theological and economic perspectives, which theologians are prone to deny and which economic determinists emphasize to the point of making religion a mere tool of economic interest, is one aspect of historical reality which refutes the pretensions of pure idealists, whether religious or secular. Even the most abstract theological controversy, as also the seemingly most objective scientific debate, is never free of accents which interest and passion have insinuated into the struggle. These interests are, it must be observed, much more complex and never as purely economic as Marxism assumes.

If the Reformation had observed the debates and conflicts in which it was involved in the light of its own ultimate insights into the imperfect character of all human ambitions and achievements, it could have used contemporary experience to validate its doctrines and to mitigate the fury with which it supported them.

Perhaps it is idle to search for particular causes of the failure of the Reformation to do this; for we have previously noted that sinful pride is able to use as instruments the very doctrines which are intended in principle to overcome it. Yet it is necessary to look for particular causes of this failure; because there were other spiritual movements, both secular and religious, which did, in fact, approach a tolerance consonant with the Christian spirit of forgiveness, though they possessed less searching doctrinal insights into the contingencies of history and the sinful corruptions of culture than the Reformation.

Undoubtedly one cause of the failure of the Reformation in the field of culture was that its Bibliolatry implied "sanctificationist" principles in the realm of culture and truth, despite its generally more paradoxical conception of grace. Thomas Hobbes was one, among many, critics of the church, who observed this effect of the Reformation: "After the Bible was translated into English," he wrote, "every man, nay, every boy and wench that could read English, thought they spoke with God Almighty . . . and every man became a judge of religion, and an interpreter of the scriptures to himself." The certain conviction of the faithful that the Bible gave them the final truth, transcending all finite perspectives and all sinful corruptions, thus contributed to individual spiritual arrogance, no less intolerable than the collective arrogance of the older church. This pride expressed itself despite the fact that contrary interpretations of scripture, against which the arrogance was directed, contradicted the pretension of an absolutely valid interpretation. For they proved that men interpreted Scripture variously, according to the variety of social and historical perspectives from which they severally approached it.

Though Reformation Bibliolatry (to which, as we have previously observed, Calvinism was more prone than Lutheranism) is thus one explanation of the fanaticism of the Reformers and their disciples, it is an explanation which must itself be explained.

Perhaps it was possible for the Reformation to take this simple jump out
of the relativities and ambiguities of history, because it did not labor with
sufficient earnestness and seriousness on those ultimate problems of human
culture, where both the possibilities and the limits of human wisdom are
discovered and defined. When this is done the gospel truth, which both
negates and fulfills human wisdom, cannot be claimed as a simple possession. For men are persuaded to the contrite recognition that their effort to
explicate this truth by human wisdom (which is the task of theology) is subject to historical contingencies, influenced by egoistic passions, corrupted by
sinful pretensions and is, in short, under the same judgment as philosophy.

Theology may differ from philosophy in that it has broken with the
principle of self-centeredness in culture "in principle." It has done so in
principle because it recognizes that the "world by its wisdom knew not
God"; that it is not possible to complete the structure of meaning from any
particular human perspective, or with any finite value as the center and
source of meaning. But the whole history of theology proves that this "in
principle" does not mean "in fact." When the truth which transcends all
partial and particular perspectives is made relevant to the truths of history
and culture (a task which theology must perform despite its perils) these
applications are subject to the same contingent elements which the history
of philosophy reveals. Luther's contemptuous attitude towards philosophy
is therefore without justification; more particularly because in practice philosophy sometimes achieves a greater spirit of humility than theology. It is
saved from *hybris* by its lack of any quick means of escape from the obvious
limitations of all human knowing. It has no Jacob's ladder upon which the
angels of grace rightly ascend and descend, but which is used falsely when
the theological Jacob imagines it an instrument of climbing into heaven.

In short, the intolerance of the Reformation is the consequence of a
violation of its own doctrinal position. Its doctrine of justification by faith
presupposed the imperfection of the redeemed. Logically this includes the
imperfection of "redeemed" knowledge and wisdom. Its intolerant fanaticism sprang from its failure to apply this insight to the cultural problem so
that it would mitigate the spiritual pride of man. Its actions thus proved its
theory to be correct; but they also revealed it to be ineffective. It is a theory
which must not only be apprehended by the mind but which must enter
into the heart and break its pride. The authority of the Bible was used to
break the proud authority of the church; whereupon the Bible became
another instrument of human pride. The secularists may be pardoned if, as
they watch this curious drama, they cry "a plague o' both your houses"; and
if they come to the conclusion that all ladders to heaven are dangerous. It
must be observed, however, that these ladders cannot be disavowed so
simply as the secularists imagine. Pride may ascend the ladder which was

meant for the descent of grace; but that is a peril which inheres in the whole human cultural enterprise. The secularists end by building ladders of their own; or they wallow in a nihilistic culture which has no vantage point from which "my" truth can be distinguished from "the" truth.

3 The Renaissance and Toleration

The toleration, whether in religious or in socio-economic disputes, which has made life sufferable amidst the cultural and social complexities of the modern world, and which enabled modern society to achieve a measure of domestic tranquility without paying the price of tyrannical suppression, is obviously the fruit, primarily, of the movement which we have defined broadly as "Renaissance." The heroes of science who defied religious authority and reopened prematurely solved problems, stood in that tradition. The Renaissance generated a wholesome attitude of skepticism which made for sanity wherever human pride had exceeded the limits of human certainty. The achievement of toleration in modern culture is sometimes regarded as due to the destruction of religious fanaticism through the destruction of religion itself. In so far as this is the case modern culture solves the problem of toleration only when the conflicts were explicitly religious; and offers no antidote for the implicity religious fanaticism generated in ostensibly secular political and social movements.

It must be observed, however, that sectarian Protestantism, which is, as we have previously noted, intimately related to Renaissance spirituality, also made very substantial contributions to the spirit of liberty and toleration.

The rationalist-humanist wing of the Renaissance made its contributions to toleration by challenging particular prejudices with the supposed universalities of reason; and by dissolving the false universalities of dogmatic religion by the force of empirical observations, proving the wide variety and relativity of all historical forms of culture. The two strategies frequently operated side by side and receive varying degrees of emphasis in the typical champions of toleration in Renaissance humanism. Bruno leans to the one, Montaigne to the other mode of attack; Descartes to the first and Locke and Voltaire to the second.

Sectarian Christianity meanwhile challenged Christian fanaticism from within the presuppositions of Christian faith. Its mystic certainties transcended the historically conditioned certainties of dogmatic faith. Its individualism challenged the orthodox passion for religious uniformity; and its social radicalism set the absolute ethical demands of the gospel against the social compromises which religious authority had prematurely sanctioned. Hans Denck, the father of Reformation pietism, in whose thought are the germs of both mystic-pietistic and radical apocalyptic sectarianism, was a champion of toleration, as was also Schwenkfeld.

While the Independents and the Levellers were the particular champions of toleration among seventeenth-century English sects, all the English sects made some contribution to the ideals of liberty. Lilburne and Walwyn, Winstanley and Roger Williams, these and many lesser known champions of liberty, are equally or more important in the history of English toleration, than the champions of liberty on the humanist side of the Renaissance.

The most distinguished of all champions of toleration, John Milton, combines Renaissance humanism and sectarian Christianity in a remarkable synthesis. Less profoundly Thomas Jefferson also achieved this synthesis, though the rationalist element in his thought is more pronounced and the Christian content more minimal.

Sectarianism was not, of course, universally tolerant. It had its own source of fanatic fury. Its simple perfectionism made it blind to the inevitability of compromises in which it saw its opponents involved. It therefore poured the fury of its self-righteous scorn upon them without recognizing that their compromises were but the obverse side of responsibilities, which the perfectionists had simply disavowed. Sometimes its individualism (and this applies to secular libertarianisms as well) rendered its preaching of toleration too cheap; for it assumed no responsibility for, nor understood the necessity of, social peace and order. It did not therefore recognize the necessity of minimal coercion in even the most liberal society.

But despite these sectarian fanaticisms, the history of sectarianism in general is as important as the more secular movement of the Renaissance in the development of toleration in the Western world.

The agreement upon this issue between secularists and sectarians rests upon two common approaches to the problem of truth, in which other differences are transcended. Both recognize the peril to truth in the coerced acceptance of it. And both are conscious of the finite character of human perspective and the variety of human viewpoints, which make perfect agreement in the search for truth impossible.

On the first point the secularists emphasize the futility of maintaining truth by coercion. "The truth," declared John Locke,

> would certainly do well enough if she were left to shift for herself. She seldom has received, and I fear never will receive, much assistance from the power of great men. . . . If truth makes not her way into the understanding by her own light, she will be but weaker for any borrowed forced violence can add to her.

The sectarian Christians give this same idea a slightly more moral–religious content. They do not see how coerced acceptance of the truth can redeem the soul. A letter of Flemish Baptists, under persecution in Elizabethan England, was a moving expression of the idea:

> We testify before God and your majesty that were we in our conscience able by any means to think or understand the contrary, we would with all our hearts receive and confess it; since it were a great folly in us not to live rather in the exercise of a right faith, than to die perhaps in a false one. . . . It is not in our power to believe this or that as evil doers who do right or wrong as they please. But the true faith must be planted in the heart by God, and to Him we pray daily that he would give us His spirit to understand His word and the Gospel.

The second point of agreement between secular and sectarian theories of toleration is derived from the appreciation and understanding by the Renaissance of the cultural task as an historical process. It understands the contingent character of all historical knowledge and appreciates the wide variety of perspectives which history and nature, geography and climate introduce into human culture. Here the Renaissance is more thoroughly in agreement with the Biblical understanding of man as "creature" and the Christian appreciation of the limits of human knowledge in history than alternative and more orthodox Christian doctrines. The Renaissance had its own ways of surmounting this historical relativity, which must be considered presently. It was led into new errors by many of them. But its provisional understanding of historical relativity gave it a great advantage over Christian orthodoxy.

This recognition of the fragmentary character of all historical apprehension of the truth is superbly expressed in Milton's *Areopagitica*, though in symbolism more Biblical than modern culture as a whole uses:

> Truth indeed came once into the world with her Divine Master and was a perfect shape most glorious to look upon; but when He ascended and His Apostles after him were laid asleep, then straight arose a wicked race of deceivers. . . . who took the Virgin truth, hewed her lovely form into a thousand pieces and scattered them to the four winds. From that time ever since the sad friends of Truth, such as durst appear, imitating the careful search that Isis made for the mangled body of Osiris, went up and down, gathering up limb by limb, still as they could find them. We have not yet found them all, Lords and Commons, nor ever shall do till the Master's second coming.

The same idea is the frequent preoccupation of sectarian and independent thought. "Let us not," wrote John Saltmarsh, ". . . assume any power of infallibility to each other; . . . for another's evidence is as dark to me as mine to him . . . till the Lord enlighten us both for discerning alike."

This provisional understanding of the relativity of human knowledge, including the relativity of various interpretations of religious revelation, is an integral part of the recovery of the sense of the historical in Renaissance thought. It is the primary cause of the ability of the Renaissance to meet one of the two tests of the problem of toleration: the willingness to entertain views which oppose our own without rancor and without the effort to suppress them.

It is in meeting the other test: the ability to remain true to and to act upon our best convictions, that modern culture most frequently fails. It finds difficulty in avoiding irresponsibility and skepticism on the one hand and new fanaticisms on the other.

Its position is safe from illusion so long as it simply seeks to preserve the free commerce of opinion, in the hope that a higher truth will emerge in the process. In the words of John Stuart Mill:

> Though silenced opinion be an error, it may, and very commonly does, contain a portion of truth; and since the general or prevailing opinion on any subject is rarely or never the whole truth, it is only [by] the collision of adverse opinion that the remainder of the truth has a chance of being supplied.[1]

The hope that fragmentary portions of the truth will finally be pieced together into the whole truth, or the belief that intellectual intercourse is a kind of competition in which the truth will finally prevail against falsehood, are admirable provisional incentives to tolerance. They are, moreover, provisionally and relatively true. The intellectual life of mankind is a process in which truth is constantly being sifted from falsehood; and the confidence that truth will finally prevail in history robs falsehood of its seeming immediate peril and mitigates the anxious fanaticism with which "our" truth is defended.

The difficulty with this solution is that it is only a provisional and not a final answer to the question of the relation of the "whole truth" to the fragmentary truths of history. Obviously this issue is a segment of the whole problem of time and eternity. The belief that history is moving towards the disclosure of the whole truth is a part of an entire conception of the relation of time to eternity, in which it is assumed that history transmutes itself into eternity, and progressively devours its own finiteness. It is typical of the combination of classical and historical viewpoints in the Renaissance, according to which the *logos* in history is not emancipated from finiteness and history but gradually prevails within history.

In so far as modern tolerance has been achieved by disavowing religion it may rest merely on indifference towards the ultimate problems of life and history, with which religion is concerned. Since religious questions have been a particularly fecund source of fanaticism and conflict, the gain in provisional toleration has therefore been great. But the weakness in the modern position is also quite apparent. Either it achieves toleration by taking an irresponsible attitude towards ultimate issues; or it insinuates new and false ultimates into views of life which are ostensibly merely provisional and pragmatic. Here are the twin perils of skepticism and a new fanaticism.

It is significant that so much of modern toleration applies merely to the field of religion; and that the very champions of toleration in this field may be exponents of political fanaticism. It is simple enough to be tolerant on issues which are not believed to be vital. The real test of toleration is our attitude towards people who oppose truths which seem important to us, and who challenge realms of life and meaning towards which we have a responsible relation. Tolerance in religion, therefore, frequently means an irresponsible attitude towards the ultimate problem of truth, including particularly the problem of the relation of *the* truth to the fragmentary truths of history. In the same way tolerance in political struggles may merely reveal irresponsibility and indifference towards the problem of political justice.

This irresponsible attitude may degenerate into complete skepticism, though there are very few consistent skeptics in the world. Absolute skepticism is rare because the very lack of confidence in the possibility of achieving any valid truth in history presupposes some criterion of truth by which all fragmentary truths are found wanting. Nevertheless, complete skepticism is always a possible consequence of the spirit of toleration; for no toleration is possible without a measure of provisional skepticism about the truth we hold. The Christian position of contrition in regard to "our" truth, the humble recognition that it contains some egoistic corruption, degenerates into irresponsibility as soon as we disavow the obligation to purge the truth we hold of its egoistic corruption. The irresponsibility degenerates into more complete skepticism if we come to the conclusion, that since history contains nothing but partial perspectives and fragmentary viewpoints, there is no possibility of discerning truth from falsehood. Complete skepticism represents the abyss of meaninglessness, a pit which has constantly threatened modern culture and into which it occasionally tumbles. Frequently, as in pre-Nazi German culture, it precedes the subordination of truth to political power. Skepticism thus becomes the forerunner of cynicism.

But new fanaticisms are the much more probable consequence of the modern position than complete skepticism. In these fanaticisms an ultimate position and a final truth are implicity or explicitly insinuated into what was provisionally regarded as a realm of partial and fragmentary truths. Thus new religions emerge in an ostensibly irreligious culture.

In the main current of Renaissance thought, the belief that the intercourse between fragmentary truths will culminate in the realization of the whole truth becomes itself a religious position as soon as it is changed from a merely provisional and tentative attitude towards the immediate problem of dealing with fragmentary truths, into an answer to the final problem of truth and falsehood. Such a religion can and does maintain tolerance towards all religious beliefs except those which challenge this basic assumption. The idea of progress is the underlying presupposition of what may be broadly defined as "liberal" culture. If that assumption is challenged the whole structure of meaning in the liberal world is imperiled. For this reason the liberal world is intolerant in regard to this article of its creed. It does not argue about its validity, precisely because it has lost every degree of skepticism in regard to it.

The creed is nevertheless highly dubious. It is true in so far as all historical processes, including the intellectual and cultural process, are meaningful and lead to fulfillment. It is false in so far as all historical processes are ambiguous. In the field of culture this means that the realization of a higher truth can lead to a new falsehood. Penetration into the mysteries of nature, for instance, may lead to false analogies between nature and history; or the discovery of the dynamic character of history may lead to the error of assuming that growth means progress.

The erroneous belief that history is its own fulfillment has been previously considered. The very structure of the human spirit refutes confidence in history as a process of cultural fulfillment as certainly as it refutes the general confidence in history. Man being a creature who both transcends and is involved in historical process cannot find perfect fulfillment in that process. His freedom over the process can be used on any level to introduce new error into the discovery of truth. But even if this were not the case his transcendence over history makes it impossible to complete his structure of meaning within the limits of history. He must ask how historical truth is related to ultimate, that is, "eternal" truth. And if he knows that historical truth is not merely imperfect but also corrupted truth, he faces a problem for which there is no answer but a divine mercy which purges the historical of its corruptions and completes its incompleteness.

But other fanaticisms grow up on the ground of the modern position baser than the mild fanaticism of the religion of progress. All of them, despite their variety, may be defined as political fanaticisms, generated by political religions. Thomas Hobbes and the French protagonist of political absolutism, Jean Bodin, may be regarded as the most typical historical exemplars of this tendency in modern culture, which finally culminated in the Nazi creed of race and nation. The tendency begins with a skeptical and irresponsible attitude towards the religious problem and an aversion to religious controversy because it imperils the tranquility of the national state. In the case of Bodin, the fratricidal religious conflict in France persuaded him to renounce his Huguenot faith for a syncretistic religion. His new religious position nicely reveals the perils of skepticism. For his highminded effort to find the truth in all religions ends with the poorly concealed conviction that all religions are equally true and *equally false*. But Bodin's real concern was the unity of France; and he solved that problem by conceiving an absolute state, which had the power and the right to suppress all opinions and vitalities which might imperil its unity. In the thought of both Hobbes and Bodin, this demand for unconditioned loyalty to the state is implicitly rather than explicitly religious. It is implicitly religious because it demands unconditioned loyalty; but not explicitly so because it does not make the overt claim that the whole meaning of life and existence is fulfilled in the individuals's relation to the national community. It was left to the Nazis to illustrate one possible kind of progress in history, by developing the logic of this state absolutism to its final conclusion. Thus they achieved the final corruption of cynicism on the soil of religious skepticism.

Thomas More, who was a Renaissance nationalist when his sovereign Henry VIII imperiled the interests of England by subservience to papal politics, and who was a Catholic universalist when the king sought to establish royal supremacy in spiritual matters, proved the validity and availability of the Christian position as a resource against this new political fanaticism. Despite its own corruption of fanaticism, the Catholic version of the Christian faith is at least a bulwark against the idolatry of political and national absolutisms. Challenged by the king to submit to his authority spiritually as well as politically, and presented with the futility of defiance in view of the submission of all other English leaders, More appealed to the authority of the universal church which had not submitted. "For," said he,

> though some nations fall away, yet likewise as how many boughs fall from the tree, though they fall more than be left thereon, yet they make no doubt which is the very tree, although each of them were planted in another place and grew to a greater tree than the stock he came first of.

This Christian universalism, despite its corruptions in both the Protestant and Catholic versions of the Christian faith, has proved as resourceful in our own day as in the day of Henry VIII. It has defied the cynical solution of the cultural problem, more successfully than any other position.

The Marxist solution of the problem of truth stands on a higher ground than the subordination of all culture to the power of the state. But it is nevertheless a political religion; and must be regarded as one of the late fruits of the soil of Renaissance thought. According to its faith the particular perspective of the proletarian class is not a relative but a transcendent vantage point for the apprehension of the truth. All truth but its own is therefore tainted with the "ideological" taint of interest. But obviously the pretension of any class or nation, of any culture or civilization, that it alone has escaped from the finiteness of human knowing, and the corruption of interest and passion, is merely another form of the taint of pride which confuses all quests for the truth. It is a secularized version of the pretension of complete sanctification. The fruit of fanaticism is the natural consequence of this claim.

However we twist or turn, whatever instruments or pretensions we use, it is not possible to establish the claim that we have the truth. The truth remains subject to the paradox of grace. We may have it; and yet we do not have it. And we will have it the more purely in fact if we know that we have it only in principle. Our toleration of truths opposed to those which we confess is an expression of the spirit of forgiveness in the realm of culture. Like all forgiveness, it is possible only if we are not too sure of our own virtue.

Loyalty to the truth requires confidence in the possibility of this attainment; toleration of others requires broken confidence in the finality of our own truth. But if there is no answer for a problem to which we do not have the answer, our shattered confidence generates either defeat (which in the field of culture would be skepticism); or an even greater measure of pretension, meant to hide our perplexities behind our certainties (which in the field of culture is fanaticism).

Gustav Mensching, "The Unity of Religions" (1955)

Mensching studied under the famed Rudolf Otto at Marburg, graduating with the doctoral degree in 1924. Thereafter he taught at Riga, and from 1936 at Bonn. He viewed religion as "experiential encounter with the holy, and the responsive action of man determined by the holy." In the work from which this excerpt is taken, he applies this definition to the problem of religious pluralism, and specifically, to the issue of toleration. Two distinctions are necessary. *Formal tolerance* is defined as "mere noninterference with another faith," as in the establishment of religious liberty in a given country. *Intrinsic tolerance* refers specifically to content, "the recognition of other religions as genuine possibilities of encounter with the sacred," which attitude, he insists, is characterized not by indifference "but presupposes critical encounter and insight" (pp. 11–12).

SOURCE: Gustav Mensching, *Tolerance and Truth in Religion*, tr. H.-J. Klimkeit (University, Alabama: University of Alabama Press, 1971 [German orig. 1955]), pp. 155–63. Reproduced with permission of the University of Alabama Press.

The most important reason why intrinsic tolerance is essentially justified and therefore necessary is the fact that there is a profound unity of religions. There are various ways of arriving at such a unity. Let us consider them one after another.

Whenever one's own religion is regarded as *the* truth in an intolerant manner, the many other religions appear as a source of annoyance and as something that must be overcome for the sake of one's own faith. If such a unity is striven for, it is attempted to be brought about *in place of* plurality. In this case, unity would be brought about by the victory of one creed over the others and elimination of all religions but one. We reject such an attempt, for it is based upon views that substantiate intolerance and that we have proven to be essentially unjustified.

A second possibility of bringing about a unity of faiths is to abstract that which is common to all of them and to regard this common core as the true religion. This unity would be an abstraction *out of* the many divergent existing faiths and beliefs. We encounter such an endeavor in the Enlightenment. It believed in a "natural religion" (*religio naturalis*) of reason concealed behind the garb of "positive" religions. In his *Speeches on Religion to its Cultured Despisers* (1799), Friedrich Schleiermacher, the great thinker who overcame the Enlightenment, characterized such a constructed faith pertinently. In talking about the consequences of such an abstraction out of the wealth of religious experiences and notions, he says, "The so-called natural religion is usually so much refined away, and has such metaphysical and moral graces, that little of the peculiar character of religion appears." And in the same place he points out, "The essence of natural religion consists entirely in denying everything positive and characteristic in religion and in violent polemics. It is the worthy product of an age, the hobby of which was that wretched generality and vain soberness which in everything was most hostile to true culture."

A rationalist view, then, fails to recognize the living nature of religion and substitutes a dead, unhistorical and abstract unity of religions for a living plurality. This type of unity is to be rejected, too, for it fails to do justice to the historical reality of religion.

But then there is a third possibility which I would like to call unity *in* plurality. With this term I would like to suggest that the plurality of positive religions is not to be eliminated for the sake of an abstract unity; but that there is, rather, an apparent unity of life in the various religions and their manifold forms of expression. This claim will now have to be substantiated.

Let us start by pointing out again that every religion has its own particular living core which gives it its unmistakable peculiarity. To study this living core is one of the most important tasks of modern history of religions. But over against these specific characteristics there are certain basic features in the life of historical religions that are, ultimately, all identical. These features belong to the very nature of each and every religion; they are often to be found under the garb of the most varying religious manifestations. Let us consider them.

It is obvious that those who truly confess a religion, no matter what it is, especially if it is basically intolerant, are all filled with "the same sincerity, the same uprightness, the same yearning and love, the same obedience, the same preparedness to make sacrifices," be they Hindus or Moslems, Jews or Christians. This fact even struck a man of such intolerant passion as Savonarola, who set the pious outside Christianity before his countrymen as an example, as it were, for true religiousness. He pointed out: "Jews and Turks keep their religion much better than Christians, who should take the reverence Turks attach to the name of God as an example. . . . They [the Turks] would have long been converted if they would not rightly have found a stumbling block in the lives of Christians."

The fact that men everywhere in all religions express the same yearning for the holy and all confess and defend the values that their religion has handed down to them, often sacrificing much, even their very lives – all this can only be explained in one way: without making an allowance for a theological bias, one must assume that such men have actually experienced an encounter with the holy and have shared in fellowship with it. Having this in view, the only attitude that is mandatory is one of respect for the convictions of men of other faith.

In addition to the motives for intolerance we have already discussed, an objectively false view of the nature of other religions is the main reason for religious polemics. In this regard, much credit is due to the scientific study of religions for correcting such historically false opinions. Friedrich Heiler, in the essay quoted above, gives examples for the positive effect of the scientific study of religions on the understanding of other traditions. First, Christian polemics denounced Mohammed as a deceiver for centuries, until finally the incorrectness of this view was proved by historical research. Second, for a long time the opinions about Hinduism were also quite false. Goethe saw in Indian religion nothing but "the maddest idols, fashioned in giant size and worshipped." Now modern research has brought to light that there is not only grotesque polytheism but also sublime mysticism and personal love of God (*bhakti*) in Indian religions. It is in this sense that most of the arguments of Christian apologetics proved untenable in view of the more developed Eastern religions.

In the fight against other religions it was, and still is, common in Christian theology and mission theology to term the adherents of non-Christian faiths indifferently "heathens." This collective devaluation is to be understood on the basis of the Christian claim to absoluteness, or rather of its rational orthodox interpretation. But if there were a greater knowledge of the profundity of worship and greatness of vision of God in wide areas of the world of non-Christian religions, and if there were an awareness of the truly determining power of religion in personal and public life there, the theoreticians of missions would perhaps be more hesitant in expressing such presumptive generalizations and depreciative verdicts as have been uttered. Luther still acknowledged a "general revelation" (*revelatio generalis*), an idea today's Protestant theology in the wake of Karl Barth has relinquished. In his *Commentary to Galatians* (1535), Luther could, with good conscience, make this distinction between non-Christian religions and Christianity:

> There is a twofold knowledge of God: the general and the particular. All men have the general knowledge, namely, that God is, that He punishes the wicked, etc. But *what God thinks of us*, what he wants to give and to do to deliver us from sin and death and to save us – which is the particular and the true knowledge of God – this men do not know. Thus it can happen that someone's face may be familiar to me, but I really do not know him, because I do not know what he has in mind . . . Now what good does it do you to know that God exists if you do not know what His Will is toward you?

Luther could make this naive distinction between Christianity with its knowledge of salvation and non-Christian religions with their mere awareness of God's existence, because he was not familiar with the high religions in the non-Christian world. But once it is realized that outside Christianity there is not only a longing for redemption but also a live, genuine experience and assuredness of salvation, this distinction cannot be maintained any longer. On the basis of our present information, there is no scientific reason why the Christian knowledge about salvation should be "true" and the non-Christian insight – often expressed in quite similar terms – "false."

There is yet another motive for an ultimate unity at the base of all religions: the fact that identical basic religious experiences are to be found in all of them. This has been established by historical research. Religion is experiential encounter with the holy, and the responsive action of man determined by the holy. Rudolf Otto, in his epoch-making work *The Idea of the Holy*, set forth what holy is and how it is experienced, taking facts from all of religious history into account. . . . Otto maintains that the primal experiences of the *mysterium tremendum* (the mystery that evokes trembling), the *fascinans* (the fascinating), and the *augustum* (the sublime) are present in all religions of the world, though with different emphasis. The ultimate unity comprehended by this insight is of a quite different type from the *religio naturalis* proposed by the Enlightenment, for the "natural religion" was a quite unhistorical product of the mind, constructed by abstracting the ideas common to all religions. That was a theoretical and bloodless religion of reason, and those who propounded it disregarded the living nature of religion and looked upon the historical phenomena as things obscuring its purity. Otto, on the other hand, in his analysis, discerns and describes the experiential encounter with the holy as it affects the religious individual and as it is reflected in the data of religious history. As opposed to Rationalism, he stresses the non-rational character of the holy and non-rational significance of religious expressions.

Religious research concerned with structural forms, or patterns, has discerned yet another kind of unity among religions. It has realized that the ethnic religions form a unity and have a common structure – we described it above – although there are differences in their respective living cores. This unity is established primarily by the circumstance that natural communities (families, sibs, tribes, nations, and states), not individuals, maintain these religions. The individual is of quite secondary importance here. His membership in the community alone ensures him contact with the divine – weal or salvation. The universal religions, too, form a unity. Here the individual, not the community, is the main thing. He has acquired self-awareness, and religiously he realizes that his situation is one of doom. In the mystical forms of universal religion, *self-centeredness* is equated with lack of salvation. This plightful situation is overcome by merging with the Absolute. In the prophetic religions, on the other hand, *selfishness*, alienation from the living God, is the source of woe. Here salvation is acquired by turning to God in faith and trust and by thus entering into communion with Him.

If we take all these facts into account, a subtle unity of all religions will become visible; it will become clear that it is impossible to mark off one faith, like Christianity, from all the rest and to uphold its absoluteness in a rational sense. Modern comparative religion is concerned not only with inner structures but also with outward phenomena of religion. The results of phenomenology justify a phrase of Schleiermacher's, who seemed to sense a crucial issue here when he pointed out: "The more you progress in the understanding of religion, the more the whole religious world will appear to you as an indivisible whole." Phenomenological research has made it evident that there are many common features in the different religions: there are similar manifestations of the holy (holy stones, mountains, trees, animals, places, times, words, scriptures, etc.), similar ways of dealing with the divine (through sacrifices, prayers, mystery cults, sacraments, etc.), and similar ideas (about God, the Otherworld, salvation). Hence by this approach, too, we can discern a unity in the way religions express their inner life.

There is yet another science that makes the unity of religions visible: psychology of religion. This field, and especially depth psychology, has shown us how religious feelings and sentiments are related everywhere in the world and have certain inner principles in common, and how conceptual images in religion are always determined by the same general psychological structures. The danger of such an approach arises when *everything* in religion is explained as a product of psychological factors. That is psychologism. But one does not have to adopt a unilateral attitude that oversteps the boundaries of psychology's competence. Other approaches are possible here, and they can be assumed without endangering the legitimate concerns of research in the field. One can legitimately strive for a discernment of the part which the human mind plays in the process and formation of religious life. Even such studies would reveal that there are typical tendencies and forms of expression of religious experience that are determined by the psyche.

Finally, a comparison of the ethical value systems in the different religions shows that a far-reaching relationship does obtain between them. Many sets of values are recognized by peoples adhering to the most different religions. The five Buddhist commands of ethical discipline, for instance, or the Decalogue in the Old Testament, or basic Islamic laws, all reflect fundamental social concerns, and they order the relationship between the people of a community; furthermore, they determine the relationship of men to worldly possessions and to their respective communities. Although these ethical values appear in different order, they are basically the same in all the different religions of the world. Beside these general values there are also others that are not discovered everywhere but at various points in religious history. Here they are then regarded as binding. The great universal religions especially proclaim particular ethical values, such as love for neighbor and foe, obedience, compassion, etc.

The far-reaching unity of religions on the ethical level allows for a certain cooperation amongst them on this basis, for there is a universal ethical consciousness common to all mankind. It was on account of such considerations that Rudolf Otto founded the "Religious League of Mankind," the goal of which was not to integrate all creeds, but rather to influence the lives of peoples on the basis of their widely common religious ethic. The pursuit of that goal is even more urgent today than it was at Otto's time.

We have endeavored to show in this chapter that, in spite of all central differences between religions – differences that must not be underestimated – an ultimate unity is clearly discernible amongst them, as various different scientific approaches show. This insight does not spring from a preconceived opinion, but arises out of a study of the realities of religious history itself. The fact that there is such a unity provides a feasible basis for intrinsic tolerance. Our academic insight is confirmed by the religious experience of unity made throughout mystical religions. Perhaps it would be better to put it the other way around: the unity of the divine and the relatedness of all ways leading to it, which is experienced everywhere in mysticism, can also be established on academic grounds. Both approaches, then, that of rational insight gained by the scientific study of religions and that of unreflected and immediate mystical experience, lead us to the same conclusion, that there is a unity of religions *in* all historical plurality.

We pointed out that the intolerance of prophetic religions is rooted, primarily, in a spontaneous, personal experience and in the conviction that this experience is absolute and incomparable. As to mysticism, tolerance belongs to its very nature; for mysticism has emotional access to the perception of the unity of religions. That is why even a minimum of formal tolerance had to be struggled for in those parts of the world where prophetic religions prevailed, as in Europe. In the East, however, this was, on the whole, not necessary. The prophetic religions have always revealed greater *naïveté* and unreflectedness than mysticism; because of their inner structure, they have shown a greater tendency toward the formation of organizations. Hence they have also greatly opposed formal and intrinsic tolerance. Their main concern was always to defend the unity of their respective communities. Their extensive and exclusive claim to absoluteness springs from the experience of an intensive union with one overpowering, universal God, but their sophisticated theologies understand that claim not in the light of its origin but in a rational sense, and they go on to defend it with utmost rigidity.

In order to come to a correct understanding of the claim to absoluteness (which was quite legitimate at an initial stage), a reorientation is necessary in prophetic religions. But such a reorientation and reinterpretation is more difficult here than in mysticism. The theological and ecclesiastical tradition of a prophetic religious organization with its authority and its characteristic tendency to preserve inherited structures always declines basically new readjustments, as the times of reformation in religious history show. Furthermore, though mystic and prophetic religions are both basically maintained by individuals who have made a personal decision for their respective faith, the masses soon dominate in prophetic religions and their organizations, and largely limit or even abolish the religious independence of the individual. Mysticism, on the other hand, remains what it always is: a religion of the individual. Organized prophetic religions necessarily have to suffer loss of the religious spontaneity and immediacy that marked their founders and early congregations. They can only accept those views and ideas that are in compliance with their fixed forms and teachings. Subsequently, this entails an intolerance that is hard to overcome. Yet the reasons brought forth above make it mandatory that intolerance be overcome.

Carrillo de Albornoz, "Are There Theological Grounds for Religious Liberty?" (1963)

The author was successively a lawyer in Spain, a Jesuit in Rome, and an Anglican who worked for the World Council of Churches' Secretariat for Religious Liberty. He performed a signal service through his publications which provided information on the contemporary situation of religious liberty throughout the world. In this essay he analyzed the thrust toward religious liberty from an ecumenical perspective, recognizing both agreement and divergence.

SOURCE: A. F. Carrillo de Albornoz, *The Basis of Religious Liberty* (London: SCM Press, 1963), pp. 55–63. Reproduced by permission of the World Council of Churches.

The title of this Second Part ["Why Christians Demand Religious Liberty"] seems to imply that Christians as such have specific religious, biblical and theological grounds for demanding that religious liberty be recognized and respected by the civil society. In fact, the existence of such particular Christian reasons in favor of religious freedom has been repeatedly proclaimed by ecumenical bodies. Nevertheless and although there is ecumenical conviction that "we hold a distinctive Christian basis for religious liberty," on the other side it is generally admitted in ecumenical circles that "there has not yet emerged a consensus concerning the theological and ethical reasons why religious freedom must be defended."

For our part, we must confess that the investigation of the Christian grounds for religious liberty has constituted the main subject of the studies and discussions of the Commission on Religious Liberty; and that there have been registered the most numerous and most important differences of opinion, which is not surprising, considering the differences of theological traditions among the member churches. We do not intend to solve all difficulties here and to formulate the theological foundation of religious liberty in such a manner that could receive a unanimous ecumenical "consensus." Our task, by far the more modest, is that of presenting to the churches the results of our discussions, underlining the main points of theological tension as well as the significant agreements reached; and to propose the questions which could be the matter of fruitful study and discussion by the churches.

To begin with, there is a conviction on which we find complete ecumenical agreement, namely that social religious liberty, such as the ecumenical movement demands, *is not a revealed truth*. This ecumenical agreement is indirectly confirmed by several official statements when they say that religious liberty is "an *implication* of the faith of the Church;" "an *implication* of the Christian faith." Consequently, not an *explicitly* revealed truth. But if such statements indirectly recognize that social religious liberty is not an explicitly revealed truth, they at the same time proclaim that liberty of religion "has its deepest foundations in the Gospel of Jesus Christ"; i.e., that our Christian faith *implies* the exigency of social religious freedom; in other words, that there is some "nexus" between Christian revelation and religious liberty. Our prime question is, therefore, to investigate this "nexus" or to see exactly how religious liberty is implied in the Christian revelation.

Particularly concerning the study of the *biblical texts*, we may also register another ecumenical agreement. Scholars generally recognize, with Amos Wilder, that the Scriptures provide "unshakable grounding" for religious liberty. As for the *method* of investigating the Bible, there is also unanimous consensus of opinion that the study cannot be confined to those single scriptural passages which are considered as dealing specifically with Christian freedom, but that it must include – as said the Commission on Religious Liberty – "the full meaning and nature of the Gospel." Or, as Professor Søe would say, "it is not single passages in the Bible, it is Christ's whole way of approaching mankind that gives us our lead." Of course, this general ecumenical opinion should be understood in the sense that, while religious liberty is not to be logically deduced from single biblical texts through some literal hermeneutic; on the other hand it would be going too far to avoid biblical citations which can certainly show the spirit and ethos of the whole revelation. On the contrary, this method of appositely using biblical citations has been employed by the most outstanding specialists.

Concerning logical reasoning in this matter, many advisers were of the opinion that not only in biblical study, but generally in our theological thinking, we should guard against the temptation to resort to abstract deduction, which would be hardly adequate to solve such a complex problem.

Here we come to the great question of ascertaining *in what manner* Scriptures and Theology give us a lead for the foundation of social religious liberty. We must confess that, in this respect, there is no more ecumenical agreement, and that we must register different and, in some cases, opposite traditions. The most discussed point in this context has been that of the *interrelations* between the *inner* Christian freedom with which Christ has set us free and the *social* or external religious freedom which ecumenical bodies claim. The point of departure of our study in this matter was the well-known statement by the Amsterdam Assembly which we must reproduce here:

> While the liberty with which Christ has set men free can neither be given nor
> destroyed by any government, Christians, because of that inner freedom, are

both jealous for its outward expression and solicitous that all men should have freedom in religious life.

We hope to be true to this text if we present its statements in the following fashion:

(a) Christian liberty, or the liberty with which Christ has set us free, is an *inner* freedom.
(b) Being inner, Christian liberty cannot be given or destroyed by any human power.
(c) Social or external religious liberty is the outward expression of the inner Christian liberty. Social religious liberty can be given (we would say: recognized) or destroyed by human powers. Social religious liberty is not identical with inner Christian freedom.
(d) Christians demand social religious liberty ("outward expression") *because* of the inner Christian liberty.

How far do theologians who participate in the ecumenical debate agree on these statements?

Firstly, they all agree on the *clear distinction* between Christian liberty and social religious liberty. We have already spoken of the ecumenical agreement on this distinction. As one of our advisers said, one thing is "what man is able to be in himself, in terms of spiritual allegiance, convictions as to right and wrong, moral judgments, personal commitment and desire and purpose on the one hand," and another quite different thing is "that which he has freedom and power to express, to manifest, and to carry into effect in the social fabric of which he is part."

Secondly, we also register ecumenical agreement on the affirmation that social religious freedom is the "outward expression" of the inner Christian liberty.

On the other hand, a most controversial question is that of knowing whether Christians should demand this "outward expression," or social religious liberty, *because* of the inner Christian liberty; and, still more, what is the exact meaning of this "because."

For some theologians (who seem to be in the minority) this "because" is altogether a mistake. They think that social religious liberty (which they sometimes call, in our opinion incorrectly, "liberty of religious exercise in a State") cannot be claimed on grounds of the inner Christian freedom. Their main argument is that both these liberties are *completely* different, so that the one cannot be the reason for the other.

The great majority of theologians believe, with the Amsterdam Assembly, that we should demand social religious liberty "because" of the inner freedom. Still more, they think that this "because" includes several inter-relations which complete each other.

The first interrelation proposed is a factual or historical one, based on the fact that inner freedom can and often is destroyed by external coercion. As one of these theologians wrote, "these two realms interact on each other so that the absolute freedom of spirit which is postulated is actually maimed and thwarted to some degree by the psychological constraints which society is able to exercise." The consequence, and not a mere abstract one but of the kind based on the concrete needs of humanity, is that the external coercion which often deprives man of the possibility of acting responsibly in religious matters (inner freedom) is "a denial of God's intention for man"; and consequently, that liberation of external coercion is demanded by the very inner Christian freedom.

There are some who simply deny the force of this argument. Based on the ecumenical statement that "the liberty with which Christ has set us free can neither be given not destroyed by any government," they think that inner religious freedom is entirely independent of external freedom. Fur-thermore, persecutions are announced in the Bible as almost the *normal* situation for the Church in many ways, and the same persecutions purify and strengthen Christianity. Therefore, they conclude, it is wrong to say that inner Christian freedom necessitates social freedom.

Other theologians think that a fundamental distinction is necessary to clarify this point. Concerning an *absolute* need, it seems obvious that inner religious freedom does not, in any way, need the protection of social liberty, for there is no human power able to destroy the very roots of our liberty in Christ. Concerning a *relative* (or "*de facto*") need, they firmly believe that external coercion may actually contradict God's intention in giving man inner freedom. Besides, these theologians think that the inner human power of resisting "*de facto*" external coercion, as well as the beneficial effects of persecution, are often exaggerated. The Reformation spread rapidly and took deep roots in Spain in the sixteenth century, but Philip II and the Spanish Inquisition, *with their external power*, not only succeeded in making martyrs, but also in completely eradicating for centuries the evangelical faith. Henry VIII of England successfully turned a Roman Catholic population into an Anglican one in just a few years, and certainly not merely by external and constrained allegiance. The flourishing and very numerous Christianity of Japan in the seventeenth century was drowned in blood by the Emperors, and the Japanese people forgot for centuries their Christian convictions. Similar examples could be multiplied. They clearly show that external coercion can quite well have destructive effects on the inner freedom and that persecution, when it is radical, has no such inner purifying and strengthening effects. God may permit in His providence such coercion but His primary intention is that man remains free and, respecting Himself this inner freedom, His will is *a fortiori* that men do the same.

But these considerations lead us to investigate whether there are, between inner Christian freedom and social religious liberty, *essential* interrelations other than the purely factual ones based on the practical need of some external protection for inner liberty.

Does inner freedom *demand in itself* social religious freedom, independently of the fact that external coercion may or may not influence internal freedom?

Many theologians answer affirmatively, based mainly on their conviction, above indicated, that inner and social freedom is not so completely different and independent as some think, particularly because the biblical conception of Christian freedom is not so *exclusively* private and inner.

We very much regret that we are not able to give here a larger exposition of Dr Wilder's article on the matter.[2] We shall indicate, nevertheless, its essentials. For Wilder, "as the Bible sees man, the freedom in question (Christian liberty) cannot be viewed only as a private and inner freedom." The inner freedom of the New Testament includes also, in his opinion, the demand that "human authorities should not trespass upon this final zone of liberty of the creature in what concerns his destiny and his dealings with eternity."

The reason for this, in Wilder's opinion, is that, for the New Testament, "the existence of the self is a social-historical existence, and its will and action involves other creatures in a public way. The self is not an atom, its life is not purely 'spiritual,' and its relation to God is not only vertical. The primordial freedom of the creature must be allowed a public-historical expression subject to the limits of the divine sovereignty which, indeed, operates in part through the social orders. But the social orders and the civil powers must act here within the terms of their mandate and subject to divine judgment."

Even Paul's distinctive understanding of Christian freedom has, for Wilder, a clear social-political implication. Here our author recognizes that the "common view" (at least the German one) is that Paul's understanding of Christian freedom has nothing to do with freedom in its political aspect nor with our modern idea of the inborn freedom of man. He also recognizes that, for superficial observers, Paul's freedom, "as an aspect of justification, 'freedom from the law, sin and death,' appears to mean an inner personal freedom of a kind which comes to clearest expression precisely under constraints, denials and persecution." Nevertheless, Wilder thinks that "Paul's

eleutheria is an eschatological freedom operating in the world, in history."
"In Stoicism and Gnosticism (and in some forms of modern idealism) it is
possible to hold a conception of religious freedom and of man in which the
soul is indifferent to the structures of the world or to that which is beyond
its disposal. But such individualism and a-historicism is not envisaged in
the New Testament. Thus Paul's radical view of Christian freedom (cf. also
John 8:32 ff. and Jesus' words in Matthew 17: 24 as to the freedom of sons)
– identified with the life of the Spirit, with *parrhesia*, joy, peace and glory
– carries with it an irresistible pressure, and one that is not only 'spiritual,'
upon all orders of the 'flesh,' whether in Church or in State. That this pressure
is defined in terms of love and suffering ('a bruised reed he will not break':
cf. the 'marks of an apostle' of Paul, 2 Corinthians 12: 10–12) does not mean
that public and worldly historical interests and patterns are not rudely
unsettled and overturned (cf. Acts 19, the impact of the Gospel on Ephesus)."

The conclusions reached by Wilder through this examination of Paul's
understanding of Christian liberty are:

1 In this freedom the ultimate responsibility for choice and decision on
   the part of the believer is presupposed.
2 This freedom is not solely inner and private freedom but is understood by Paul as having a *historical-social* and indeed cosmic outreach
   and effect.
3 The Christian is obliged to recognize the freedom of his fellow-
   believers in this sense.
4 *The temporal power* even of the pagan State *is viewed as similarly
   obliged.*

We may say that this position is accepted by many, if not by all, ecumenical theologians in the sense that they think there is some essential relationship between inner and social freedom, so that the former constitutes a
necessity of the latter; and that the inner freedom of the Christian presupposes, if not through mere *conceptual* logicality, at least in virtue of some
logicality of Christian attitude, the social respect for the inner maturity it
has achieved in man as well as for the community conditions that make it
possible for all. However, we should not forget that there are very distinguished ecumenical theologians opposed to Wilder's thesis. . . .

The different and even opposite positions of the ecumenical theologians
concerning the interrelations between inner Christian freedom and social
religious liberty have made it necessary that their theological foundations of
religious freedom follow different ways.

Those theologians who recognize essential interrelations between both freedoms believe that the fundamental principle which gives a Christian basis to the social religious liberty is God's will, revealed in the Bible, that man should be free in religious matters, both internally and socially. This insight which, rather than being an *argument* in a dialectic sense, constitutes the whole spirit and heart of the biblical revelation, has two aspects. The first is that the *status* of man, as he has been created, redeemed and called by God, including his personal destiny and his social vocation, relates primarily to the realm of freedom, so that humanity, as it is presented in the biblical revelation, is intelligible only in the hypothesis that the purpose of God is better served by leaving man free to make choices for which he has to bear the consequences, than by restraining or coercing him in order to keep him from making mistakes. The second aspect of the same Christian insight is what we could call God's ways with men: God as disclosed in Jesus Christ is neither arbitrary nor coercive. It is an essential characteristic of the Gospel that God himself does not use force to win our allegiance. And this divine respect for human freedom is a revelation, directed decisively at the world, about the source and meaning of power, for even the State and its coercive power exists by virtue of the love and power of God, who does not compel faith.

For the theologians who are reluctant to accept the above-indicated essential interrelations between inner Christian freedom and social religious liberty the latter is rather the consequence of Christian teaching on the authority of worldly powers and the limits set to them. As one of them explains, "from the Christian view the State has authority from God, not unlimited, but limited. The secular authority is not entitled to rule over the conscience of man. The government cares for peace and order, for economic and social welfare, but it is not the ruler over man's conscience. Therefore, Christian doctrine can demand from the State that it recognize the right of the Christian to exercise his religion freely."

Philip Wogaman, "An Unconscious Commitment in Search of Basis" (1967)

A Methodist seminary professor, Wogaman recognizes the importance of the concept of religious liberty and notes that its acceptance is now widespread. But he is not satisfied with this, claiming that there is an inadequate theoretical basis for its existence, which might prove disastrous under certain trying conditions. Different traditions must deal differently with religious freedom, but Wogaman desires to see each one express a foundation for it right at the center of a given set of beliefs and values.

SOURCE: Philip Wogaman, *Protestant Faith and Religious Liberty* (Nashville, TN: Abingdon Press, 1967), pp. 26–30.

Even though religious liberty is far from being a reality in many parts of the world, and even though it may not be realized *perfectly* anywhere, one can still venture the assertion that it is one of those axiomatic commitments which are common to most of mankind. It is an important part of the *ius gentium* in the emerging world civilization. Despite religious intolerance and persecution, there is evidence that most people believe in freedom of religion and that the denial of religious liberty is everywhere on the defensive.

This is curiously evident in the fact that guarantees for freedom of worship are to be found in so many national constitutions – even in those of governments which are committed to viewpoints which seem irreconcilable with religious liberty. For instance, even the Soviet Constitution (in Article 124) states: "In order to guarantee to the citizens the freedom of conscience, the church in the USSR is separated from the state and the school is separated from the church; freedom for the performance of the religious rites and freedom of anti-religious propaganda are guaranteed to every citizen." That such provisions are ambiguous, that they may have been enacted through sheer expediency, or that they may be understood cynically does not change their importance. It is expedient to affirm at least some degree of freedom of worship because it is demanded by large numbers of people. Even cynicism in these matters is not to be discounted entirely, for it contains at least a silent tribute to a norm even though it may not genuinely accept commitment to it. Inclusion of freedom of worship as a constitutional provision bears public witness that there *ought* to be freedom in religious matters.

This commitment is even more manifest in the pronouncements of universal bodies which reflect the emerging world community. The United Nations, for instance, has since its inception affirmed religious liberty to be one of man's fundamental rights. At several points the Universal Declaration of Human Rights supports religious liberty indirectly. In Article 18 it forthrightly declares that "everyone has the right to freedom of thought, conscience and religion; this right includes freedom to change his religion or belief, and freedom, either alone or in community with others and in public or private, to manifest his religion or belief in teaching, practice, worship and observance." The United Nations Commission on Human Rights has continued to show the keenest interest in the subject. It currently has under discussion a draft of a wide-ranging "Declaration on the Elimination of all Forms of Religious Intolerance" which seeks to anticipate and condemn every possible kind of religious intolerance and persecution.

The World Council of Churches has similarly given categorical support to religious liberty as a universal principle ever since the founding of that body in 1948. In a lengthy declaration the Amsterdam Assembly of the World Council, which was held in that year, carefully analyzed the meaning of religious liberty and asserted that "the rights of religious freedom herein declared shall be recognized and observed for all persons without distinction as to race, color, sex, language, or religion, and without imposition of disability by virtue of legal provision or administrative acts."

As suggested above, it is also of the greatest significance that the Vatican Council has committed Roman Catholicism in a declaration supporting religious liberty. No matter how one may wish to criticize this declaration, strong movement in this direction by so vast and worldwide a religious community is profoundly important. The fact that Catholicism has often been associated with the denial of religious liberty only underscores this as evidence of an emerging worldwide consensus of the human community concerning the rightness of the principle. Significantly, the Declaration itself places great stress upon the "growing consciousness" of mankind that man must enjoy freedom if he is to be fully human, and that this "is particularly applicable in matters of religion." Both the Declaration and its principal architect, Father John Courtney Murray, strongly suggest that it is precisely the emerging human consciousness of the importance of freedom which has made it possible for the church to affirm religious liberty and still be true to its own nature. More will need to be said about the Declaration later. Here I am simply suggesting that its form and adoption are a kind of crowning evidence of the near-universal commitment to religious commitment to religious liberty which is emerging.

But despite this general commitment, there is by no means a universal consensus as to *why* there should be religious liberty. I have referred to the commitment as an "unconscious" one. This is not to say that people are committed to the idea without being aware of it, which would be absurd. But it is to say that people are committed to the idea without having consciously grounded it in relation to other things they believe. Indeed, it is probable that many people believe in religious liberty *in spite of* their other beliefs. Among the friends of religious liberty there are to be found adherents of groups which are exclusivistic, intolerant, and even arrogant. This is splendid witness to the contemporary power of the idea and to the universality of commitment to it. But it also suggests danger.

In the first place, it raises the question why we are supporting this principle. Is it really only because we find it expedient at the present time? Is it because we have already rejected elements in our own less tolerant traditions and that religious liberty now represents a more fundamental faith for some unknown reason? What will happen when there is a direct conflict between the two commitments – as when our religious group gains overwhelming social and political power and ventures to use that power against others?

In the second place, it raises the question how far we would be willing to apply religious liberty as a principle. Until we know the basis of the principle, the manner and extent of its application must remain uncertain. It may remain the kind of popular slogan which can mean one thing to one person but quite a different thing to others.

In the third place, it raises the question of the extent to which persons of different faiths can trust one another with respect to a common commitment to this principle.

There is little ground for hope that reflection about the basis of the principle will result in a universal consensus. Anticipating later discussion, it is possible that a kind of natural-law understanding based upon the common sense of mankind will be able to develop into a consensus. It is my hope that the idea of a responsible state might serve in this way. But so long as there are religious differences, persons reflecting such differences will need to come to grips with religious liberty *in terms of the deepest insight of their own traditions*. While this in itself will not yield a consensus (short of the unlikely future merging of all religious faiths or the conversion of everybody to any one faith), it can at least lead to communication and a form of reassurance. To illustrate, I am not a Marxist and the prospect of my becoming a Marxist is remote. But as a non-Marxist who must live in the same world with Marxists I would be reassured if good Marxist theoreticians could find convincing support for religious liberty at the center of their doctrine, and if this fresh interpretation of Marxism were to become accepted generally throughout the Communist movement. I would similarly be reassured by such support coming from the center of Buddhist, Moslem, and Hindu religious thought. And I assume that persons of such faiths would, in turn, be pleased to discover that Protestant and Catholic Christians and adherents of the various Jewish traditions find support for religious liberty at the center of their theologies. While this effort may never produce a universal consensus as to the religious basis for religious liberty, it cannot fail to promote greater security for the idea and greater clarity in its political application.

For the present, however, it must be said merely that the search for the most profound basis for religious liberty is on. The fate of the principle ultimately depends upon that search. If the age-old problem of religious persecution and coercion is to be abolished in our time, it will largely be because the principle of religious liberty has become grounded in the central beliefs and values of mankind.

John Rawls, "Equal Liberty" (1971)

In his controversial work on justice Harvard philosopher Rawls considers liberty "in connection with constitutional and legal restrictions. In these cases liberty is a certain structure of institutions, a certain system of public rules defining rights and duties" (p. 202). One cannot rely on the religious perspective to ensure liberty of conscience; this must be grounded in fairness – what is right for one is right for another.

SOURCE: John Rawls, *A Theory of Justice* (Cambridge, MA: Harvard University Press, 1971), pp. 208, 211–12, 214–16.

33 Equal Liberty of Conscience

. . . It may be said against the principle of equal liberty that religious sects, say, cannot acknowledge any principle at all for limiting their claims on one another. The duty to religious and divine law being absolute, no understanding among persons of different faiths is permissible from a religious point of view. Certainly men have often acted as if they held this doctrine. It is unnecessary, however, to argue against it. It suffices that if any principle can be agreed to, it ought to recognize the same beliefs and first principles that he does, and that by not doing so they are grievously in error and miss the way to their salvation. But an understanding of religious obligation and of philosophical and moral first principles shows that we cannot expect others to acquiesce in an inferior liberty. Much less can we ask them to recognize us as the proper interpreter of their religious duties or moral obligations. . . .

34 Toleration and the Common Interest

Justice as fairness provides, as we have now seen, strong arguments for an equal liberty of conscience. I shall assume that these arguments can be generalized in suitable ways to support the principles of equal liberty. Therefore the parties have good grounds for adopting this principle. It is obvious that these considerations are also important in making the case for the priority of liberty. From the perspective of the constitutional convention these arguments lead to the choice of a regime guaranteeing moral liberty and freedom of thought and belief, and of religious practice, although these may be regulated as always by the state's interest in public order and security. The state can favor no particular religion and no penalties or disabilities may be attached to any religious affiliation or lack thereof. The notion of a confessional state is rejected. Instead, particular associations may be freely organized as their members wish, and they may have their own internal life and discipline subject to the restriction that their members have a real choice of whether to continue their affiliation. The law protects the right of sanctuary in the sense that apostasy is not recognized, much less penalized, as a legal offense, any more than is having no religion at all. In these ways the state upholds moral and religious liberty.

Liberty of conscience is limited, everyone agrees, by the common interest in public order and security. This limitation itself is readily derivable from the contract point of view. First of all, acceptance of this limitation does not imply that public interests are in any sense superior to moral and religious interests; nor does it require that government view religious matters as things indifferent or claim the right to suppress philosophical beliefs whenever they conflict with affairs of state. The government has no authority to render associations either legitimate or illegitimate any more than it has this authority in regard to art and science. These matters are simply not within its competence as defined by a just constitution. Rather, given the principles of justice, the state must be understood as the association consisting of equal citizens. It does not concern itself with philosophical and religious doctrine but regulates individuals' pursuit of their moral and spiritual interests in accordance with principles to which they themselves would agree in an initial situation of equality. By exercising its powers in this way the government acts as the citizens' agent and satisfies the demands of their public conception of justice. Therefore the notion of the omnicompetent laicist state is also denied, since from the principles of justice it follows that government has neither the right nor the duty to do what it or a majority (or whatever) wants to do in questions of morals and religion. Its duty is limited to underwriting the conditions of equal moral and religious liberty. . . .

The characteristic feature of these arguments for liberty of conscience is that they are based solely on a conception of justice. Toleration is not derived from practical necessities or reasons of state. Moral and religious freedom follows from the principle of equal liberty; and assuming the priority of this principle, the only ground for denying the equal liberties is to avoid an even greater injustice, an even greater loss of liberty. Moreover, the argument does not rely on any special metaphysical or philosophical doctrine. It does not presuppose that all truths can be established by ways of thought recognized by common sense; nor does it hold that everything is, in some definable sense, a logical construction out of what can be observed or evidenced by rational scientific inquiry. The appeal is indeed to common sense, to generally shared ways of reasoning and plain facts accessible to all, but it is framed in such a way as to avoid these larger presumptions. Nor, on the other hand, does the case for liberty imply skepticism in philosophy or indifference to religion. Perhaps arguments for liberty of conscience can be given that have one or more of these doctrines as a premise. There is no reason to be surprised at this, since different arguments can have the same conclusion. But we need not pursue this question. The case for liberty is at least as strong as its strongest argument; the weak and fallacious ones are best forgotten. Those who would deny liberty of conscience cannot justify their action by condemning philosophical skepticism and indifference to religion, nor by appealing to social interests and affairs of state. The limitation of liberty is justified only when it is necessary for liberty itself, to prevent an invasion of freedom that would be still worse.

The parties in the constitutional convention, then, must choose a constitution that guarantees an equal liberty of conscience regulated solely by forms of argument generally accepted, and limited only when such argument establishes a reasonably certain interference with the essentials of public order. Liberty is governed by the necessary conditions for liberty itself. Now by this elementary principle alone many grounds of intolerance accepted in past ages are mistaken. Thus, for example, Aquinas justified the death penalty for heretics on the ground that it is a far graver matter to corrupt the faith, which is the life of the soul, than to counterfeit money which sustains life. So if it is just to put to death forgers and other criminals, heretics may *a fortiori* be similarly dealt with. But the premises on which Aquinas relies cannot be established by modes of reasoning commonly recognized. It is a matter of dogma that faith is the life of the soul and that the suppression of heresy, that is, departures from ecclesiastical authority, is necessary for the safety of souls.

Again, the reasons given for limited toleration often run afoul of this principle. Thus Rousseau thought that people would find it impossible to live in peace with those whom they regarded as damned, since to love them would be to hate God who punishes them. He believed that those who regard others as damned must either torment or convert them, and therefore sects preaching this conviction cannot be trusted to preserve civil peace. Rousseau would not, then, tolerate those religions which say that outside the church there is no salvation. But the consequences of such dogmatic belief which Rousseau conjectures are not borne out by experience. *A priori* psychological argument, however plausible, is not sufficient to abandon the principle of toleration, since justice holds that the disturbance to public order and to liberty itself must be securely established by common experience. There is, however, an important difference between Rousseau and Locke, who advocated a limited toleration, and Aquinas and the Protestant Reformers who did not. Locke and Rousseau limited liberty on the basis of what they supposed were clear and evident consequences for the public order. If Catholics and atheists were not to be tolerated it was because it seemed evident that such persons could not be relied upon to observe the bonds of civil society. Presumably a greater historical experience and a knowledge of the wider possibilities of political life would have convinced them that they were mistaken, or at least that their contentions were true only under special circumstances. But with Aquinas and the Protestant Reformers the grounds of intolerance are themselves a matter of faith, and this difference is more fundamental than the limits actually drawn to toleration. For when the denial of liberty is justified by an appeal to public order as evidenced by common sense, it is always possible to urge that the limits have been drawn incorrectly, that experience does not in fact justify the restriction. Where the suppression of liberty is based upon theological principles or matters of faith, no argument is possible. The one view recognizes the priority of principles which would be chosen in the original position whereas the other does not.

Notes

1 Niebuhr's citation is rather free, containing five different variants from the original.
2 *Ecumenical Review*, XIII (1961), pp. 409–20.

8

POST-WORLD WAR II DECLARATIONS

As Philip Wogaman has pointed out, it has become a commonplace in the modern world for societies to make some statement in favor of religious liberty. Included in this section are a number of declarations, originating both in religious and political contexts. One will find expressed in them many of the ideas canvassed in the first seven chapters of this anthology.

One of the most famous – and most significant – is the declaration *Dignitatis Humanae Personae*, from the Roman Catholic Vatican II Council. It is included here in its proper chronological location, but because it represents a vast area of its own, it is dealt with more specifically at that point.

LITERATURE: Herbert G. Wood, *Religious Liberty Today* (Cambridge: Cambridge University Press, 1949); Arcot Krishnaswami, *Study of Discrimination in the Matter of Religious Rights and Practices* (New York: United Nations, 1960); Angel F. Carrillo de Albornoz, *Religious Liberty: A General Review of the Present Situation in the World* (Geneva: World Council of Churches, 1964); Angel F. Carrillo de Albornoz, *Religious Liberty in the World: A General Review of the World Situation in 1965* (Geneva: World Council of Churches, 1966); Charles Humana (ed.), *World Human Rights Guide* (New York: Pico Press, 1984); Leonard Swidler (ed.), *Religious Liberty and Human Rights in Nations and in Religions* (Philadelphia, PA: Ecumenical Press, 1986); David Little (ed.), *Human Rights and the Conflict of Cultures: Western and Islamic Perspectives on Religious Liberty* (Columbia, SC: University of South Carolina Press, 1988); Elizabeth Odio Benito (ed.), *Elimination of all Forms of Intolerance and Discrimination based on Religion or Belief* (New York: United Nations, 1989); Ian Brownlie (ed.), *Basic Documents on Human Rights*, 3rd edn (Oxford: Clarendon Press, 1992); Ninan Koshy, *Religious Freedom in a Changing World* (Geneva: World Council of Churches Publications, 1992).

Churches of Great Britain, *Human Rights and Religious Freedom* (1947[1])

I *Religious Freedom and Secular Authority*

(1)   In Christian belief the essential meaning of all human freedom is free-dom to live according to the will of God, which includes the opportunity to exercise and develop in full measure the capacities with which He has endowed human nature, and a corresponding deliverance from conditions which thwart His purpose for mankind.

(2)   In the State we recognize an instrument to this end, to be honored as belonging to a natural order grounded in God's will, and to be wielded with responsibility towards God as the ultimate source and sanction of all authority. The primary functions of the State are to protect its citizens against attack from without and disorder within its own borders; to frame, administer, and uphold a body of law expressive of prevailing conceptions of right; and thus to secure to its citizens freedom from violence and injustice. The due discharge of these high and heavy responsibilities entitles the State to loyalty and obedience from the citizen who enjoys the freedoms thus secured.

Under modern conditions there is a tendency to entrust the State with further general responsibilities for the public good, notably in the fields of education, health, and employment. Believing that freedom from ignorance, freedom from disease, and freedom from want belong to the Divine purpose for men, we recognize that an obligation rests upon the citizen to cooperate loyally with the State in the pursuit of these good ends.

(3)   But, in Christian belief, the highest capacity of human nature, and the most important in that its due exercise gives meaning, direction and co-herence to all others, is that of knowing, obeying and worshipping God. This capacity for religion is innate in every human being; it can be exercised by the individual in his solitariness at any time and in all circumstances; and it must be thus exercised at certain critical turning-points in personal development. Yet the capacity for religion is essentially also a social capa-city requiring for its due development the disciplines and fellowship of a religious community, and demanding expression in appropriate forms of social life.

The freedom proper to religion is therefore two-fold: on the one hand, it consists in the individuals's right of direct approach to God, and response to God according to conscience, and of adherence to that religious community which in his private judgment shall best minister to this religious and moral welfare; on the other hand, it consists in the right of a religious community freely to order its own forms of worship and social life for the religious and moral welfare of its members, and to give open witness to the faith which informs its common life.

We claim that such religious freedom is the fundamental human freedom in which alone the true dignity of human personality can be fostered and its highest capacities flower. The right to it is therefore inalienable at all times and in all circumstances, and ought to be acknowledged and duly safeguarded by the State.

But we recognize that this right, while inalienable, is nevertheless in the following sense not an unconditional right: if the adherents to any form of religion so exercise their right or religious freedom as to disturb public order, or endanger public security, or outrage the basic moral conceptions which are essential to both, they do so at their own risk, and the State to which they belong, or in which they are resident, is entitled to invoke the sanctions of law against them. Yet, in the light of history, it must be added that States sometimes unjustifiably curtail religious freedom on an alleged plea of its abuse.

Thus understood and subject to the limit thus indicated, freedom of religion is not a special privilege claimed for minority groups, but rather a universal human right. As such, it ought to be embodied in any International Bill of Rights which may be framed, and to be under-written by all the signatories.

II A Charter of Religious Freedom

When analyzed more closely and reduced to terms of particular civil rights, religious freedom will be found to require safeguards at least as comprehensive and as specific as those contained in a charter such as the following:

1 Freedom of religion is an essential and integral aspect of human freedom. It includes the freedom of all human beings to choose for themselves their religious belief and adherence, and to change them if they so desire.

2 The rights which guarantee the full development of human beings, in the integrity and dignity of their human personality, include the religious rights not only of freedom to worship according to conscience, but also of freedom to educate, to propagate and to persuade, and to conduct social and charitable activities.

3   The rights of meeting guaranteed by a community to its members
    include the right of meeting for the purpose of worship according to
    conscience.
4   The rights of association guaranteed by a community to its members
    include the right of association for religious purposes – that is to say,
    not only for the purpose of worship according to conscience, but also
    for the purposes of religious education, propagation and persua-
    sion, and of social and charitable activities. Religious associations are
    accordingly free, on the same basis as other associations and subject
    to the same limits imposed by the necessities of public order, security
    and morality, to acquire and hold property, and to act generally for
    the fulfillment of their purposes.
5   The rights of freedom of expression of thought (by speech, writing,
    printing and publishing) guaranteed by a community to its members
    include the rights of expression of religious thought, of the propaga-
    tion of religious belief, and of religious persuasion, subject to the
    same limits as are imposed on the general freedom of expression of
    thought by the necessities of public order, security and morality.
6   The rights of children to receive instruction and education with a
    due regard to their freedom include the right to receive religious
    instruction and education when such instruction and education is
    desired by their parents.
7   The rights of religious freedom – in meeting for worship, in associ-
    ation, in the expression of thought, and instruction, education, and
    persuasion – include the right of persons and groups to be guar-
    anteed against legal provisions and administrative acts which are
    calculated to impose disabilities on grounds of religion.

III   Explication of Certain Points in the Charter

The experience of the Committee, gathered from many parts of the world,
puts it beyond doubt that, if religious freedom is to be materially effective,
the last provision in the Charter given above requires considerable elaboration, especially as it affects the provisions contained in the first, fourth and
sixth paragraphs.

1   *The individual's right to choose or change his religious belief and adherence*
will not be materially effective if by reason of its exercise he should:

(a)   lose complete and full protection of life and liberty;
(b)   forfeit equality before the law in respect of any civil or political right;

(c) be deemed to be under a legal incapacity to take any share in a succession to property or to take under a will.

2 *The right of association for religious purposes* will be materially ineffective if it omits any one of the following specific rights of religious communities:

(a) to be recognized as legal corporations;

(b) to appoint without hindrance their own leaders and officers;

(c) to train their leaders and workers in theological institutions, and in other ways;

(d) to erect, repair and lease buildings for worship and for educational, social and charitable purposes, to open and maintain institutions for such purposes, and to appoint their own staff in them, provided their qualifications conform to the minimum technical standards required by the State in such institutions;

(e) to maintain, in religious, educational, social and charitable activities, free connexion with their co-religionists in other countries, and to receive from other countries contributions towards such activities without deduction;

(f) to enjoy, without discrimination, all privileges which are given to any religion in respect of taxation, customs dues, the ownership, sale and transfer of property, etc.

3 *The right of religious instruction and education* will be materially ineffective if it is not safeguarded by the following specific provisions:

(a) no minor shall be taught a religion other than that of his parents or guardians without their consent;

(b) in any State which contains substantial religious minorities and in which religious instruction is given in the State schools, there shall be opportunity for the minority communities to provide special religious teaching for their own children;

(c) all citizens shall have the right, whether individually or in association with others, to open schools and other educational institutions for members of their own religious communities and for others in which:

(i) they may teach their own religion freely, subject to a conscience clause in the case of members of other faiths;

(ii) they are free from the obligation to teach any religion, *qua* religion, other than their own;

(iii) they may appoint their own staff in all subjects, provided their scholastic qualifications are adequate;

(iv) if the schools are unaided, they may follow their own cur-
      ricula and their own methods of instruction, provided these
      do not contravene Government requirements regarding
      health and sanitation, financial administration and technical
      efficiency;

(v)   they may participate in Government grants to non-govern-
      ment schools without discrimination on religious grounds;

(vi) their students are admitted without discrimination to Gov-
      ernment examinations.

IV   The Problem of Religious Minorities

(1) Religious freedom is a matter of groups as well as of individuals;
indeed it is perhaps even more a matter of groups as well as of individuals.
As a matter of groups, it raises – and has always raised in the course of
history – the problem of religious minorities. The dominant religious group
of a territory or state, confronted by other and smaller groups, has often
felt impelled either to demand conformity or to impose disabilities. That
impulse partly proceeds from an instinct, common to all groups, directed to
the establishment of what may be called a common pattern; but the instinct
is reinforced, and may even seem to be sublimated, when a religious group
has the additional sense of being a custodian of truth, and feels itself moved
by the motive of making the truth prevail. Nor are group-instincts and the
sense of a special custodianship of truth the only factors. Motives and
impulses are generally mixed in the tangle of human affairs; and an issue
which at first sight may seem to be purely a religious issue will often be
found, on further inquiry, to be complicated by other factors. Religious
feeling, consciously or unconsciously, may be mixed with nationalism; and
it may similarly be mixed with racialism. A nation, for example, in which
the predominant religious group is Mohammedan may feel that Mohammedanism is the core of its nationality; and if such a nation should also
cherish the sense of a racial kinship with other nations in which the predominant religious group is equally Mohammedan, it may proceed to feel
that Mohammedanism is not only the core of its own nationality, but also
the core of a general racial unity which draws the kindred nations together.
The problem of religious minorities may thus be something more than a
problem of religion.

(2) In the course of history three stages or methods may be traced in the
handling of the problem of religious minorities.

The first stage or method is one which remits the handling of the problem to the internal jurisdiction of each State. In England, for example, there was a long struggle between the Established Church and the Dissenting Churches; and that struggle formed a great issue of English domestic politics. Gradually the demand for conformity and the imposition of disabilities were abandoned; but the process took more than two centuries. Eventually, however, by a process of domestic settlement, the problem may be said to have reached a solution; and the assurance of complete freedom and equality before the law did justice, and brought contentment to English religious minorities. The question may naturally be raised why the problems of religious minorities should not similarly be treated as a matter of internal jurisdiction in *all* States. The answer may perhaps be found in a brief review of the actual exercise of such jurisdiction during the course of modern history. Such a review suggests that the English precedent, if it be a precedent, does not afford a basis of general policy. Internal jurisdiction has too often resulted in measures which are repugnant to the general conscience of men. Sometimes religious minorities have been simply expelled: sometimes an attempt has been made, short of this extreme policy, to effect an interchange of minorities; but in either case minorities so treated have been torn up from their roots in the soil and deprived of old social attachments. Sometimes, again, minorities have been retained; but the retained minorities have been either subjected to measures intended to absorb them by force into the life of the majority group, or condemned to live a life of segregation on an inferior level of citizenship and rights, with various disabilities – political, civil, social and economic. Not that these policies of expulsion, or compulsory absorption, or enforced segregation, have been generally or uniformly pursued. States have varied in their attitudes to religious minorities; and if some States have followed these policies, others – alike in the East and West – have followed a policy of justice, and of the freedom and equality of all religious confessions. In the same way as States have varied in their attitude to minorities, minorities also have varied in their attitude to the State. Some have shown loyalty to the States in which they were contained, and a readiness to co-operate with their authorities: others, looking to larger bodies of co-religionists in other States, and with a mixture of motives which might include secular factors of nationality or race as well as the motive of religion, have been intransigent. There are minorities which are apt to think in terms of their rights, and to forget the corresponding duties.

(3) In this position, and under these conditions, a second method of handling the problem of religious minorities emerged. This is a method of international action which takes the form of stipulations contained in

treaties. A number of causes led to the adoption of this form of international action. Under modern conditions of communication and commerce, which bring all States into closer contact, a problem of religious minorities in one State may present itself clearly and vividly to their co-religionists in other States: it may affect, and even embitter, international relations. Again, and on a higher level, there may also be traced – not only in the present century, but also in the nineteenth – the growth of a general public opinion, common to many States, which deprecates, and may even resent injustices and inequalities (or what it regards as such) inflicted upon minorities in contravention of its own standards. Under the influence of such causes the principle began to be asserted that the relations between States and minorities (among them religious minorities) cannot be left entirely to the internal jurisdiction of all the States concerned. This principle (which had already been at work in the nineteenth century) was adopted in some of the treaties concluded after the war of 1914–18. In these treaties, and also in the mandates formulated under the Covenant of the League of Nations, specific provisions were incorporated for the protection of minorities; and it was stipulated, in some cases, that issues raised by the treatment of minorities were matters of international concern affecting the League of Nations.

The purpose of these provisions was to ensure (1) that the States affected by them should recognize the rights of minorities in their constitution and laws, and (2) that their courts and administrative officials should give actual and practical effect to such constitutional and legal recognition. The second of these purposes was no less important than the first. Much was bound to depend on the action of courts and administrative officials in the actual interpretation and the practical enforcement of constitutional and legal provisions. If they took their duties seriously, they would make the safeguards for the liberty and equality of religious minorities effective and valuable. If, on the other hand, they gave a large latitude to considerations of "public order," and brought such considerations largely to bear on their treatment of religious minorities, they might render the safeguards for these minorities contained in constitutional and legal provisions comparatively ineffective.

In any case, and even if this difficulty is surmounted, the handling of the problem of religious minorities by the method of international action which takes the form of stipulations contained in treaties presents other difficulties. A State bound by such stipulations may resent them, as an infringement of its "national sovereignty" – especially when it sees them peculiarly and (as it thinks) invidiously imposed on itself, while many other States are free from any such obligation. Again the handling of the problem of religious minorities by the method of treaty brings it into the sphere of diplomacy, and may thus subject it to the considerations of national interest and national policy, which inevitably play their part in the conduct of diplomacy. It would thus appear that something further than international action proceeding through treaty stipulations is necessary. Such action is indeed an advance on the unfettered action of the internal jurisdiction of States. But it seems to invite and demand a still further advance.

(4) A third method of handling the problem of religious minorities is now beginning to emerge in the thought and discussion of today; and this is the method which invites and demands exploration. Briefly it is the method of making a just treatment for religious minorities incumbent on all States alike, without any particular and possibly invidious reference to particular States. This would involve, as a speaker in the British Parliament has recently suggested, some general declaration by all the United Nations; some general statement of a standard to which all the members of the United Nations would be expected, and would expect one another, to conform: and in the last resort, some application of sanctions by the collective authority of the United Nations in the event of failure to conform. This would be a method of international action which was fully and entirely international; and it would transcend the method of international action which takes the form of stipulations in treaties binding only on particular States. The best hope may thus be argued to be, as the Archbishop of York recently stated in Parliament, "to find a place in the proposed Charter or Bill of Human Rights for a declaration insisting on civil and religious freedom for individuals and minorities." Whether or no any sanction were added, such a declaration, proceeding from the whole body of the United Nations, would be a new milestone of advance. It would be a Magna Carta of the rights of religious minorities; and it might well be the case that if breaches of that Magna Carta were reported to and ventilated in the meetings of the United Nations, such report and ventilation would themselves be sufficient sanction.

The conclusion of the whole matter would thus seem to be this – that the British public should strengthen the hands of its government, and urge it to associate with other governments, in pressing for the formulation of a Declaration of Human Rights to which all States would be invited to become signatories. Such a Declaration should include, as one of its articles, the rights of religious minorities to profess and practise their faith freely, on terms of equality with religious majorities, with no disabilities (whether political, legal, social or economic), and with a full recognition of all the safeguards proposed in sections II and III above.

It only remains to add that in urging the need of a Declaration of the Human Rights which it believes should be secured to all religious groups in all States, the Joint Committee on Religious Liberty is concerned *not* with privileges claimed for any particular religious minority (Christian,

Mohammedan, Jewish, or other), but with the creation of a general standard, and the formulation of general principles of action. It would deprecate, and deprecate strongly, the conducting and carrying on of political or other non-religious activities by any religious minority on the plea of religious rights, as it would equally deprecate any curtailing of the religious rights of such a minority under the plea and on the ground of public order, which must indeed always be maintained, but should never be made a plea for curtailing the genuine exercise of religious rights by any religious group.

World Council of Churches, *Declaration on Religious Liberty* (Amsterdam, 1948[2])

An essential element in a good international order is freedom of religion. This is an implication of the Christian faith and of the worldwide nature of Christianity. Christians, therefore, view the question of religious freedom as an international problem. They are concerned that religious freedom be everywhere secured. In pleading for this freedom, they do not ask for any privilege to be granted to Christians that is denied to others. While the liberty with which Christ has set men free can neither be given nor destroyed by any government, Christians, because of that inner freedom, are both jealous of its outward expression and solicitous that all men should have freedom in religious life. The nature and destiny of man by virtue of this creation, redemption and calling, and man's activities in family, State and culture establish limits beyond which the government cannot with impunity go. The rights which Christian discipleship demands are such as are good for all men, and no nation has ever suffered by reason of granting such liberties. Accordingly:

> The rights of religious freedom herein declared shall be recognized and observed for all persons without distinction as to race, color, sex, language, or religion, and without imposition of disabilities by virtue of legal provision or administrative acts.

(1) *Every person has the right to determine his own faith and creed.*
   The right to determine faith and creed involves both the process whereby a person adheres to a belief and the process whereby he changes his belief. It includes the right to receive instruction and education.
   This right becomes meaningful when man has the opportunity of access to information. Religious, social and political institutions have the obligation to permit the mature individual to relate himself to sources of information in such a way as to allow personal religious decision and belief.

The right to determine one's belief is limited by the right of parents to decide sources of information to which their children shall have access. In the process of reaching decisions, everyone ought to take into account his higher self-interests and the implications of his beliefs for the well-being of his fellow-men.

(2) *Every person has the right to express his religious beliefs in worship, teaching and practice, and to proclaim the implications of his beliefs for relationships in a social or political community.*

The right of religious expression includes freedom of worship both public and private; freedom to place information at the disposal of others by processes of teaching, preaching and persuasion; and freedom to pursue such activities as are dictated by conscience. It also includes freedom to express implications of belief for society and its government.

This right requires freedom from arbitrary limitation of religious expression in all means of communication, including speech, press, radio, motion pictures and art. Social and political institutions should grant immunity from discrimination and from legal disability on grounds of expressed religious conviction, at least to the point where recognized community interests are adversely affected.

Freedom of religious expression is limited by the rights of parents to determine the religious point of view to which their children shall be exposed. It is further subject to such limitations, prescribed by law, as are necessary to protect order and welfare, morals and the rights and freedoms of others. Each person must recognize the rights of others to express their beliefs and must have respect for authority at all times, even when conscience forces him to take issue with the people who are in authority or with the position they advocate.

(3) *Every person has the right to associate with others and to organize with them for religious purposes.*

This right includes freedom to form religious organizations, to seek membership in religious organizations, and to sever relationship with religious organizations.

It requires that the rights of association and organization guaranteed by a community to its members include the right of forming associations for religious purposes.

It is subject to the same limits imposed on all associations by non-discriminatory laws.

(4) *Every religious organization, formed or maintained by action in accordance with the rights of the individual persons, has the right to determine its policies and practices for the accomplishment of its chosen purposes.*

The rights which are claimed for the individual in his exercise of religious liberty become the rights of the religious organization, including the right to determine its faith and creed; to engage in religious worship, both public and private; to teach, educate, preach and persuade; to express implications of belief for society and government.

To these will be added certain corporate rights which derive from the rights of individual persons, such as the right: to determine the form of organization, its government and conditions of membership; to select and train its own officers, leaders and workers; to publish and circulate religious literature; to carry on service and missionary activities at home and abroad; to hold property and to collect funds; to co-operate and to unite with other religious bodies at home and in other lands, including freedom to invite or to send personnel beyond national frontiers and to give or to receive financial assistance; to use such facilities, open to all citizens or associations, as will make possible the accomplishment of religious ends.

In order that these rights may be realized in social experience, the State must grant to religious organizations and their members the same rights which it grants to other organizations, including the right of self-government, of public meeting, of speech, of press and publication, of holding property, of collecting funds, of travel, of ingress and egress, and generally of administering their own affairs.

The community has the right to require obedience to non-discriminatory laws passed in the interest of public order and well-being. In the exercise of its rights, a religious organization must respect the rights of other religious organizations and must safeguard the corporate and individual rights of the entire community.

Universal Declaration of Human Rights (1948[3])

Article 2:   Everyone is entitled to all the rights and freedoms set forth in this Declaration, without distinction of any kind, such as race, color, sex, language, religion, political or other opinion, national or social origin, property, birth or other status.

Article 16:   (1) Men and women of full age, without any limitation due to race, nationality or religion, have the right to marry and to found a family. . . .

Article 18:   Everyone has the right to freedom of thought, conscience and religion; this right includes freedom to change his religion or belief, and freedom, either alone or in community with others and in public or private, to manifest his religion or belief in teaching, practice, worship and observance.

Article 19: Everyone has the right to freedom of opinion and expression; this right includes freedom to hold opinions without interference and to seek, receive and impart information and ideas through any media and regardless of frontiers.

Article 26: (2) Education shall be directed to the full development of the human personality and to the strengthening of respect for human rights and fundamental freedoms. It shall promote understanding, tolerance and friendship among all nations, racial or religious groups, and shall further the activities of the United Nations for the maintenance of peace.

Vatican II, *Dignitatis Humanae Personae* (1965)

Of the *Decree on Religious Freedom* (Vatican II) J. C. Murray wrote that its highly controversial nature was due to the challenge it seemed to pose in the area of the development of doctrine. "The notion of development, not the notion of religious freedom, was the real sticking-point for many of those who opposed the *Declaration* even to the end. The course of the development between the *Syllabus of Errors* (1864) and *Dignitatis Humanae Personae* (1965) [i.e., the *Decree on Religious Freedom*] still remains to be explained by theologians" (Abbott (ed.), *Documents of Vatican II*, p. 673). Another commentator says that the concept was generally granted by Roman Catholics, the church's position being nothing more than "a relic of a nineteenth-century polemic" (Regan, *Conflict and Consensus*, p. 1). This is not quite obvious.[4] The declaration represented a reversal of centuries of official intolerance by the church both in its own right and in its support for state action against Christian dissent. As such, it is one of the landmark documents in the history described by this anthology.

SOURCE: Walter M. Abbott (ed.), *The Documents of Vatican II* (New York: Guild Press, 1966), pp. 675–96. Reproduced with permission of America Press, Inc., 106 West 56th Street, New York, NY 10019; © 1966, all rights reserved.

LITERATURE: John Courtney Murray (ed.), *Religious Liberty: An End and a Beginning* (New York: Macmillan, 1966); H. E. Cardinale, *Religious Tolerance, Freedom and Inter-Group Relations in the Light of Vatican Council II* (London: Council of Christians and Jews, 1966); Richard J. Regan, *Conflict and Consensus: Religious Freedom and the Second Vatican Council* (New York: Macmillan, 1967); H. Vorgrimler (ed.), *Commentary on the Documents of Vatican II*, 5 vols (Montreal: Palm Publishers, 1967–9); for a Protestant perspective, Philip Wogaman, *Protestant Faith and Religious Liberty* (Nashville, TN: Abingdon Press, 1967), pp. 30–41; Albert C. Outler, *Methodist Observer at Vatican II* (Westminster, MD: Newman Press, 1967).

Declaration on Religious Freedom

On the right of the person and of communities to social and civil freedom in matters religious

> Paul, bishop
> Servant of the servants of God
> together with the fathers of the sacred council
> for everlasting memory

(1) A sense of the dignity of the human person has been impressing itself more and more deeply on the consciousness of contemporary man. And the demand is increasingly made that men should act on their own judgment, enjoying and making use of a responsible freedom, not driven by coercion but motivated by a sense of duty. The demand is also made that constitutional limits should be set to the powers of government, in order that there may be no encroachment on the rightful freedom of the person and of associations.

This demand for freedom in human society chiefly regards the quest for the values proper to the human spirit. It regards, in the first place, the free exercise of religion in society.

This Vatican Synod takes careful note of these desires in the minds of men. It proposes to declare them to be greatly in accord with truth and justice. To this end, it searches into the sacred tradition and doctrine of the Church – the treasury out of which the Church continually brings forth new things that are in harmony with the things that are old.

First, this sacred Synod professes its belief that God himself has made known to mankind the way in which men are to serve Him, and thus be saved in Christ and come to blessedness. We believe that this one true religion subsists in the catholic and apostolic Church, to which the Lord Jesus committed the duty of spreading it abroad among all men. Thus He spoke to the apostles: "Go, therefore, and make disciples of all nations, baptizing them in the name of the Father, and of the son, and of the Holy Spirit, teaching them to observe all that I have commanded you" [Matthew 28: 9–20]. On their part, all men are bound to seek the truth, especially in what concerns God and His Church, and to embrace the truth they come to know, and to hold fast to it.

This sacred Synod likewise professes its belief that it is upon the human conscience that these obligations fall and exert their binding force. The truth cannot impose itself except by virtue of its own truth, as it makes its entrance into the mind at once quietly and with power. Religious freedom, in turn, which men demand as necessary to fulfill their duty to worship God, has to do with immunity from coercion in civil society. Therefore, it leaves untouched traditional Catholic doctrine on the moral duty of men and societies toward the true religion and toward the one Church of Christ.

Over and above all this, in taking up the matter of religious freedom this sacred Synod intends to develop the doctrine of recent Popes on the inviolable rights of the human person and on the constitutional order of society.

I General Principle of Religious Freedom

(2) This Vatican Synod declares that the human person has a right to religious freedom. This freedom means that all men are to be immune from coercion on the part of individuals or of social groups and of any human power, in such wise that in matters religious no one is to be forced to act in a manner contrary to his own beliefs. Nor is anyone to be restrained from acting in accordance with his own beliefs, whether privately or publicly, whether alone or in association with others, within due limits.

The Synod further declares that the right to religious freedom has its foundation in the very dignity of the human person, as this dignity is known through the revealed Word of God and by reason itself. This right of the human person to religious freedom is to be recognized in the constitutional law whereby society is governed. Thus it is to become a civil right.

It is in accordance with their dignity as persons – that is, beings endowed with reason and free will and therefore privileged to bear personal responsibility – that all men should be at once impelled by nature and also bound by a moral obligation to seek the truth, especially religious truth. They are also bound to adhere to the truth, once it is known, and to order their whole lives in accord with the demands of truth.

However, men cannot discharge these obligations is a manner in keeping with their own nature unless they enjoy immunity from external coercion as well as psychological freedom. Therefore, the right to religious freedom has its foundation, not in the subjective disposition of the person, but in his very nature. In consequence, the right to this immunity continues to exist even in those who do not live up to their obligation of seeking the truth and adhering to it. Nor is the exercise of this right to be impeded, provided that the just requirements of public order are observed.

(3)   Further light is shed on the subject if one considers that the highest norm of human life is the divine law – eternal, objective, and universal – whereby God orders, directs, and governs the entire universe and all the ways of the human community, by a plan conceived in wisdom and love. Man has been made by God to participate in this law, with the result that, under the gentle disposition of divine Providence, he can come to perceive ever increasingly the unchanging truth. Hence every man has the duty, and therefore the right, to seek the truth in matters religious, in order that he may with prudence form for himself right and true judgments of conscience, with the use of all suitable means.

Truth, however, is to be sought after in a manner proper to the dignity of the human person and his social nature. The inquiry is to be free, carried on with the aid of teaching or instruction, communication, and dialogue. In the course of these, men explain to one another the truth they have discovered, or think they have discovered, in order thus to assist one another in the quest for truth. Moreover, as the truth is discovered, it is by a personal assent that men are to adhere to it.

On his part, man perceives and acknowledges the imperatives of the divine law through the mediation of conscience. In all his activity a man is bound to follow his conscience faithfully, in order that he may come to God, for whom he was created. It follows that he is not to be forced to act in a manner contrary to his conscience. Nor, on the other hand, is he to be restrained from acting in accordance with his conscience, especially in matters religious.

For, of its very nature, the exercise of religion consists before all else in those internal, voluntary, and free acts whereby man sets the course of his life directly toward God. No merely human power can either command or prohibit acts of this kind.

However, the social nature of man itself requires that he should give external expression to his internal acts of religion: that he should participate with others in matters religious; that he should profess his religion in community. Injury, therefore, is done to the human person and to the very order established by God for human life, if the free exercise of religion is denied in society when the just requirements of public order do not so require.

There is a further consideration. The religious acts whereby men, in private and in public and out of a sense of personal conviction, direct their lives to God transcend by their very nature the order of terrestrial and temporal affairs. Government, therefore, ought indeed to take account of the religious life of the people and show it favor, since the function of government is to make provision for the common welfare. However, it would clearly transgress the limits set to its power were it to presume to direct or inhibit acts that are religious.

(4)   The freedom of immunity from coercion in matters religious which is the endowment of persons as individuals is also to be recognized as their right when they act in community. Religious bodies are a requirement of the social nature both of man and of religion itself.

Provided the just requirements of public order are observed, religious bodies rightfully claim freedom in order that they may govern themselves according to their own norms, honor the Supreme Being in public worship, assist their members in the practice of the religious life, strengthen them by instruction, and promote institutions in which they may join together for the purpose of ordering their own lives in accordance with their religious principles.

Religious bodies also have the right not to be hindered, either by legal measures or by administrative action on the part of government, in the selection, training, appointment, and transferral of their own ministers, in communicating with religious authorities and communities abroad, in erecting buildings for religious purposes, and in the acquisition and use of suitable funds or properties.

Religious bodies also have the right not to be hindered in their public teaching and witness to their faith, whether by the spoken or by the written word. However, in spreading religious faith and in introducing religious practices, everyone ought at all times to refrain from any manner of action which might seem to carry a hint of coercion or a kind of persuasion that would be dishonorable or unworthy, especially when dealing with poor or uneducated people. Such a manner of action would have to be considered an abuse of one's own right and a violation of the right of others.

In addition, it comes within the meaning of religious freedom that religious bodies should not be prohibited from freely undertaking to show the special value of their doctrine in what concerns the organization of society and the inspiration of the whole of human activity. Finally, the social nature of man and the very nature of religion afford the foundation of the right of men freely to hold meetings and to establish educational, cultural, charitable, and social organizations, under the impulse of their own religious sense.

(5)   Since the family is a society in its own original right, it has the right freely to live its own domestic religious life under the guidance of parents. Parents, moreover, have the right to determine, in accordance with their own religious beliefs, the kind of religious education that their children are to receive.

Government, in consequence, must acknowledge the right of parents to make a genuinely free choice of schools and of other means of education. The use of this freedom of choice is not to be made a reason for imposing unjust burdens on parents, whether directly or indirectly. Besides, the rights of parents are violated if their children are forced to attend lessons or instruction which are not in agreement with their religious beliefs. The same is true if a single system of education, from which all religious formation is excluded, is imposed upon all.

(6)   The common welfare of society consists in the entirety of those conditions of social life under which men enjoy the possibility of achieving their own perfection in a certain fullness of measure and also with some relative ease. Hence this welfare consists chiefly in the protection of the rights, and in the performance of the duties, of the human person. Therefore, the care of the right to religious freedom devolves upon the people as a whole, upon social groups, upon government, and upon the Church and other religious Communities, in virtue of the duty of all toward the common welfare, and in the manner proper to each.

The protection and promotion of the inviolable rights of man ranks among the essential duties of government. Therefore, government is to assume the safeguard of the religious freedom of all its citizens, in an effective manner, by just laws and by other appropriate means. Government is also to help create conditions favorable to the fostering of religious life, in order that the people may be truly enabled to exercise their religious rights and to fulfill their religious duties, and also in order that society itself may profit by the moral qualities of justice and peace which have their origin in men's faithfulness to God and to His holy will.

If, in view of peculiar circumstances obtaining among certain peoples, special legal recognition is given in the constitutional order of society to one religious body, it is at the same time imperative that the right of all citizens and religious bodies to religious freedom should be recognized and made effective in practice.

Finally, government is to see to it that the equality of citizens before the law, which is itself an element of the common welfare, is never violated for religious reasons whether openly or covertly. Nor is there to be discrimination among citizens.

It follows that a wrong is done when government imposes upon its people, by force or fear or other means, the profession or repudiation of any religion, or when it hinders men from joining or leaving a religious body. All the more is it a violation of the will of God and of the sacred rights of the person and the family of nations, when force is brought to bear in any way in order to destroy or repress religion, either in the whole of mankind or in a particular country or in a specific community.

(7)   The right to religious freedom is exercised in human society; hence its exercise is subject to certain regulatory norms. In the use of all freedoms,

the moral principle of personal and social responsibility is to be observed. In the exercise of their rights, individual men and social groups are bound by the moral law to have respect both for the rights of others and for their own duties toward others and for the common welfare of all. Men are to deal with their fellows in justice and civility.

Furthermore, society has the right to defend itself against possible abuses committed on pretext of freedom of religion. It is the special duty of government to provide this protection. However, government is not to act in arbitrary fashion or in an unfair spirit of partisanship. Its action is to be controlled by juridical norms which are in conformity with the objective moral order.

These norms arise out of the need for effective safeguard of the rights of all citizens and for peaceful settlement of conflicts of rights. They flow from the need for an adequate care of genuine public peace, which comes about when men live together in good order and in true justice. They come, finally, out of the need for a proper guardianship of public morality. These matters constitute the basic component of the common welfare: they are what is meant by public order.

For the rest, the usages of society are to be the usages of freedom in their full range. These require that the freedom of man be respected as far as possible, and curtailed only when and in so far as necessary.

(8) Many pressures are brought to bear upon men of our day, to the point where the danger arises lest they lose the possibility of acting on their own judgment. On the other hand, not a few can be found who seem inclined to use the name of freedom as the pretext for refusing to submit to authority and for making light of the duty of obedience.

Therefore, this Vatican Synod urges everyone, especially those who are charged with the task of educating others, to do their utmost to form men who will respect the moral order and be obedient to lawful authority. Let them form men too who will be lovers of true freedom – men, in other words, who will come to decisions on their own judgment and the light of truth, govern their activities with a sense of responsibility, and strive after what is true and right, willing always to join with others in cooperative effort.

Religious freedom, therefore, ought to have this further purpose and aim, namely, that men may come to act with greater responsibility in fulfilling their duties in community life.

II *Religious Freedom in the Light of Revelation*

(9) The declaration of this Vatican Synod on the right of man to religious freedom has its foundation in the dignity of the person. The requirements

of this dignity have come to be more adequately known to human reason through centuries of experience. What is more, this doctrine of freedom has roots in divine revelation, and for this reason Christians are bound to respect it all the more conscientiously.

Revelation does not indeed affirm in so many words the right of man to immunity from external coercion in matters religious. It does, however, disclose the dignity of the human person in its full dimensions. It gives evidence of the respect which Christ showed toward the freedom with which man is to fulfill his duty of belief in the Word of God. It gives us lessons too in the spirit which disciples of such a Master ought to make their own and to follow in every situation.

Thus, further light is cast on the general principles upon which the doctrine of this Declaration on Religious Freedom is based. In particular, religious freedom in society is entirely consonant with the freedom of the act of Christian faith.

(10)   It is one of the major tenets of Catholic doctrine that man's response to God in faith must be free. Therefore no one is to be forced to embrace the Christian faith against his own will. This doctrine is contained in the Word of God and it was constantly proclaimed by the Fathers of the Church. The act of faith is of its very nature a free act. Man, redeemed by Christ the Savior and through Christ Jesus called to be God's adopted son, cannot give his adherence to God revealing Himself unless the Father draw him to offer to God the reasonable and free submission of faith.

It is therefore completely in accord with the nature of faith that in matters religious every manner of coercion on the part of men should be excluded. In consequence, the principle of religious freedom makes no small contribution to the creation of an environment in which men can without hindrance be invited to Christian faith, and embrace it of their own free will, and profess it effectively in their whole manner of life.

(11)   God calls men to serve Him in spirit and in truth. Hence they are bound in conscience but they stand under no compulsion. God has regard for the dignity of the human person whom He himself created; man is to be guided by his own judgment and he is to enjoy freedom.

This truth appears at its height in Christ Jesus, in whom God perfectly manifested Himself and His ways with men. Christ is our Master and our Lord. He is also meek and humble of heart. And in attracting and inviting His disciples he acted patiently. He wrought miracles to shed light on His teaching and to establish its truth. But His intention was to rouse faith in His hearers and to confirm them in faith, not to exert coercion upon them.

He did indeed denounce the unbelief of some who listened to Him; but He left vengeance to God in expectation of the day of judgment. When He sent His apostles into the world, He said to them: "He who believes and is baptized shall be saved, but he who does not believe shall be condemned" [Mark 16: 16]; but He Himself, noting that cockle had been sown amid the wheat, gave orders that both should be allowed to grow until the harvest time, which will come at the end of the world.

He refused to be a political Messiah, ruling by force; He preferred to call Himself the Son of Man, who came "to serve and to give his life as a ransom for many" [Mark 10: 45]. He showed Himself the perfect Servant of God; "a bruised reed he will not break, and a smoking wick he will not quench" [Matthew 12: 20].

He acknowledged the power of government and its rights, when He commanded that tribute be given to Caesar. But He gave clear warning that the higher rights of God are to be kept inviolate: "Render, therefore, to Caesar the things that are Caesar's, and to God the things that are God's" [Matthew 22: 21].

In the end, when He completed on the cross the work of redemption whereby He achieved salvation and true freedom for men, He also brought His revelation to completion. He bore witness to the truth, but He refused to impose the truth by force on those who spoke against it. Not by force of blows does His rule assert its claims. Rather, it is established by witnessing to the truth and by hearing the truth, and it extends its dominion by the love whereby Christ, lifted up on the cross, draws all men to Himself.

Taught by the word and example of Christ, the apostles followed the same way. From the very origins of the Church the disciples of Christ strove to convert men to faith in Christ as the Lord – not, however, by the use of coercion or by devices unworthy of the gospel, but by the power, above all, of the Word of God. Steadfastly they proclaimed to all the plan of God our Savior, "who wishes all men to be saved and to come to the knowledge of the truth" [1 Timothy 2: 4]. At the same time, however, they showed respect for weaker souls even though these persons were in error. Thus they made it plain that "every one of us will render an account of himself to God" [Romans 14: 12], and for this reason is bound to obey his conscience.

Like Christ Himself, the apostles were unceasingly bent upon bearing witness to the truth of God. They showed special courage in speaking "the word of God with boldness" [Acts 4: 31] before the people and their rulers. With a firm faith they held that the gospel is indeed the power of God unto salvation for all who believe. Therefore they rejected all "carnal weapons." They followed the example of the gentleness and respectfulness of Christ. And they preached the Word of God in the full confidence that there was

resident in this Word itself a divine power able to destroy all the forces
arrayed against God and to bring men to faith in Christ and to His service.
As the Master, so too the apostles recognized legitimate civil authority.
"For there exists no authority except from God," the Apostle teaches, and
therefore commands: "Let everyone be subject to the higher authorities
. . . he who resists the authority resists the ordinance of God" [Romans
13: 1–2].

At the same time, however, they did not hesitate to speak out against
governing powers which set themselves in opposition to the holy will of
God: "We must obey God rather than men" [Acts 5: 29]. This is the way
along which countless martyrs and other believers have walked through all
ages and over all the earth.

(12)   The Church therefore is being faithful to the truth of the gospel, and
is following the way of Christ and apostles when she recognizes, and gives
support to, the principle of religious freedom as befitting the dignity of man
and as being in accord with divine revelation. Throughout the ages, the
Church has kept safe and handed on the doctrine received from the master
and from the apostles. In the life of the People of God as it has made its
pilgrim way through the vicissitudes of human history, there have at times
appeared ways of acting which were less in accord with the spirit of the
gospel and even opposed to it. Nevertheless, the doctrine of the Church
that no one is to be coerced into faith has always stood firm.

Thus the leaven of the gospel has long been about its quiet work in the
minds of men. To it is due in great measure the fact that in the course of
time men have come more widely to recognize their dignity as persons, and
the conviction has grown stronger that in religious matters the person in
society is to be kept free from all manner of human coercion.

(13)   Among the things which concern the good of the Church and indeed
the welfare of society here on earth – things therefore which are always and
everywhere to be kept secure and defended against all injury – this certainly
is pre-eminent, namely, that the Church should enjoy that full measure of
freedom which her care for the salvation of men requires. This freedom is
sacred, because the only-begotten Son endowed with it the Church which
He purchased with His blood. It is so much the property of the Church that
to act against it is to act against the will of God. The freedom of the Church
is the fundamental principle in what concerns the relations between the
Church and governments and the whole civil order.

In human society and in the face of government, the Church claims
freedom for herself in her character as a spiritual authority, established by
Christ the Lord. Upon this authority there rests, by divine mandate, the

duty of going out into the whole world and preaching the gospel to every creature. The Church also claims freedom for herself in her character as a society of men who have the right to live in society in accordance with the precepts of Christian faith.

In turn, where the principle of religious freedom is not only proclaimed in words or simply incorporated in law but also given sincere and practical application, there the Church succeeds in achieving a stable situation of right as well as of fact and the independence which is necessary for the fulfillment of her divine mission. This independence is precisely what the authorities of the Church claim in society.

At the same time, the Christian faithful, in common with all other men, possess the civil right not to be hindered in leading their lives in accordance with their conscience. Therefore, a harmony exists between the freedom of the Church and the religious freedom which is to be recognized as the right of all men and communities and sanctioned by constitutional law.

(14) In order to be faithful to the divine command, "Make disciples of all nations" [Matthew 28: 19], the Catholic Church must work with all urgency and concern "that the Word of God may run and be glorified" [2 Thessalonians 3: 1]. Hence the Church earnestly begs of her children that, first of all, "supplications, prayers, intercessions, and thanksgivings be made for all men. . . . For this is good and agreeable in the sight of God our Savior, who wishes all men to be saved and to come to the knowledge of the truth" [1 Timothy 2: 1–4].

In the formation of their consciences, the Christian faithful ought carefully to attend to the sacred and certain doctrine of the Church. The Church is, by the will of Christ, the teacher of the truth. It is her duty to give utterance to, and authoritatively to teach, that Truth which is Christ Himself, and also to declare and confirm by her authority those principles of the moral order which have their origin in human nature itself. Furthermore, let Christians walk in wisdom in the face of those outside, "in the Holy Spirit, in unaffected love, in the word of truth" [2 Corinthians 6: 6–7]. Let them be about their task of spreading the light of life with all confidence and apostolic courage, even to the shedding of their blood.

The disciple is bound by a grave obligation toward Christ his Master ever more adequately to understand the truth received from Him, faithfully to proclaim it, and vigorously to defend it, never – be it understood – having recourse to means that are incompatible with the spirit of the gospel. At the same time, the charity of Christ urges him to act lovingly, prudently and patiently in his dealings with those who are in error or in ignorance with regard to the faith. All is to be taken into account – the Christian duty to Christ, the life-giving Word which must be proclaimed, the rights of the human person, and the measure of grace granted by God through Christ to men, who are invited freely to accept and profess the faith.

(15)   The fact is that men of the present day want to be able freely to profess their religion in private and in public. Religious freedom has already been declared to be a civil right in most constitutions, and it is solemnly recognized in international documents. The further fact is that forms of government still exist under which, even though freedom of religious worship receives constitutional recognition, the powers of government are engaged in the effort to deter citizens from the profession of religion and to make life difficult and dangerous for religious Communities.

This sacred Synod greets with joy the first of these two facts, as among the signs of the times. With sorrow, however, it denounces the other fact, as only to be deplored. The synod exhorts Catholics, and it directs a plea to all men, most carefully to consider how greatly necessary religious freedom is, especially in the present condition of the human family.

All nations are coming into even closer unity. Men of different cultures and religions are being brought together in closer relationships. There is a growing consciousness of the personal responsibility that weighs upon every man. All this is evident.

Consequently, in order that relationships of peace and harmony may be established and maintained within the whole of mankind, it is necessary that religious freedom be everywhere provided with an effective constitutional guarantee, and that respect be shown for the high duty and right of man freely to lead his religious life in society.

May the God and Father of all grant that the human family, through careful observance of the principle of religious freedom in society, may be brought by the grace of Christ and the power of the Holy Spirit to the sublime and unending "freedom of the glory of the sons of God" [Romans 8: 21].

Each and every one of the things set forth in this Declaration has won the consent of the Fathers of this most sacred Council. We too, by the apostolic authority conferred on us by Christ, join with the Venerable Fathers in approving, decreeing, and establishing these things in the Holy Spirit, and we direct that what has thus been enacted in synod be published to God's glory.

Rome, at St Peter's, December 7, 1965

I, Paul, Bishop of the Catholic Church

International Covenant on Civil and Political Rights (1976⁵)

Part III

Article 18

1   Everyone shall have the right of freedom of thought, conscience and religion. This right shall include freedom to have or to adopt a religion or belief of his choice, and freedom, either individually or in community with others and in public or private, to manifest his religion or belief in worship, observance, practice and teaching.

2   No one shall be subject to coercion which would impair his freedom to have or to adopt a religion or belief of his choice.

3   Freedom to manifest one's religion or beliefs may be subject only to such limitations as are prescribed by law and are necessary to protect public safety, order, health, or morals or the fundamental rights and freedoms of others.

4   The States Parties to the present Covenant undertake to have respect for the liberty of parents and, when applicable, legal guardians to ensure the religious and moral education of their children in conformity with their own convictions.

Article 27

In those States in which ethnic, religious or linguistic minorities exist, persons belonging to such minorities shall not be denied the right, in community with the other members of their group, to enjoy their own culture, to profess and practice their own religion, or to use their own language.

Declaration on the Elimination of all Forms of Intolerance and of Discrimination based on Religion or Belief (1981⁶)

The General Assembly,

Considering that one of the basic principles of the Charter of the United Nations is that of the dignity and equality inherent in all human beings, and that all Member States have pledged themselves to take joint and separate action in co-operation with the Organization to promote and encourage universal respect for and observance of human rights and fundamental freedoms for all, without distinction as to race, sex, language or religion,

Considering that the Universal Declaration of Human Rights and the International Covenants on Human Rights proclaim the principles of non-discrimination and equality before the law and the right to freedom of thought, conscience, religion and belief,

Considering that the disregard and infringement of human rights and fundamental freedoms, in particular of the right to freedom of thought, conscience, religion or whatever belief, have brought, directly or indirectly, wars and great suffering to mankind, especially where they serve as a means of foreign interference in the internal affairs of other States and amount to kindling hatred between peoples and nations,

Considering that religion or belief, for anyone who professes either, is one of the fundamental elements in his conception of life and that freedom of religion or belief should be fully respected and guaranteed,

Considering that it is essential to promote understanding, tolerance and respect in matters relating to freedom of religion and belief and to ensure that the use of religion or belief for ends inconsistent with the Charter of the United Nations, other relevant instruments of the United Nations and the purposes and principles of the present Declaration is inadmissible,

Convinced that freedom of religion and belief should also contribute to the attainment of the goals of world peace, social justice and friendship among peoples and to the elimination of ideologies or practices of colonialism and racial discrimination,

Noting with satisfaction the adoption of several, and the coming into force of some, conventions, under the aegis of the United Nations and of the specialized agencies, for the elimination of various forms of discrimination,

Concerned by manifestations of intolerance and by the existence of discrimination in matters of religion or belief still in evidence in some areas of the world,

Resolved to adopt all necessary measures for the speedy elimination of such intolerance in all its forms and manifestations and to prevent and combat discrimination on the ground of religion or belief,

Proclaims this Declaration on the Elimination of All Forms of Intolerance and of Discrimination Based on Religion or Belief:

Article 1

1   Everyone shall have the right to freedom of thought, conscience and religion. This right shall include freedom to have a religion or whatever belief of his choice, and freedom, either individually or in community with others and in public or private, to manifest his religion or belief in worship, observance, practice and teaching.

2 No one shall be subject to coercion which would impair his freedom to have a religion or belief of his choice.

3 Freedom to manifest one's religion or beliefs may be subject only to such limitations as are prescribed by law and are necessary to protect public safety, order, health or morals or the fundamental rights and freedoms of others.

Article 2

1 No one shall be subject to discrimination by any State, institution, group of persons, or person on grounds of religion or other beliefs.

2 For the purposes of the present Declaration, the expression "intolerance and discrimination based on religion or belief" means any distinction, exclusion, restriction or preference based on religion or belief and having as its purpose or as its effect nullification or impairment of the recognition, enjoyment or exercise of human rights and fundamental freedoms on an equal basis.

Article 3

Discrimination between human beings on grounds of religion or belief constitutes an affront to human dignity and a disavowal of the principles of the Charter of the United Nations, and shall be condemned as a violation of the human rights and fundamental freedoms proclaimed in the Universal Declaration of Human Rights and enunciated in detail in the International Covenants on Human Rights, and as an obstacle to friendly and peaceful relations between nations.

Article 4

1 All States shall take effective measures to prevent and eliminate discrimination on the grounds of religion or belief in the recognition, exercise and enjoyment of human rights and fundamental freedoms in all fields of civil, economic, political, social and cultural life.

2 All States shall make all efforts to enact or rescind legislation where necessary to prohibit any such discrimination, and to take all appropriate measures to combat intolerance on the grounds of religion or other beliefs in this matter.

Article 5

1 The parents or, as the case may be, the legal guardians of the child have the right to organize the life within the family in accordance with

their religion or belief and bearing in mind the moral education in which they believe the child should be brought up.

2   Every child shall enjoy the right to have access to education in the matter of religion or belief in accordance with the wishes of his parents or, as the case may be, legal guardians, and shall not be compelled to receive teaching on religion or belief against the wishes of his parents or legal guardians, the best interests of the child being the guiding principle.

3   The child shall be protected from any form of discrimination on the ground of religion or belief. He shall be brought up in a spirit of understanding, tolerance, friendship among peoples, peace and universal brotherhood, respect for freedom of religion or belief of others, and in full consciousness that his energy and talents should be devoted to the service of his fellow men.

4   In the case of a child who is not under the care either of his parents or of legal guardians, due account shall be taken of their expressed wishes or of any other proof of their wishes in the matter of religion or belief, the best interests of the child being the guiding principle.

5   Practices of a religion or beliefs in which a child is brought up must not be injurious to his physical or mental health or to his full development, taking into account Article 1, paragraph 3, of the present Declaration.

Article 6

In accordance with Article 1 of the present Declaration, and subject to the provisions of Article 1, paragraph 3, the right to freedom of thought, conscience, religion or belief shall include, *inter alia*, the following freedoms:

(a)   To worship or assemble in connection with a religion or belief and to establish and maintain places for these purposes;

(b)   To establish and maintain appropriate charitable or humanitarian institutions;

(c)   To make, acquire and use to an adequate extent the necessary articles and materials related to the rites or customs of a religion or belief;

(d)   To write, issue and disseminate relevant publications in these areas;

(e)   To teach a religion or belief in places suitable for these purposes;

(f)   To solicit and receive voluntary financial and other contributions from individuals and institutions;

(g)   To train, appoint, elect or designate by succession appropriate leaders called for by the requirements and standards of any religion or belief;

(h) To observe days of rest and to celebrate holidays and ceremonies in accordance with the precepts of one's religion or belief;

(i) To establish and maintain communications with individuals and communities in matters of religion and belief at the national and international levels.

Article 7

The rights and freedoms set forth in the present Declaration shall be accorded in national legislation in such a manner that everyone shall be able to avail himself of such rights and freedoms in practice.

Article 8

Nothing in the present Declaration shall be construed as restricting or derogating from any right defined in the Universal Declaration of Human Rights and the International Covenants on Human Rights.

Notes

1 Issued by the Joint Committee on Religious Liberty. See Wood, *Religious Liberty Today*, Appendix I, pp. 131–43.

2 A. F. Carrillo de Albornoz, *The Basis of Religious Liberty* (London: SCM Press, 1963), pp. 157–9.

3 Humana (ed.), *World Human Rights Guide*, pp. 13–17; Brownlie (ed.), *Basic Documents*, 3rd edn, pp. 21–7; extracts reproduced in Wood, *Religious Liberty*, Appendix II.

4 See M. Searle Bates, *Religious Liberty: An Inquiry* (New York: International Missionary Council, 1945), pp. 432–68.

5 This covenant was intended to be incorporated into United Nations treaty provisions and made obligatory on member states which ratified it. The full text may be consulted in Humana (ed.), *World Human Rights Guide*, pp. 18–23.

6 Reprinted in Brownlie, *Basic Documents*, pp. 109–12. For the text of the "Preliminary Draft Declaration on the Elimination of all Forms of Religious Intolerance," see Carrillo de Albornoz, *Religious Liberty*, pp. 28–32.

INDEX

Abelard, 11
Acontius, Jacob, 12, 115
Acton, Lord, 12
Ad abolendam, 72
Albigensians, 11, 207, 213
Ambrose of Milan, 78
Amnesty International, 2
anabaptism, anabaptists, 95, 98,
   142–3, 182, 196, 280, 285
Anglican, *see* England, Church of
Aquinas, Thomas, 5, 11, 55, 81,
   315–16
Aristotle, 55, 68, 76, 259
Arius, Arianism, 53, 56, 71, 75,
   121–3, 145, 148
Arminius, Arminians, 12, 127, 150,
   182
atheism, atheist, 8, 23, 159, 165,
   174, 187, 210, 224, 235, 265, 273,
   316
Athens, 8, 21–2, 50, 198, 208
Augustine, 9, 10, 39, 59–60, 63, 65,
   67–71, 76–8, 88, 128, 148–50,
   159, 171–4, 270
auto da fé, 212

Bacchanalia, 7
Bainton, Roland, 7
Baptists, 3, 4, 132, 136, 273, 291;
   Baptist World Alliance, 4
Barth, Karl, 299

Bayle, Pierre, 11, 39, 165
blasphemy, 44, 52, 59, 86, 89, 97,
   100, 107, 109, 143, 147–51, 155,
   187, 243, 264
Bodin, Jean, 294–5
Bohemia, *see* Hussites
Bossuet, Jacques Bénigne, 165
Britain, churches of, *Human Rights
   and Religious Freedom* (1947), 318
Brownlow, John, 225
Buddhism, Buddhists, 6, 301, 312
Butler, Samuel, 1

caesar, 25, 77, 90, 101, 133, 135,
   138–9, 226, 270, 337
Calas, Jean, 187
Calvin, John, 101, 251, 266, 285
Calvinists, 3, 125, 206, 214, 227, 230,
   234, 279, 287
Cambridge Platonists, 159
Cardinale, Archbishop H. E., 6, 16
Carillo de Albornoz, Angel F., 303
Carter, Stephen L., 14
Castellio, Sebastian, 86, 100–1
catacombs, 244
Cathars, *see* Albigensians
Celsus, Mino, 147
Charles V, Holy Roman Emperor,
   88, 112, 153, 190, 271
China, 2
Chrysostom, John, 36, 59–60, 74–5

Circumcelliones, 40
cockle, *see* tares
compelle intrare, 21, 42, 59, 166–70
conscience, as inadequate basis for
    religious pluralism, 11, 81, 165
Constantine, 9–10, 29, 47, 65, 74,
    121, 136, 189
Constantius, 121
Creighton, Mandell, 257
Crusades, 11
Cyril of Alexandria, 148

D'Arcy, Eric, 55
"Declaration on the Elimination
    of all Forms of Religious
    Intolerance," 310, 341
De haeretico comburendo, 221
deism, deists, 188, 203–4, 211, 215,
    265, 272
Denck, Hans, 289
Descartes, René, 222, 289
Dignitatis humanae vitae, *see* Vatican
Diocletian, 226
Dominic, Dominicans, 11, 207,
    282–3
Donatists, 39, 46–7, 49–50, 148, 150,
    165, 171–4, 189
Dort, synod of, 127

England, English, 3, 125, 199, 220,
    228, 230–1, 241, 248, 273, 323;
    Church of (Anglican), 1, 132,
    202, 220, 225, 252, 257, 306;
    Elizabeth I, 202, 221, 247;
    Glorious Revolution, 3; Henry
    VIII, 295, 306; Mary, 135, 226,
    247; James I, 132; James II, 174
Enlightenment, 12
Erastianism, 280
exterminare, 11

fanaticism, fanatics, 23, 39, 103, 161,
    187–8, 191–2, 208, 212–14, 217,
    224, 257, 264, 276, 282–3, 285–90,
    292–6
Fascists, 272

Flanders, 195, 247
France, 100, 114–15, 129, 195, 205,
    213, 222, 230–1, 267, 277, 294;
    Charles IX, 207; Francis I, 188,
    190; Francis II, 188, 190; Henry
    IV, 6, 186; Louis XIV, 6, 11, 165;
    Revolution, 13, 265, 267, 273
Franciscans, 11

Galerius, 187
Galileo, 210, 222
Gamaliel, 21, 190
Germany, 124–5, 212, 293
Gerson, Jean, 208
Goodwin, John, 150
Gregory VI, pope, 53, 58, 63

Heber, Reginald, 141
Helvétius, Claude Adrien, 205
Helwys, Thomas, 132
heresy, defined, 66–8, 155–7, 207
Hesiod, 7
Hick, John, 1
Hilary of Poitiers, 74–5
Hinduism, Hindus, 262, 298, 312
Hobbes, Thomas, 287, 294–5
Holland, 195, 212–13
Hübmaier, Balthasar, 94–5
Huguenots, 6, 129, 165, 207, 231,
    295
Hume, David, 7, 10
Hussites, 124–5, 247

Immortale Dei, 283
Incas, 7
index, 274
inquisition, inquisitors, 5, 10–11,
    22, 55, 96, 105, 155, 195, 222–3,
    230–1, 242, 274, 283; Spanish,
    306
International Covenant on Civil and
    Political Rights, 4, 341
intolerance, natural to humans, 212,
    245, 258
Ireland, 228, 235–6
Isidore, 68

Islam, Muslims, 6, 93, 96, 107, 109, 124–5, 161, 182, 188, 190, 195, 203, 206, 214, 227, 262, 298, 312, 326
Italy, 231, 277

Jansenius, Jansenism, Jansenists, 170, 211, 215
Japan, 306
Jefferson, Thomas, 219–20, 290
Jerome, 65–6, 68, 70–3
Jesuits, 117, 171, 188, 215, 283
Jews, Judaism, 6, 45, 55–69, 93, 98, 101, 103, 107, 109, 119, 148, 151–2, 161, 182, 192–3, 203, 207–8, 227, 229, 234, 238–9, 264, 276, 298, 312, 326
Johnson, Dr Samuel, 246–7, 261
Julian the Apostate, 121
jurisdictionalism, 272, 280
Justinian, 86, 121

King, Preston, 5
Knox, John, 202, 251
Knox, Ronald A., 13, 17

Lactantius, 9, 28, 145–8, 184
Lammenais, Felicité de, 13, 242
Lea, Henry Charles, 271
League of Nations, 324
Lecler, J., 73
Leo XIII, pope, 283
Lessing, Gotthold Ephraism, 12, 215, 224
levellers, 196, 290
Lewis, Bernard, 2
libertines, libertinism, 142–3, 178
liberty, distinct from toleration, 5–6, 255
Lilburne, John, 290
Littell, Franklin H., 2
Locke, John, 4, 6, 12, 174, 252, 255–6, 262, 289–90, 315
Lollards, 234, 247
Lombard, Peter, 78

Luther, Martin, 8, 12, 82, 85, 86, 111, 124, 206, 247, 285, 299
Lutherans, Lutheranism, 190, 206, 214, 279, 287

Madison, James, 219
Mani, Manichees, 10, 51–2, 57, 68, 128
Mariana, Juan de, 117
Markham, Ian, 1
Marsilius of Padua, 73
Martin of Tours, 10, 54–5, 81
Marxism, Marxists, 287, 295, 312
Maternus, Julius Firmicus, 9, 32
Maximin, 55
Mendelssohn, Moses, 215, 224
Mendus, Susan, 5
Mensching, Gerd, 296
Mill, John Stuart, 12, 34, 244, 262, 292
Milton, John, 12, 152, 290–1
Mirabeau, Comte de, 276
Mohammed, Mohammedans, see Islam
monotheism, 7–8, 10
Moore, R. I., 11
More, Henry, 159, 182
More, Sir Thomas, 82, 295
Mullett, Michael, 7
Murray, John Courtney, 311, 329

Nantes, edict of, 6, 165, 195
Nathan the Wise, see Lessing
natural law, 65–6, 151, 161, 164, 174, 188, 208–9, 213–14, 266–7, 312
natural religion, 166–9, 265, 297, 299
natural right, 9, 25, 27, 55, 146, 160, 165, 183, 198, 212, 221, 226, 228, 241–2, 267
Nazism, 294
Nebuchadnezzar, 8, 45, 121
Nestorius, Nestorians, 56, 69, 148, 190
New England, 3, 136, 195, 220

New York, 223
Newman, Jay, 5, 8
Niebuhr, Reinhold, 12, 281
Noonan, John, 5

Optatus, 39, 121
Otto, Rudolf, 296, 299–301
Owen, John, 174

Paine, Thomas, 5
Paramo, Ludovico of, 10
Parsons, Robert, 283
Paul VI, pope, 330, 340
Pennsylvania, 195, 203, 223
Philips, Dirk, 98
Plato, 21–2, 25, 50, 191
Poissy, colloquy of, 129
Poland, Polish, 195, 214
polytheism, 7–8, 298
Pospielovsky, Dimitry, 3
predestination, 12, 127, 136
presbyterianism, presbyterians, 143,
    156, 182, 204, 286
Priestley, Joseph, 12, 193
Priscillian, Priscillianists, 10, 55, 81
Prussia, 213, 280
Przywara, Erich, 282–3
puritans, 286

quakers, 159, 182, 192, 203–4, 220

Rabb, T. K., 2
Rawls, John, 313
Reformed, see Calvinists
relativism, 5, 268
religious pluralism, 1–2, 4
Remonstrants, see Arminius
Rome, Roman Empire, Romans, 7, 9,
    26, 89, 189, 191, 198, 222, 247,
    251
Rommen, Heinrich, 5
Rorty, Richard, 2
Rousseau, Jean Jacques, 3, 185, 208,
    273, 315
Ruffini, Francesco, 73, 271

Rushdie, Salman, 2
Rutherford, Samuel, 141–2

Saltmarsh, John, 291
Saracens, see Islam
Savonarola, 247
Schleiermacher, Friedrich, 297, 300
Schwenkfeld, Caspar, 290
Scotland, 3, 202
separatism, 272, 280
Septuagint, 188, 224
Servetus, Michael, 86, 100, 215
Singulari nos, 243
skepticism, skeptics, 115, 127, 265,
    272–3, 289, 292–6, 315
Smyth, John, 132
Socrates, Socratic philosophy, 8, 22,
    50, 208, 248
Søe, Niels H., 304
Sophocles, 8
Soviet Union, 3, 310
Sozzini, Lelio, and Socinians, 115,
    145, 273, 280; see also unitarians
Spain, 107, 117, 230–1, 247; Philip
    II, 195, 306; Philip III, 117
Sparta, Spartans, 198–9
Stanhope, Lord, 276
Star Chamber, 230–1
Stephen, James Fitzjames, 244
Sudan, 2
Syllabus of Errors (1864), 329

tares, parable of, 9, 18, 20, 36–8,
    53–4, 58–9, 70–1, 95–6, 99, 115,
    136–7, 154–5, 243, 337
Tertullian, 9, 24–5, 146, 184, 189
Themistius, 8, 34
Theodosius, Theodosian Code, 10,
    65, 121, 271
toleration, contrasted with
    intolerance, 4–6, 276
Tracy, David, 14
Trent, Council of, 270
Troeltsch, Ernst, 3
Turkey, 214, 238

Turks, *see* Islam
typology, 12, 132, 136, 151

Ulster, 2
unitarians, 193, 233, 246, 273
United Nations, 15, 310, 325, 329, 341–3
United States of America, Americans, 264, 272, 276, 280–1; constitution, 220
Universal Declaration of Human Rights, 310, 328, 342, 345

Vatican, Second Council of, 13, 311, 316, 329
Vermeersch, Albert, 263
Vinet, Alexander, 273, 279
Virginia, 219–20
Voltaire, 187, 289

voluntarism, voluntary, 3, 109–10, 169, 174, 180–1, 236, 252

Waldensians, 234
Walwyn, William, 290
Warburton, William, 196, 224
Wazo, bishop of Liège, 10, 51, 55
Westphalia, Peace of, 279
Wiggins, James, 1
Wilder, Amos, 304, 307–8
Williams, Roger, 12, 136, 152, 174, 290
Winstanley, Gerard, 290
Wogaman, Philip, 2, 309, 317
World Council of Churches, 303; Amsterdam Assembly, 188, 305, 311; Declaration on Religious Liberty, 326

Zwingli, Huldreich, 95, 112, 266, 285